VIEW OF AMERICA

A
VIEW

OF THE

UNITED STATES

OF

AMERICA

*IN A SERIES OF PAPERS
WRITTEN AT VARIOUS TIMES, IN THE YEARS
BETWEEN 1787 AND 1794*

By TENCH COXE

[1794]

REPRINTS OF ECONOMIC CLASSICS

Augustus M. Kelley, Bookseller
New York 1965

Library of Congress Catalogue Card Number
64 - 24342

PRINTED IN THE UNITED STATES OF AMERICA
by SENTRY PRESS, NEW YORK, N. Y. 10019

A

VIEW

OF THE

UNITED STATES

OF

AMERICA,

IN A SERIES OF PAPERS,

WRITTEN AT VARIOUS TIMES, BETWEEN THE YEARS
1787 AND 1794,

By *TENCH COXE*, OF PHILADELPHIA;

INTERSPERSED WITH

AUTHENTIC DOCUMENTS:

THE WHOLE TENDING TO EXHIBIT THE PROGRESS AND PRE-
SENT STATE OF CIVIL AND RELIGIOUS LIBERTY, POPU-
LATION, AGRICULTURE, EXPORTS, IMPORTS, FISHE-
RIES, NAVIGATION, SHIP-BUILDING, MANUFAC-
TURES, AND GENERAL IMPROVEMENT.

———————

PHILADELPHIA:
PRINTED FOR WILLIAM HALL, Nº· 51, Market Street, and
WRIGLEY & BERRIMAN, Nº· 149, Chesnut Street.

1794.

A TABLE of the CONTENTS.

BOOK I.

CONTENTS.

BOOK II.

BOOK I.

A

PREFATORY NOTE

CITIZENS of PENNSYLVANIA.

AFTER the following pages were delivered from the press some observations upon those parts of their contents, which relate to our particular state, occurred with very considerable force. These were accompanied by interesting reflections upon the existing circumstances of the country. It appeared useful to introduce them in a prefatory note, that they might encourage our perseverance in the ancient line of policy and conduct, which have produced effects so transcendently favourable to our local interests, without injustice to our sister states, or to the foreign world.

It appears by the return on the 476th page, that the state of Pennsylvania (or the city of Philadelphia) exported in the year, ending in September, 1793, of foreign and domestic goods, nearly seven eighths of the sum exported by New-York, Con-

necticut, *Rhode-Island, Massachusetts, and New-Hampshire ;
and that those exports of Philadelphia were* 1,717,572 *dollars, more than all the exports of New-England. At the same
time, it is well known, that Baltimore received a considerable
part of the produce of this state, and that some of it is usually
sent out by land to the Patowmac, and by water through the
river Ohio. The migrators from New-England, New-York,
New-Jersey, Delaware and Maryland, from Europe and in
that year, from the West-Indies, were consuming largely of
articles, which would otherwise have greatly increased the value of our exportations.*

*Having reference to the number of tons and to the quality, it
will be found, that we built new vessels in the same year to an
amount double that of any other port in the United States.*

*The increase of the exports of the United States in flour
since the year* 1786, *has been about* 800,000 *barrels. This
article is received by New-England, the Carolinas and Georgia,
in a much greater degree from the middle states, than it is exported from the former seven. This very great increase is
therefore confined to Pennsylvania, New-Jersey, New-York,
Delaware, Maryland and Virginia; and it is not the principal
staple of the two last states, which export more in value of tobacco
than of flour. The difference in the value of the flour shipped
from those six states, in* 1786, *and that in* 1793, *is about six
millions of dollars, calculating as well upon the increase of price
as of quantity. The whole increase of the exports of the union,
since March* 1789, *is about eight millions of dollars, of which
more than two millions were in foreign goods.*

Pennsylvania, and Maryland (which exports considerably for
Pennsylvania) shipped, of domestic and foreign goods, in 1792,
Dollars,   6,370,904

The same two states shipped in 1793,   10,645,855

The difference in favour of the latter year was 4,274,951
dollars. This was about seventeen twentieth parts of the in-
crease of the exports of the United States in the same time.

The whole exports of New-York, in 1793, *were*   2,934,370

The mere increase *of the exports of Pennsylvania,*
between 1792 *and* 1793, *was*   3,138,090

The exports of Pennsylvania, for the half *year*
only, ending on the 30th March, 1794, *were, Dols.* 3,533,597

The increase *of the exports of the United States, in* 1793,
beyond those of 1792, *was about* 5,000,000 *dollars, of which*
the above increase of Pennsylvania alone, in that time, was
thirty-one fiftieth parts : or more than three fifths.

The population of Pennsylvania appears to have increased,
in 23 *years, nearly in the proportion of* 39 *to* 91, *though the*
whole term of a revolutionary and invasive war of seven years
was included.* This considerably exceeds Dr. Franklin's es-
timate of doubling in twenty years. Now, that all New-Eng-
land is full, except Main and Vermont, the contiguous states of
New-Jersey and Delaware are overstocked, and Maryland

* *See page* 481.

*nearly fo; and above all, now that Europe is full and much
difturbed, a curious rapidity of population is to be expected in
a ftate with fo much unimproved land, difpofition and capacity
for manufactures, wealth, foreign intercourfe, energy and enterprife as Pennfylvania. The furplus population of New-
England, New-Jerfey, Delaware, and Maryland, at five per
cent. is above 60,000 perfons per annum; and the furplus of
the old fettlements of this ftate is above twenty-two thoufand
per annum.*

*The plenty of pit-coal in Pennfylvania will very foon give it
an immenfe advantage over all the interior country north and
eaft of it, in which, though colder than Pennfylvania, it is not
known, that there is one coal mine open, or that there is any
confiderable appearance of that invaluable foffil. Wood and
timber are very much decreafed in the principal part of New-
England and in New-Jerfey, but is abundant in Maine and
Vermont, and in many parts of NewYork.*

*It cannot be too much enforced and reiterated, that the inte-
rior and weftern counties of Pennfylvania, and the weftern
country in general, ought to procure, at any expence, the* moft
valuable *breeding animals, which can be obtained—Horfes,
mares, horned cattle and fheep: becaufe their diftance from
the fea-ports dictates the moft intelligent and particular attention to the grazing hufbandry. Horned cattle have been
driven to Philadelphia, from Maffachufetts and North-Carolina, and mules from Connecticut to Baltimore. The journey
from the Ohio to Philadelphia, is not more difficult.*

*The practice of the eaftern ftates, in regard to fchools de-
ferves the moft ferious attention of the wife and good. It*

appears to have refulted in New-England from their fettling in townfhips of four, five and fix miles fquare. Perhaps it would be moft eafily accomplifhed in Pennfylvania by dividing the ftate into fuch townfhips. The utmoft diftance from a fchool, in the centre of a divifion of four miles fquare, would be very little more than a mile.

It is obvioufly of the greateft importance to this country and to Pennfylvania, that its citizens fhould continue to be firmly attached to the union of the American ftates. An oppofite difpofition would be an error the moft fatal and the moft extreme.

There was never applied, to the improvement and advancement of Pennfylvania, fo great an aggregate of money as is employed directly or indirectly at the prefent time. The improvements at the falls of Delaware, at Alexandria on the fame river, oppofite to Bucks, at Wilfonville on the Walenpaupack, at Affylum on the Sufquehannah, at Connewaga by that company, at the Brandywine, Schuylkill and Tulpehocken canals, at the Lancafter turnpike road, at the Black Friar falls of Sufquehanna, in the private buildings at Pittfburg, the mills, work-fhops and dwelling houfes in every town and every quarter of the ftate, together with the expenditures upon roads, bridges and rivers, amount to a prodigious fum, have attracted artifts, mechanics and labourers from other ftates, and even from Europe, and have catched the ftream of emigration ere it paffed from eaft to weft, and from north to fouth. It may be truly faid, that the profits, not only of agriculture, but of trade, manufactures, funds and banks are turned, to a great amount, to the promotion of the landed intereft, by Pennfylvanians, by many other Americans and foreigners of feveral nations.

The manufactured imports of the state of Pennsylvania, are somewhat less than those of New-York; though the exports of this state are so much greater. This is a clear proof of the magnitude of the manufactures of Pennsylvania. Gunpowder, linseed oil, glue, paper, books, engravings, carriages, braziery, copper ware, tin and pewter wares, iron castings, saddlery, hats, carriages for pleasure and work, paper hangings, pasteboards, boots, shoes, tanned and tawed leather, parchments, earthen and stone ware, cedar ware, corn-fans, Windsor and rush bottom chairs, household manufactures of woolen, cotton and linen, set work, gold work, silver plate, rolled and slit iron and steel, and manufactures thereof and of lead, leather breeches, whips, gloves, horsemens' caps, cartouch boxes, canteens, sword blades, bayonets, musquets, rifles, drums, boats, ships and vessels, beer, distilled spirits, and many other articles to a great amount indeed, are manufactured in the city of Philadelphia, in the boroughs, and in the counties of Pennsylvania; are transported, in many instances, by land and water, to several other states; and, in many instances, are exported to foreign countries. This is the real cause of a difference, which has attracted some observation; and this important circumstance is conceived to be one of the strongest points in favour of the resources, powers and efficiency of Pennsylvania. From this solid truth it is obvious, that upon an accurate and comprehensive statement of her commerce, foreign and domestic, by sea and land, a great balance would appear in favour of this state.

The people of Pennsylvania owe very little money indeed, to their American brethren, but on the contrary, have always much due to them on all sides. They partake more largely in the ready money branches of foreign commerce, because of *their own valuable ſtaples and of the extent of their capital and their habits of exporting to foreign countries, from the ſouthern ports, the productions of thoſe ſtates. In the credit trades, they take a very large ſhare and are ſecond to none in punctuality of payment.*

The citizens of Philadelphia conſume in their arts, trades and families, and export tō foreign countries ſo much of the produce of the fiſheries, that they appear to have a ſtrong intereſt to participate in them. While the Britiſh and French partake in the American fiſheries, and in the whale fiſhery of every ſea, it will continue to be a matter of certainty, that the enterprizing ſhip owners and mariners of Philadelphia may at any time make the experiment.

The facts aud ideas in this note, relative to the ſtate of Pennſylvania, together with thoſe in the 4th chapter of the firſt book and in the 6th chapter of the ſecond book will tend to prove to us, who are of that proſperous ſtate, its very deep intereſt in maintaining juſt government and public order.

V I E W

OF THE

U N I T E D S T A T E S.

―――――――

C H A P T E R I.

INTRODUCTORY REMARKS.

THE progreffive courfe of things, in young countries, renders the tafk of thofe, who undertake to treat of their affairs, particularly difficult. The inceffant changes, produced by public operations and private induftry, occafion the reprefentations of one year to be imperfect and diffimilar pictures, in thofe which follow foon after. In no country have thefe obfervations been more ftrikingly exemplified, than in the United States of America. The actual fituation of many parts of their affairs is nearly *the reverfe* of what it was at times within the memory of children. This circumftance has fuggefted the idea, that collections of papers, which have been publifhed at the different ftages of American affairs during the exifting peace, (like thofe, which occupy this volume) introduced in each inftance by concife explanatory remarks, and clofed by fuch brief obfervations on its particular fubject, as arife in the prefent time, would be of confiderable utility to thofe, who may defire to know, and thoroughly to underftand the fituation of the United States. The publications, now difpofed in that form, were all produced in America by the ftate of things at the moment, and were given to the world without any refervation as to the writer's name. It is an interefting prefumption, therefore, to perfons abroad, that confiderable dependance may be reafonably placed by them upon facts, which have been, in moft inftances, brought forward with a view to the ufe of the inhabitants of the United States, and which have been ftated and afferted, in the moft public manner, before the beft informed people of the country. Grofs deceptions, or many erroneous reprefentations are not very likely to be found in fuch a collection. It is, however, prudent and neceffary to obferve, that the field of information and enquiry in the United States is fo extenfive, diverfified and variable, that many very interefting facts remain unknown to their moft attentive inhabitants. There is no doubt, therefore, that thofe, who are well acquainted with any portion of the United States, will perceive many inftances of advantages, which are not contemplated in this collection. All that is intended to be affirmed, in regard to the matter they comprize, is, that the various allegations they contain were really warranted by truth or by fincere belief at the time when they were written.

CHAPTER II.

FACTS AND CONSIDERATIONS RELATIVE TO THE AGRICUL-
TURE, MANUFACTURES, FISHERIES, NAVIGATION, AND
THE IMPORT, EXPORT AND COASTING TRADE; INTENDED
TO ELUCIDATE THE COMMERCIAL INTERESTS OF THE
UNITED STATES.

NOTWITHSTANDING the actual profperity of the United States of America at this
time, it is a fact which ought not to be concealed,
that their affairs had fallen into a very difagreeable
condition in the year 1786. The derangements
and injuries of a civil and invafive war, of more
than feven years duration, the defects of the late
national confederation and government, the confu-
fed mafs of debts, both public and private, which
had arifen from various caufes, with other unfavorable circumftances, had reduced the country to
a painful fituation. Commerce, among other things,
was of courfe deeply affected. From the difpofitions of free governments to fofter trade, and from
the facility with which the mercantile citizens
communicate with each other, meafures were taken
in a majority of the ftates for the appointment of a
convention of commiffioners to devife fome mode
of relief. The defective reprefentation, which that
body contained, when affembled at Annapolis, *
and the alarming complexion of public affairs in
general at that juncture, produced an unanimous
conviction in the commiffioners, that the falvation

* In the autumn of 1786.

of the country required the appointment of another convention, with more general powers. Such
a body was foon after conftituted, and commenced
its fittings at Philadelphia in the fpring of 1787.
The following confiderations relative to the American trade, were publifhed in that city, and in-
fcribed to the members of the convention at an
early period of their bufinefs. It is proper to remark (and by the kindnefs of heaven it can be faid
with truth) that the unfavorable part of the circumftances, which are detailed in this effay, have given
place to that profperous ftate of commerce, which
a country of diverfified and productive agriculture
muft ever poffefs, either in the foreign or domeftic
line, while it maintains with fincerity and vigilance
the freedom of its citizens, and with energy and firmnefs, *the rights of property.*

*An enquiry into the principles, on which a commer-
cial fyftem for the United States of America fhould
be founded ; to which are added fome political obfervations connected with the fubject.—Read before
the fociety for political enquiries, convened at the
houfe of Benjamin Franklin, in Philadelphia, May
11, 1787.*

There are in every country certain important
crifes when exertion or neglect muft produce confequences of the utmoft moment. The period at
which the inhabitants of thefe ftates have now arrived, will be admitted, by every attentive and ferious perfon, to be clearly of this defcription.

Our money abforbed by a wanton confumption of imported luxuries, a fluctuating paper medium fubftituting in its ftead, foreign commerce* extremely circumfcribed and a federal government not only ineffective but disjointed, tell us indeed too plainly, that further negligence may ruin us forever. Impreffed with this view of our affairs, the writer of the following pages has ventured to intrude upon the public. But as neither his time nor opportunities will permit him to treat of all the great objects, which excite his apprehenfions or engage his wifhes, he means principally to confine himfelf to that part of them, which have been moft fubjected to his obfervations and enquiries.

Juft opinions on our general affairs, muft neceffarily precede fuch a well devifed fyftem of commercial regulations, as will extend our trade as far as it can be carried, without affecting unfavorably our other interefts. It may therefore be ufeful in the firft place, to take a comparative view of the two moft important objects in the United States— our agriculture and commerce.

In a country bleft with a fertile foil, and a climate admitting fteady labour, where the cheapnefs of land tempts the European from his home, *and the manufacturer from his trade*,† we are led by a

* In regard to its old channels under the Britifh monopoly— and the new channels not having then difcovered themfelves, or their importance.

† It may be truly affirmed in the middle ftates that agriculture draws more of the emigrating European artizans from manufactures than manufactures draw of the farmers from agriculture.

few moments reflexion to fix on agriculture as the great leading intereft. From this we fhall find moft of our other advantages refult, fo far as they arife from the nature of our affairs, and where they are not produced by the operation of laws—the fifheries are the principal exception. In order to make a true eftimate of the magnitude of agriculture, we muft remember that it is encouraged by few or no duties on the importation of rival produce*— that it furnifhes outward cargoes not only for all our own fhips, but thofe alfo which foreign nations fend to our ports, or in other words, that it pays for all our importations†—that it fupplies a part of the clothing of our people and the food of them and their cattle—that what is confumed at home, including the materials for manufacturing, is many times the value of what is exported—that the number of people employed in agriculture, is at leaft nine parts in ten of the inhabitants of America‡—that therefore the planters and farmers compofe the body of the militia, the bulwark of the nation—that the value in property, occupied by agriculture, is manifold greater than that employed in every other way—that the fettlement of our wafte lands, and fubdividing our improved farms is every year increafing the pre-eminence of the agricultural intereft—that the refources we derive from it are

* A. D. 1787, and under the laws of the feveral ftates.

† The fifheries were then the only exception, but manufactures are beginning to form another, tho’ much lefs important, yet: A. D. 1789.

‡ A. D. 1787.

at all times certain and indifpenfibly neceffary—
and laftly, that the rural life promotes health and
morality by its active nature, and by keeping our
people from the luxuries and vices of the towns.
In fhort, agriculture appears to be the fpring of
our commerce, and the parent of our manufactures.

The commerce of America, including our exports,
imports, fhipping, manufactures and fifheries, may be
properly confidered as formirg one intereft. So
uninformed and miftaken have many of us been,
that it has been ftated as our greateft object, and it
is feared that it is yet believed by fome to be the
moft important intereft of New-England. But calculations carefully made do not raife the proportion of property, or the number of men employed in
manufactures, fifheries, navigation and trade,* to
one-eighth of the property and people occupied by
agriculture, even in that commercial quarter of the
Union. In making this eftimate fomething has
been deducted from the value and population of
the large towns for the idle and diffipated, for thofe
who live upon their incomes, and for fupernumera-
ry domeftic fervants. But the difproportion is
much greater, taking the union at large, for feveral
of the ftates have little commerce, and no manufactures—others have no commerce and fcarcely manufacture any thing. The timber, iron, cordage
and many other articles neceffary for building fhips
to fifh or trade—nine parts in ten of their cargoes

---

* As regular occupations, &c. A. D. 1787. The manufacturers are but little more than half of the people of England.

—the fubfiftence of the manufacturers, and much of their raw materials are the produce of our lands. In almoft all the countries of Europe, judicious writers have confidered commerce as the handmaid of agriculture : if true there, with us it muft be unqueftionable. The United States have yet few factories to throw into the fcale againft the landed intereft. We have in our lands full employment for our prefent inhabitants, and inftead of fending colonies to newly difcovered iflands, we have adjoining townfhips and counties, whofe vacant fields await the future increafe of our people.

If a comparative view of the importance of our various interefts fhould terminate in a conviction of the great fuperiority of agriculture over all the reft combined—if emigration and natural increafe are daily adding to the number of our planters and farmers—if the ftates are poffeffed of millions of vacant acres, that court the cultivator's hand—if the fettlement of thefe immenfe tracts will greatly and fteadily increafe the means of fubfiftence, the refources and powers of the country—if they will prove an inherent treafure of which neither folly nor chance can deprive us, let us be careful to do nothing, which may interrupt this happy progrefs of our affairs. Should we, from a mifconception of our true interefts, or from any other caufe, form a fyftem of commercial regulations, prejudicial to this great mafs of property, and to this great body of the people, we muft injure our country during the continuance of the error, and we muft finally return, under the difadvantages of further changes,

to that plan, which it muft be our fincere defire,
as it is our ferious duty, at this time to devife*.

While we feel an abfolute conviction, that our
true interefts fhould reftrain us from burdening or
impeding agriculture in any way whatever, we muft
be ready to admit, that found policy requires our
giving every encouragement to commerce and its
connexions†, which may be found confiftent with
a due regard to agriculture.

The communication between the different ports
of every nation is a bufinefs entirely in their power—The policy of moft countries has been to fecure this domeftic navigation to their own people.
The extenfive coafts, the immenfe bays and numerous rivers of the United States have already made
this an important object, and it muft increafe with
our population‡. As the places at which the cargoes of coafting veffels are delivered muft be fupplied with American produce from fome part of
the Union, and as the merchant can always have

---

* The ftate of information, connected with commercial legiflation was very unfatisfactory in 1787. We had very few ftate documents, and lefs of national. To legiflate then on the fubject was
a more difficult and uncertain bufinefs than it now is.—A. D.
1793.

† The fifheries and manufactures.

‡ The coafting veffels, entered at the cuftom-houfe of Philadelphia in the year 1785, were 567 fail; all the other entries of fea-
veffels in the fame year were 501.

American bottoms to transport the goods of the
producing state to the state consuming them, no
interruption to the market of the planters and farmers can be apprehended from prohibiting tranfportation in foreign bottoms from port to port
within the United States—A single exception may
perhaps be proper, permitting foreign veffels to
carry from port to port, *for the purpofe of finifhing
their fales,* any goods that fhall be *part of the cargoes they brought into the Union, from the laft foreign
place at which they loaded.* The fleets of colliers
on the Britifh coaft evince the poffible benefits of
fuch a regulation*.

The confumption of fifh, oil, whalebone and
other articles obtained through the fifheries, in the
towns and counties that are convenient to naviga
tion, has become much greater than is generally
fuppofed. It is faid that no lefs than five thoufand
barrels of mackarel, falmon and pickled cod-fifh,
are vended in the city of Philadelphia annually.
Add to them the dried fifh, oil, fpermaceti candles,
whalebone, &c. and it will be found that a little
fleet of floops and fchooners muft be employed in
the bufinefs.

The demand for the ufe of the inhabitants of
thofe parts of the Union to which thefe fupplies

* The freight made by a foreign veffel from Bofton to Philadelphia, or from New-York to Virginia, or from Philadelphia to
Charlefton, is a total lofs to the United States.

can be carried, is already confiderable, and the increafe of our towns and manufactures will render it more fo every year. In the prefent ftate of our navigation we can be in no doubt of procuring thefe fupplies by means of our own veffels. The country that interferes moft with us in our own market is Nova Scotia, which alfo, it is faid, has had fome emigrants from our fifhing towns fince the decline of their bufinefs. Such encouragement to this valuable branch of commerce, as would fecure the benefits of it to our own people, without injuring our other effential interefts, is certainly worth attention. The Convention will, probably, find on confideration of this point, that a duty or prohibition of foreign articles, fuch as our own fifheries fupply, will be fafe and expedient*.

The article in the Britifh trade laws, which confines the importation of foreign goods to the bottoms of the country producing them, and of their own citizens, appears applicable to our fituation. By means of thofe two flags we fhould be certain of the neceffary importations, and we fhould throw out of each department of the carrying trade every competitor, except the fhips of the nation by which the goods were produced or manufactured. All trade whit feveral countries, fuch as China and India,

---

* The plan of the Convention was not at that time known. Inftead of a power to lay particular duties being granted to Congrefs, the better grant of a power to regulate our national commerce was made.

whole veffels feldom or never make foreign voyages, would be fecured in our own hands. It will
be found, that a modified application of this regulation in practice, will be attended with no difficulties or inconveniencies, and befides the immediate benefits already mentioned, our merchants
will be led *directly* to the *original* market for the
fupplies of which we ftand in need. Inftead of
purchafing the goods of Ruffia or the Eaft-Indies
in England, France or Holland, our own fhips
will fail directly to the fountain from whence they
have hitherto flowed to us through foreign channels. The credits given to us in Europe after the
peace, kept us in the practice of going to a very
few places, for all our importations. But they
have trufted us in many inftances at a dear rate
indeed, and however ufeful credit may be as a fup-
plement to our means of trade in this young country, it is very certain that we fhould firft lay out,
to the beft advantage, our funds in hand.

These are the principal encouragements to foreign commerce, which occur at prefent as proper
to form a part of a permanent fyftem for the United States. Regulations for temporary purpofes,
fuch as reftrictions and prohibitions affecting particular nations, it is not meant to fpeak of here.
It muft be obferved, however, that they fhould be
adopted with great prudence and deliberation, as
they may affect us very unfavourably, if they
fhould be tried in vain.

In taking measures to promote manufactures, we must be careful, that the injuries to agriculture and the general interests of commerce do not exceed the advantages resulting from them. *The circumstances of the country, as they relate to this business, should be dispassionately and thorougly examined**. Tho' it is confessed that the United States have full employment for all their citizens in the extensive field of agriculture, yet as we have a valuable body of manufacturers already here, as many more will emigrate from Europe, most of whom may chuse to continue at their trades, and as we have some citizens so poor as not to be able to effect a little settlement on our waste lands, there is a real necessity for some wholesome general regulations on this head. By taking care not to force manufactures in those states, where the people are fewer, tillage much more profitable, and provisions dearer than in several others, we shall give agriculture its full scope in the former, and leave all the benefits of manufacturing (so far as they are within our reach) to the latter. South-Carolina, for example, must, in many instances, manufacture to an evident loss†, while the advancement of that business in Massachusetts will give the means of subsistence to many, whose occupations have been rendered unprofitable by the consequences of the revolution. A liberal policy on this subject should be adopted, and the

---

* This has been frequently done since 1786, and the subject is now reduced to some plain and safe principles.

† Domestic manufacturing must be always excepted.

produce of the fouthern ftates fhould be exchanged
for fuch manufactures as can be made by the northern, free from impoft*.

Another inducement to fome falutary regulations
on this fubject, will be fuggefted by confidering
fome of our means of conducting manufactures.
Unlefs bufinefs of this kind is carried on, certain
great *natural powers* of the country will remain inactive and ufelefs. Our numerous mill feats, for
example, by which flour, oil, paper, fnuff, gunpowder, iron work, woolen cloaths, boards and fcantling, and fome other articles are prepared or per-
fected, would be given by Providence in vain. If
properly improved, they will fave us an immenfe
expence for the wages, provifions, cloathing and
lodging of workmen, without diverting the people
from their farms—Fire, as well as water, affords,
if we may fo fpeak, a fund of affiftance, that cannot lie unufed without an evident neglect of our
beft interefts. Breweries, which we cannot eftimate too highly, diftilleries, fugar houfes, potteries, cafting and fteel furnaces, and feveral other
works are carried on by this powerful element, and
attended with the fame favings, as were particularized in fpeaking of water machines—'Tis probable alfo that a frequent ufe of fteam engines will
add greatly to this clafs of factories. In fome cafes,

* From the claufe in the Federal Conftitution, which fecures
this advantage, a great fpring is given to the coafting trade, and
to American manufactures.

where fire and water are not employed, horfes are
made to ferve the purpofe as well, and on much
lower terms than men. The cheapnefs and the eafy encreafe of thefe ferviceable animals infure us
this aid to any extent that occafion may require,
which however is not likely to be very great.

The encouragement to agriculture, afforded by
fome manufactories, is a reafon of folid weight in
favour of carrying them on with induftry and fpirit. Malt liquors, if generally ufed, linfeed oil,
ftarch (and were they not a poifon to our morals
and conftitutions we might add grain fpirits) would
require more grain to make them, than has been
exported in any year fince the revolution*.—We
cannot omit to obferve here, that beer ftrengthens
the arm of the labourer without debauching him,
while the noxious drink now ufed enervates and
corrupts him—The workers in leather too of every kind, in flax and hemp, in iron, wood, ftone
and clay, in furs, horn, and many other articles
employ either the fpontaneous productions of the
earth, or the fruits of cultivation.

If we are convinced, by thefe confiderations, that
regular factories of many kinds fhould be promoted
in the moft fuitable part of the Union, let us next
confider, whether the encouragements now held
out to them are at prefent fufficient and proper.

* A fenfible and well-informed Englifh writer ftates the quantity of grain *made into drink* in Britain at twenty-four millions of
bufhels, valued at £.3,000,000 fterling.

The neareſt rivals of our manufacturers are thoſe of Europe, who are ſubjeĉted to the following charges in bringing their goods into our market: The merchant's commiſſion for ſhipping from the foreign port, and the ſame charge for ſelling here, the coſt of packages, cuſtom-houſe papers in Europe, and the ſame charge with a duty of five *per cent.* here*, porterages, freight, inſurance, damage, intereſt of money, waſte, and loſs on exchange—Theſe may be rated at twenty-five *per cent.* on the leaſt bulky of our manufactures†. Here

* The duties have been raiſed, with a view to revenue, to at leaſt 7½ per cent. on all manufactured goods: and with a view to the protection of manufactures, they have been advanced upon ſeveral claſſes of articles to 10, 12½, 15, and 15½ per cent. The ſpecific duties are much higher. *See table of duties.* A. D. 1793.

† We have no manufacture more compact than a piece of yard wide linen, equal to what coſt 15d. ſterling in Europe. The following minute calculation will ſhew the charges, under which a package of 100l. ſterling value of that article can be imported.

	Currency.		
64 pieces of linen of 25 yards each, will be 1600 yards, which, at 15d. amount to 100l. ſterling, - -	166	13	4
Outward entry, debenture certificate, and ſearchers fees, porterage, wharfage, bill of lading in Europe are 15s. ſterling, or in currency - - -	1	5	0
Inſurance to cover charges, commiſſion for effecting and part policy, £.3 3s. ſterling, or currency, -	5	5	0
Coſt of caſe, ropes, and packing, 15s. ſterling, -	1	5	0
One year's intereſt on firſt coſt, and European charges on the goods, £.5 5s. ſterling, - - -	8	15	0

[*N. B.* This is too low, for the manufacturing houſes put twice that advance upon what the goods are worth in *caſh.*]

Carried over,	£.183	3	4

is a folid premium, operating like a bounty, while it happily cofts the confumer nothing but what he would otherwife be obliged to pay ; for the charges of importation are unavoidable, and the duty being *merely for the purpofe of revenue,* is applied to pay the public debts and expences of which he owes his proportion. This encouragement can be fome-what encreafed *by exempting raw materials from duty,* which may be very fafe and proper, and by addi-

C

		Currency.		
Brought forward,	- - -	£.183	3	4
Duty on the value of goods in America eftimated at 160l. currency for 100l. fterling coft, at 5 per cent.		8	0	0
Commiffion on fhipping, £.183 4 4 in Europe, at 2½ per cent.	- - -	4	11	7
Part cuftom-houfe bond and permit, and primage,		0	1	6
Commiffion on the fales and remitting, fuppofing the goods to fell for 210l. currency, per 100l. fterling coft, at 7½ per cent.	- - -	11	5	0
Freight of 13 1-3 feet, at 1/3 fterling per foot,	-	1	7	9
Porterage,	- - - -	0	1	0
		208	10	2
Deduct the firft coft as above,	- -	166	13	4

£.25 2 1 fterling, being the charges, is equal to £. 41 16 10

In this calculation, wafte, which of fome articles is great, da-mages below 5 per cent. which the underwriters do not pay, in-juries not within the rifk infured, difference of exchange now 6 per cent. above par ,and other loffes on remitting, poftages of letters, and bad debts on fales at a long credit, as well as the pro-fit of the importer and the higher rate of duties, which feveral claffes of goods pay are not taken notice of, though feveral of them really occur in every importation.

tional duties and prohibitions, which might induce the lofs of the revenue and an injury to morals from fmuggling, and would throw upon the
other members of the commercial interest and the
cultivators and improvers of our lands an unneceffary burden. The manufacturers are a judicious body of men, and love their country. There
is every reafon to confide therefore, that when
they fee a fubftantial advantage of twenty-five *per
cent.* at leaft in favour of their goods, *which cannot
be taken from them*, they will defire that government fhould refrain from further duties and prohibitions. This eftimate being made upon the fineft of our manufactures, it is evident that the more
bulky and weighty would exhibit the advantages
of our own workmen in a yet ftronger light.

The clear air and powerful fun of America are
other advantages which our manufacturers enjoy.
When the linen and cotton branches fhall become
confiderable, a great faving of time and money will
be made by the climate, and where bleaching is effected principally by the fun and water, the quality
of the cloth is known to be more excellent. The European procefs by drugs and machines impairs the
ftrength. Ireland, it is confeffed, with a climate very
different from ours, is remarkable for the quality of
its linens, but they do not equal the American home-
fpun in ftrength. In confirmation of the above
opinion, it may be mentioned, that there was a
plan formed before the revolution, by a number
of English merchants, of eftablishing a company

with a large capital, to import the *brown* linens of Europe to be bleached here for the fupply of our markets.

In this country the confumer's money follows the delivery of the manufacture, therefore lefs capital is required. In every part of Europe extenfive credits are given upon their goods. For tho' fome nations have not got into the habit of truſting us, their own merchants are known to buy on eafy terms of payment. France is, perhaps, as little accuſtomed to give thefe indulgencies as any other great country in Europe, yet nothing is paid for there, in lefs than two months, and the credits are extended from that time to twelve months according to the article. At the expiration of the term an accepted bill at fixty days is confidered as prompt payment, fo that the actual term of credit is from four months to fourteen.

To thefe might be added feveral other little advantages, the joint benefits of which are fenfibly felt, but it is prefumed that enough has been faid to fatisfy the juſt and patriotic mind, though concerned in the bufinefs, that a further addition of duties would not promote the general interefts of the country. We muſt here beg leave however ſtrenuouſly to recommend, that every duty on American produce or manufaćtures, impoliticly and unkindly impofed by the laws of feyeral of the ſtates, fhould be taken off, and that the juſtice and found policy of the alteration fhould be declared

and admitted in some public inftrument: and as
fhips may be very properly confidered as the greateft article we make, the tonnage on our own bottoms fhould be equalized throughout the Union,
and the extra duties on goods imported in veffels not belonging to the ftate in which they are
landed, fhould be done away—Complaints againft
the trade laws of foreign nations come not confift-
ently from thofe who lay fimilar burdens on their
fifter ftates.

A further encouragement to manufactures will
refult from improvements and difcoveries in agriculture—There are many raw materials, that could
be produced in this country in abundance, which
have hitherto been very limited. *Cotton* for many
years before the revolution was not worth more
than nine pence fterling in the Weft-India Iflands.
The perfection of the factories in Europe has raifed
it to fuch a pitch, that befides the prohibition
againft fhipping it from the colonies to any foreign
port, the price has rifen fifty per cent. The confumers in Pennfylvania have paid near two fhillings
fterling for the importation of this year. This article
muft be worth the attention of the fouthern planters.

If the facts and obfervations in the preceding
part of this paper be admitted to be true and juft,
and if we take into confideration with them the fuperiority of foreign commerce, and the fifheries
over our manufactories*, we may come to the fol-

* A. D. 1787.

lowing conclusions—That the United States of America cannot make a proper use of the natural advantages of the country, nor promote her agriculture and other interests without manufactures, that they cannot enjoy the attainable benefits of commerce and the fisheries, without some general restrictions and prohibitions affecting foreign nations, that in forming these restrictions and prohitions, as well as in establishing manufactories, there is occasion for the greatest deliberation and wisdom, that nothing may be introduced, *which can interfere with the sale of our produce, or with the settlement and improvement of our new lands.*

Among the political considerations, which must necessarily be admitted in treating of this subject, the force that may be required for our protection is not to be forgotten. It is certainly the greatest that attends it. America, we may assume, can have no inducement to engage in European wars. From our local situation we may keep ourselves long disengaged from them. The principal European nations would find us an unprofitable and troublesome enemy. The trade of France, Great-Britain, Spain, Holland and Portugal, which passes by our coasts, are a security against their hostilities. A war among them, in which we should take no part, would be more beneficial to our farmers, merchants and manufacturers than all the advantages we could obtain, if engaged in it ourselves. Our ships would carry for them, or instead of theirs, and our lands and manufactories would furnish the

supplies of their fleets and iflands in the Weft-Indies. To counterbalance thefe advantages, and to
pay the expences of a war would require captures
rich and numerous indeed; but what would compenfate us for the drain of peafantry and the loft
opportunity of cultivating commerce and the arts
of peace. A war merely offenfive cannot be apprehended. The fortune of the Britifh arms againft
America undifciplined and divided, will inftruct
our enemies to beware of invafions after the military leffons taken from that long and ferious conteft. Having no foreign colonies whofe fituation and weaknefs would fubject them to their at-
tacks, and having all our refources at hand to defend our own coafts, and cut up their trade in its
paffage by our doors, no European power will be
inclined to infult or moleft us. Should any of them
be fo infenfible to their own interefts, as to depart
from the policy, which evidently ought to govern
them, America, by acting in concert with the moft
powerful enemy of fuch hoftile country, muft commence a war, which however inconvenient and
difagreeable to us, would be ruinous to their Weft-
India trade, and fatal to their colonies. We are
not deftitute of refources and powers to injure
them or defend ourfelves. Our inland navigation,
coafting trade and fifheries, and the portion of foreign commerce we muft inevitably enjoy, are no
inconfiderable nurferies for feamen. Good naval
officers we fhould not want: they have never been
fcarce, and one happy effect of the revolution has
certainly been to raife the reputation of the marine

life, and to increafe the talents and refpectability of its followers. Foreign feamen too, would find great temptations to enter on board our privateers and fhips of war, and might be hired in any numbers we could pay. The increafe of the ftrength and riches of the country, by filling up our vacant lands, is the infallible method by which the neceffary means may be acquired.

It will not be amifs to draw a picture of our country, as it would really exift under the operation of a fyftem of national laws formed upon thefe principles. While we indulge ourfelves in the contemplation of a fubject at once fo interefting and dear, let us confine ourfelves to fubftantial facts, and avoid thofe pleafing delufions into which the fpirits and feelings of our countrymen have too often mifled them.

In *the foreground* we fhould find the mafs of our citizens—the cultivators (and what is happily for us in moft inftances the fame thing) the independent proprietors of the foil. Every wheel would appear in motion that could carry forward the interefts of this great body of our people, and bring into action the inherent powers of the country. A portion of the produce of our lands would be confumed in the families or employed in the bufinefs of our manufacturers—a further portion would be applied in the fuftenance of our merchants and fifhermen and their numerous affiftants, and the remainder would be tranfported by thofe that could

carry it at the loweſt freight (that is with the ſmalleſt deduction from the aggregate profits of the buſineſs of the country) to the beſt foreign markets.
On one ſide we ſhould ſee our manufacturers encouraging the tillers of the earth by the conſumption and employment of the fruits of their labours,
and ſupplying them and the reſt of their fellow citizens with the inſtruments of their occupations,
and the neceſſaries and conveniencies of life, in
every inſtance wherein it could be done without
unneceſſarily diſtreſſing commerce and increaſing
the labours of the huſbandmen, and the difficulties
of changing our remaining wilds into ſcenes of cultivation and plenty. Commerce, *on the other hand*,
attentive to the general intereſts, would come forward with offers to range through foreign climates
in ſearch of thoſe ſupplies, which the manufacturers could not furniſh but at too high a price, or
which nature has not given us at home, in return
for the ſurplus of thoſe ſtores, that had been drawn
from the ocean or produced by the earth.

On a review of the preceding facts and obſervations there appears good reaſon to believe, that
the neceſſary meaſures might be taken to render
our farms profitable and to improve our new lands,
and that our manufactures, fiſheries, navigation
and trade, would ſtill be conſiderable. The long
voyage by which all interfering foreign articles
muſt be brought to theſe markets, and *the inevitable neceſſity for a revenue*, give us, as hath been
demonſtrated, a virtual bounty of twenty-five *per*

cent. in favor of our own commodities, and this in
the leaft favorable inftances. When *returning* œ-
conomy, and the fall of rents and provifions fhall
have reduced the expences of living, when our increafing farms fhall have poured in their addition
of raw materials, and we fhall have felt the fhort-
nefs of importation produced by the fuffering of
our credit abroad, and by the check which has been
given to foreign adventurers in our trade, this difference of twenty-five *per cent.* will have a fenfible effect*. Being rated on the whole value of the article, that is, as well on the labour as the raw materials, it is in fact fifty *per cent.* on the labour in all
cafes wherein the workmanfhip is half the value
of the manufactured goods, and fo in proportion
where it is more. Beer, diftilled liquors, pot-afh,
gun-powder, cordage, loaf fugar, hanging and writing paper, fnuff, tobacco, ftarch, anchors, nail
rods, and many other articles of iron, bricks,
tiles, potters ware, mill-ftones, and other ftone
work, cabinet work, corn fans, Windfor chairs,
carriages, fadlery, fhoes and boots, and other wearing apparel, coarfe linens, hats, a few coarfe wool-
en articles, linfeed oil, wares of gold and filver,
tin and copper, fome braziery, wool cards, worms
and ftills, and feveral other articles may be confidered as eftablifhed. Thefe are tending to greater
perfection, and will foon be fold fo cheap as to
throw foreign goods of the fame kind entirely out
of the market.

* This has now become very evident. A. D. 1793.

Many of the fame circumftances, that favour the manufacturer, will render the fifheries more profitable, and from the cheapnefs of veffels, they will be carried on at lefs expence than in the few laft years. The American market, where the confumption (with population) is increafing faft, may be entirely fecured to them. Our manufactories and towns will annually make larger demands for candles, oil, whalebone and pickled fifh, and it would be good policy to extend the confumption of the dried cod. The Danifh and French iflands, and the free ports in the Weft-Indies, receive fome of the produce of the fifheries—France is likely to take off a confiderable quantity, as alfo are the Spaniards, Portuguefe and Italians, and the Englifh will always want certain articles for their manufactories, though not to any great amount—New-England, the feat of the fifheries, has the great advantage of being the cheapeft and moft populous part of America. Its inhabitants are healthy, active and intelligent, and can be frugal; wherefore there appears good reafon to be believe, that many factories will in the courfe of a very few years revive their declining towns.

The commercial citizens of America have for fome time felt the deepeft diftrefs. Among the principal caufes of their unhappy fituation were the inconfiderate fpirit of adventure to this country, which pervaded almoft every kingdom in Europe, and the prodigious credits from thence given to our merchants on the return of peace. To thefe may be added the high fpirits and the golden dreams, which naturally followed fuch a war, clofed with fo much honor and fuccefs.—Triumphant over a great ene-my, courted by the moft powerful nations in the world, it was not in human nature that America fhould immediately comprehend her new fituation. Really poffeffed of the means of future greatnefs, fhe anticipated the moft diftant benefits of the revolu-tion, and confidered them as already in her hands. She formed the higheft expectations, many of which however, ferious experience has taught her to relin-quifh, and now that the thoughtlefs adventures and imprudent credits from foreign countries take place no more*, and time has been given for cool reflec-tion, fhe can fee her real fituation and need not be difcouraged.

Our future trade may comprehend the fifheries, with the exclufive benefit of fupplying our own markets, as hath been already obferved. The coafting trade† will be entirely fecured to us. The right of bringing the commodities of foreign countries may be divided with the fhips of the nation from whom they come, or in thofe cafes where they have no native fhips, the carrying

* An application of the foregoing obfervations to the commerci-al fubject, can only be admiffible into this effay.

† This, though not in form, is yet, in effect, fecured to us. The coafting trade will receive a great fpring from the Chefapeak collieries in a few years, fhould no others be difcovered on naviga-ble water.

trade may be our own*. The revolution has opened to us some new branches of valuable commerce.
The intercourse with France was next to none before the war, and with Russia†, India and China
not thought of. With activity and strict economy
we may pay Europe with some of the *produce* of
India, for a part of the goods with which they supply us, and if we do not over-regulate trade, we
shall be an *entrepot* of certain commodities for their
West-Indian and South-American colonies. Besides these objects all the manufacturing countries
and many free ports will be open to us, and we
may adventure in foreign ships to a considerable
extent, though it would be more desirable to employ our own. As the proposed regulations would
compel the British or Dutch merchants, to import
into the United States a part of the produce of
France and Spain in American bottoms, so may
ours serve the general interests of their country by
sending tobacco to Sweden, or flour, rice and live
stock to the British colonies in the vessels of the
respective nations.

The foundations of national wealth and consequence are so firmly laid in the United States, that
no *foreign* power can undermine or destroy them.
But the enjoyment of these substantial blessings is

---

* This idea remains for consideration as before observed.

† With Russia it is not at present likely to be very great. Our
products and manufactures are similar and bulky: Our positions
remote.

rendered precarious by domeſtic circumſtances. Scarcely held together by a weak and half formed federal conſtitution, the powers of our national government, are unequal to the complete execution of any ſalutary purpoſe, foreign or domeſtic. The evils reſulting from this unhappy ſtate of things have again ſhocked our reviving credit, produced among our people alarming inſtances of diſobedience to the laws, and if not remedied, muſt deſtroy our property, liberties and peace. Foreign powers, however diſpoſed to favor us, can expect neither ſatisfaction nor benefit from treaties with Congreſs, while they are unable to enforce them. We can therefore hope to ſecure no privileges from them, if matters are thus conducted. We muſt immediately remedy this defect or ſuffer exceedingly. Deſultory commercial acts of the legiſlatures, formed on the impreſſion of the moment, proceeding from no uniform or permanent principles, claſhing with the laws of other ſtates and oppoſing thoſe made in the preceding year by the enacting ſtate, can no longer be ſupported, if we are to continue one people. *A ſyſtem which will promote the general intereſts with the ſmalleſt injury to particular ones has become indiſpenſibly neceſſary.* Commerce is more affected by the diſtractions and evils ariſing from the uncertainty, oppoſition and errors of our trade laws, than by the reſtrictions of any one power in Europe. A negative upon all commercial acts of the legiſlatures, if granted to Congreſs wold be perfectly ſafe, and muſt have an excellent effect*. If thought expedient it fhould be given as well with regard to thofe that exift, as to thofe that may be devifed in future. Congrefs would thus be enabled to prevent every regulation, that might oppofe the general interefts, and by reftraining the ftates from impolitic laws, would gradually bring our national commerce to order and perfection.

We have ventured to hint at prohibitory powers, but fhall leave that point and the general power of regulating trade to thofe who may undertake to confider the political objects of the Convention, fuggefting only the evident propriety of enabling Congrefs to prevent the importation of foreign commodities, fuch as can be made from our own raw materials†. When any article of that kind can be fupplied at home, upon as low terms as thofe on which it can be imported, a manufacture of *our own produce*, fo well eftablifhed, ought not by any means to be facrificed to the interefts of foreign trade, or fubjected to injury by the wild fpeculations of ignorant adventurers. In all cafes careful provifion fhould be made for refunding the duties on exportation, which renders the impoft a virtual excife without being liable to any of the objections which have been made againft an actual one, and is a great encouragement to trade.

* The power over commerce granted by the federal conftitution is far preferable to this.

† Though this fhould be moft cautioufly done, it merits careful attention.

The reſtoration of public credit at home and abroad ſhould be the firſt wiſh of our hearts, and requires every economy, every exertion we can make. The wiſe and virtuous axioms of our political conſtitutions, reſulting from a lively and perfect ſenſe of what is due from man to man, ſhould prompt us to the diſcharge of debts of ſuch peculiar obligation. We ſtand bound to no common creditors. The friendly foreigner, the widow and the orphan, the truſtees of charity and religion, the patriotic citizen, the war-worn ſoldier and a magnanimous ally—theſe are the principal claimants upon the feelings and juſtice of America. Let her apply all her reſources to this great duty, and wipe away the darkeſt ſtain, that has ever fallen upon her. The general impoſt—the ſale of the lands and every other unneſſary article of public property—reſtraining with a firm hand every needleſs expence of government and private life—ſteady and patient induſtry, with proper diſpoſitionsin the people, would relieve us of part of the burden, and enable Congreſs to commence their payments, and with the aid of taxation, would put theſinking and funding of our debts within the power of the United States.

The violence committed on the rights of property under the authority of tender laws in ſome of the ſtates, the familiarity with which that pernicious meaſure has been recurred to, and the ſhameleſs perſeverance with which it has been perſiſted in after the value of the paper was confeſſedly gone, call aloud for ſome remedy. This is not merely a

matter of juſtice between man and man. It diſho-
nors our national charaćter abroad, and the engine
has been employed to give the *coup de grace* to public credit. It would not be difficult perhaps to
form a new article* of confederation to prevent it
in future, and a queſtion may ariſe whether fellow-
ſhip with any ſtate, that would refuſe to admit it,
can be ſatisfaćtory or ſafe. To remove difficulties
it need not be retroſpećtive. The preſent ſtate of
things inſtead of inviting emigrants, deters all who
have the means of information, and are capable of
thinking. The ſettlement of our lands, and the
introdućtion of manufaćtories and branches of trade
yet unknown among us or requiring a force of capital, which are to make our country rich and
powerful, are interrupted and ſuſpended by our
want of public credit and the numerous diſorders
of our government."

———————

The meaſures of the convention of 1787, iſſued,
as it is univerſally known, in impoſing a *conſtitution-
al* prohibition upon paper emiſſions, paper tenders
and other pernicious violations of the rights of
property, in the confirmation of the foreign treaties by an aćt of the people, in the eſtabliſhment of
a national legiſlature with complete powers over

* This idea is moſt happily carried to the utmoſt length we
could deſire in the federal conſtitution and the clauſe is no leſs favorable to commerce than to private virtue and national honour.

commerce and navigation, defence, war and peace, money, and all the other great objects of national economy. The confequences of this wife and fingular effort of the American people are beginning to be known to the world, and fome of them will appear in the latter chapters of this volume.

CHAPTER III.

Sketches of the subject of American Manufactures in 1787, preparatory to exertions for their advancement and increase.

THE various political diforders of 1787, and the want of *national* fyftem, affected very feverely a number of perfons in the large towns, who were engaged in the different branches of manufactures. Thefe were more numerous and much more important, than was at that time perceived by perfons of the clofeft obfervation. The laws of fome of the ftates impofed confiderable duties upon the fabrics of all the reft; in fome inftances as high as the impoft on fimilar articles manufactured in foreign countries. The remains of the exceffive importations of the four preceding years were conftantly offered for fale at prices lower than their coft in Europe, and lefs than they could be made for in America. From a deep fenfe of thefe inconveniencies exertions were commenced, in various parts of the United States, by perfons of all defcriptions, to relieve the manufacturing citizens; which appeared the more defirable to many, becaufe the neceffary meafures tended, at the fame time, to promote *the great caufe of union among the ftates,* and to reprefs habits of expenfe, which the war, and the peace likewife, though from very different caufes, had introduced into moft of the towns, and into too many parts of the country.

The citizens of Philadelphia took a very active part in these salutary measures, and instituted a society, which afterwards proved of considerable utility, to carry their views into execution. The address, which is comprized in this chapter, was prepared in consequence of a request from one of the meetings, which were held by the promoters of the institution, and other patrons of the internal trade and manufactures of the United States.

An Address to an assembly of the friends of American manufactures, convened for the purpose of establishing a Society for the encouragement of Manufactures and the useful arts, in the University of Pennsylvania, on Thursday, the 9th of August, 1787, and published at their request.

GENTLEMEN,

WHILE I obey with sincere pleasure the commands of the respectable assembly whom I have now the honor to address, I feel the most trying emotions of anxiety and apprehension in attempting to perform so difficult and serious a duty, as that prescribed to me at our last meeting. The importance and novelty of the subject, the injurious consequences of mistaken opinions on it and your presence necessarily excite feelings such as these. They are lessened however, by the hope of some benefit to that part of my fellow citizens, who depend for comfort on our native manufactures, and by an ardent wish to promote every measure, that will give to our new-born states the strength of man-

hood. Supported by thefe confiderations and rely-
ing on the kind indulgence, which is ever fhewn
to well-meant endeavours, however unfuccefsful, I
fhall venture to proceed.

Providence has beftowed upon the United States
of America means of happinefs, as great and numerous, as are enjoyed by any country in the world.
A foil fruitful and diverfified—a healthful climate—
mighty rivers and adjacent feas abounding with fifh
are the great advantages for which we are indebted
to a beneficent creator. Agriculture, manufactures
and commerce, naturally arifing from thefe fources,
afford to our induftrious citizens certain fubfiftence
and innumerable opportunities of acquiring wealth.
*To arrange our affairs in falutary and well digefted
fyftems*, by which the fruits of induftry, in every
line, may be moft eafily attained, and the poffeffion
of property and the bleffings of liberty may be completely fecured—thefe are the important objects,
that fhould engrofs our prefent attention. The interefts of commerce and the eftablifhment of a juft
and effective government are already committed to
the care of THE AUGUST BODY* now fitting
in our capital.—The importance of agriculture has
long fince recommended it to the patronage of numerous affociations, and the attention of all the legiflatures—but manufactures, at leaft in Pennfylvania, have had but few unconnected friends, till
found policy and public fpirit gave a late, but au-
fpicious birth, to this Society.

* The Federal Convention.

The fituation of America before the revolution was very unfavourable to the objects of this inftitution. The prohibition of moft foreign raw materials—confiderable bounties in England for carrying away the unwrought productions of this country to that, as well as on exporting Britifh goods from their markets—the preference for thofe goods, which habit carried much beyond what their excellence would juftify, and many other circumftances, created artificial impediments which appeared almoft infuperable. Several branches however were carried on with great advantage. But as long as we remained in our colonial fituation, our progrefs was very flow; and indeed the neceffity of attention to manufactures was not fo urgent, as it has become fince our affuming an independent ftation. The employment of thofe, whom the decline of navigation† has deprived of their ufual occupations—*the confumption of the encreafing produce of our lands and fifheries,* and *the certainty of fupplies in the time of war* are very weighty reafons for eftablifhing new manufactories now, which exifted but in a fmall degree, or not at all, before the revolution.

While we readily admit, that in taking meafures to promote the objects of this fociety, *nothing fhould be attempted, which may injure our agricultural interefts,* they being undoubtedly the moft important, we muft obferve in juftice to ourfelves, that very many of our citizens, who are expert at

† A. D. 1787.

manufactures and the useful arts, are entirely un-
acquainted with rural affairs, or unequal to the
expences of a new settlement; and* *many* we may
believe, will come among us invited to our shores
from foreign countries, by the blessings of liberty,
civil and religious. We may venture to assert too,
that more profit to the individual and riches to
the nation will be derived from some manufactures,
which promote agriculture, than from any species
of cultivation† whatever. The truth of this remark however, will be better determined, when
the subject shall be further considered.

Let us first endeavour to disencumber manufactures of the objections, that appear against them,
the principal of which are, *the high rate of labour,*
which involves the price of provisions—*the want of
a sufficient number of hands* on any terms,—*the
scarcity and dearness of raw materials—want of skill*
in the business itself and *its unfavorable effects on
the health of the people.*

Factories which can be carried on by water-mills,
wind-mills, fire, horses and machines ingeniously
contrived, are not burdened with any heavy expense of boarding, lodging, clothing and paying

* This has been the great dependance and the great means in
the business of handicraft manufactures in Pennsylvania.

† The manufacture of malt liquors and fruit and corn spirits
might be the means of preventing the importation of rum, brandy, gin, &c. which must amount to two millions of dollars per annum taking in all our ports.

workmen, and they fupply the force of hands to a great extent without taking our people from agriculture. By wind and water machines we can make pig and bar iron, nail rods, tire, fheet-iron, fheet-copper, fheet-brafs, anchors, meal of all kinds, gun-powder, writing, printing and ha nging paper, fnuff, linfeed oil, boards, plank and fcantling*; and they affift us in finifhing fcythes, fickles and woolen cloths. Strange as it may appear they alfo card, fpin and even weave, it is faid, by water in the European factories. Bleaching and tanning† muft not be omitted, while we are fpeaking of the ufefulnefs of water.

By fire we conduct our breweries, diftilleries, falt and potafh works, fugar houfes, potteries, cafting and fteel furnaces, works for animal and vegetable oils and refining drugs‡. Steam mills have not yet been adopted in America, but we fhall probably fee them after a fhort time in places, where there are few mill feats and in this and other great towns of the United States. The city of Philadel-

---

* One mill of Ramfey's (the improvement on Barker's) near Philadelphia, grinds by water, chocolate, flour, fnuff, hair-powder, and muftard, and fhells chocolate nuts; alfo preffes and cuts tobacco for chewing and fmokeing, and boults meal.

† The leather branch in Great-Britain is eftimated at eleven millions of pounds fterling, or more than a fifth of all their ftaple manufactures, and we eat more meat than they, and have the command of much more deer-fkins.

‡ The American improvements in fteam have been brought forward fince this publication.

phia, by adopting the ufe of them, might make a great faving on all the grain brought hither by water, which is afterwards manufactured into meal, and they might be ufefully applied to many other valuable purpofes.

Horfes give us, in fome inftances, a relief from the difficulties we are endeavouring to obviate. They grind the tanners bark and potters clay; they work the brewers and diftillers pumps, and might be applied, by an inventive mind, as the moving principle of many kinds of mills*.

Machines ingenioufly conftructed, will give us immenfe affiftance.—The cotton and filk manufacturers in Europe are poffeffed of fome, that are invaluable to them. Several inftances have been afcertained, in which a few hundreds of women and children perform the work of thoufands of carders, fpinners and winders. In fhort, combinations of machines with fire and water have already accomplifhed much more than was formerly expected from them by the moft vifionary enthufiaft on the fubject. Perhaps I may be too fanguine, but they appear to me fraught with immenfe advantages to us, and not a little dangerous to the manufacturing nations of Europe; for fhould they continue to ufe and improve them, as they have heretofore done, their people may be driven to us for want of employment, and if, on the other hand, they fhould

* We might cut ftone and marble by horfe and *water* mills. In Italy the *latter* is the mode.

return to manual labour, we may underwork them
by thefe invaluable engines. We may certainly
borrow fome of their inventions*, and others of the
fame nature we may ftrike out ourfelves; for on the
fubjeƈt of mechanifm America may juftly pride her-
felf. Every combination of machinery may be expeƈted from a country, A NATIVE SON of which,
reaching this ineftimable objeƈt at its higheft point,
has epitomized the motions of the fpheres, that
roll throughout the univerfet.

The lovers of mankind, fupported by experienced phyficians, and the opinions of enlightened politicians, have objeƈted to manufaƈtures as unfavourable to the health of the people. Giving to this
humane and important confideration its full weight,
it furnifhes an equal argument againft feveral other
occupations, by which we obtain our comforts and
promote our agriculture. The painting bufinefs
for inftance—reclaiming marfhes—clearing fwamps
—the culture of rice and indigo and fome other
employments, are even more fatal to thofe, who are
engaged in them. But this objeƈtion is urged
principally againft carding, fpinning and weaving,
which *formerly* were entirely manual and fedentary
occupations. Our plan, as we have already fhewn,
is not to purfue thofe modes unlefs in cafes parti-

---

* 1790. We have fince obtained the mill for fpinning flax,
hemp and wool.

† David Rittenhoufe, of Pennfylvania.

cularly circumſtanced, for we are ſenſible that our people muſt not be diverted from their farms. *Horſes, and the potent elements of fire and water, aided by the faculties of the human mind, are to be in many inſtances, our daily labourers**. After giving immediate relief to the induſtrious poor, theſe unhurtful means will be purſued and will procure us private wealth and national proſperity.

Emigration from Europe will alſo aſſiſt us. The bleſſings of civil and religious liberty in America, and the oppreſſions of moſt foreign governments, the want of employment at home and the expectations of profit here, curioſity, domeſtic unhappineſs, civil wars and various other circumſtances will bring many manufacturers to this aſylum for mankind. Ours will be their induſtry, and, what is of ſtill more conſequence, ours will be their ſkill. Intereſt and neceſſity, with ſuch inſtructors, will teach us quickly. In the laſt century the manufactures of France were next to none; they are now worth millions to her yearly. Thoſe of England have been more improved within the laſt twelve years, than in the preceding fifty. At the peace of 1762, the uſeful arts and manufactures were ſcarcely known in America. How great has been their progreſs ſince, unaided, undirected and diſcouraged. Countenanced by your patronage and promoted by your aſſiſtance, what may they not be 'ere ſuch another ſpace of time ſhall elapſe ?

---

* So far as we depend on our own reſources.

Wonderful as it muſt appear, the manufacturers
of beer, that beſt of all our commodities, have lately been obliged to import malt from England.
Here muſt be inexcuſable neglect, or a ſtrange blind-
neſs to our moſt obvious intereſts. The cultivation of barley ſhould certainly be more attended to,
and if I miſtake not exceedingly, the preſent abundant crop of wheat* will ſo fill our markets, that
the farmer, who ſhall reap barley the enſuing year,
will find it the moſt profitable of all the grains.
We cannot, however, have any permanent difficulty on this article†.

Of flax and hemp little need be ſaid, but that we
can encreaſe them as we pleaſe, which we ſhall do
according to the demand.

Wool muſt become much more abundant, as our
country populates. Mutton is the beſt meat for
cities, manufactories, ſeminaries of learning, and
poor houſes, and ſhould be given by rule as in
England. The ſettlement of our new lands, remote from water carriage, muſt introduce much
more paſturage and graizing, than has been heretofore neceſſary, as ſheep, horſes and horned
cattle will carry themſelves to market through
roads impaſſable by waggons. The foreign re-

* The price of flour had fallen in December, 1788, to 30ſ. per
barrel. The French demand then took place and raiſed it on a
medium ſince to 38ſ. and 40ſ. and often more.

† The importation of malt has ceaſed, and the breweries are
greatly encreaſed. A. D. 1793.

ftrictions on our trade will alfo tend to encreafe the number of fheep. Horfes and horned cattle ufed to form a great part of the New-England cargoes for the Englifh Weft-India iflands. Thefe animals are exported to thofe places now in fmaller numbers, as our veffels are excluded from their ports.—The farms, capital and men, which were formerly employed in raifing them, will want a market for their ufual quantity, and the nature of that country being unfit for grain, fheep muft occupy a great proportion of their lands.

Cotton thrives as well in the-fouthern ftates, as in any part of the world. The Weft India iflands and thofe ftates raifed it formerly, when the price was not half what it has been for years paft in Europe*. It is alfo worth double the money in America, which it fold for before the revolution, all the European nations having prohibited the exportation of it from their refpective colonies to any foreign country†. It is much to be defired, that the fouthern planters would adopt the cultivation of an article from which the beft informed manufacturers calculate the greateft profits, and on which fome eftablifhed factories depend.

* A. D. 1787.

† There was a long and great mercantile fpeculation that had a great artificial effect. But this bubble being broken by the increafe of cotton from their iflands, and the importations from Su_rat, Bombay, &c. the price is now much reduced. It is fuppofed to be now in America about 25 per cent. higher than in the five years preceding the revolution war. We have imported cotton into America fince this publicationfrom Bombay and Mauritius.

Silk has long been a profitable production of Georgia and other parts of the United States, and may be encreafed, it is prefumed, as faft as the demand will rife. This is the ftrongeft of all raw materials and the great empire of China, though abounding with cotton, finds it the cheapeft cloathing for her people*.

Iron we have in great abundance, and a fufficiency of lead and copper, were labour low enough to extract them from the bowels of the earth.

Madder has fcarcely been attempted, but this and many other dye ftuffs may be cultivated to advantage, or found in America.

Under all the difadvantages which have attended manufactures and the ufeful arts, it muft afford the moft comfortable reflection to every patriotic mind, to obferve their progrefs in the United States and particularly in Pennfylvania. For a long time after our forefathers fought an eftablifhment in this place, then a dreary wildernefs, every thing necef-

---

* A. D. 1789. Forty-three chefts of this article were imported from China in the laft fhips and re-fhipped to Europe advantageoufly. We have a large nurfery of the white Italian mulberry eftablifhed here this fummer. Within ourfelves little can be expected, but the idea of the nurfery has been encouraged upon this principle that it prepares things for an emigration from a filk country. This perhaps is refining, but the expence is fmall—the trees are wanted to replace thofe deftroyed by the Britifh army—and the meafure falls in with our plan to *fofter and encourage*, but *not to force* manufactures.

fary for their fimple wants was the work of European hands. How great—how happy is the change. The lift of articles we now make ourfelves, if particularly enumerated would fatigue the ear, and wafte your valuable time. Permit me however to mention them under their general heads: meal of all kinds, fhips and boats, malt liquors, diftilled fpirits, pot-afh, gun powder, cordage, loaf fugar, pafteboard, cards and paper of every kind, books in various languages, fnuff, tobacco, ftarch, cannon, mufquets, anchors, nails and very many other articles of iron, bricks, tiles, potters ware, millftones and other ftone work, cabinet work, trunks and Windfor chairs, carriages and harnefs of all kinds, corn fans, ploughs and many other implements of hufbandry, fadlery and whips, fhoes and boots, leather of various kinds, hofiery, hats and gloves, wearing apparel, coarfe linens and woolens, and fome cotton goods, linfeed and fifh oil, wares of gold, filver, tin, pewter, lead, brafs and copper clocks and watches, wool and cotton cards, printing types, glafs and ftone ware, candles, foap and feveral other valuable articles with which the memory cannot furnifh us at once.

If the nations of Europe poffefs fome great advantages over us in manufacturing for the reft of the world, it is however clear, that there are fome capital circumftances in our favour, when they meet us *in our own markets*. The expences of importing raw materials, which in fome inftances they labour under, while we do not—the fame charges

in bringing their commodities hither—the duties
we muſt lay on their goods for the purpoſes of revenue—the additional duties, which we may venture to impoſe without riſquing the corruption of
morals or the loſs of the revenue by ſmuggling—the
prompt payment our workmen receive—the long
credits they give on their goods—the ſale of our
articles by the piece to the conſumer, while they
ſell theirs by great invoices to intermediate pur-
chaſers—the durable nature of ſome American
manufactures, eſpecially of linens—the injuries
theirs often ſuſtain from their mode of bleaching—theſe things taken together will give us an
advantage of twenty-five to fifty *per cent.* on many articles, and muſt work the total excluſion of
ſeveral others.

Beſides the difference in the qualities of American and European linens, ariſing from the mode of
bleaching, there is a very conſiderable ſaving of
expence from the ſame cauſe. So much and ſo
powerful a ſunſhine ſaves a great loſs of time and
expence of bleaching ſtuffs and preparations, and
this will be ſenſibly felt in our manufactures of
linen and cotton.

We muſt carefully examine the conduct of other
countries in order to poſſeſs ourſelves of their
methods of encouraging manufactories and purſue
ſuch of them, as apply to our ſituation, ſo far as it
may be in our power—exempting raw materials, dye
ſtuffs, and certain implements for manufacturing

from duty on importation is a very proper meafure. Premiums for ufeful inventions and improvements, whether foreign or American, for the beft
experiments in any unknown matter, and for the
largeft quantity of any valuable raw material muft
have an excellent effect. They would affift the
efforts of induftry, and hold out the noble incen-
tive of honourable diftinction to merit and genius.
The ftate might with great convenience enable an
enlightened fociety, eftablifhed for the purpofe, to
offer liberal rewards in land for a number of objects of this nature. Our funds of that kind are
confiderable and almoft dormant. An unfettled
tract of a thoufand acres, as it may be paid for at
this time, yields little money to the ftate. By of-
fering thefe premiums for ufeful inventions to any
citizen of the union, or to any foreigner, who would
become a citizen, we might often acquire in the
man a compenfation for the land, independently of
the merit which gave it to him. If he fhould be
induced to fettle among us with a family and property, it would be of more confequence to the ftate
than all the purchafe money.

It might anfwer an ufeful purpofe, if a committee
of this fociety fhould have it in charge to vifit every fhip arriving with paffengers from any foreign
country, in order to enquire what perfons they may
have on board capable of conftructing ufeful machines, qualified to carry on manufacture , or coming among us with a view to that kind of employment. It would be a great relief and encourage-

ment to thofe friendlefs people in a land of ftrang-
ers, and would fix many among us whom little difficulties might incline to return*.

Extreme poverty and idlenefs in the citizens of
a free government will ever produce vicious habits
and difobedience to the laws, and muft render the
people fit inftruments for the dangerous purpofes
of ambitious men. In this light the employment,
in manufactures, of fuch of our poor, as cannot
find other honeft means of fubfiftence, is of *the
utmoft confequence.* A man oppreffed by extreme
want is prepared for all evil, and the idler is ever
prone to wickednefs; while the habits of induftry,
filling the mind with honeft thoughts, and requiring
the time for better purpofes, do not leave leifure
for meditating or executing mifchief.

† An extravagant and wafteful ufe of foreign
manufactures, has been too juft a charge againft
the people of America, fince the clofe of the war.
They have been fo cheap, fo plenty and fo eafily
obtained on credit, that the confumption of them
has been abfolutely wanton. To fuch an excefs has
it been carried, that the importation of the finer
kinds of coat, veft and fleeve buttons, buckles,

* There are many focieties in Philadelphia, New-York, &c. for
the patronage of emigrators from foreign countries.

† In this particular there has been a meritorious reform, amply
compenfating every good citizen for the exertions he may have
made to promote manufactures.

broaches, breaft-pins, and other trinkets into this
port only, is fuppofed to have amounted in a fingle
year to ten thoufand pounds fterling, which coft
wearers above 60,000 dollars. This lamentable
evil has fuggefted to many enlightened minds a
wifh for fumptuary regulations, and even for an un-
changing national drefs fuitable to the climate, and
the other circumftances of the country. A more
general ufe of fuch manufactures as we can make
ourfelves, would wean us from the folly we have
juft now fpoken of, and would produce, in a lefs
exceptionable way, fome of the beft effects of fumptuary laws. Our dreffes, furniture and carriages
would be fafhionable, becaufe they were American
and proper in our fituation, not becaufe they were
foreign, fhewy or expenfive. Our farmers, to
their great honour and advantage, have been long
in the excellent economical practice of domeftic
manufactures for their own ufe, at leaft in many
parts of the union. It is chiefly in the towns that
this madnefs for foreign finery rages and de-
ftroys—There unfortunately the diforder is epide-
mical. It behoves us to confider our untimely
paffion for European luxuries as a malignant and
alarming fympton, threatening convulfions and dif-
folution to the political body. Let us haften then
to apply the moft effectual remedies, ere the difeafe becomes inveterate, left unhappily we fhould
find it incurable.

I cannot conclude this addrefs, gentlemen, without taking notice of *the very favourable and prodi-*

gious effects upon the landed interest, which may result from manufactures. The breweries of Philadelphia, in their present infant state, require forty
thousand bushels of barley annually, and when the
stock on hand of English beer shall be consumed,
will call for a much larger quantity*. Could the
use of malt liquors be more generally introduced,
it would be, for many reasons, a most fortunate
circumstance. Without insisting on the pernicious
effects of distilled spirits, it is sufficient for our present purpose to observe, that a thousand hogsheads
of rum and brandy†, mixt with water for common
use, will make as much strong drink as will require
one hundred and twenty thousand bushels of grain
to make an equivalent quantity of beer, besides the
horses, fuel, hops, and other articles of the country, which a brewery employs. The fruits of the
earth and the productions of nature in America are
also required by various other manufacturers, whom
you will remember without enumeration. But it
is not in their occupations only, that these valuable
citizens demand our native commodities. They
and their brethren, who work in foreign articles,
with their wives, children and servants, necessarily
consume in food and raiment a prodigious quantity
of our produce, and the buildings for the accommodation of their families and business are princi-

* This presumption has been fully realized. We have besides,
a very lively export trade in malt liquors and if we had a sufficiency of black beer bottles, it must become very great.

† Worth about £.20,000, and our imports of ardent spirits are
estimated at ten times that sum in the port of Philadelphia only.

pally drawn from our lands. Their effects upon agriculture are of more confequence than has ever been fuppofed by thofe, who have not made the neceffary eftimates. So great are the benefits to the landed intereft, which are derived from them, that I venture to affert without apprehenfion of miftake, that the value of American productions annually applied to their various ufes as above ftated, without including the manufacturers of flour, lumber and bar-iron, is double the aggregate amount of all our exports in the moft plentiful year with which Providence has ever bleffed this fruitful country. How valuable is this market for our encreafing produce—How clearly does it evince the importance of our prefent plan. But we may venture to proceed a ftep further—Without manufactures the progrefs of agriculture would be arrefted on the frontiers of Pennfylvania*. Though we have a country practicable for roads, fome of our weftern counties are yet unable to fupport them, and too remote perhaps to ufe land carriage of the moft eafy kind. Providence has given them, in certain profpect, a paffage by water; but the natural impediments, though very inconfiderable, and the more cruel obftructions arifing from political circumftances, are yet to be removed. The inhabitants of the fertile tracts adjacent to the waters of

* Manufacturing eftablifhments on the banks of Sufquehaunah are of the utmoft confequence to our weftern and mid-land counties. It is fuppofed that the manufacture of diftilled fpirits in the country on the waters of the Ohio around Pittfburg, has occafioned, a furplus to be fent down that river of 100,000 gallons.

the Ohio, Patowmac and Sufquehannah, befides the cultivation of grain, muft extend their views immediately to pafturage and grazing and even to manufaĉtures. Foreign trade will not foon take off the fruits of their labour *in their native ſtate.* They muſt manufaĉture firſt for their own confumption, and when the advantages of their mighty waters ſhall be no longer fufpended, they muſt become the greateſt faĉtory of American raw materials for the United States. Their refources in wood and water are very great, as are their mines of coal. As they do not fell much grain, but for home confumption and muſtpropagate ſheep and cattle for the reafons above ſtated, their country will in a ſhort time be the cheapeſt upon earth.

How numerous and important then, do the benefits appear, which may be expeĉted from this falutary defign ! It will confume our native productions now encreafing to fuperabundance—it will improve our agriculture, and teach us to explore the foffil and vegetable kingdoms, into which few refearches have heretofore been made—it will accelerate the improvement of our internal navigation and bring into aĉtion the dormant powers of nature and the elements—it will lead us once more into the paths of public virtue by reſtoring frugality and induſtry, thofe potent antidotes to the vices of mankind ; and will gave us real independence by refcuing us from the tyranny of foreign fafhions, and the deſtruĉtive torrént of luxury*.

* There is one *peculiar* means of advancement in the United States of the moſt ſtriking and ferious importance, as it regards ma-

Should these blessed consequences ensue those severe restrictions of the European nations, which have already impelled us to visit the most distant regions of the eastern hemisphere, defeating the schemes of short-sighted politicians, will prove, through the wisdom and goodness of Providence, the means of our POLITICAL SALVATION.

———————

Opinions had prevailed in America, that manufacturing employments were injurious to the best interests of the country, that the pursuit of agriculture should occupy all our citizens, and that labour was so dear as to preclude all chances of success. Yet it was observed that many emigrators, and others in the manufacturing branches, had actually succeeded, and it was manifest that the civil and

nufactures. Being an unimproved country, we have the inestimable advantage of importing skillful cultivators of raw materials and *manufactures* from nations, which are more advanced than we are, together with their capital and their skill. We can have no doubt of the fulfilling of this expectation, for every town and county of the middle and southern states, and many of those in the eastern states abound with proofs, that the hope has been already realized in numerous instances. But were these proofs wanting there could be no doubt that strangers of every description will resort to a country so fit for their reception—so pregnant with the means of human happiness.

relgious freedom of the country, and the low price
of food, of fuel and of raw materials would continue to attract perfons of that defcription. Further
inveftigation and reflection threw new and pleafing
lights upon the fubject. It was perceived, that
children, too young for labour, could be kept from
idlenefs and rambling, and of courfe from early
temptations, to vice, by placing them for a time
in manufactories, and that the means of their pa-
rents to clothe, feed and educate them could be
thereby increafed; that women, valetudinarians
and old men could be employed; that the portions
of time of houfewives and young women, which
were not occupied in family affairs, could be pro-
fitably filled up, that machinery, horfes, fi.e, water
and various proceffes requiring only fome incipient labour, were the principal means of manufacturing in Britain, that manufactures, inftead of impeding agriculture in that country, are actually its
greateft and moft certan fupport, and that, in truth,
*they are indifpenfibly neceffary to the profperity of
its landed intereft.* It has been afcertained on further examination, that wages in feveral parts of
the United States are not higher than in parts of
Britain, as had been erroneoufly fuppofed, efpecially taking into confideration the prices of provifions and the fame degree of comfortable living.
It was therefore confidently expected by many, who
carefully examined the fubject, that great advantages would refult from a rational, and fteady courfe
of attention, private and public, to the advancement of manufactures. It will appear in the fequel,

that the prudent exertions, which have been inceſ-
ſantly made have been crowned accordingly with
abundant ſucceſs, conſidering the ſhortneſs of the
time and how many other matters of great importance have called for attention, induſtry and capital in the United States.

CHAPTER IV.

A SUMMARY VIEW OF THE STATE OF PENNSYLVANIA, INTEND-
ED TO EXHIBIT TO THE INHABITANTS OF THE POPULATED
DISTRICTS OF THE OTHER STATES, AND TO FOREIGNERS
THE REAL, AND GREAT ADVANTAGES TO BE OBTAINED BY
TRADE, MANUFACTURES AND PURCHASES OF ESTATES THERE-
IN, AND BY MIGRATION THITHER.

THE judicious and temperate proceedings of
the American people in the reform of their
national conftitution in 1787, 1788, and 1789, the
magnanimous refolution *to impofe upon themfelves
the wholefome reftraints of a juft government,* which
they exhibited to each other and to mankind, the
moderation and impartiality of their deportment to
foreign nations under their new government, and
their early attention to the reftoration of public
credit at home and abroad were followed by the
moft beneficial confequences in the beginning of
1790. The little effay, which enters into the compofition of this chapter, was publifhed about the
middle of that year in order to remind the people
of the ftate of Pennfylvania, in which it was written, of their profpeсts of future comfort, and to
facilitate the anfwers to numerous enquiries, which
were beginning to be made concerning that ftate
by perfons of various defcriptions in other countries. It was fincerely intended to be an unexaggerated ftatement of the principal faсts on which

depend the comforts and profperity of the inhabitants of that part of the American union.

Notes on the ftate of Pennfylvania.

THE ftate of Pennfylvania is an oblong, of
about one hundred and fifty-fix miles wide from
north to fouth, by about two hundred and ninety
miles in length from eaft to weft. On the eaft of
it lies the Delaware river, dividing it from Weft-
Jerfey and New-York; on the north New-York,
and a territory of about two hundred thoufand
acres on lake Erie, which Pennfylvania purchafed
of Congrefs. On the north weft lies lake Erie,
on which it has a confiderable front and a good port,
lying within the purchafe from Congrefs, on the
weft are the new lands called the weftern territory,
and a part of Virginia : On the fouth lie another
part of Virginia, Maryland, and the ftate of Delaware. The contents of Pennfylvania are about
twenty-nine millions of acres, including the lake
Erie territory. It lies between 39° 43" and 42°
of north latitude. The bay and river of Delaware
are navigable from the fea up to the great falls at
Trenton, and have a light-houfe, buoys, and piers,
for the direction and fafety of fhips. On this
river are the fmall towns of Chefter and Briftol,
and the city of Philadelphia, which is the capital
of the ftate, and by much the largeft and moft
populous fea-port and manufacturing town in the
United States. The diftance of this city from
the fea is about fixty miles acrofs the land to the
New-Jerfey coaft, and one hundred and twenty

miles by the ship-channel of the Delaware. A seventy gun ship may lie before the town, and at many of the wharves, which occupy the whole east front of the city for near two miles, affording every vessel an opportunity of unlading and lading without the expense of lighterage. Rafts of masts, timber, boards, hoops and staves, with other articles upon them, can be brought down the Delaware from the counties of Montgomery and Otsego, in New-York, two hundred miles above the city, by the course of the river. Some money was expended by the government and landholders in improving the navigation up towards the source, before the revolution; and there has been a survey lately begun, for the purpose of proceeding in the improvement of this and other principal rivers of Pennsylvania, and for making communications by canals in the improved part, and by roads in the unimproved part of the state. The Pennsylvanians are much inclined to such enterprises, having found great benefit from them. On the completion of the present plan, the state will be more conveniently intersected by roads than any other of its size in the union, which will greatly facilitate the settlement of its new lands. A slight view of the map of Pennsylvania, by Howell, that in Mr. Jefferson's notes on Virginia, or that in Morse's geography, will shew how advantageously this state is watered by the Delaware and its branches, the Schuylkill, the Juniata, the Susquehanna and its branches, the Ohio, Allegeny, Youghiogeny, and Monongahela. The Patowmac and lake Erie also afford profpects of confiderable benefit from their navigation. Nature has done much for Pennfylvania in regard to inland water carriage, which is ftrikingly exemplified by this fact, that although Philadelphia and lake Erie are diftant from each other above three hundred miles, there is no doubt that the rivers of the ftate may be fo improved, as to reduce the land carriage between them nine tenths. In the fame way the navigation to Pittfburg, after due improvement, may be ufed inftead of land carriage for the whole diftance, except twenty or thirty miles—By thefe routes it is clear, that a large proportion of the foreign articles, ufed on the weftern waters, will be tranfported; and that their furs, fkins, ginfeng, hemp, flax, pot-afh, and other valuable commodities, may be brought to Philadelphia. The hemp and oak timber for the Ruffian navy is tranfported by inland navigation one thoufand two hundred miles: and yet hemp is fhipped from that kingdom on lower terms than from any other part of the world. Ruffia, for fome time after the fettlement of Pennfylvania by civilized and enlightened people, was in a ftate of abfolute barbarifm, and deftitute of thefe improvements. Much therefore is to be expected from the continued exertions of the prudent, induftrious and intelligent inhabitants of Pennfylvania, in the courfe of the prefent century*

* In the laft three years more public funds and private capital have been applied to the improvement of roads and rivers and the cutting of canals than in all the time between the year 1790 and the firft fettlement of the ftate. A. D. 1793.

Confiderable bodies of new lands in this ftate remain for fale by individuals. Purchafes can be always made, partly or wholly on credit, from thofe perfons, who take mortgages on the lands they fell to emigrants, and indulge them fometimes with a very eafy credit. The Pennfylvanians having no difputes with the Indians about boundaries. All the lands within the ftate having been purchafed at a fair and open treaty, and there being fome fettlements weftward of Pennfylvania on the new lands of Congrefs, we have little apprehenfions from the Indians any where; and in moft of our new country there is no danger at all.

Improved lands, in the old counties of this ftate, fell generally at a certain fum for a farm, including the buildings. This, before the war, was, in moft of the thick fettled counties within a day's ride of Philadelphia, from four pounds ten fhillings fterling, to thirty fhillings per acre, and lefs, according to the quality, unlefs in fituations very near the city or fome town, or in cafes of very valuable buildings, mills, taverns, or fituations for country trade. In one or two counties, remarkable for therichnefs of the lands, they fold higher, fometimes confiderably. Farms can be purchafed upon terms as favourable as then, owing to the quantity of new lands for fale in this and feveral other ftates; and owing to the many new and profitable ufes for money, which did not exift before the revolution.

The produce, manufactures, and exports of Pennfylvania are very many and various, viz. wheat, flour, midlings, ſhip-ſtuff, bran, ſhorts, ſhip-bread, white water biſcuit, rye, rye flour, Indian corn, or maize, Indian meal, buckwheat, buckwheat meal, bar and pig iron, ſteel, nail rods, nails, iron hoops, rolled iron tire, gun-powder*, cannon ball, iron cannon, muſquets, ſhips, boats, oars, hand-ſpikes, maſts, ſpars, ſhip-timber, ſhip-blocks, cord-age, ſquare timber, ſcantling, plank, boards, ſtaves, heading, ſhingles, wooden hoops, tanners' bark, corn fans, coopers' ware, bricks, coarſe earth-en or potter' ware, a very little ſtone-ware, glue, parchment, ſhoes, boots, ſoal-leather, upper lea-ther, dreſſed deer and ſheep ſkins, and gloves and garments thereof, fine hats, many common, and a few coarſe; thread, cotton, worſted, and yarn hoſiery; writing, wrapping, blotting, ſheathing and hanging paper; ſtationary, playing cards, paſte-boards, books; wares of braſs, pewter, lead, tin-plate, copper, ſilver and gold; clocks and watches, muſical inſtruments, ſnuff, manufactured tobacco, chocolate, muſtard-ſeed and muſtard, flaxſeed, flax-ſeed oil, flax, hemp, wool, wool and cotton cards, pickled beef, pork, ſhad, herrings, tongues and ſturgeon, hams and other bacon, tallow, hogs' lard, butter, cheeſe, candles, ſoap, bees-wax, loaf-ſugar, pot and pearl aſhes, rum and other ſtrong waters, beer, porter, hops, winter and ſummer barley, oats, ſpelts, onions, potatoes, turnips, cabbages, carrots,

---

* It is ſaid there are at this time near 50,000 quarter caſks of gun-powder in the Philadelphia magazine, manufactured in the ſtate of Pennſylvania —A. D. 1793.

parfnips, red and white clover, timothy, and moſt
European vegetables and graſſes, apples, peaches,
plumbs, pears, and apricots, grapes, both native and
imported, and other European fruits, working and
pleaſurable carriages, horſes, horned cattle, ſheep,
hogs, wood for cabinet makers, lime-ſtone, coal,
free-ſtone and marble.

Some of theſe produ&ions are fine, ſome indif-
ferent. Some of the manufa&ures are confiderable, for a young country, circumſtanced as this has
been; ſome inconfiderable: but they are enumerated, to ſhew the general nature of the ſtate, and
the various purſuits of the inhabitants. In addition to them we may mention, that a lead-mine and
two or three ſalt-ſprings have been diſcovered in
our new country, which will, no doubt, be worked,
as ſoon as the demand for lead and ſalt to the weſtward increaſes. We ought alſo to notice our great
foreſts for making pot aſhes, and glaſs.

The manufa&ures of Pennſylvania have increaſed exceedingly within a few years, as well by maſ-
ter-workmen and journeymen from abroad, as by
the increaſed ſkill and induſtry of our own citizens.
Houſehold or family manufa&ures have greatly
advanced; and valuable acquiſitions have been
made of implements and machinery to ſave labour,
either imported or invented in the United States.
The hand-machines, for carding and ſpinning cotton, have been introduced by foreigners, and improved, but we have obtained the water mill for

spinning cotton, and a water mill for flax, which is applicable also to spinning hemp and wool. These machines promise us an early increase of the cotton, linen, and hempen branches, and must be of very great service in the woolen branch. Additional employment for weavers, dyers, bleachers, and other manufacturers must be the consequence. Paper-mills, gun-powder-mills, steel works, rolling and slitting mills, printing figured goods of paper, linen, and even of cotton, coach making, book printing, and several other branches, are wonderfully advanced: and every month seems to extend our old manufactures, or to introduce new ones.

The advancement of the agriculture of Pennsylvenia is the best proof that can be given of the comfort and happiness it affords to its farming, manufacturing, and trading citizens. In the year 1786, our exports of flour were one hundred and and fifty thousand barrels : in 1787, they were two hundred and two thousand barrels : in 1788, they were two hundred and twenty thousand barrels : and in 1789 they were three hundred and sixty-nine thousand barrels : which exceed any exports ever made in the times of the province, or in the times of the commonwealth*. The produce of flax is increased in a much greater degree : and that of wool is considerably more than it was before

* The exports of flour in the year 1792 from Philadelphia, amounted to above 420,000 barrels, and in the spring quarter of 1793 it exceeded 200,000 barrels.

the revolution. A new article is added to the lift of our productions, which is a well-tafted and wholefome fugar, made of the maple tree. It has been proved, by many fair and careful experiments, that it is in the power of a fubftantial farmer who has a family about him, eafily to make twelve hundred weight of this fugar every feafon, without hiring any additional hands, or utenfils, but thofe that are neceffary for his family and farm ufe. The time, in which it can be made, is from the middle of February to the end of March, when farmers in this country have very little to do, as it is too early to plough or dig. The price of fugar being lower here than in Europe, this article may be reckoned at one hundred and fifty dollars per annum, to every careful and fkilful farmer, who owns land bearing the fugar maple. Of thefe there are fome millions of acres in Pennfylvania and the adjacent ftates. It feems alfo highly probable, that this valuable tree may be tranfplanted, and thus be obtained by almoft any farmer in the ftate ; and that men of property, who will purchafe kettles, and hire hands for the above fhort period, may make larger quantities.

The fituation of religion and religious rights and liberty in Pennfylvania is a matter, that deferves the utmoft attention of all fober and well-difpofed people, who may have thoughts of this country. This ftate always afforded an afylum to the perfecuted fects of Europe, and of the other ftates in former times. No church or fociety ever was efta-

blifhed here; no tythes or tenths can be demanded: and though fome regulations of the crown of
Britain excluded two churches* from a fhare in
our government, in the times of the province, that
is now done away with regard to every religious fociety whatever, except the Hebrew church.
But at this time a convention of fpecial reprefentatives of the citizens of Pennfylvania have under
confideration all the errors which have inadvert-
ently crept into our conftitution and frame of government; and in the act which they have publifhed for the examination of the people, they have rejected the half-way doctrine of toleration, and have
eftablifhed upon firm and perfectly equal ground,
all denominations of religious men. By the provifions of the new code, a Proteftant, a Roman
catholic, and a Hebrew, may elect or be elected to
any office in the ftate, and purfue any lawful calling, occupation, or profeffion†. The conftitution
of general government of the United States alfo
guarantees this ineftimable and facred right—and
it is furely a facred right; for it belongs to the
Deity to be worfhipped according to the free-will
and confciences of his creatures.

We lay no difficulty in the way of any perfon,
who defires to become a free and equal citizen. On
the day of his landing, he may buy a farm, a houfe,
merchandife, or raw materials; he may open a

* The Roman and Hebrew.

† This code has been confirmed in Pennfylvania.

work-fhop, a counting-houfe, an office, or any
other place of bufinefs, and purfue his calling,
without any hindrance from corporation rules
or monopolifing companies, or the payment of any
fum of money to the public. The right of elect-
ing and being elected (which does not affect his
bufinefs or his fafety) is not granted till the expiration of two years; which prudence requires.

A privilege, almoft peculiar to this ftate, has
been granted to foreigners by the legiflature of
Pennfylvania, that of buying and holding lands
and houfes within this commonwealth, without re-
linquifhing their allegiance to the country in which
they were born. They can leafe, hire, fell or be-
queath the lands, receive the rents, and, in fhort,
have every territorial and pecuniary right, that
a natural-born Pennfylvanian has; but no civil
rights. As they profefs to owe allegiance to a foreign prince or government, and refide in a foreign
country, where they, of courfe, have civil rights,
they cannot claim them, nor ought they to defire
them here: for if they choofe, at any time after
the purchafe to come out to this country, and make
themfelve citizens—or if they choofe to give their
eftates to their children or other perfons, who will
do fo, any of them may become citizens to all in-
tents and purpofes. This indulgence to purchafe
is granted for three years from January 1789:
and all lands bought by foreigners before January
1792, may be held forever on thofe terms. Whether a right to make purchafes upon thofe terms

will be allowed to foreigners, after that time, is
uncertain, and will entirely depend upon the opinion of our then legiflature, as to the fafety or
utility of it*.

Ufeful knowledge and fcience have been favourite objects of attention here. We have an univer-
fity, three colleges, and four or five public academies, befides many private academies and free
fchools, in the city and feveral of the county-towns
of this ftate. Confiderable grants of monies, rent
charges and particularly of new lands, have been
made for this purpofe by our legiflature, and very
liberal private fubfcriptions have been added at
various times. Though our government and citizens have been always attentive to the important
object of ufeful and liberal knowledge, yet an
increafed regard for learning has been manifefted
fince the revolution. Rifing from a provincial to
an independent fituation, appears, and very naturally, to have expanded our ideas, and to have
given an enhanced value to improvements of the
human mind†.

Among the natural advantages of Pennfylvania,
her almoft innumerable mill-feats ought not to be
omitted. They are conveniently diftributed by

* This law has been continued till the year 1795, when it
may be renewed.

† Much has been done fince 1790 in regard to fchools.
A. D. 1793.

Providence throughout the ftate, and afford the means of eftablifhing every fpecies of mill-work and labour-faving machines, to meet the produce and raw materials almoft at the farmers' doors. In the prefent fituation of this country, wanting hands for farming, and in the prefent ftate of manufactures, when ingenious mechanifm is every day and every where invented, to leffen the neceffity for manual labour, this natural advantage muft appear of ineftimable importance. Hemp and flax are among the moft profitable productions of our rich midland and new counties, the cream of which is yet to be fkimmed. It is therefore a moft pleafing fact, that we have in the ftate the full-fized and complete movements or works of a water mill and machinery, to fliver, rove, and fpin flax and hemp into threads or yarns, fit for linen of thirty cuts to the pound, or any other coarfer kind, fheetings, towelling, fail-cloth, ozanbrigs, twine, and the ftrands or yarn for cordage. The fame machinery is calculated for the roving or preparing, and fpinning combed wool into worfted yarn. We have alfo the movements and complete machinery of Sir Richard Arkwright's water-mill for fpinning yarns of cotton. And though the climate of this ftate is not fit for cultivating that raw material, yet cotton can be raifed with profit in every ftate in our union fouthward of Pennfylvania, and imported from the Eaft and Weft-Indies.

It is certain, that this extraordinary capacity of our country for mechanical works has either called forth, in an unufual degree, the mechanical powers of the human mind, or that Providence has beftowed upon the people of this and our fifter ftates an uncommon portion of that talent, which its nature and fituation require. Our Rittenhoufe and Franklin ftand unrivalled in mechanical philofophy: and thofe, who know our country, are well informed, that to thefe two great names we could add a confiderable lift of philofophical and practical mechanicians, in a variety of branches.

So many of the neceffary and convenient arts and trades depend upon the plenty and cheapnefs of fuel, that it appears proper to take notice of this article. Till the revolution, our dependence was almoft entirely upon wood fuel, of which, in the moft populous places, we have ftill a great abundance, and in all interior fituations immenfe quantities: but the increafe of manufactures has occafioned us to turn our attention to coal. Of this ufeful foffil, Providence has given us very great quantities, in our middle and weftern country. The vicinity of Wyoming, on the Sufquehanna, is one bed of coal, of the open-burning kind, and of the moft intenfe heat. On the head waters of Schuylkill and Lehi are fome confiderable bodies. At the head of the weftern branch of Sufquehanna is a moft extenfive body, which ftretches over the country fouth-wefterly, fo as to be found in the greateft plenty at Pittfburgh, where the Allegeny and Youghiogeny unite, and form the head of the Ohio. It has been lately difcovered on the waters of Nefcopeck.

All our coal has hitherto been accidently found on the furface of the earth, or difcovered in the digging of common cellars or wells: fo that when our wood-fuel fhall become fcarce, and the European methods of boring fhall be fkilfully purfued, there can be no doubt of our finding it in many other places. At prefent, the ballafting of fhips from coal countries abroad, and the coal mines in Virginia, which lie convenient to fhip-navigation, occafion a good deal of coal to be brought to the Philadelphia market. From this great abundance and variety of fuel, it refults, that Pennfylvania, and the United States in general, are well fuited to all manufactories which are effected by fire, fuch as furnaces, founderies, forges, glafs-houfes, breweries, diftilleries, fteelworks, fmiths' fhops, and all other manufactories in metal, foap-boiling, chandlers' fhops, pot afh works, fugar and other refineries, &c. &c.

Ship-building is a bufinefs in which the port of Philadelphia exceeds moft parts of the world. Mafts, fpars, timber, and plank, not only from our own ftate and the other ftates on the Delaware, are conftantly for fale in our market: but the mulberry of the Chefapeak, and the evergreen or live oak, and red cedar of the Carolinas and Georgia, are fo abundantly imported, that nine-tenths of our veffels are built of them. No veffels are better than thefe: and in proof of it, Englifh writers of rank might be quoted, who have publifhed for and againft us. A live oak and cedar ſhip of two hundred tons, carpenter's meaſurement, can be fitted to take in a cargo for fourteen pounds currency per ton* : and there is not a port in Europe, in which an oak ſhip can be equally well built and fitted for twenty pounds per ton in our money, or twelve pounds ſterling. This fact may appear doubtful or extraordinary; but it is certainly true; and it is greatly in favour of our ſhip carpenters and other tradeſmen employed in fitting and building ſhips, as well as our merchants and farmers, whoſe intereſts are ſo much connected with navigation.

The diſtance of Philadelphia from the ſea, has been made an objection by ſome, and the cloſing of our river by the ice, which happens almoſt every winter. Amſterdam, the greateſt port in Europe, is inacceſſible in the winter. But it is a fact, that, notwithſtanding theſe objections, our veſſels make as many Weſt-India voyages as thoſe of the two other principal ſea ports of the middle ſtates : and though the river is frozen from three to nine weeks almoſt every winter, yet there are occaſional openings, which give opportunities for fleets of merchantmen to go out and come in. The fine corn and proviſion country, which lies near Philadelphia, enables the merchants to load their veſſels in the winter : and the market is regularly ſupplied with flour, pork, beef, lumber, ſtaves, iron and many other of our principal articles of exportation.

* A. D. 1790.

Little time is therefore loft: and we find that our
trade increafes. The crop of 1789, and other exports from the harveft of that year to that of 1790,
it is fuppofed, will load one hundred and twenty
thoufand tons of fhipping. We have a very extenfive back country; and many large bodies of new
land, which muft fend their produce to the Philadelphia market, are fettling faft. The population
of Pennfylvania, by the laft accounts taken, was
three hundred and fixty thoufand men, women and
children: but, as fome years have fince elapfed,
it is fuppofed it will not fall much fhort of four hundred thoufand when the prefent enumeration fhall
be completed.*

No country in Europe has paid off fo much of
her public debt, fince the late general war, as this
ftate, notwithftanding the paft diforders and difficulties of the United States, arifing from the weaknefs of our late general government, and the fhocks
of an invafive war. She has paid off and funk a fum
equal to her full fhare of the intereft and a confiderable part of the principal of her ftate and federal
debts. Yet fhe has laid no excife or internal duty,
but eight pence currency upon fpirituous liquors,
which has fince been repealed.

The inhabitants of Pennfylvania are principally
defcendents of Englifh, Irifh, and Germans, with

---

* It proved to be 434,000 by the cenfus of 1791.

fome Scotch, Welfh, Swedes, and a few Dutch.
There are alfo many of the Irifh and Germans, who
emigrated when young or in the middle time of life:
and there is a number of each of thofe two nations
now in legiflative, executive, and judicial ftations
among us. It has ever been the policy of our government, before and fince the revolution, and the
difpofition of our people, to receive all fober emigrants with open arms, and to give them immediately the free exercife of their trades and occupations, and of their religion.*

Such is the prefent fituation of things in Pennfylvania, which is more or lefs the fame in feveral
other of the American ftates, viz. New-York,
Main, Virginia, the Carolinas, Georgia, Vermont,
and Kentucky: but though not fo in the reft, the principal difference is, that they are fo fully peopled,
that there are no new lands of any value unfold;
and farming lands, which are improved, are of
courfe dearer than with us. In thofe ftates, however, agriculture, commerce, manufaĉtures, the
fifheries, and navigation, afford comfortable fubfiftence and ample rewards of profit to the induftrious and well difpofed, amidft the bleffings of civil and religious liberty.

Before this paper fhall be concluded, it may be
ufeful to recapitulate the various productions and
exports of the United States, which are the fure

* Latterly there are many French.

foundations of a grand fcene of agriculture—the refources for an extenfive trade—and the materials for a great variety of ufeful and elegant manufactures. From our new country we have ginfeng, and feveral kinds of fkins and furs; in the fettled parts of the ftates, rice, indigo, cotton, filk, tobacco, flaxfeed, wheat, rye, barley, oats, fpelts, Indian corn, hemp, flax, wool, iron, lead, copper, coal, freeftone, limeftone, marble, fulphur, faltpetre, a great variety of fhip timber, fhip plank, mafts, fpars, tar, pitch and turpentine, pork, beef, cider, fifh oil, fpermaceti, whalebone, driedfifh, pickled fifh, hides, leather, black cattle, fheep, cheefe, butter, tallow, hops, muftard feed, ftaves, heading, fhingles, boards, plank, fcantling, fquare timber, black walnut, wild cherry and curled maple for cabinet wares, potafh, pearl afhes, potters clay, brick clay, &c. &c. with apples, and all the other principal fruits, and potatoes, and all the other principal vegetables. During the late war, confiderable quantities of fea-falt were manufaÉured on our coaft, as far north as New Jerfey : and this article will no doubt one day become an objeÉ of attention. It may be fafely affirmed, that no European nation whatfoever unites in its dominions, even including diftant colonies, fuch a variety of important and capital produÉions; nor can there be any doubt, in the mind of a candid and ferious obferver, that fuch a country muft rife with common prudence, in agriculture, manufaÉures and commerce, affording to every induftrious and virtuous citizen, and emigrant, the certain means of comfortable fubfiftence, and the faireft profpect of eftablifhing a family in life.

———————

THE progrefs of the ftate of Pennfylvania in the great bufinefs of agriculture, fince the return of peace, is ftrikingly evinced by the increafed exportation of flour between 1786 and 1792, which being extracted from the public records may be relied on as accurately true. The extenfion of the grain diftilleries and breweries, in the fame term, has been at leaft equally great: the demand of bread for the increafing manufacturers has been enlarged in full proportion: fhip-building has made a correfponding progrefs: and the opening of roads through the new country, the improvements of the old roads, the building of bridges, the clearing of rivers, and the cutting of canals in the three laft years have exceeded the fimilar operations of any other equal term, either before, during, or fince the revolution, beyond all comparifon*.

* It has aftonifhed thofe beft acquainted with the affairs of Pennfylvania to find, that the exports from Philadelphia (the only port in that ftate) proved to be near feven millions of dollars during the year ending on the 30th September, 1793. For the particulars fee the return of exports of the United States for that year, in this volume.

CHAPTER V.

Containing some information relative to Maple Sugar, and its possible value in certain parts of the United States.

THE difpofition of the people of America to examine and difcufs the topics of the day, the increafed intercourfe among the ftates fince the late war, and the diffufion of knowledge thro' the channels of their numerous gazettes naturally occafion information, which ufed to be local, to be much more generally extended. The eafy and profitable practice of making *fugar* from the fap or juice of the maple tree, had prevailed for many years in the nothern and eaftern ftates. The facility and advantages of this pleafing branch of hufbandry, had attracted little attention in Pennfylvania, tho a few of its inhabitants were in the habit of manufacturing fmall quantities of this kind of fugar. In the year 1790, it became more generally known to the Pennfylvanians, that their brethren in the eaftern and nothern parts of the union, had long made confiderable quantities, with their family utenfils, and without the expenfe of hiring affiftance, that the fame tree might be carefully tapped without injury for many fucceffive years, that the procefs was fimple and very eafy, and only required to be carried on between the middle of February and the end of March, when the farmer has little to

do, and that a very large proportion of the unfettled lands of the ftate abound with this valuable tree.
The great and increafing diflike to negro flavery,
and to the African trade among the people of that
ftate, occafioned this new profpeft of obtaining a
fugar, not made by the unhappy blacks, to be particularly interefting to them. The following eftimate, which was founded on the beft materials attainable at that time, was publifhed among other
things to elucidate the fubjeft.

*An eftimate of the capacity of fugar maple lands
of Pennfylvania and New-York, to fupply the
demand of the United States for fugar and molaffes.*

THE DEMAND.

By authentic documents obtained from the cuftom-houfe of Philadelphia, it appears————

That the medium importation of brown
fugar, for each year, from 1785 to 1789
was   lbs. 5,692,848

Of loaf fugar, on a medium   4,480

And of molaffes—543,900 gallons,
which at 10lb. per gallon, is 5,439,000
lbs. half of which weight in fugar may
be confidered as equal to 543,900
gallons of molaffes   2,719,500

Total quantity of fugar required—lbs. 8,416,828

The information of William Cooper, Efquire, of Coopers town,* is that there are ufually made from a tree five pounds weight of fugar, and that there are fifty trees on an acre at a medium, but fuppofe only four pounds to be produced by a tree and forty trees on an acre, then 52,605 acres will yield 8,416,828 lbs. and fuppofing the whole demand of the union 42,084,140 lbs. or five times the importation into Philadelphia, then 263,000 acres will yield a fupply for the United States. It need not be obferved, that there are *very many* more than 263,000 acres of fugar maple lands in each of the eight following counties.

Albany,
Montgomery,
Otfego,   } in New-York.
Tyoga,
Ontario,

Northampton,
Luzerne,   } in Pennfylvania.
Northumberland,

Alfo that the fugar maple tree is found in many other parts of thofe two ftates, and of the United States.

It will be frankly admitted, that *the refult* of the above eftimate has a wild and vifionary appearance; but as it is made upon facts, very carefully

* One of the judges of the court of common pleas in the county of Otfego, and ftate of New-York.

afcertained, and as the whole calculation is expo-
fed to examination, it will not be unreafonable to
give fome faith to it, until exaggeration of fact or
error fhall be pointed out.

Philadelpha, 1790*.

* In the fpring of the year 1793, the following letter was received from judge Cooper, and feveral other perfons, who had emigrated from Pennfylvania, New-Jerfey and France, into the prefent
county of Otfego (at the heads of the rivers Delaware and Sufquehanna) which is diftant from Philadelphia about 137 miles, and
from the city of New-York about 100 miles, in direct lines.

Coopers Town, April 9th, 1793.

GENTLEMEN,

Being convinced that you feel an intereft in the
manufactory of *maple* fugar, and that your wifhes and exertions to
prevent the deftruction of the trees from whence it is produced,
have been of public utility—We are encouraged to tranfmit to you
the ftatement we have been able to make from actual obfervation
of the quantity of fugar, which has been made this feafon, in the
former townfhip of Otfego, and which was an entire wildernefs in
1786—We find upon a moderate calculation, that there has been
made at leaft one hundred and fixty thoufand pounds weight, which
at nine pence per pound is equal in value to 15000 dollars. This
plain demonftration of the importance of this article, will we hope,
induce you to continue your endeavours to promote and encourage
it, and we would fubmit to your confideration whether it is not an
object of fufficient confequence to claim the encouragement of the
legiflature of your ftate.

WILLIAM COOPER,
RICH. R. SMITH,
RENSSEL. WILLIAMS, jun.
CHARLES FRANCIS,
LEWIS DE VILLERS,
EBBAL.

To HENRY DRINKER,
    BENJAMIN RUSH,
    TENCH COXE, Philadelphia.

Since the publication of the foregoing calculation, it has been afcertained, that the balance of the
medium imports and exports of foreign fugar, (that
is the confumption of that article in the United
States) is about 20,000,000 of pounds weight per
annum. The quantity of molaffes, ufed in fubftance (and exclufively of diftillation) probably
does not exceed 1,500,000 gallons, which may be
deemed equal to about half their weight in fugar,
or fix millions of pounds. The total fum of thefe,
being the whole confumption of fugar and molaffes
in fubftance, is 26,000,000 of pounds. It is certain
that every farmer having one hundred acres of fugar maple land, in a ftate of ordinary American
improvement, (that is, one third covered with judicious referves of wood and timber, and two thirds
cleared for the culture of grafs and grain) can
make one thoufand pounds weight of fugar with
only his neceffary farming and kitchen utenfils, if
his family confifts of a man, a woman and a child of
ten years, including himfelf. It would therefore require the attention of 26,000 of fuch fmall families
occupying (at one hundred acres each) 2,600,000
acres of thofe lands to make (at 1,000lbs. each)
26,000,000 of pounds, or a quantity of fugar equal
to all the molaffes and fugar, annually confumed in
fubftance in the United States. The operation in
a family is as eafy, as to make houfhold foap or
cheefe, or to brew ale or beer, and as there is in
this country much more than twice the above quan-

tity of fugar maple lands, in fituations not too fouthern, the only object that requires attention is *to give, as faft as poffible, generality to this fimple, profitable, and comfortable manufacture.*

CHAPTER VI.

A CONCISE GENERAL VIEW OF THE UNITED STATES, FOR THE INFORMATION OF MIGRATORS FROM FOREIGN COUNTRIES.

CIRCUMSTANCES of the fame nature, as thofe, which led to the notes on the ftate of Pennfylvania, fuggefted the utility of a fimilar detail concerning the United States ; which will be found in this chapter. A difpofition to promote general profperity and the wifdom of a reliance upon collective national advantages, in preference to detached local interefts gave additional force to thefe confiderations. However true the account of Pennfylvania might be, it was well known that fcenes, promifing great comfort and a rapid profperity, were to be found in other parts of this country. The diftrict of Maine, parts of New Hampfhire, Vermont, the Genefee country and other parts of the ftate of New-York, the wefternmoft parts of Maryland, of Virginia, of the two Carolinas and Georgia, with the ftate of Kentucky, containing large quantities of fparfely fettled and, of courfe, cheap lands, it appeared really inequitable to pafs them over in filence. The beft information concerning them, which could be promptly collected, was therefore confolidated into the little publication, which forms the body of this chapter.

Notes concerning the United States of America, &c.

THE United States of America are fituated in the northern divifion of that extenfive portion of the globe, between the thirty-firft and forty-fixth degrees of northern latitude. The extreme length of their territories is about 1250 miles, the breadth about 1040. Their fuperficies is computed to be 640,000,000 acres of land and water : and, after deducting the fpace occupied by the capacious lakes and mighty rivers, which fertilize and accommodate this country, and occupy above a feventh part of its furface, there remain about 590,000,000 of acres of faft land.

In fo very extended a fcene, it will be naturally expected, that the fruits of the earth are many and various : and accordingly we find, in the prefent half-tried ftate of the capacities of our foil and climate, a lift of invaluable productions prefent themfelves, fome found by the firft difcoverers of the country—others introduced by mere accident— and others tranfported from Europe, during the fimple ftate of agriculture in the laft century. In our fouthe n latitudes, including the ftates of Georgia, South Carolina and North Carolina, rice, much fuperior to that of Italy or the Levant, is raifed in very great quantities. The comparative value of this grain was twenty five per cent. in the Englifh markets, for the American more than the Italian or Levant rice, as long as the latter was fold there : but, from the ample quantity and goodnefs of our rice, it seems probable, that no Mediterranean rice is now imported into England, as it has been omitted for some time in their general accounts of prices. The South Carolina crop alone, of 1789, appears to have been above 100,000 tierces,* weighing sixty millions of pounds. It is expected that Virginia will add this article to her list of exports; as it is supposed, a large body of rich swamp in her most eastern counties, is capable of producing it; and mountain rice has been raised by way of experiment, in her new country near the head of the Ohio.

Tobacco is a staple article of all the states, from Georgia as far north as Maryland, including both. Virginia, alone, generally exported before the revolution, 55,000 hogsheads, weighing fifty-five millions of pounds—Maryland 30,000 hogsheads. The Carolinas and Georgia, which raised but little of this article before the revolution, have, of late years, produced very large quantities: and as Virginia and Maryland are turning more of their attention to the cultivation of wheat, Indian corn, flax, and hemp, the Carolinas and Georgia will probably extend the cultivation of this plant, to which their soil and climate are well suited†.

---

* 141,762 Tierces were exported from the United States in the year ending on the 30th September 1792, though the consumption in the middle and nothern states has increased considerably.

† 112,428 Hogsheads were exported in the year ending on 30th September 1793, besides snuff and manufactured tobacco.

Indigo is produced by North Carolina, South
Carolina, and Georgia : but this, and the other two
articles before mentioned, are raifed in much lefs
proportions in North Carolina, than in South Carolina and Georgia. The uniform of our national
troops has been heretofore of *blue* cloth, as alfo of
the militia in general. Our clergy are alfo permitted by our cuftoms to wear this colour : and it is
generally liked among the moft frugal and moft expenfive people. Thefe circumftances will no doubt
be duly attended to in our future laws and regulations, and will operate very favourably for the indigo planters, without any expenfe to the country.

Cotton has been lately adopted as an article of
culture in the fouthern ftates : and if the prices of
rice, tobacco, and indigo decline, it muft be very
beneficial to the owners and purchafers of lands
in that part of our union. This article is raifed
with eafe in Spain, every part of which kingdom
lies further north than the Carolinas, and in the
fame latitudes as Virginia, Maryland and the Delaware ftate. It is alfo raifed in all that part of
Afiatic Turkey, which lies between Scanderoon
and Smyrna, which are in the latitudes of the three
laft ftates. As our people will increafe very rapidly by emigration, and the courfe of nature, it
is certain we cannot procure wool from our own
internal refources in fufficient quantities. The
owners of cotton plantations may therefore expect
a conftant and great demand for this article, as a

fubſtitute for wool, beſides its ordinary uſes for light goods.

Tar, pitch, and turpentine are produced in immenſe quantities in North Carolina, which ſtate ſhips more of theſe articles, particularly the laſt, than all the reſt of our union. Tar and pitch are alſo produced in the ſouthern parts of Jerſey, and more or leſs in all the ſtates ſouthward of that.

Beſides theſe, myrtle wax, and thoſe two invaluable timbers, the live oak and red cedar, are abundant in the Carolinas and Georgia : and they have Indian corn, hemp, flax, boards, ſtaves, ſhingles, leather, beef, pork, butter, minerals, foſſils, and many other articles in common with the middle, or eaſtern ſtates; alſo ſkins, furs and ginſeng from their Indian country.

The wheat country of the United States lies in Virginia, Maryland, Delaware, Pennſylvania, New-Jerſey and New-York, and the weſternmoſt parts of Connecticut, as alſo the weſtern parts of the two Carolinas, and probably of Georgia, for their own uſe. The character of the American flour is ſo well known, that it is unneceſſary to ſay any thing in commendation of it here. Virginia exported before the war 800,000 buſhels of wheat—Maryland above half that quantity. The export of flour from Pennſylvania (with the wheat) was equivalent to 1,200,000 buſhels in 1788, and about

2,000,000 of bushels in 1789, which, however, was a very favourable year. New-York exports in flour and wheat equivalent to 1,000,000 of bushels. In the wheat states are also produced great quantities of Indian corn, or maize. Virginia formerly exported half a million of bushels*. Maryland ships a great deal of this article, and considerable quantities, raised in Virginia, Delaware, Pennsylvania, New-Jersey, New-York, and Connecticut, are exported—as are the wheat and flour of the last five states, from Philadelphia and New-York, there being little foreign trade from Delaware or Jersey—and the western parts of Connecticut shipping with less expense from the ports on Hudson's river than those of their own state.

Hemp and flax are raised in very large quantities throughout the United States: and though South Carolina and Georgia produce less than any other states, of these two articles, they are capable of raising immense quantities. From the advantage they have in the Savannah and other rivers, they could produce hemp with great profit. Large portions of the new lands of all the states are well suited to hemp and flax.

Though sheep are bred in all parts of America, yet the most populous scenes in the middle states, and the eastern states which have been long settled,

* Virginia exported in the above year 684,627 bushels of Indian corn, besides her increased shipments coastwise.

and particularly the latter, are the places where they thrive beſt. In the eaſtern or New-England ſtates, they form one of the greateſt objeƈts of the farmer's attention, and one of his ſureſt ſources of profit. The demand for wool, which has of late increaſed exceedingly with the rapid growth of our manufaƈtures, will add conſiderably to the former great profits of ſheep: and the conſumption of their meat by the manufaƈturers, will render them ſtill more beneficial.

Horned or neat cattle are alſo bred in every part of the United States. In the weſtern counties of Virginia, the Carolinas, Georgia, and Kentucky, where they have extenſive ranges, and mild winters, without ſnows of any duration, they run at large, and multiply very faſt. In the middle ſtates, cattle require more of the care and attention they uſually receive in Europe, and they are generally good; often very large. But in the eaſtern ſtates, whoſe principal objeƈts on the land, have until lately been paſturage and grazing, cattle are very numerous indeed, and generally large. Cheeſe is, of courſe, moſt abundant in thoſe ſtates. No European country can exceed the United States in the valuable article of ſalt proviſions. Our exports of this kind are every day increaſing; as the raiſing of cattle is peculiarly profitable to farmers, the greater part of whom have no more land, than they can cultivate even with the plough. Barley and oats are the produƈtions of every ſtate, though leaſt culti-

vated to the fouthward. Virginia however is turning her attention to barley, as alfo Maryland, and
can raife great quantities.

Mafts, fpars, ftaves, heading, boards, plank, fcantling, and fquare timber, are fhipped from almoft all
the ftates : New-Hampfhire, and the adjoining province of Maine, which is connected with Maffachufetts, are among the moft plentiful fcenes. In New-
York they abound : and in North Carolina and
Georgia, the pitch-pine plank, and fcantling, and
white oak ftaves, are excellent, and abundant, efpecially in the former. The ftock of thefe articles
on the Chefapeak and Delaware bays is more ex-
haufted : but yet there is a great deal on the rivers
of both for exportation, befides abundance for
home confumption. Confiderable quantities are
alfo brought to the Charlefton market, but a large
part of them is from the adjacent ftates of Georgia
and North Carolina. When their internal navigation fhall be improved, South-Carolina will open
new fources of thefe articles.

Pot-afhes and pearl-afhes have become very valuable articles to both the land-holders and merchants
of the United States : but their importance was comparatively unknown twenty years ago. A fingle
faft will illuftrate the wealth that may be accquired
by this manufacture. The ftate of Maffachufetts,
which has been fettled twice as long the other
ftates on a medium—which contains about a fiftieth part of the territory of the United States—which

is among the moſt populous of them—and conſequently muſt have far leſs wood to ſpare than many other parts of the union—has nevertheleſs ſhipped two hundred thouſand dollars worth of theſe two
articles in a year. New-England and New-York
have derived great advantage from their attention
to pot and pearl-aſhes : but it has hitherto been
made in very inconſiderable quantities, in the ſtates
to the ſouthward of them. In moſt of them it has
been entirely overlooked. New-Jerſey and Delaware have more foreſts than Maſſachuſetts: and
as there is no part of either of thoſe ſtates, that lies
twenty-five miles from navigable water, they may
venture to expend their wood, and to depend upon
coal. In the other ſix ſtates, which lie ſouth of
Hudſon's river, the materials for pot-aſh are immenſe—as alſo in the ſtate of New-York.

A grand dependence of the eaſtern ſtates is on
their valuable fiſheries. A detail of theſe is unneceſſary. It is ſufficient to ſay, that, with a ſmall exception in favour of New-York, *the whole great ſea
fiſhery* of the United States, is carried on by New-
England: and it is in a variety of ways highly beneficial to our landed and manufacturing intereſts.
Maſſachuſetts very far exceeds all the other ſtates,
in the fiſhing buſineſs.

Iron is abundant throughout the union, except
in the Delaware ſtate ; which can draw it as conveniently from the other ſtates on the Delaware

river, as if it were in her own bowels. Virginia is
fuppofed to be the ftate moft pregnant with minerals and foffils of any in our union.

Deer-fkins, and a variety of furs, are obtained
by all the ftates from the Indian country; either directly, or through the medium of their neighbours. Hitherto they have been exported in
large quantities. : but from the rapid progrefs of
our manufactures, that exportation muft diminifh.

The article of pork, fo important in war, navigation and trade, merits particular notice. The plenty
of maft or nuts of the oak and beech, in fome places,
and Indian corn every where, occafion ours to be
very fine, and abundant. Two names among us
are pre-eminent—Burlington and Connecticut:
the firft of which is generally given to the pork of
Pennfylvania, and the middle and northern parts
of Jerfey: the fecond is the quality of all the pork
north of Jerfey. It may be fafely affirmed, that
they are fully equal to the pork of Ireland, and
Britanny, and much cheaper.

Cider can be produced with eafe in confiderable
quantities, from Virginia inclufive to the moft
northern ftates, as alfo in the weftern country of the
Carolinas and Georgia : but New-Jerfey and New-
England have hitherto paid moft attention to
this drink. An exquifite brandy is diftilled from
the extenfive peach-orchards, which grow upon the

the numerous rivers of the Chefapeak, in North Carolina, in Georgia, and in Pennfylvania, and may be made in the greater part of our country.

Silk has been attempted with fuccefs in the foutheernmoft ftates, fo far as due attention was paid to it: but is not well fuited to the nature of their labourers, who, being blacks, are not fufficiently careful or fkilful: and there are many other objects of more importance and profit in the agriculture of thofe fertile ftates. In Connecticut, where there is a fenfible and careful white population, and where land is comparatively fcarce and dear, it is found to be practicable and beneficial. A project to extend the white Italian mulberry-tree over all the ftates, has been formed by fome perfevering individuals, acquainted with the propagation of them. A great part of Connecticut is already fupplied. An extenfive nurfery has been eftablifhed near Philadelphia; another at Princeton, in New-Jerfey; and two more are at this time commenced on New-York and Long Iflands.

Rye is produced generally through all the ftates north of the Carolinas, and in the weftern parts of the three fouthern ftates. But the detail of American productions, and the parts in which they moft abound, would be very lengthy. It will therefore be fufficient to fay, that, in addition to the above capital articles, the United States produce or contain flaxfeed, fpelts, lime-ftone, allum, faltpetre,

lead, copper, coal, free-ftone, marble, ftone for
wares, potters' clay, brick clay, a variety of
fhip-timber, fhingles, holly, beech, poplar, curled
maple, black walnut, wild cherry, and other
woods fuitable for cabinet makers, fhingles of
cedar and cyprefs, myrtle-wax, bees-wax, butter,
tallow, hides, leather, tanners' bark, maple fugar,
hops, muftard-feed, potatoes, and all the other principal vegetables; apples, and all the other principal fruits; clover, and all the other principal graf-
fes. On the fubject of our productions, it is only
neceffary to add, that they muft be numerous, diverfified, and extremely valuable, as the various
parts of our country, lie in the fame latitudes as
Spain, Portugal, the middle and fouthern provinces
of France, the fertile ifland of Sicily, and the greater part of Italy, European and Afiatic Turkey,
and the kingdom of China, which maintains by its
own agriculture more people than any country in
the world.

The lands of the United States, though capable
of producing fo great a variety of neceffary and
ufeful articles, are much cheaper than in Europe.
Farms which lie in fuch of our ftates as have been
longeft fettled and improved, can be purchafed for
lefs money than the medium value of farming lands
in any civilized part of the world: and our new
lands, as well within the particular bounds of the
feveral ftates, as thofe in the weftern territory of
our confederated republic, are to be procured at

very low prices, either for cafh at the time of purchafe, a reafonable credit for a part, or a long credit on mortgage for the whole. This difference in
the price of new or unfettled lands is occafioned by
the difference of fituation and quality, their near-
nefs to good roads and water carriage, the quantity
wanted by the purchafer, his capacity to pay cafh,
the length of the credit given, the wants or neceffities of the fellers, and other circumftances, which
reafon will naturally fuggeft. The moft advantageous mode is, for a number of perfons to emigrate
together, with a minifter and fchoolmafter. If fuch
fmall bodies of people can only command money
enough to erect their little buildings, where timber
and ftone coft nothing and are abundant, and to
buy provifions to live on for a year, they may procure lands upon very convenient and eafy terms
for feveral years, with little advance, and in many
inftances without the leaft advance of purchafe
money.

Labouring people in the farming, manufacturing,
and mechanical trades, can have conftant employment, and better wages, than in the dearest
countries of Europe; becaufe we have fo much
land, fo many new dwelling-houfes, work-fhops,
barns, and other buildings to erect, and fo many
new trades and manufactories to eftablifh. And
though the wages of the induftrious poor are very
good, yet the neceffaries of life are cheaper than
in Europe, and the articles ufed are more comfortable and pleafing. The medium price of meat and

fish in many parts of America, is lower than the price of flour in Europe, especially if bought by the carcase. The French fleet were supplied with their beef last year, at ten shillings sterling, for one hundred pounds weight, in the city of Boston.— Pickled beef was sold in the same year, in the city of New-York, for twenty to twenty-two shillings sterling per barrel, of two hundred pounds weight, including the cost of salt and cask. Beef was sold by the side and carcase at Trenton, in New-Jersey, at less than ten shillings sterling per hundred pounds; and in Philadelphia, at ten shillings sterling, in 1789. These parcels were of the inferior kind. The first cuts of the finest cattle are higher as must be supposed, especially in those three cities, which are the largest in the United States; but it may be safely affirmed that an American cent (being equal to the hundredth part of a Mexican dollar) will buy as good butchers' meat in the capitals of the several states, as a penny sterling will buy in Amsterdam, Paris, or London. Fish, in all our cities and towns near the sea, are excellent, abundant, and cheaper far than butchers' meat: and poultry is so low, that a turkey, of fourteen or fifteen pounds weight, may be bought for three shillings and nine-pence to four shillings and six-pence sterling. Add to this, many principal necessaries and conveniencies of life are entirely free from excise or duty, at this time; and will be lightly charged for a long while to come—such as home-made malt liquors and cider, coal and fire-wood, candles, oil, soap, tobacco, and leather, none of which pay excise, and even foreign falt pays only about fix-pence fterling duty on importation, and no excife whatever. Nor have we any window-tax or hearth-money, nor feveral other taxes, by which large fums are raifed in Europe.

Many things are daily prefenting themfelves, by which the profits of land will be greatly enhanced in this country. We have hitherto imported a great part of our drink from abroad, viz. rum, brandy, gin, &c. but we find, if we extend our breweries fo far as to render thefe fpirituous liquors unneceffary, that we fhall want above two millions of bufhels of barley for the purpofe, and large quantities of hops, befides having ufe for a further part of the immenfe quantities of fire-wood and coal with which our country abounds. We have alfo obtained the European cotton mill, by means of which, and a few of our innumerable mill feats, the owners of lands, in the fix fouthern ftates, will be called upon to fupply great quantities of cotton. The movements of a mill for fpinning flax, hemp, and combed wool, have alfo been conftructed here, by which our farmers, throughout the union, will be called upon to fupply further quantities of flax and hemp, and to increafe their fheep. The rolling mill for iron and other metals—and the tilthammer for all large iron work—have been brought into extenfive ufe, and will no doubt be erected in all the ftates. But the detail of water-works, and mechanifm which may be introduced into a country, that has, moderately fpeaking, ten thoufand (and probably nearer twenty thoufand) mill-feats, would be endlefs.

There is a ftriking invaluable difference between the navigable waters of the United States and thofe of any country in the old world. The Elbe is the only river in Europe, which will permit a fea veffel to fail up it for fo great a length as feventy miles. The Hudfon's, or North-River, between the ftates of New-York and New-Jerfey, is navigated by fea veffels one hundred and eighty miles from the ocean ; the Delaware, between Pennfylvania, New-Jerfey and the Delaware ftate, one hundred and fixty miles; the Patowmac, between Virginia and Maryland, three hundred miles: and there are feveral other rivers, bays, and founds, of extenfive navigation, far exceeding the great river Elbe. The inland boatable waters and lakes are equally numerous and great.

In a country thus circumftanced, producing the great raw materials for manufactures, and poffeffing unlimited powers by water and refources of fuel, fubject alfo to confiderable charges upon the importation of foreign fabrics, *to neglect manufactures would have been highly criminal.* Thefe important ideas have taken full poffeffion of the American mind. The theory is now every where approved: and in New England, Pennfylvania, and feveral other ftates, the practice has been taken up with confiderable fpirit and very extenfively.   Mafter

workmen in every manufacturing and mechanical
art (except thofe of fuperfluous or luxurious kinds)
with their journeymen and labourers, muft fucceed
here. The freight, infurance, and other charges
of a long voyage, of more than three thoufand miles
and the duties laid here, operate greatly in favour
of American fabrics. Manufactures by fire, water,
and emigrating workmen, muft fucceed even in
the moft agricultural of our ftates, and will meet
every encouragement in the New England ftates,
and others whofe lands are nearly full. A regard
for the republican manners of our country, renders
it a duty to warn the manufacturers of very fine,
fuperflous, and luxurious articles, not to emigrate
to thefe ftates. Gold and filver and other laces,
embroidery, jewellery, rich filks and filk velvets,
fine cambrics, fine lawns, fine muflins, and articles
of that expenfive nature, have yet few wearers
here.

Ship-building is an art for which the United
States are peculiarly qualified by their fkill in the
conftruction, and by the materials, with which
this country abounds: and they are ftrongly tempt-
ed to purfue it by their commercial fpirit, by the
capital fifheries in their bays and on their coafts,
and by the productions of a great and rapidly increafing agriculture. They build their oak veffels on
lower terms than the cheapeft European veffels of
fir, pine, and larch. The coft of an oak fhip in
New England, is about twenty-four Mexican dollars per ton fitted for fea: a fir veffel cofts in the

ports of the Baltic, thirty-five Mexican dollars : and the American ship will be much the moft durable. The coft of a veffel of the American live-oak and cedar, which will laft (if falted in her timbers) thirty years, is only thirty-fix to thirty-eight dollars in our different ports ; and an oak ship, in the cheapeft part of England, Holland, or France, fitted in the fame manner, will coft fifty-five to fixty dollars. In fuch a country, the fifheries and commerce, with due care and attention on the part of government, muft be profitable.

The public debt of the United States, occafioned by the revolution war, is eftimated at about eighteen millions of pounds fterling ;* but as they have an extenfive fettled territory—above two hundred and forty millions of acres of vacant land—as their duties upon foreign articles are not more than one fourth of thofe of Great Britain—as they have no excifes or duties upon articles of their own growth or manufacture—and laftly, as they are every year faving large fums by the introduction of new manufactures and the extenfion of old ones, this debt cannot be confidered as heavy. The intereft of the public debts of France and Great Britain (which are nearly equal to each other) is, in each inftance, above nine millions fterling : And as our debt, like the debt of all nations, is fold below its nominal value, lefs than two years intereft of the debts of either of thofe two nations would entirely fink it.

* It proves to be lefs.

The capital of the Britifh debt is above fourteen times as great as ours—and the annual expenfes of their government exceed ours beyond all compa-rifon. The annual expences of France are ftill greater, being about one hundred and five mil-lions of dollars. If nations thus circumftanced can have comfort and eafe, under fuch debts and ex-penfes, America can have no hardfhips or difficul-ty to apprehend.

The people of the principal European nations will find themfelves more *at home* in America than in any foreign country, to which they can emigrate. The Englifh, German, and Dutch languages are fluently fpoken by large bodies of our citizens, who have emigrated from thofe countries, or who are the defcendants of emigrants. The French language is alfo fpoken by many in our towns. There are many emigrants from other nations, and the defcendants of fuch emigrants. Our popula-tion has been derived from England, Scotland, Wales, Ireland, Germany, the United Netherlands, Sweden, and France, and a few from feveral other countries. It is computed to be above three mil-lions at this time :† and the population of no coun-try can increafe fo rapidly : becaufe living is no where fo cheap, and we are conftantly gaining peo-ple from the nations of the old world.

The ftate of literature in the Uuited States is

† It was a matter of agreeable furprife, that our population in 1791, proved to be about 4,000,000.

respectable, and is rapidly advancing and extending. Seminaries of learning are spread from north to south. There are five universities, no one of which, however is on a very extensive scale—fourteen colleges, and forty eight public academies, besides very many establishments of schools, in the townships or hundreds, and under the care of religious corporations and societies. There is scarcely an instance of a state constitution, which does not recognize the utility of public schools, and the necessity of supporting and increasing them. Liberal grants of land and other real estates, and of monies, for these salutary purposes, have been and are continually made.

The situation of civil liberty in America is so universally known that it is scarcely necessary to add any thing upon that head. Yet it may not be amiss briefly to mention, that no man can be convicted of any crime in the United States, without the unanimous verdict of twelve jurymen—that he cannot be deprived of any money, lands, or other property, nor punished in his person, but by some known law, made and published before the circumstance or act in question took place—that all foreigners may freely exercise their trades and employments, on landing in our country, upon equal terms with our own natural born citizens—that they may return at any time, to their native country, without hindrance or molestation, and may take with them the property they brought hither, or what they may have afterwards acquired here—that if they choose

to remain among us, they will become completely
naturalized free citizens by only two years refi-
dence; but may purchafe and hold lands on the day
of their arrival, and that a free citizen of the United States has a right, directly or indirectly, to elect
every officer of the ftate in which he lives, and
every officer of the United States.

The fituation of religious rights in the American
ftates, though alfo well known, is too important,
too precious a circumftance, to be omitted. Almoft every fect and form of chriftianity is known
here—as alfo the Hebrew church. None are merely tolerated. All are admitted, aided by mutual
charity and concord, and equally fupported and
cherifhed by the laws. In this land of promife for
the good men of all denominations, are actually to
be found, the independent or congregational
church from England, the Proteftant Epifcopal
church (feparated by our revolution from the
church of England) the Quaker church, the Englifh,
Scotch, Irifh and Dutch Prefbyterian or Calvinift
churches, the Roman Catholic church, the German
Lutheran church, the German reformed church,
the Baptift and Anabaptift churches, the Hugonot
or French Proteftant church, the Moravian church,
the Swedifh Epifcopal church, the Seceders from
the Scotch church, the Menonift church, with other
Chriftian fects, and the Hebrew church. Mere toleration is a doctrine exploded by our general conftitution; inftead of which have been fubftituted
an unqualified admiffion, and affertion, that their

own modes of worſhip and of faith equally belong to all the worſhippers of God, of whatever church, ſect, or denomination*.

———————

AT the time of the foregoing publication, the the exports of the United States amounted to above 18,000,000 of dollars. The progreſs of induſtry had advanced them in 1792, to the ſum of 21,000,000 of dollars†. A very large proportion of this increaſe, conſiſts in articles for the ſuſtenance of man—the food of our increaſing manufacturers, or the prime neceſſaries of other countries. The uſeful art of ſhip-building has kept more than equal pace with our agriculture, becauſe it has felt the impulſe of the revival of the fiſheries, and of foreign demand. The price of iron, which is a good general index of induſtry and

* The writer of the foregoing publication has found himſelf reſtrained in the ſtatement of facts concerning the United States, by the want of that accurate and various information, which a full account of ſo extenſive and grand a ſcene neceſſarily requires: and his narrow limits obliged him to omit ſeveral important facts, very intereſting to emigrants of every deſcription. He hopes that ſome of the excellent pens, which abound in every part of our union, will be employed in ſhewing the true ſituation of things in each ſtate, that, from the ſeveral details, *the extraordinary capacity of the United States of America, to promote the comfort and happineſs of the human race, may be duly manifeſted.*

† In the year ending on the 30th September 1793, the exports of the United States were 26,000,000 of dollars.

arts, has been greatly advanced by the progrefs of public and private improvements, and ufeful ma- nufaêtures: and eleven great and important canals have been aêtually commenced in a country, which before the late revolution did not exhibit a fingle inftance of thofe invaluable improvements.

CHAPTER VII.

CONCERNING THE DISTILLERIES OF THE UNITED STATES.

THE importance of molaffes to the United States has been fo frequently a topic of obfervation, that it is prefumed to be generally underftood. No lefs than 7,194,606 gallons were regularly entered in the cuftom-houfes, from various places, during the year ending in September 1791. When the diforders in the French part of the ifland of St. Domingo commenced in the autumn of that year, apprehenfions arofe, that thofe citizens of the United States, who were interefted in the diftilleries from foreign materials, might fuftain a grievous fhock, unlefs they would adopt the fubfti-tutes, which our own agriculture afforded. It was manifeft, that thefe individual inconveniencies, by due anticipation, might be confiderably diminifhed; and it was no lefs evident, that the agriculture of the United States might be exceedingly benefited by the diftillation of fruit and grain, inftead of molaffes. From a defire to bring thefe circum-ftances into that notice, which their importance required, the following paper was introduced into public view in the ftate of Maffachufetts, in which the molaffes diftillery greatly exceeds thofe of all the other ftates together.

Reflections on the present situation of the distilleries of the United States heretofore employed on foreign materials.

IT has been a subject of frequent apprehension, to attentive observers on the internal industry of our country, that the distilleries in the sea-port towns would one day be deprived of their necessary supply of foreign materials: the obvious possibility of various events suggested these fears. A contingency as deplorable as it was unexpected, has at length happened, which menaces a long interruption, perhaps a total privation, of that large part of those supplies, which has been drawn from Hispaniola; and the late disorders in Martinico, have conspired to heighten the evil.

In consequence of these events, the ordinary operations of above one hundred distilleries will be affected, and the subsistence of those numerous families, that are dependant on them, will be for a time or in a degree cut off. The ravages already committed in the West Indies, must occasion a defalcation of produce, which it will require several years of industry to restore, after tranquility shall be established. To supply our demand for the raw materials from any other source, is impracticable; and if it were possible to procure from the islands of other nations, distilled spirits, equal to our consumption, yet the importation would be excessively expensive, as well as impolitic. Little more than

eight millions of gallons are annually made in thofe
iflands; and the demand for the expected Spanifh
war advanced the price of rum in Jamaica, fifty
per cent.—What then would be the effect of a
new and conftant demand for feveral millions of
gallons?

But were it practicable to procure the diftilled
fpirits from abroad, upon moderate terms, what
would be the fate of the American diftillers, their
workmen and affiftants ? Would not their capitals become unproductive, and their diftilleries,
fink into ruin? It is to be feared, too, that the fhipping connected with this branch of induftry, will
feel a fhare of thefe unfortunate events.

To avoid evils fo great and extenfive, muft be
the wifh and fhould be the endeavour of every
good citizen. If, however, they cannot be altogether prevented, prudence may perhaps mitigate
them. It is thought that a diminution of them
may be found in the application of our diftilleries
to the manufacture of grain and fruit fpirits.

The harvefts of Europe are faid to have been
abundant; thofe of the United States are known
to be fo; and a reduction of the prices of grain
feems to be a probable confequence: the prefent
time, therefore, is the proper one to commence
this bufinefs. The tranfportation of grain and cider coaftwife, to the diftilleries; and of the diftil-

led spirits to the consumers, on all the navigable waters of the United States, will give employment to those vessels which may necessarily relinquish the French West-India trade.

It will not escape the observation of those who meditate the establishment or extension of breweries, that the present is a favourable moment for proceeding in that most beneficial branch. It is well known that brewing, and the distillation of spirits from grain, are two very profitable manufactures in Great-Britain; although the brewer and distiller there pay fifty per cent. higher for grain than the ordinary price of the same article in this country. Holland also brews extensively, and in distillation from grain exceeds Great-Britain; yet she imports more grain than she manufactures, and more fuel than her breweries and distilleries consume.

The difference of eleven cents per gallon (about forty per cent. on the value of the article) in favour of spirits distilled from native materials, when compared with imported spirits, gives an advantage to the home manufacture, which will be duly estimated by every judicious calculator: there can be no doubt, that this advantage will be always preserved, and probably increased by the laws of the United States*.

* Among the inducements which the national government have to adhere to this policy, is this *very important one*, that the encouragement to the culture of grain, which would be derived from the use of it in brewing and distillation, would prove the most effectual security against a scarcity of bread.

The ſtrongeſt inducement to reaſonable men, for the employment of their capital and induſtry in any undertaking, is the hope of permanent profit, founded on fair calculation: this calculation the diſtillers are beſt able to make: to them, therefore, the ideas herein ſuggeſted are all ſubmitted.

T H E great ſtock of molaſſes, which was left on hand from the unuſual importation of 1791, and the exertions of the merchants and diſtillers to procure ſupplies of that article from new ſources, have occaſioned the mutation of the molaſſes diſtilleries into fruit and grain diſtilleries, to be yet inconſiderable. It is certain however, that the new diſtilleries have been principally confined to fruit and grain, and that the manufacture of ſpirits, from domeſtic materials, has greatly increaſed. The high price of grain, ariſing from the European demand, has occaſioned the gradual manner, in which the change of our diſtilleries is taking place, to be perfectly convenient. The inhabitants of the United States are thoroughly prepared, by their own reflections on this branch of their buſineſs, to make ſuch further alterations, as circumſtances may require, whenever they ſhall become neceſſary*

* Breweries, which are more eſtimable kind of liquor manufactory, have greatly increaſed. 1793.

CHAPTER VIII.

STATEMENTS, RELATIVE TO THE AGRICULTURE, MANU-
FACTURES, COMMERCE, POPULATION, RESOURCES AND
PUBLIC HAPPINESS OF THE UNITED STATES, IN REPLY
TO THE ASSERTIONS AND PREDICTIONS OF LORD SHEF-
FIELD.

THE misconceptions in regard to American
affairs which prevailed in many parts of Europe in the year 1791, and particularly in the British dominions, were deemed to be very great.
They appeared to be founded, in no small degree,
on the disquisitions of an English writer* whose errors, it was therefore, necessary to demonstrate.

An examination of his work was commenced in
the American Museum and continued monthly, as
circumstances permitted. Further reflection and
opportunity produced additional facts and some relative considerations, which, on a re-publication,
were intermixed with the original materials, or
were comprised in a seventh number, and in two
additional notes on American manufactures.

It is possible, that a question may have arisen,
why an examination of a work, first published in
1783, should have been instituted in 1791? The
observations of lord Sheffield had gone through six

* Lord Sheffield.

enlarged editions, and the fame writer having dif-
feminated ideas, very unfavourable to the United
States, in his book upon the commerce of Ireland,
it was conceived that a developement of his errors
was due no lefs to thofe who are mifinformed in
Europe, than to thofe interefts, which are not underftood in this country. It had been frequently
obferved, that when American affairs were difcuffed in Britain, lord Sheffield's work was quoted
with fymptoms of conviction and belief. Under
circumftances like thefe, an examination of his allegations, predictions and remarks, even at that day,
would not, it was hoped, appear unfeafonable.

*A Brief examination of Lord Sheffield's Obferva-
tions on the Commerce of the United States, with
two fupplementary notes on American manufactures.*

SECTION I.

THE facts and obfervations of this writer have.
in the opinion of many of his countrymen, fo firmly endured the touchftone of experience, that an
attempt to demonftrate errors in both, may appear
to deferve little attention. The brevity, however,
which is intended to be obferved, may induce the
parties concerned, to give thefe papers an attentive perufal.

It is remarked, in the laft edition of the publication referred to, " that a knowledge and con-

fideration of the American trade fhould dictate to Great-Britain the meafures fhe ought to purfue." The good fenfe of that obfervation, in relation to the time when it was written, is admitted, without hefitation, and it is confidered as equally proper, in regard to the prefent. It is believed, indeed, to comport moft perfectly with the dignity and true interefts of nations, not to induce into injurious grants thofe foreign powers, with whom they may find occafion to treat. No obfervations need be offered, to fhow the refpectability, which is acquired by negociations conducted with a liberal and mag-nanimous policy. It will be fufficient to remark, that arrangements, folidly founded in the mutual interefts of the contracting parties, will always be fatisfactory to the intelligent part of their refpective citizens, and confequently moft permanent; but that injudicious grants of unreafonable advantages, efpecially if obtained by deceptive means, difho-nour the character of the over-reaching party—lead to murmers among the people of the miftaken na-tion, often to expenfive and bloody wars—and give immenfe hazard to the commercial enterprizes, which are ufually inftituted in confequence of new treaties. It may be confidered, therefore, as wif-dom in negociating nations, diligently to fearch for their *common interefts,* as the fitted ground of treaty. In order to difcover *thefe* with eafe, and to view them with juft impreffions, it is a meafure not only of primary importance, but of indifpenfible necef-fity, to remove eftablifhed errors in the public creed of either country. It is not by way of apology, that thefe prefatory remarks are offered to all concerned, but to fhow, that a rational purfuit of the interefts of their refpective countries, fhould lead both Americans and Englifhmen, to develope the errors, in regard to facts and opinions, difcoverable in a publication,* which appears to have been the caufe of a change of meafures in the Britifh nation, or to have been intended to vindicate one, which it was pre-determined to make.

It is not propofed to go into a full and regular reply to the writer of the obfervations, but rather to point out fo many real and important errors in his facts and predictions, as may fhake the unlimited confidence, which has been repofed in him by his countrymen, in order to lead to a different legiflative deportment towards us. Little regard will be paid to order, in this curfory examination; but any important object, which prefents itfelf, will be concifely noticed.

THE CARRYING TRADE,

in the opinion of lord Sheffield, is loft to the people, inhabiting thefe ftates, by their choice of independence. Let us examine the proofs. His feventh table ftates the inward tonnage of all the Britifh provinces in North-America, in 1770, to have been 365,100 tons. From this amount are

* Lord Sheffield's Obfervations, &c.

to be deducted the entries in Newfoundland, Canada, Nova-Scotia, the two Floridas, the Bahamas,
and Bermuda, being 33,458 tons, which leaves the
entries in thofe provinces, which are now the
United States, at 331,642 tons. We are alfo to
deduct the fhips owned by Britifh fubjects, not
refident in thofe thirteen provinces. *Champion*
confiders thefe to have been nearly the whole in
the European trade, it is believed erroneoufly ;
but they muft have been very confiderable : yet
the return of entries of American veffels for the
laft year, rendered by our treafury to the Houfe of
Reprefentatives, though known to have been incomplete from inevitable caufes, amounts to above
363,000 tons, exclufive of fifhing veffels*.

It is manifeft, then, that the carrying trade, which
refults almoft unaided from an agriculture, that fully lades 650,000 tons of veffels to foreign ports, is
confiderably greater than what we enjoyed as Britifh provinces.   A very beneficial coafting trade
(employing above 100,000 tons*) has moreover
grown up, partly from the variety of our productions
and mutual wants, and partly from the introduction
of manufactures, which it was believed we could
never attain, and with which Great Britain alone
ufed to fupply us.   The building of fhips has alfo
increafed, as we undertake hereafter to fhow, and

* Our *numerous* coafters alfo not being entered, but only renew-
ing their licences in that trade, once a year, form no part of
the 363,000 tons.

the tonnage owned by the merchants of the United States or late American provinces, was never fo great as at the prefent moment. It is believed, moreover, that the American carriers derive greater profit from the bufinefs, than the Britifh nation, who builds fhips two-thirds dearer, and who maintain themfelves in what they poffefs of the carrying trade, at the expenfe of great bounties out of their public treafury, by burdenfome reftrictions on all their dominions, but the ifland of Great-Britain, and by regulations to favour their fhipping, which increafe *the price of raw materials* for their manufactures, and of bread and other *food* for their workmen and for their poor.

BEEF AND PORK,

in the opinion of our author, are not likely to become confiderable articles of export, fo as to interfere with Ireland for fome time. The medium annual quantity exported from the United States, before the revolution, he ftates at 23,635 barrels. Our treafury return, for the laft year, exhibits 66,000 barrels, befides 2,500 barrels of bacon, 5,200 head of horned cattle, and an equal number of hogs. The medium price of the pork was thirty-feven fhillings fterling, or about $8\frac{1}{4}$ dollars per barrel, and that of beef twenty-eight fhillings fterling, or about $6\frac{1}{4}$ dollars per barrel. Befides this exportation, 263,000 tons of foreign veffels, in a great degree, and all our own, were victualled from our markets.

But a moments reflection will convince any man, who knows this country, that it will, in the courfe of a few years, offer to all foreign nations fuch quantities of falt provifions, efpecially of beef, as muft ferioufly affect Ireland, where that article is fold at eight dollars per barrel. It is a fact no lefs curious, than important to our provifion trade, that the French fleet has been fupplied with beef in the port of Bofton, at prices lower than the then current value of wheat-flour in any of our feaports, although our expors of the latter article are fourteen times as great as thofe of Ireland. The owners of the interior lands of the United States, on which fettlements have but lately become confiderable, find a particular advantage in raifing cattle, becaufe thofe animals tranfport themfelves to the feaports at a very fmall expenfe.*

TEAS.

It is known to perfons acquainted with American commerce, that teas of various kinds form a very confiderable proportion of our importations. The rich and the poor confume them freely. Their value, as they were entered in our cuftom-houfes, for the year preceding the firft of October, 1790, was 2,784,000 dollars, which was about a feventh of our imports. On this very capital article of commerce and confumption, lord Sheffield hazards the following opinions—

* The exportation of beef and pork, in the year ending on the 30th September, 1792, was 112,456 barrels.

" That as the Englifh Eaft-India company can afford to fell this tea, on full as good, if not better, terms, than the Dutch, or any other nation in Europe, *there is no danger of lofing the American market*." And

" That the allowing the drawback upon teas exported from Great-Britain, will generally enable the Englifh *to command the tea trade to America*."

His lordfhip had forgotten that Canton is an open market, *equally acceffible* to all nations. The American fhips have accordingly gone thither, not only in the ordinary feafons, but in thofe, *which ufually reftrain European expeditions*. The United States produce the great article of *ginfeng* in large quantities, which renders this trade convenient to them. The teas, imported by our merchants directly from China, in the laft year, were *two millions fix hundred and one thoufand eight hundred and fifty two pounds*, which is fully equal to our confumption, could we obtain coffee, and the requifite quantity of Mufcovado fugars, of which our people are univerfally and paffionately fond. There were imported alfo from Europe, 416,652 pounds of teas, fhipped from foreign ports, *other than Britifh*, to the extreme difadvantage of the fhippers, and to the great injury of our merchants. But the values of commodities in any two markets are the beft illuftration of the relation of thofe markets to each other. The article of tea will therefore be paffed over, after the following ftatement of the current prices on a given day in America and Great-Britain.

In Philadelphia, on the 5th day of November, 1790, after paying the duty inward.	In London, on the 5th day of November, 1790, after deducting the drawback of 12l. 10s. per cent.
Sterling.	Sterling.
Bohea, 1/3½ or 30 cents,	Bohea, 1/5½ or 32 cents,
Souchong, 3/4½ or 75 cents,	Souchong, 4/6 or 100 cents,
*Hyfon, 4/6 or 100 cents.	Hyfon, 6/ or 133¼ cents.

The fame circumftances, which facilitate and infure the attainment of the requifite quantity of teas, not only by means other than Britifh, but indeed by *American* means, certify to us the acquifition of the neceffary fupplies of porcelain, nankeens, filks, and all other China commodities: and upon the whole,' we dare venture to appeal to the books of the infpector general of the Britifh commerce, when we affirm that Great Britain does not fupply us with with a fortieth fhilling of the various kinds of China merchandize, confumed in America, though they probably fall little fhort of a fixth of our importations.

SALT FROM EUROPE.

This article, the writer of the obfervations fays, will be taken indifcriminately from Europe: thereby mifleading the government and people of En-

---

* No teas have been imported from Britain into the United States fince the firft publication of this work. A. D. 1793.

gland into a belief, that they will have a chance of
supplying a confiderable proportion. The quantity imported into the United States, from various
countries, in the laft year, was 2,337,920 bufhels;
befides which it was manufactured in interior fituations. The price of falt in Kentucky, where it is
home made, is about one third of the market rate
at Pittfburgh, where foreign falt is ufed.

The Britifh falt is what is called *fine* in America, from the fmall fize of the cryftals. Of this
kind the price is greater than that of the coarfe,
and not a twentieth bufhel was imported before
the prefent year, it being little ufed but at the table, and inconvenient to tranfport to the interior
country; but the new duty, near the eighth of a
Mexican dollar, will render its importation very
unprofitable in future. A bufhel of rock or allum
falt, as it is termed, from the fize of the cryftals,
will go as far in ufe, as a bufhel and an half or two
bufhels of the finer kind; and the duty is equal.
The price, as before obferved, is lefs. Befides, our
grain and lumber fhips to Portugal, our tobacco
fhips to France, our corn, flour and lumber fhips
to Spain, our veffels to the Cape-de-Verd and Weft-
India iflands, are accommodated by ballafts of falt,
which is cheap and abundant in thofe places. It
never fails to yield fome profit to the owner of the
fhip, (though it will very feldom pay a freight) and
it is exceedingly beneficial to the timbers of a veffel. The liberation of this article in France will

occafion it to be better made there in future, and the French will confequently fupply us with larger parcels than heretofore. The approximation of our fettlements to the falt fprings, and the increafe of white population on the fouthern fea coafts, will occafion additions to the quantity made at home. Should any impediment be thrown in the way of the reception of our lumber and other bulky articles, and of our veffels in Great Britain, the importation of falt, and indeed of moft other coarfe Britifh articles, will be exceedingly diminifhed, as they are brought now to ballaft our return veffels. It appears, however on examining better documents than were procurable at the firft publication of this paper, that our Britifh lumber trade had induced a greater return in falt, than was at that time fuppofed; and as truth is the fole objeĉt of this examination, the error is made known without hefitation.

SHOES,

Our writer fays, were, and muft continue to be imported in confiderable quantities, and principally from Britain! 'Tis probable that not lefs than eight millions of pair of fhoes, boots, half boots, guetres, flippers, clogs, and golofhoes, are annually confumed in or exported from the United States. Our population proves to be about 4,000,000; and if each perfon wears a quantity of the above fhoemakers' wares, *equivalent* to two pair of fhoes per annum, the number will be made up. If the medium value be taken at 75 cents or 3/4½ fterling per pair, this valuable article will amount to six millions of dollars. Of this prodigious quantity, only 70,450 pair of shoes, boots, &c. were imported into the United States in the last year.† Tanned leather, weighing 22,698 pounds, was exported within the same time, and 5,700 pairs of boots and shoes. Of *unmanufactured* hides, only 230 were shipped abroad. Leather and shoes were sent in some degree from the western country. The leather branch is the *second* in England, and it is equal to one-fifth of their staple manufactures. Our shoemakers' wares alone appear to be more in value than one fourth of our exports: and as New England is our greatest cattle country, and the most advanced in handicraft-manufactures, it is plain that its inhabitants must be in a considerable degree indemnified for the effects of those regulations which injured their fisheries. The coarser oils, it may be also observed, are demanded in large quantities by the leather dressers, whose requisitions of them will increase with our population, and exports of leathern manufactures.

PAPER.

This article, it is alledged by our author, will continue to be sent in considerable quantities from

† It must be highly satisfactory to the people of the United States, that they actually make of *one* necessary article *by hand* so very great an aggregate value, as six millions of dollars. All argument against the possibility of manufacturing *by hand* with profit is ended by this fact.

England; and that " although fome coarfe paper for newfpapers is made in America, it is not equal to the demand." From a return made to the manufacturing fociety of Philadelphia, it appears, that there are forty-eight paper mills in Pennfylvania alone. Five more are building in one county of that ftate. Others are known to exift in North Carolina, Delaware, Maryland, New Jerfey, New York and New England. The United States, till very lately, were infenfible of the facility with which this branch can be carried on, of the profit which refults from it, and of the great degree in which it is eftablifhed. The treafury of the United States, and the feveral banks, have paper of the moft perfect kind, fpecially made for them; the printing of books has increafed in an aftonifhing degree; and factories of paper hangings are carried on with great fpirit in Bofton, New-Jerfey, and Philadelphia. In fhort, there are abundant proofs of eftablifhment and progrefs towards perfection, in this valuable branch, in which every thing is made, as it were, *out of nothing*.

RUM.

It is the opinion of lord Sheffield, that the whole of *the Weft-India rum* ufed in America, except a fmall quantity from Demarara, and fome from St. Croix, may be fupplied by the Britifh iflands* The following fcale may be relied on, as the pre-

---

* The Britifh Weft-India iflands do not make as much diftilled fpirits, as are confumed in the United States.

fent ftate of this bufinefs in the United States. If the whole quantity of molaffes, of diftilled fpirits imported, and of diftilled fpirits made at home of fruit and grain, fhould be divided into 132 parts, it would ftand thus.

parts.

Molaffes imported would be   -   -   60

Britifh, Danifh, and other rum, taffia, brandy, geneva, arrack, cordials, and other diftilled fpirits imported, would be*.   37

Spirits diftilled from the native fruits and grain of the United States would be at leaft   35

Total   132

It is afcertained, that the Britifh fpirits are not more than twenty-one parts of the fecond item of thirty-feven; and it appears that *the Weft-India rum*, fupplied by all nations, is reduced to about one fourth of our confumption and fale to foreign nations of diftilled fpirits. How long we fhall continue to take even that proportion is very uncertain. Breweries are multiplying: as their value is becoming manifeft. Grain and fruit diftilleries are rifing up every where. From interior fituations two gallons of fpirit, extracted from a bufhel of rye,

---

* There is reafon to affirm, that the two firft articles have decreafed, and that an increafe in the quantity of the article which follows them, has taken place. A. D. 1793.

can be brought to markets where it will realize to
the farmer two thirds of a dollar for his grain, at
lefs expenfe than if made into flour, and carted to
the fame fpot. The country is abundantly fupplied with ftills; and were the Britifh iflands to be
refufed our flour and grain by their own government, as lord Sheffield advifes, this country would
be compelled to indemnify itfelf by making grain
fpirits and malt liquors in lieu of their rum, which
it is reafonable to fuppofe we fhould no longer import. Indeed the exportation of liquors of all kinds,
made from grain, will probably become very confiderable. Some countries refufe our flour: and
the freight to Europe is a heavy charge upon grain.
This will induce brewing and diftillation, even
when markets abroad are not bad; but when
prices in Europe are very low, we fhall be more
ftrongly impelled to them. Fruit fpirits muft be
made continually, and will add much to the aggregate of diftilled liquors. The grain confumed in
Great-Britain, in their breweries and diftilleries, is
computed to be twenty-four millions of bufhels,
though they are obliged to import confiderable
quantities of flour, meal and grain and though
they have rum colonies to fupport, and to fupply
with fpirits. Holland alfo carries on the liquor
manufactories to a great extent, though far from
able to feed itfelf. The ability in the United States
to do the fame, cannot be doubted, and will certainly increafe. The facilities, which are or may
be granted to our fhips and trade by foreign nations, who make fpirits from the vine, the cane, or

the several kinds of grain, will induce returns in brandy, rum, or gin, which will diminish the American demand for British rum.

The idea that the United States are a country, sui generis.

This position the writer of the observations treats " as perfectly whimsical—" As a figure of rhetoric " conveying no distinct idea, or an effort of cunning " to unite, at the same time, two inconsistent cha- " racters." Yet it will not be difficult to demonstrate to an unprejudiced mind, that the circumstances, in which the people of these states were placed at the peace of 1783, were different from those of any other nation; and that there were some peculiarities in them, considered with respect to British affairs, which rendered it a serious question, whether they did not require a particular arrangement. It is true, that the citizens of the United States had " renounced the duties of British subjects," or, in other words, that they had assumed an independent station : but this measure was fully justified, if we may so speak, by Britain's abandoning the ground, which produced the war—*the assertion of the right to bind the people of America in all cases whatsoever.* It will be acknowledged, too, that we manufactured less at that time than any other nation in the world; consequently we were a more profitable commercial connexion. We shipped, in proportion to our population, more raw materials, and provisions, which they want, than any other nation; for it appears we load 650,000 tons of ship-

ping, and our cargoes were then almoſt entirely
unmanufaĉtured. We were, by much, the firſt cuſ-
tomer for Britiſh manufaĉtures; for it appears by
their exports for 1784, that the greateſt value was
ſhipped to the United States, being £. 3,648,0007,
ſterling, including no raw articles; and that the
next greateſt foreign ſhipment was to Holland, being only £. 1,277,480, part of which was for German conſumption, and ſome part probably was in
raw articles—and that in the year 1785, alſo, the
greateſt value was ſhipped to the United States, being £. 2,308,023, ſterling, and that the next greateſt
foreign ſhipment was likewiſe to Holland, amounting to £. 1,605,303, part of which was not manufaĉtures. The exports to Ruſſia in each of thoſe
two years were leſs than half the exports to New-
York or Pennſylvania. It is to be remembered,
too, how very great a proportion of the Britiſh export trade theſe ſhipments to America conſtituted.
In 1784, their whole exportations were £.15,733,847
and in 1785, £. 16,770,228*.

In additi_n to merchandize from Britain, we took
very large quantities of linen and other dry goods
from Ireland, and an enormous value in rum and

---

* Recent and authentic information warrants the aſſertion,
that the United States, for ſix years ſubſequent to the treaty of
Paris in 1783, imported more goods from Great-Britain than were
imported from thence by any other foreign country, by the difference of at leaſt half a million of ſterling money, and probably
more, though their exports to foreign nations were compoſed in
part of our tobacco, rice, indigo, &c.

other produce of their Weſt India iſlands: and further we were a nation of planters and farmers, whoſe quantities of unimproved and uncultivated lands were manifold greater than thoſe which were or are yet brought into uſe, and conſequently a great and conſtant demand might have been reaſonably expected to exiſt for thoſe ſupplies, which Britain, upon reaſonable terms of intercourſe, would be able to furniſh. Our diſtant ſituation, and the tranſportation of goods, which will lade 650,000 tons of ſhipping, were circumſtances favourable to the carrying trade of our liberal connexions and allies, which no other country preſented to Great-Britain.—We have hitherto ſuffered her to participate freely in this, for it appears, that in the laſt year, 230,000 tons of Britiſh veſſels, a fourth of all their private ſhips, were loaded in our ports.

If then the United States actually furniſh the moſt ſolid items of Britiſh foreign commerce—if the raw materials they afford be the precious elements of a large proportion of the Britiſh manufactures—if our demands from that nation be not only much the largeſt, but alſo of kinds the moſt profitable to them—if our peculiar ſituation would have drawn us, in a greater degree, than any other country to agriculture, and from manufactures—if our language, our religion, our theories of liberty and law, were in many reſpects the ſame as theirs—the idea of our being a people *peculiarly* circumſtanced, ſuch a people as exiſt not elſewhere cannot, in candour, be treated as fanciful: and, indeed, did not the ferioufnefs of a fubject, which involves the interefts of two nations, fupprefs every feeling, which might tend to obfcure them, the indecorum and acrimony, with which this and other pages of "the obfervations" are marked, ought not to pafs without due animadverfion.

The profecution of this examination will be continued in a fubfequent paper. In the mean time, what has been already thrown out, may be duly and temperately confidered. The prefent feafon is interefting andcritical. The policy, which the United States ought to obferve, in *the legiflation of commerce*, is likely to be formally difcuffed. At fuch a moment, facts, accurately afcertained and candidly ftated, are of the utmoft importance ; for how fhall we fo well reafon, as from what we know ? It is to be defired, that *the light of indifputable truth* may enable our own legiflators and thofe of foreign nations, to difcover the ground of common intereft, and that no erroneous maxims, however fanctioned, may clofe one avenue of mutually beneficial communication.

SECTION II.

I T was premifed, in the firft fection, that no particular attention would be paid to order in this examination. We fhall therefore proceed to remark upon timber, fcantling, boards, fhingles, ftaves, heading, and hoops, under the general denomination of

Thefe articles are of the greateft importance to
the Irifh provifion trade, to every branch of the
fifhery, to Britifh navigation, commerce and manufactures in general, and particularly to the profitable management of Weft-India eftates. Lord Sheffield is of opinion, that " moft of them may be imported from Canada and Nova-Scotia, on as good,
if not better terms, than from thefe ftates;" and
that Nova-Scotia will, at leaft for fome time, have
little elfe to depend on, but her fifheries, provifions
and cutting of lumber." But the experience of
1790, feven years after thofe provinces began to
regain order, inftructs us, that there were fhipped
in that year, from the United States to Nova-Scotia alone, 540,000 of ftaves and heading, 924,980
feet of boards, 285,000 fhingles, and 16,000 hoops.

The legiflature of Jamaica (the imports of which
ifland directly from the United States, might be eftimated, in 1784, at half our fhipments to the Britifh Weft Indies) accompanied their addrefs to the
parliament of Britain, with proofs that only 20
bundles of hoops, 301,324 fhingles and ftaves, and
510,088 feet of lumber, were imported into that
ifland from Canada, Nova-Scotia, and St. John's,
between the 3d of April 1783, and the 26th of October 1784, a term of nearly nineteen months! It
appears probable, then, that they did not fupply their
Weft India brethren with more than one half of
what they import, at this mature ftage of their fet-

tlements, from us. It is to be remembered, that
Jamaica drew no fupplies of our lumber through
the Dutch and Danifh iflands; though the more
windward iflands at that time did. From 1768,
to 1772, only 36,100 fhingles and ftaves, and
27,235 feet of lumber, were fhipped annually from
the northern Britifh colonies to the ifland of Jamaica.

In another page of the obfervations, we are told,
that hoops, ftaves, and boards may be fent out to
the Weft-Indies from England, " becaufe the
freight is lower than from the United States."
Here again, the writer of the obfervations is unfortunate in his propofed means of fupply : for it appears, that there were fhipped, in the year above
mentioned, to the *European* dominions of Great-
Britain, 13,306,000 ftaves and heading, 3,000,000
feet of boards, 4,000,000 feet of timber, 253,000
fhingles, and 6000 of hoops. We learn, too, from
Mr. Anderfon's hiftory of commerce, that there
were imported from England to the Weft-Indies,
in 1787, the value of £80 : 12 : 5 fterling and no
more, in boards, ftaves and other lumber, towards
the fupply of the demand of thofe iflands, which
lord Sheffield admits to have been, in 1770, about
thirty-five millions of boards, fcantling, ftaves and
hoops, and fifteen millions and a half of fhingles,
It will appear to him an extraordinary fact, (and
muft excite a fmile in the graveft countenance,)
that the balance of the lumber account between
Great Britain and her Weft-India colonies, is actu-

ally againſt the former : for we learn, from another
of Mr. Anderſon's documents, that there were ſhipped thither from thoſe colonies, between Michael-
mas 1786, and the ſame day in 1787, £.3070 : 13 : 11
ſterling, in boards, ſtaves, and timber.† But if the
projeɛt of ſhipping from Europe were as rational,
as it is wild, what would become of the low freights,
upon which it is chiefly founded? The lumber actually taken by the Britiſh Weſt Indies from the
United States, " exhauſted," as this writer miſre-
preſents them to be, would load all the veſſels that
depart from Great Britain to the Weſt Indies ; for
it would fill above 100,000 tons of ſhipping ; and a
large quantity of tonnage would ſtill be required for
the coal, malt-liquors, wines, loaf ſugar, candles,
ſoap, proviſions, cordage, bale goods, earthen ware,
nails, tallow, lime, carriages, &c. which are conſtantly ſhipped thither from Europe.

The prices of lumber, in London and the United
States have been gravely compared ; and December 1783, was taken as the common ſeaſon. It is
unneceſſary to loſe time in diſproving an allegation
about a period ſo long paſſed, which, however,
could be ſatisfaɛtorily done, or to animadvert upon the ſuppreſſion of the price of boards in which
we had ſo much more the advantage. Our public
returns from the ſeveral ports, which cannot be
ſuppoſed to undervalue the article, nor indeed do
they vary materially from the ſhipping prices give

* Theſe were probably for dunnage, or the ſtowage of cargoes
Of ſugar, coffee, pimento, &c.

the medium rate of twelve and two-thirds dollars
or £.2 : 17 fterling for red oak and white oak ftaves,
and heading, fit for barrels, hogfheads, and pipes.
The prices of ftaves vary exceedingly in the different markets of the United States ; and that, which was
felected by the writer of the obfervations, is known
not to be among the cheapeft. Even there the article is at this time thirty per cent. below the quo-
tation in the obfervations. But we have already
noticed the very large exportation of lumber from
the United States to the Britifh European dominions, which alone is a fufficient contradiction of the
fact, and is a fatisfactory correction of the obfervations.

The following statement of the prices in St. Domingo and Jamaica will not be deemed uninteresting, as tending to shew the rates at which French and American vessels supply the former, and British vessels supply the latter, although the home dominions of France were incapacitated from furnishing their usual quantity of provisions.

At Kingston in Jamaica, 1790.

	June.	Oct.	Nov.
	dolls. dolls.	dolls.	dolls. dolls.
Super. flour, per lb.	10. 20 to 10. 50	7.50	7.50 to 8.25
Common do. do.	9.37½	6.75	7.12 to 7.50
Ship bread, do.	5.25	4.50	4.87
Indian meal, do.	5.25	4.50	5.25
Rice, per 100 lbs.	3.37½	4. 2½	4.50 to 5.25
Pork, do.		14.	12.
Hams, per lb.	.12½	.16¼	15.
Butter, do		.15	15.
Pine boards,	24.	27.	30.
R. O. hhd. staves,	24.	31.	27.
Wooden hoops,	30.	36.	30.

At Cape Francois*, 1790.

	July.	Oct.	Nov.
	dolls.	dolls.	dolls. dolls.
Superfine flour, per bbl.	10.	6.50	6 to 6.50
Common do. do.	9.	5.	5 to 5.45
Ship bread,	3.52		
Indian meal, do.	3.64	2.50	
Rice, per 108 lb.	3.50	2.91	
Beef, do.	6.6	7.	7. to .8
Hams, per lb.	.9	9.	.9
Butter, do.		9.	.12
Pine boards,	15.76	12.12	10.91
R. O. hhd. staves†.	14.	16.	12.

N. B. Wooden hoops vary in Cape-Francois from 14 to 28 dollars.

* The duties, from one to twelve and a half per cent. are included.

† The French West-Indians use very few white oak hhd. staves, making little rum, or taffia, and having a sufficiency of old casks, in which brandy has been imported.

It is not eafy to afcertain the precife degree in which the Britifh Weft-India iflands are fupplied with lumber from their own dominions. But much light is thrown upon the enquiry, by the information of the Jamaica legiflature : and it appears, that the Britifh European ports furnifh none. Their northern colonies are proved to import from us now, more than they exported in 1784: and as our return of exports of lumber to the Weft-India iflands, for the laft year, exceeds the quantity fhipped thither before the revolution, the fupplies from Canada and Nova-Scotia, even now, muft neceffarily be very inconfiderable*.

* After the firft publication of this examination a proclamation of the governor of Nova Scotia was received in the United States, permitting the importation of every fpeices of lumber, from hence into that province, for fix months of 1791, during all which the St. Lawrence is free from ice. As they would have preferred to draw their fupplies during the term of the licence, from Canada, if that country could have furnifhed them—and as lumber does not depend on feafons, and is not, like crops of grain, liable to fudden failures, an irrefragable proof is afforded, that Canada cannot fupply the demand of *Nova Scotia*, much lefs of the Weft-Indies, and that Nova Scotia wants population, or timber, or both, to enable her to furnifh lumber enough *for her own demand*. It feems highly probable, *that without our lumber, the Weft-India trade of the northern Britifh colonies would fuffer deeply*, they having neither grain, flour, bifcuit, nor lumber, to fill up the veffels, which take out their parcels of fifh ; and, it is alfo probable, that a prohibition on our part, were we inclined to it, would affect their fifheries, by enhancing the price of cafks for its package. The coft of cafks in Nova Scotia, at this time, is a heavier charge on their fifh, than our impoft, as it now ftands.

The opening of the nothern Britifh colonies has been repeated twice fince, and a fimilar meafure has been recently adopted in the Britifh Weft-India iflands. A. D. 1793.

The state of Georgia, which is penetrated by large rivers, would probably furnish more lumber and timber than the British dominions will require in the next twenty years. It can be cut at all seasons from the nature of the climate, and her ports, which are more conveniently situated, to supply the West-Indies (though lord Sheffield says, those of Canada are more so!) are open in the middle of winter. The improvement of the inland navigation of South-Carolina will bring into the abundant lumber-market of Charleston, a new and large supply. North-Carolina has very great magazines of timber, and the openings of the Pasquotank canal will give it to all the ports of the Chesapeak. The middle and eastern states are more exhausted; but large quantities will long be exported from the Delaware, much larger from the Hudson, and still greater from the province of Maine.

NOVA-SCOTIA AND CANADA.

Great reliance is placed by this and other Engglish writers on the supplies, which may be derived by the West-India islands from the northern British colonies. It has been already shown, that they hitherto afford little or no lumber. Of rice and naval stores they cannot furnish any, producing none. Of flour, Canada can yet have supplied but a small proportion, having very few mill, having to support cattle through long winters, and the climate preventing shipments during half the year*. The voyage is a very heavy one, being long and on a single freight. Nova Scotia can never supply much of this article, and has taken from the United States above 40,000 barrels of meal and bread, within the laft year, befides 80,000 bufhels of grain.† Canada is too remote to fend fupplies of cattle, hogs, fheep, and horfes; and our exports of thefe animals to Nova Scotia, prove they have not yet any to fpare. Of horned cattle 899, of horfes 12, of fheep 2,244, of hogs 267, and of poultry 2376, were fhipped from the United States to the northern Britifh colonies, in a little more than one year, from the autumn of 1789 to that of 1790. Very little beef, pork, hams, tongues, tallow, lard, butter, cheefe, candles, or foap, can be fpared to the Weft-Indies, by countries which import neat cattle, hogs, fheep, and poultry.

The documents adduced by the Jamaica legifla-ture went further to fhow, that between the 3d of April, 1783, and the 26th of October, 1784, they had received in that populous and extenfive ifland, from Canada, St. John's‡ and Nova Scotia, no flour—no Indian corn, beans, or oats—no fhip bread or other bifcuit—no Indian or other meal—no horfes, cattle, fheep, hogs or poultry—10 bar-

---

* Canadian flour will always be fubject to fpoiling, as it muft be made in fummer.

† There are fewer mills there than in Canada.

‡ Meaning New-Brunfwick.

rels of rice—160 bushels of potatoes—751 hogsheads, 37 tierces, 39 half tierces, and 457 barrels of fish, 45 barrels of oil, 100 oars, 710 shaken casks (or puncheon packs) 21 masts and spars, with the small parcels of lumber mentioned under that head, and no other goods. They also show, that all the imports of Jamaica from Canada, Nova Scotia, and St. John's,* were, on an average of the five years, from 1768 to 1772 but 33 barrels of flour, 7 hogsheads of fish, 8 barrels of oil, 3 barrels of tar, pitch and turpentine, 36 thousand of shingles and staves, and 27,235 feet of lumber.

How far it has been in the power of the northern British colonies, or of the British European dominions to furnish their West-India islands with flour, bread and Indian corn will further appear from the following facts. It is stated by lord Sheffield, that there were imported from hence into those islands, in a year of great plenty and trade, before the revolution, 132,426 barrels of flour and biscuit; but our returns for $13\frac{1}{2}$ months, already mentioned, show that their late demand from us in that term, was 139,286 barrels of flour alone, and 77,982 barrels of Indian meal, middlings, ship-stuff, rye meal, and biscuit. Their former annual supply of Indian corn, received from hence, was 401,471 bushels; and their recent importations prove to have been 516,794 bushels, in the space of time stated in our late return.

* Meaning New-Brunswick.

It is unneceffary to dwell longer upon the fupplies which the remaining Britifh American colonies were expected to afford to their Weft-India
plantations. An experiment of years has been fairly made—The returns from their cuftom houfes,
and from thofe of the iflands, will inform the government of Great-Britain what they really furnifh
at this time, and the proportion it bears to the whole
demand. This head will therefore be paffed over
with the reiteration of a few remarks—that the
Britifh Weft-India iflands are proved to have been
indebted to the United States in 1790, for more
lumber, more grain, and more bread and flour,
than they imported from thefe ftates before the revolution—that their remaining colonies can therefore have furnifhed them, in their prefent mature
ftate, but in very fmall quantities—that thofe colonies have required of us near half the amount in cattle, hogs and fheep, which the Weft-India iflands
formerly took off*—and that the high prices of falt
and fmoked provifions in the Britifh Weft-Indies,
which are greater than thofe in the French iflands,
where thofe articles are prohibited or heavily duti-
ed, fully prove, that they depend for them on Ireland alone, and receive no fenfible relief from the
Britifh American colonies. Their inability to furnifh fupplies of provifions to the Weft-India iflands
is fairly to be prefumed from the proclamation of
the governor of Nova Scotia, already mentioned,
which, befides the article of lumber, permits the

* Befides what go to upper and lower Canada by land.

importation from the United States, of grain, flour, bifcuit, cattle, fheep, poultry, &c. through the whole feafon of 1791, when the St. Lawrence and bay of Fundy are certainly navigable, and the province of Canada is exporting whatever it has of furplus produce.

LINSEED OIL.

This article is faid, in the obfervations, to be made in fome parts of America, from the refufe of the flaxfeed, and that the quantity is trifling compared with the confumption. It is added, that confiderable quantities went from Britain to America, before the war; and the Englifh nation are left to believe, that this will continue to be the cafe, though they actually import feed from hence to make oil.

The cultivation of flax is exceedingly increafed in this country, particularly in interior fituations, and is very general. Oil mills having become more numerous, the feed in inland places is manufactured into oil. This will bear an expence of tranfportation, which fo bulky an article as the feed, cannot fuftain. Hence the prefent price of linfeed oil, after it is brought down to the Philadelphia market, is about 2/1 fterling, while the price in London is from 2/3 to 2/4. The Irifh demand for our feed is about 42,000 hogfheads: after deducting that, the remainder muft be made into oil here, or fhipped to Europe for that purpofe. This manufactory being effected by water mills, there can be no doubt that the former difpofition of the furplus feed will be made.

PAINTERS' COLOURS.

Several of the ochres are found in abundance in Virginia, Connecticut, and other parts of the United States. The interior fituation of the Virginia lead mine, which now yields very copioufly, will foon occafion the manufacture of white lead, and of all the preparations of lead, from the fame caufe that has been mentioned in the cafe of linfeed oil, and rye fpirits—economizing in the tranfportation. The patent colours have been imitated with great fuccefs. The trade with Holland and the Hanfe towns, as alfo with the Mediterranean and the Eaft-Indies, gives us many colours, which were formerly imported from Britain, like apothecaries articles, at immenfe advances.

COACHES AND OTHER CARRIAGES.

The importation of thefe was formerly **very** great. Virginia, in 1788, had 360 coaches and chariots, 365 phaetons and other pleafurable fourwheeled carriages, and 1,967 one-horfe chairs and folas. New-Jerfey, in 1789, had 38 coaches, chariots, and phaetons, 1,549 one-horfe chairs and folas, and a very great number of plain decent lightwaggons, on fteel or wooden fprings. From thefe facts, and fimilar truths in the other parts of the union, it is certain that the pleafurable carriages of the United States amount to a very large fum. Though to be obtained on credit from Britain, no more than £.5,000 fterling in carriages, or parts of carriages, were imported in the year following Auguft 1789, including thofe of numerous travellers and emigrators : and 220 carriages were exported to foreign countries, within the fame year. All the wood and iron work, the harnefs and other leathern materials, frequently the brafs work, fringe, lace, and lately the plated work, are made in America. Lord Sheffield feems to have expected a confiderable importation of thefe articles : but he did not advert to the poffibility, that the manufacturers themfelves would emigrate to us; which is every month taking place.

" MEDICINES AND DRUGS

" will be imported from Great-Britain," fays the writer of the obfervations, " on account of the knowledge, which the phyficians, furgeons and apothecaries, in the American ftates, have of the method of preparing and procuring them there." Many drugs and medicines are imported without preparation. There is, in many important inftances, no difference in the modes of different nations. The Materia Medica, Chymiftry, &c. are taught in America from the books of Europe. Men of the requifite fkill from other countries are to be found in moft of our principal feaports. To thefe many of the chymical and Galenic operations of Holland, France, and Germany are not un-known. Saltpetre, mufk, camphor, rhubarb, and other Eaft-India articles in this line, have been fhipped occafionally from the United States, in confiderable parcels. Bark, fulphur, balfam ca-pivi, and many other medicinal productions, have been obtained from Spain, the Mediterranean, the Weft-Indies, and other places. Holland partici-pates largely in our importations of chymical pre-parations; but many, which ufed to be imported, are begun to be manufactured here: and exporta-tions of them to advantage, have, in fome inftances taken place. The knowledge which our medical gentlemen have acquired abroad, and in their pro-feffional reading at home, of the methods of procu-ring drugs, has been communicated to our mer-chants: and their information of the methods of preparing chymical articles, has been often put in practice here. There is, no doubt, a confiderable trade in thefe commodities from Great-Britain. But it is, even now affected by the above circum-ftances, and is not by any means a monopoly. From our free and enterprifing commerce, the natural productions of the country, and chymical fkill, it muft decreafe every year. Great-Britain poffeffes, from nature, lefs of thefe commodities than the United States. Foreign trade, and fkill employed at home, will give us a great fhare of thofe, which are not fpontaneous productions of our various foil and climate.

are placed second on the list of articles, in which
it is alledged Great-Britain will sustain little competition : and lord Sheffield remarks, that " whatever we make of them, is at the expense of at least
three times the amount of what the same articles
could be imported for from Europe." The iron
branch is highly important and growing in the
United States. In Massachusetts, there were se-
venty-six iron works, many of them small, in 1784.
The Virginia works make above 5,300 tons of iron.
The slitting and rolling mills of Pennsilvania, are
ascertained to cut and roll 1500 tons or 3,360,000lbs.
per annum : and so completely do they obviate the
objection of manual labour, which is constantly
urged against American manufactures, that they
employ but twenty five hands. In that state, there are
also sixteen furnaces and thirty-seven large forges.
In New Jersey alone, in the year 1789, the number
of forges were seventy-nine and of furnaces eight.
And though the details are not so well known, they
are very numerous in Maryland and most of the
states. These works are annually increasing, and
particularly in interior situations. The nails and
spikes consumed yearly in the United States, (calculating on 4,000,000 people, at ten to a house,
including negroes, which gives 400,000 houses)
allowing ten pounds for the average use of all the
persons living in each house, in building, repair-
ing, fencing, and in their business, and manufactur-

ing, would be 4,000,000lbs. Of this quantity there were imported in the returned year, 1,800,000lbs: and about 2,200,000lbs. muſt, therefore, have been made at home. The remainder of the ſlit and rolled iron is either exported or made into tire, hoops, ſprings for carriages, or ſome other ſubſtitutes for foreign imported articles. Ship-building alſo demands very large quantities of iron work. Ploughſhears, carriages, axes, ſaws, hoes, ſpades, ſhovels, kitchen utenſils, and many other articles employ the, American workers in this raw material. About one half of the ſteel, conſumed in the United States, is home made, and new furnaces are building at this moment. The works being few, and the importation aſcertained, this faĉt is known to be accurate. Bar iron before the revolution, was uſually ſold for ſixty four dollars. It fell, after the war, to the ſame price; and large quantities of iron in bars and pigs were exported. The progreſs of manufaĉtures has raiſed theſe articles to the higheſt prices ever known in peace; and only 200 tons in bars, and 3,555 tons in pigs were exported in thirteen months and a half of 1789, and 1790. The exportation of this quantity was principally to throw the requiſite weight into the bottoms of the ſhips laden with cargoes of tobacco or lumber. Lord Sheffield ſtates, that we ſhipped 2,592 tons of bar iron, and 4,624 tons of pig metal per annum, in ſeveral years before the revolution, when it is known our commerce and population were not at the higheſt. It is alſo to be obſerved, that we now import conſiderable quantities of bar iron from the Baltic

and its vicinity, particularly into the eaftern ftates.
One thoufand two hundred and eighty-eight tons of
bar iron, were imported from St. Peterfburg alone,
in the year 1790, and above forty tons of iron hoops
and nail rods.   From thefe facts may be collected
convincing proofs of the ftate of the iron manufactures of this country, ftrongly oppofed to the prefumptions of lord Sheffield, as well with refpect to
the dearnefs of thofe manufactures, as the monopoly of our fupplies.

FLOUR AND WHEAT.

Thefe ineftimable commodities are not, in the
opinion of lord Sheffield, the beft ftaples for the
United States to depend on; becaufe as he obferves,
in general the demand in Europe is uncertain. He
again repeats his unfounded notion of a competition between us and Nova Scotia for the fupply of
Europe, in thefe articles; and adds, that it is a fortunate confequence of American independence,
that the Britifh European iflands may regain the
fupply of their Weft-Indies, with bread and flour,
and that they can furnifh them cheaper than we.   In
regard to the profpects from Nova Scotia, enough
has been already faid, and particularly till they difcover fymptoms of internal refources for their own
ufe, by ceafing to import grain and flour from the
United States.   As to the European corn trade,
authentic and important information, indeed, is to
be derived from a report of the Britifh privy council, of March 1790, which is faid to have been

drawn by lord Hawkſbury. It is wiſely obſerved, in that report, that the culture of grain is the moſt important objeƈt, that can receive the public attention : and it is ſtated that the demand of Great Britain, for flour and grain, has produced an average balance againſt the nation, of £.291,000 ſterling, for the laſt nineteen years, although from the year 1746, to the year 1765, they had annually gained, by their corn trade, £.651,000 ſterling on a medium. Ireland, it is true, has greatly increaſed its exports of grain, flour, and biſcuit, but by no means in proportion to this falling off by Great Britain, and its whole exports of flour and grain are much leſs than our ſhipments to the Britiſh Weſt Indies. Their lordſhips proceed to ſtate, that in conſequence of information received by them from the principal corn countries of Europe, they are of opinion, that the quantity of grain raiſed in Europe, in common years, is not more than equal to the ordinary conſumption of its inhabitants ; and that, in the event of a failure of their crops, *a ſupply can only be expeƈted from America*. In verification of this formal official communication, on a ſubjeƈt of ſuch high importance, we find, that the influence of the late ſcarcity in France, not only pervaded all Europe, but was extended to the moſt interior counties of theſe ſtates. Wheat was ſold on that occaſion three hundred miles from the ocean, for prices which have been uſually acceptable in our ſea-port towns : and at the places of ſhipment, it was advanced to rates beyond what had ever occurred ſince the ſettlement of the country.

When we remember, that by grain liquors we may avoid the purchase of eleven millions and a half of gallons of the spirits, or ingredients for spirits of foreign nations; that by grain these states are rendered the alternate ground of dependance of every European nation, in time of need; that we are protected from the possibility of dreadful famine by this blessed production; that grain is the raw material in which some considerable manufacturers work, and which all must necessarily consume; we must smile at the ideas which lord Sheffield has hazarded, in regard to those precious staples, wheat and flour.

GUNPOWDER,

It is asserted, will be imported cheaper than it can be manufactured in America. The price of this important article has been reduced in the Philadelphia market to sixteen dollars, or £.3:12 sterling per 100 wt. by the free importation of brimstone and saltpetre from India and other countries. Our merchants usually pay for it in England at the rate of 75 to 76 shillings sterling, after deducting the drawback on exportation. Twenty-one powder mills have been erected in Pensylvania alone, since the year 1768 or 1770—much the greater part of them since the commencement of the revolution war : four new ones are now building in that state, one at Baltimore, and others in different parts of the United States; and it is certain they will be multiplied in proportion to the demand, whether it be for home confumption or exportation. Of the quantity commonly on hand in the Philadelphia magazine, not more than feven per cent. is of foreign manufacture*. Saltpetre and fulphur are found in confiderable quantities, particularly in the interior parts of Virginia: but at prefent the commercial fupplies are fo plentiful and cheap, that our internal refources are little ufed. Saltpetre is cheaper in Philadelphia than in London.

THE ABILITY OF GREAT-BRITAIN TO MAKE HER SHIPS THE CARRIERS FOR THE UNITED STATES.

It is explicitly declared, in the 39th page of lord Sheffield's introduction, that the adoption of the ground propofed by him, will infure to Britifh fhips the carrying trade of the United States; "for (he adds) it is certain, if our navigation laws be maintained, it will not anfwer the Americans to keep many fhips." This it will be admitted, is to us, if true, a very interefting pofition, and demands our moft ferious attention. It will, however, be very eafy to fhow, that the private fhipping of the United States does not depend upon Britifh laws. The tables, which accompany the report on the American fifheries, from the department of ftate, clearly prove, that we are not dependent on Great-Britain for that branch of commerce. In the regulation of our coafting trade, which employs above 100,000 tons of fhipping, and which will

---

* None, but American powder is now received there. A. D. 1793.

conftantly increafe with our population, manufactures, and ufe of coal, Britifh laws can have no operation. In our commerce with the Baltic, and the North, with all the Netherlands, the Hanfe towns, France, Spain, .Portugal, through the ftreights, with moft parts of Africa and India, and the colonies of the European nations, except the Britifh, their navigation act cannot affect us. It appears moreover, that our fhips are fo " many," as to have amounted to 360,000 tons of veffels laden in our ports, by a return which is incomplete, while thofe of Great-Britain and her dominions were 225,000 tons. But it is poffible, that confiderable deductions from the Britifh tonnage may happen. There is little doubt, that the diminutions of our importations from their dominions, which have taken place, in regard to China merchandize, and other India goods, Italian, Ruffian, Dutch, and German goods, paper, nails, fheet iron, fteel, fhoes, and boots, gunpowder, lead, coal, falt, malt liquors, loaf and brown fugars, coffee, cocoa and fpirituous liquors, by reafon of our intercourfe with other nations, and the great improvement of our own refources and manufactures, will be followed by further commercial acquifitions from liberal nations, by the conftant introduction of new foreign manufactures, and the difcovery and attainment of new internal refources. If, for example, cotton be raifed and imported, and fpinning mills be erected, Manchefter importations will decreafe: if flax and hemp be raifed and imported, in greater quantities, and flax

and hemp fpinning mills be erected, fail-cloth fheet-
ing, and fhirting linens, checks, oznabrigs, table
and towel linen, &c. will be imported more fpar-
ingly. If by thefe and other means, our imports
from Great-Britain fhould be finally reduced to
fuch a fum, as will purchafe only fo much rice, tobacco, and other articles as its people confume,
thofe articles will not be fhipped indirectly to foreign countries, through Britifh ports, as is now
the cafe. Thefe indirect fhipments afford Britifh
veffels more than an equal chance in the competition with ours from America to England; becaufe
the property is generally on Englifh account,
and it gives them fo far the command of the carriage from England to other parts of Europe.
From thefe circumftances, it will be perceived,
that it is interefting to our private fhipping, and
confequently to our fuccefs in the eftablifhment
of a navy, that we continue by prudent and
falutary means, to decreafe our importations from
each foreign country, fo as in a greater degree to
equalize them with the confumption, which that
country actually makes of our productions: this,
however, it is conceived, ought not to be attempted, by any precipitate or coercive means; but by
the eftablifhment of our mercantile credit in other
countries, by commercial enterprife, capital and
and manufacturing induftry.

A fecond caufe, which renders the intercourfe
in the fhape of exportation to Great-Britain inordi-
nately great, is to be found in the old private debts

due to that country from this. Thefe, fo far as
they will be paid by money or goods, are confiderably diminifhed. The rife of our ftocks, and the
fales of them to foreigners, have enabled many to
leffen thofe debts : and Britifh fubjeȼts will continue to find it their intereft to buy into them. Thefe
are payments, which occafion only a remittance of
the intereft; and the commutation of private for
public debts is therefore to be defired. Part of the
old debts which remain due to the Englifh merchants, muft be received in the foil and buildings
of this country. When thefe fhall be accepted by
the creditor, they will ftill remain immoveable: and
he will find himfelf, or his child, transformed into
an American freeholder, to his profit and that of
the United States, though to the injury, and fometimes the ruin of the unfortunate debtor. This
change of the creditor's fituation, will not be un-
pleafing to a liberal mind of any country, and, if
properly underftood, may greatly meliorate the
profpeȼts of the family and connexions of many in
Britain, who are concerned in American debts. A
country, of great native ftrength, becoming energetic, intelligent, free, not difpofed to provoke either infults or injuries, and in a fituation not to
fubmit to a wanton impofition of either, holds out
as great promifes of human happinefs, as any, of
which the foreign creditor can have been a citizen.
He is fure of a kind reception, and of the protection of the laws and conftitution in his perfon, property, and religion.

A third caufe, which has produced an extraordinary intercourfe in the fhape of importations from
Great-Britain, has been the want of credit from
other nations. We now annually import from
that kingdom about 900,000 dollars, in articles not
of its growth, produce, or manufacture; and
though we have reduced this from about 2,200,000
dollars fince the feparation of the two countries,
there is yet that great value expenfively, becaufe
circuitoufly, imported. The purfuit of this accuftomed track, eftablifhed in the time of the old Britifh monopoly, has been one caufe of thefe unna-
tural importations—but the chief caufe was *the credit* we found from England. The Britifh merchants
will probably continue to afford the greateft accomodations of this kind; but it is evident, that the
citizens of other countries will furnifh us with credits, and fometimes in more eligible fhapes. They
will give us their cafh articles and their coin, to be
employed in ready-money trades at home and
abroad, in manufactures and foreign commerce. In
proof of this may be adduced the refpondentia credits in India and China, the purchafes into our feveral bank ftocks, the inveftment of monies in our
lands,* and in our navigation, trade, and manufactures. The medium imports from Great-Britain for
feveral years before the revolution, appear, from
European accounts, to be to the medium imports for

* Thefe continue in numerous and great inftances—6,500,000
acres of our new lands have been purchafed by foreigners within
the laft two years. A. D. 1793.

an equal term of years antecedent to 1790, as 27 to
23, though our population has probably almoſt
doubled ; and though much larger importations
than heretofore, by perſons intending to remain
here, have alſo contributed to ſwell the quantity in
the latter term. What is to follow in this way,
time, it is believed, will very quickly ſhow.

In addition to the foregoing cauſes, which ſeem
likely to occaſion a diminution of the proportion of
ſhipping employed directly and indirectly by Great-
Britain in the American trade (including the exportation of our productions from the Britiſh ports
to other markets in Europe) one other, which does
not ſeem to have ſufficiently engaged their attention, may produce, it is believed, very conſiderable effects. The regulations of the Britiſh navigation act do not appear to have been duly examined
by other European powers, with a view to the
adoption of ſuch of them as will apply beneficially
to their own affairs. If they have had effects ſo
favourable to the ſhipping and naval power of Britain, it is poſſible, and highly probable they might
be, in a greater or leſs degree, beneficial to other
countries. The preſent appears a fit ſeaſon for ſuch
an examination in America : and we cannot ſuffer,
if we enter on it with temper and diſcretion. That
it would diminiſh the number of Britiſh veſſels, for
example, if the United States and all other maritime
countries, ſhould deem it expedient to enact into a
law of their reſpective nations, *the clauſe of the
Britiſh ſtatute, by which the importation of all*

*foreign goods is confined to native bottoms and
to thofe of the nation producing the articles,* cannot be doubted. Whether this regulation will
be convenient to the United States—to France
—to Spain—to Portugal—to Ruffia—to Pruffia,
who, exporting twenty or thirty times the bulk
of goods, that Great-Britain fhips, do not, altogether enjoy a part of the carriage for foreign nations,
equal to what fhe poffeffes, is a queftion thofe nations are feverally to confider and determine,
Facts, in the mean time, are highly interefting. In
the year 1772, as Mr. Anderfon informs, the imports and exports of the Baltic were made in 6680
veffels, of which the Britifh were 1894, the French,
Spanifh, Portuguefe, and Ruffian only 45. The
commodities carried thither (in addition to their own
manufactures) were the produce and fabrics of all
the countries of Europe and of the Eaft and Weft-
Indies, which, by their navigation act, could not
have been imported into Great-Britain in like manner. The fame may be faid of the cargoes they
brought away, fo far as they were carried directly
to the ports of other nations, or were re-fhipped
from their own ports in their original form. The
fame writer ftates the Britifh entries in Lifbon, in
the year 1788, to have been 351, and thofe of
Portugal, in her own metropolis and emporium,
to have been only 283. The Spaniards had but 31,
the Ruffians one, the Pruffians one, and Dantzickers one. By the fame authority we are inftructed,
that the Britifh entries in Malaga in 1787, were
189, the Dutch 24, the Portuguefe five, the Ruffi-

ans, Pruffians, and Dantzickers, none. In the
year 1778, the Britifh entries in Cronftadt, the
port of the city of St. Peterfburgh, were 252;
thofe of Ruffia, though in her own capital, were
only twelve, of Spain fix, of Portugal two, of
Hamburg and Bremen five. In the year 1790, the
Britifh entries, in the fame port, were 517 out of
932 : and we have recently feen, that the Britifh
have fupplied themfelves and the other nations of
Europe, with cargoes of our commodities amount.
ing to 230,000 tons, while thofe Europeans carried for themfelves no more than one fixth of the
quantity! It is not intended to difcufs, in this
place, the policy of adopting fo momentous a regulation as that alluded to, obfervations on which
are rendered peculiarly delicate by the fituation in
which it is placed by the national legiflature. The
inftance, it is conceived, however, will forcibly
inculcate the utility of the examination fuggefted
in the beginning of this paragraph, and will lead
to ufeful refleftions on the confequences, which
fuch an examination may induce. The fafts, by
which it is illuftrated, appeared too ferious and
important to Americans and to foreigners, not to
be adduced. It will be perceived, that it is equally the intereft of thofe who are Englifhmen, to confider the certain effefts of fuch an examination of
the Britifh trade laws, and of thofe who are not.
Some of the convifions, which fuch an enquiry,
made with judgment, would create in the minds of
candid men, would probably be, that Great-Bri-

tain cannot not make her fhips the carriers for the
United States : and that rather than make the attempt, it would be better far to commence the formation of liberal arrangements, folidly founded in
the mutual interefts of the two nations.

S E C T I O N III.

I N the profecution of this examination, our attention is drawn to the article of

FINE AND COARSE HATS.

The writer of the obfervations remarks, that the
high price of wool and labour muft induce the
Americans to import the felt and common hats.
The increafe of our population, as in other new
countries, has been accompanied by an increafe
of the quantity of wool. Sheep have been found,
on frequent and fair experiments, to be very profitable to the farmer†. Importation, though hitherto cafual, has fupplied us with fome wool.
Hatters are found in every part of the United
States. The following table, which was contained
in a report made by a committee to the manufacturing fociety of Philadelphia, will fhow the ftate
of the hatting bufinefs in Pennfylvania, and difco-
vers a faĉt little known even to her own citizens,
that 12,340 hats are annually made in the four
counties beyond the Allegany mountains*.

† The American farmers are become very generally fenfible of
the great profits of breeding fheep.

	Hatters.	Fur hats.	Wool hats.
In the city and county of Philadelphia,	68	31,637	7,600
Montgomery, - -	10	800	1,000
Delaware, - - -	14	1,500	4,000
Weſt-Cheſter, - -	14	1,300	4,000
Lancaſter, - -	16	3,000	15,000
Dauphin, - - -	10	1,200	4,000
Bucks, - - -	12	1,000	1,000
Berks, - - -	38	2,200	54,000
York, - -	26	2,600	30,000
Cumberland, -	16	1,300	9,000
Northumberland, -	10	700	5,000
Northampton, - -	12	1,000	7,000
Bedford, - -	8	800	2,000
Franklin, - - -	10	800	2,000
Luzerne, - - -	6	400	1,400
Huntington, - -	6	1,400	2,000
Mifflin, - - -	6	400	2,000
Weſtmoreland*,	10	600	3,000
Fayette*,	7	400	1,540
Allegany*,	6	400	1,600
Waſhington*,	10	800	4,000
	315	54,237	161,140

From this return, it appears that every county in the ſtate participates in the hatting buſineſs, there being none but what are in the above liſt†.

† The county of New-London, in Connecticut, contains ſeventeen hatters, who make yearly 10,000 wool and fur hats. The

The United States are found to contain near 4,000,000 inhabitants, and of that number the whites are conjectured to be about 3,300,000. If a hat per annum, be allowed for every third person of this last number, 1,100,000 hats per annum, would be a supply for the United States, and the above 215,000 made in a single state, may be confidered as more than equal in value to one fifth of the demand, a quarter of the number being of fur. It is to be remembered, that leathern hats and fur caps are not rarely feen in the interior country. This branch has not grown up fuddenly in America ; but was commenced among our firft manufactures, and has made a regular progrefs with the population. The furs of the country have at once held out a ftrong temptation, and afforded the eafy means. Latterly, the increafe of wool has given a great extenfion to the manufacture. The practical difficulties, fuggefted by lord Sheffield, can gain little credit under fo fuccefsful a courfe of the bufinefs ; but the truth is, that few handicrafts are more quickly acquired by apprentices, who can open fhops for themfelves long before they are permitted in many parts of Europe. Foreign fhops have alfo been eftablifhed here, by emigrants from Germany, France and Britain.*

army of the United States has been furnifhed with American hats, made by contractors, who did and could obtain the contract only by underbidding, in fealed propofals received from importers and hat-makers. A. D. 1791.

* This is likewife a branch effected by manual induftry.

BOOKS.

" All fchool and common books," in the opinion of lord Sheffield, may be fent cheaper from Britain, than they can be printed in America." The
great and conftant increafe of paper mills in the
United States, the extention of thofe longeft
erected, the eftablifhment of type founderies and
the introduction of engravers and book-bind-
ers, have made a greater change in regard to
the bufinefs of book printing, than has happened
with refpect to any other equally valuable branch
of manual art.* The Latin and Greek fchool books
are imported in greater numbers than heretofore ;
becaufe our population is confiderably increafed,
fince the feparation from Great-Britain, and the
ufe of them is too limited to render an edition profitable : but a very great proportion of the Englifh fchool books (which are in general ufe) are
printed here. Of fome kinds there are none imported ; and feveral of them, with alterations and improvements, have been publifhed. A number of
the law books, which are moft demanded, have
been reprinted with advantage : and an edition of
the Encyclopœdia, in fifteen large quartos, containing about 5 per cent. more matter than that
printed in Great-Britain, is now publifhing at fe-

---

* The advertifement of a fingle book-ftore in Philadelphia, publifhed in the gazettes of the prefent year, contains feventy editions
of different books printed in the United States. This, it is to be
obferved, is alfo a branch effected *by hand.*

venty dollars, or fifteen guineas—precifely the price charged to *fubfcribers* for the Britifh edition. The cuts in the American copy are equally numerous, and are really the beft.

There are two circumftances, which will eftablifh the book-printing bufinefs in this country—the opportunity of publifhing immediately, for the American demand, all books in every European language,* within the term of the copy right; and the printing of moderate fized and plain editions, inftead of the large, ornamented, and expenfive copies which are now the fafhion in Europe. A fuperb quarto, on the beft vellum paper, with an elegant but unneceffary copperplate frontifpiece, richly gilt and lettered, (the drefs in which modern writers often introduce their works) cofts more than is agreeable to the people of this country, who defire valuable matter for their money. The freight, duties, and other charges of importation, depending either on the bulk or value, are very much enhanced; and our printers find it eafy to embrace the opportunity which thefe circumftances afford them to furnifh their counrty with a

---

* The firft premium for excellency in printing was adjudged by the Penfylvania manufacturing fociety to the publifhers of a book in the *German* language, in the inland town of Lancafter, in that ftate feveral attempts at French gazettes have been made; and French advertifements are frequent in our newfpapers. German gazettes are conftantly printed. The laws of Pennfylvania, and of the United States are publifhed in the German language.

cheap octavo, and fometimes even a duodecimo, in its ftead.

German fchool books are much demanded in this country, as may be fuppofed, when it is remembered how numerous, in the United States, the perfons are, who read and fpeak that language —probably 150,000 to 180,000 of our people. Thefe books are either imported from Holland, or the Hanfe towns, or printed in America. England fupplies none of them.

The extenfion of the French language, together with the intercourfe between the United States and that nation, which took place in the year 1776, and the alliance in 1778, with which it was followed, will naturally be fuppofed to have increafed the demand for French books. Thefe are principally imported from France, the Hanfe towns, Holland, and Flanders; and fome few are printed in America.

Books in thefe two languages could not be imported, before the revolution, from any country, except Great-Britain: but are now drawn, as above mentioned, from other foreign fources, or the American printing preffes.

THAT THE AMERICANS WILL IN FUTURE GIVE A PREFE-
RENCE TO BRITISH MANUFACTURES BEFORE ALL OTHERS
—THAT IT WILL BE A LONG TIME BEFORE THE AMERI-
CANS WILL MANUFACTURE FOR THEMSELVES—AND THAT
OUR DEMAND FOR BRITISH GOODS WILL INCREASE IN
PROPORTION TO OUR POPULATION.

The manufactures of Great-Britain and Ireland*
are very generally good, often excellent, and almoſt
always as handſome as the nature of the article
will admit. Yet, there are not wanting proofs,
that we ſhall take conſiderable quantities of goods
from other countries. Twenty-two ſhips, for example, arrived in the United States from St. Pe-
terſburg, in the year 1790, with cordage, ticking,
drillings, diaper, broad linens, narrow linens, printed linens, craſh, ſheetings, ravens duck, Ruſſia
duck, nail rods, and rolled iron for hoops. The
remainder of their cargoes were bar iron, hemp,
and flax, which were intended to be manufactured here. Nankeens, ſilks, long-cloths, porcelain
and ſome ſmall articles, are imported regularly
from China: and muſlins, plain, ſtriped, figured,
and printed, with ſilks, and a variety of other articles, are imported from India. It being manifeſtly very injurious to the manufacturing intereſt of
every nation in Europe, even to import, and much
more ſo to conſume theſe goods, there can be no

* The linens, and flaxen hoſiery of Britain and Ireland are however much fallen off in goodneſs, ſince they have applied the
tow and worſt flax to the manufacture of coarſe goods, wherein
ſtrength is indiſpenſible.

doubt, that they will be supplied to us in the East-Indies, with more readiness every year; and if a few more callico printers were to establish themselves among us, the importation of printed linens, callicoes and cottons might be exceedingly diminished. The importation also of dowlafs, oznaburghs, ticklenburgs, and other German linens, and of Haerlem stripes, and tapes, from Bremen, Hamburgh, and Amsterdam, together with the manufactory of every ton of hemp, and almost every ton of flax, which we raise or import, together with some cotton, has very much affected the British and Irish linen trade*. It appears from various documents, that the average exports of their manufactures to the United States for several years prior to the year 1789, were near half a million of dollars less than the average exports of several years immediately antecedent to the war, though our population has probably doubled in the last twenty-five years. It is not improbable, however, that the great quantities of goods shipped since 1789, in consequence of the jealousy of American manufactures, the apprehension of a rupture with Spain, and the efforts of the British cotton manufacturers to banish East-India goods from our markets, would show a considerable increase in the last and present years. In short, the United States are an open market: the American merchants are men of judgment and enterprise; and consequently the goods of every

* The use of cotton shirts is extending in America, being thought very favourble to health. A. D. 1793.

country in the world, which are adapted to our confumption, are found in our ware-houfes. It is certainly true, that among them are very large quantities of Britifh manufactures, being much and juftly
approved, and being imported on convenient credits
by our merchants, and copioufly fhipped by Britifh
merchants and manufacturers on their own account,
to their correfpondents here. If properly conducted on both fides, it may yet be a very beneficial
trade to the two countries; but it has not excluded
the valuable goods of other nations, nor has it prevented a very great progrefs of our own manufactures, particularly in the family way. Cordage,
gunpowder, fteel, nails, paper, paper-hangings,
books, ftationary, linfeed oil, carriages, hats, wool
and cotton cards, ftockings, fhoes, boots, fhot, and
many other articles are made in confiderable quantities, fome of them as far as fifty per centum on the
demand, and other in quantities nearly equal to the
confumption. Subftantial freedom, liberal wages,
and cheap and excellent living, free from any ex_
cife, except a very fmall one, (compared with any
in Europe) upon fpirituous liquors, operate daily to
bring us manufacturers and artizans in the manual
branches; and we are beginning to fee the great, and
to us, the *peculiar* value of labour-faving machines.
The rate of manual labour is no objection againft them,
but a bfolutely in their favour; for it is clear, that
they muft yield the greateft profit in countries where
the price of labour is the higheft. The firft judicious
European capitalifts, who fhall take good fituations
in the United States, and eftablifh manufactories,

by labour-faving machines, muft rapidly and certainly make fortunes. They cannot, it is prefumed, be long infenfible of this; but if they fhould continue fo, the appreciation of our public flocks will probably bring fome of our own capitalifts into the bufinefs. The public creditors, the owners of perhaps fifteen millions fterling of now inactive wealth, might at this moment do much towards the introduction of the cotton mills, wool-mills, flax and hemp-mills, and other valuable branches of machine manufacturing. It is paft a doubt, that were a company of perfons of character and judgment to fubfcribe a flock for this purpofe of 500,000 dollars in the public paper, they might obtain upon a depofit of it, a loan of as much coin from fome foreign nation, at an intereft lefs than fix per cent. Was fuch a company to be incorporated, to have its flock transferable as in a bank, to receive fubfcriptions from 400 dollars upwards, to purchafe 500 or 1000 acres of land well fituated for receiving imported materials and exporting their fabrics—were they to erect works in the centre of fuch a body of land, to lay out their grounds in a convenient town-plat, and to proceed with judgment and fyftem in their plan, they would be fure of fuccefs in their manufactories; they would raife a valuable town upon their land, and would help to fupport the value of the public debt.* Were a

* This meafure, which was in contemplation at the time when thefe papers were written, has been fince digefted and commenced. The capital already engaged amounts to above 600,000 dollars. A. D. 1791. The proprietors of all the inland towns in the Uni-

few eftablifhments, like that defcribed, to take place (and there are room and funds for many of them) even the manufactories of *piece goods*, of every kind in which machinery could be applied, would foon be introduced with profit into the United States. It cannot, on cool reflexion, be expected, that a country remote from all the manufacturing nations, able to produce the requifite raw materials and provifions, and fubject to many interruptions in their exportation to foreign markets, will continue to depend on diftant tranfmarine fources, for the mafs of her neceffary fupplies. The wonderful progrefs of other nations, which have commenced manufactures under difadvantages much greater than any we have to contend with, will powerfully incite us to exertion. Until the year 1667, a piece of woolen cloth was never dyed and dreffed in England. This great manufacture was quickly after improved by the fkill of foreign emigrants, (a mean at our command ;) and fo rapidly has the woolen branch advanced, that it was eftimated, in 1783, at the immenfe fum of £. 16,800,000 fterling (above feventy-four millions of dollars) per annum, and was equal in value to all the exports, and fuperior to all the revenues of Great-Britain. It may, perhaps, be afked, why manufactures were not eftablifhed in the late war? Any man, who makes a comparifon of a variety of branches, as they were in 1774, and as they ftood in 1782, will

ted States appear to have become fenfible of the advantages, which will arife from attracting manufacturers to them. A. D. 1793.

perceive a great advance to have actually taken place, though manufactures were little encouraged through the intermediate eight years, by reason of the total occupation of government in the prosecution of the war: their importance moreover was not duly estimated. The British manufacturers, who can now emigrate with the greatest convenience, then viewed the people of this country as enemies. Neither they, nor the people of other nations (who indeed knew little of us) cared to risk themselves in an invaded country, nor would they hazard a capture in their passages hither. Notwithstanding these impediments, the manufacturers of the United States have been found to be the most successful competitors with those of Great-Britain in the American market. They have not made fine linens, fine cloths, silks, stuffs, and other articles requiring a great degree of skill, labour, or capital; but they have made common cloths of linen, woollen, and cotton, steel, nails, sheet iron, paper, gunpowder, cannon and musquets, cabinet work, carriages, shoes, and fabrics of the simple but most important and necessary kinds. ☞ *See the supplementary note, concerning the progress and present state of American domestic or household manufactures,* which follows, No. VII.

THAT IT WOULD BE IMPOLITIC IN GREAT-BRITAIN, TO AD-
MIT AMERICAN VESSELS INTO HER WEST-INDIA ISLANDS.

This is a very momentous queſtion to Great-Britain ; and therefore whatever may be the real merits of it, the people of that country might have
been expeΰed to conſider it with firſt impreſſions
unfavourable to the admiſſion of foreigners. It is
alſo probable, that the Americans may have taken
a partial view of the ſubjeΰ, from the great intereſt, they ſuppoſe they have, to obtain a participation in the Britiſh Weſt-India trade. There are
two poſitions of lord Sheffield, relative to this ſubjeΰ, which appear conformable with truth and reaſon, and in which it is of great conſequence, that
we ſhould, on mature refleΰion, agree. The firſt
is, " *That the cultivation of the Britiſh Weſt-India
iſlands might be carried much farther than it is,*"
which he ſupports by obſerving " *that the produce of
the iſland of Jamaica might be trebled at leaſt.*" The
ſecond is, " *That the nation which may hereafter be
in poſſeſſion of the moſt extenſive and beſt cultivated
ſugar iſlands,* will take the lead at ſea.*"

If the firſt of theſe poſitions be true, both in regard to the Britiſh Weſt-Indies in general, and the
iſland of Jamaica in particular, then it becomes a
matter of the utmoſt importance to Great-Britain,

* Or tranſmarine colonies.

by reafon of the fecond pofition, to adopt *the beft poffible fyftem for promoting the cultivation of the vacant lands and improved eftates in the feveral iflands.* Perfons, who have contended with the difficulties and expences of fettling new plantations, and who are acquainted with the management of Weft-India eftates, will be fenfible, that cheap fupplies of building materials, and other neceffary incipient articles, give the greateft facility and certainty to thofe who are ftruggling to effect a new fettlement: and keeping down the contingent expences of planting and raifing produce, and of packing and preparing the crop for market, is manifeftly a fure mean of increafing the profits of an eftate. In this point of light, it muft be immenfely againft the Britifh Weft-India producers of 7,500,000 gallons of rum, and 2,000,000 cwt. of fugars, with cotton, coffee, pimento and other articles, that they receive their ftaves, boards, provifions, and other fupplies, on terms fo much higher than the French, the Dutch, and the Danes. While the iflands of France were furnifhed in the laft year, by French and American bottoms, with red oak hogfhead ftaves, at 12, 14, and 16 dollars—with hoops, at 14 to 28 dollars—with pine boards, at 11 to 16 dollars—with Indian meal, at $2\frac{1}{2}$ to 3 and two third dollars per barrel—with fhip-bread, at $3\frac{1}{2}$ dollars per 108 pounds; the Britifh planters in Jamaica were obliged to pay for red oak hogfhead ftaves, 24, 27, and 31 dollars; for wooden hoops, 27, 30, and 36 dollars; for pine boards 24, 27, and 30 dollars; for Indian meal $4\frac{1}{4}$, to $5\frac{1}{4}$ dollars ; for fhip-bread the fame ; and for rice per 100 pounds $3\frac{1}{3}$ to $5\frac{1}{4}$ dollars. Let confiderate men determine, whether the Britifh colonial agriculture muft not be depreffed, and that of the French be exceedingly elevated, under fuch circumftances. It is plain that the latter will find it eafy to extend their plantations into grounds now uncultivated, if the Britifh planters fhould be able to endure their difadvantages. In conformity with this reafoning, we find that the produce of French St. Domingo, fhipped to Europe, which, before the late war, is ftated by lord Sheffield to have employed no more than 450 fhips, was fufficient, in the year 1788, to load for France 580 fhips, of $370\frac{3}{4}$ tons on a medium, and 110 of 740 tons, (exclufive of the numerous French and foreign veffels employed in the trade with North and South America,) amounting in the whole to 296,435 tons, nearly equal to one third of the private fhips of Britain. The whole of the veffels loaded in 1787, from all the Britifh Weft-India iflands to England and Scotland, amounted to but 132,222 tons. In 1788 the quantity was the fame, and as the writer of the obfervations admits that the produce of Jamaica was before the war two thirds in value (though lefs in bulk) of that of St. Domingo, the Britifh colonial agriculture muft have advanced, if at all, in a much lefs degree than that of the French. This great increafe of the French navigation, refulting from *a profperous Weft-Indian agriculture, abundantly and cheaply fupplied,* is a verification of the prediction of lord Sheffield, which

was mentioned above, and induces the moft reafonable doubts, whether it would be really impolitic in Great-Britain to admit American veffels into
her Weft-India iflands. As it is of great importance to this argument, to eftablifh the actual increafe of the French produce upon ftronger ground
than even the higheft probability, it may be ufeful
to ftate, that the fugars exported from St. Domingo, in 1786, were near 133 millions of pounds; in
1788, near 163 millions and an half; that the coffee in 1786 was about 51 millions of pounds; and,
on the average of 1787 and 1788, near 70 millions;
and that the cotton, in 1786 was 5,200,000 pounds
—and, on the average of 1787 and 1788, above
6,500,000 pounds—alfo that the molaffes, which in
1786 was 21,855 hhds. was increafed in 1788, to
29,503.

The augmentation of the French veffels, employed from St. Domingo alone, appears to be equal
to 108,000 tons. If the whole of their fugar colonies have profpered in the fame degree, it is probable their acquifition of fhipping may be fafely eftimated at 162,000 tons, which is 47,000 tons more
than lord Sheffield fuppofes to have been employed, before the American revolution, between
the Britifh fugar iflands and *all* the American provinces, and is very far beyond the tonnage employed at this time in the trade of thofe iflands
with the United States. The Britifh publications
reprefent it to be lefs than 21,000 tons, making

three voyages per annum, the aggregate entries of which, they confider, as about 62,000 tons.

It is alledged, American veffels cannot be ad-mitted without offence to other countries: but that has not been found an objection to the admiffion by the French. Nor, if the regulation were pro-perly made, would the allies of England have any caufe of complaint; for they might participate in the trade, if they could find advantage in fo doing, which, however, would not be the cafe. The fhips of Ruffia, of Holland, of Great-Britain, of Spain, of Portugal, of the United States, and of all other foreign countries, may enter the French iflands with the fame kind of goods, even American arti-cles. The Englifh, indeed, would be much more protected in the ifland trade than the French; be-caufe by other claufes in their laws, the goods brought by each flag muft be its own national pro-ductions.

It may be argued that the Americans would take a large proportion of the carriage to the Britifh iflands: but this, if true, is the ftrongeft proof, that can be adduced, of the expediency of the meafure, as calculated to promote the colonial agriculture, and thus aid and fupport the navy of Great-Britain. France, it is feen, by the mode propofed, has ad-ded nearly as much to her fhipping, in the trade of a fingle ifland, as England enjoys in the monopoly of the intercourfe with all her iflands, by the mode fhe purfues. The Britifh fhipping, too, if ours were admitted, would certainly maintain themfelves in a confiderable portion of the trade : and in proof of this, it may be obferved, that the French employ of their own veffels in their Weft-India trade from this country, nearly two-thirds of the tonnage that is engaged in their commerce between thefe ftates and France. It is material to obferve, that in the intercourfe between the French iflands and the United States, the tonnage of the Britifh, Dutch, Spanifh, Danes, Swedes, and Portuguefe, does not amount to two per cent. upon the whole of the veffels employed.

THAT IT WOULD BE BETTER FOR BRITAIN TO GIVE UP THE ISLANDS THAN THEIR CARRYING TRADE.

As the arguments on this point, adduced by lord Sheffield, relate only to the carrrying trade between the United States and the Britifh Weft-India iflands, the obfervations will proceed on the fame ground. The whole freight betweeen the two countries prior to the war, he eftimates at £.245,000, rather than lofe which, he thinks it better to give up thofe valuable iflands, the produce whereof, according to various eftimations, is worth three or four millions fterling, and whofe inhabitants arc very free confumers of Britifh and Irifh manufactures. A prudent adminiftration fhould beware of a writer, who palpably deceives himfelf by too ardently maintaining a favourite hypothefis. But a relinquifhment of the trade, on the part of Great-Britain, is not defired ; nor can a lofs of it be fuppofed to follow the admiffion of our veffels to a

participation in it. The ſhips always employed in
the circutious voyage would ſtill continue to purſue it ; thoſe belonging to the Weſt Indians themſelves, the Bahamans, the Bermudians, and the
northern Britiſh colonies, would ſtill enjoy a large
portion : the remainder would be done by the
Americans, who now ſuffer the Britiſh nation to
employ a very large quantity of tonnage in imports
from, and exports to foreign countries, other than
Britiſh, without any reciprocation.

THAT THE SHIPPING GREAT-BRITAIN GAINS, BY EXCLUD-
ING THE AMERICANS, WILL BE AT HAND.

Lord Sheffield undertakes to ſay, that the navigation of thoſe provinces, which are now the
United States, operated as a drain of Britiſh ſea-
men ; and conveys an idea, that the ſailors employed here, were of no uſe to Britain. The
prompt manning of their ſhips on this ſtation, the
cheap and certain ſupply of their Weſt-Indies, in
the war of 1755 to 1762, the diſtreſs to the French
and Spaniſh trade by American privateers, the af-
fair of cape Breton, the great exportation of prize
goods from this country, and other weighty faƈts,
might be adduced to prove this not the ſmalleſt of
his errors. Aſſuming that we were too remote to
be of any uſe in time of war, he proceeds to a con-
cluſion, that the navigation employed in the ſupply of the iſlands, will be hereafter nearer home,
inferring that it will belong to the merchants of
their European dominions. This may be in a

great degree the cafe, as to the fugar fhips, which make the circuitous voyage from Europe to the United States, the Weft-Indies and Europe; and it was equally fo, as to that defcription of traders, before the revolution: but the direct intercourfe between thefe ftates and the Britifh Weft-India iflands, from which we are excluded, muft, from the nature of the trade, be carried on principally in veffels owned in thofe iflands, whofe fituation is more remote than ours, and by Britifh fubjects refiding in our ports, Bermudians, and the people of the northern Britifh colonies, all of whom are as diftant as we.

THAT AMERICA COULD NEVER BE UNITED AGAIN,

Was a fettled opinion of the writer of the obfer-vations. He did not perceive that accident, prin-cipally, had caft us into the form of thirteen ftates. It is true, that the extreme injuries of difunion were not generally forefeen by many of our own citizens. The utility—the neceffity of ftrengthen-ing the national government, had not come home, as it has fince done, to the minds of the American people. Many of their friends, however, faw with regret, and fome of thofe who were not their friends, perceived with a fatisfaction not the moft honourable, that the profpects of individual happi-nefs, and of national profperity had ceafed to be fair. The moft miferable ill that can afflict the po-litical body, *the want of a fit organization*, had brought on alarming convulfions; and there were no evils which were not to be apprehended, unlefs a change of fyftem could be effected. In this moment, the friends of order came forth. The jarring interefts, on the effects of which the writer relies, were made to harmonize. The difference of " manners, of climates, and of ftaples," did not intervene, according to his expectations, as infurmountable obftacles to amity and union. That hearty co-operation, the hope of which is treated as prepofterous, has actually taken place : and the American people now univerfally perceive, " that whatever meafures have a tendency to diffolve their union, or contribute to violate or leffen the fovereign authority, ought to be confidered as hoftile to their liberty and independency."

It remains, then, for thofe, who have believed in thefe predictions of ruinous contentions among the people, and an enfeebling difcord in the councils of the United States, to confider, in fo different a courfe of things, the conduct which ought to be obferved : and for us it remains fteadily to proceed in the good work of *reftoring* and *firmly fecuring* public order, as the certain and only means of private and public happinefs.

SECTION IV.

The article, which next prefents itfelf, is that of

NAVAL STORES.

It appears to lord Sheffield, that Ruffia will interfere much with the American ftates, in the fupply of thefe commodities. The quantities exported, agreeably to his table for 1771, and our return in 1791, appear to have been,

In 1771.	Barrels.			Barrels.	*In the re-*
of pitch,	9,144			8,875	*turn for*
tar,	82,075			85,067	*13 ½ mo.*
turpentine,	17,014	worth then		28,326	worth now
rofin,	223	156,000		316	217,945
fpirits of tur-		dollars.			dollars.
pentine,	41			193	
Total,	108,497			122,777	

From this increafe of value, it appears, that the
United States have not fuffered from the competition of Ruffia, or any other country; but that in
this article, like moft others, we experience the advantage of being *an open market,* free from the
Britifh monopoly, which exifted before the revolution. In addition to this large exportation, confiderable quantities have been confumed, in manufactures which have been introduced or extended fince the year 1771 : and a very large quantity
has been purchafed for the repairs and ftores of

770,000 tons of veffels, of various nations, employed in the foreign trade, the coafting trade, and
the fifheries, and in the building of new fhips, which
greatly exceed the number built on a medium of
1769 to 1771.

POT AND PEARL ASHES.

Thefe articles, lord Sheffield ventures to affirm,
can be made to greater advantage in Canada and
Nova Scotia, than elfewhere in America, on account of the plenty of wood, and owing to the great
quantity of fuel confumed in a long and fevere winter.
It is well known, that the people of this continent
do not attempt to make thefe falts out of any of the
terebinthine woods,* (though it is faid to be prac-
tifed in the north of Europe,) and that the growth
of trees in the remaining Britifh colonies, is principally of thofe kinds. Abundant proof that they
have little oak, is derived from the fmall quantity
of ftaves, heading, oak timber, and oak planks,
which they export, and from the quantities of them,
which they import from the United States. But
had they the proper kinds of fuel, that would not
be fufficient; for a certain degree of population is
neceffary to this manufacture. The number of
people in the whole of the northern Britifh colonies,
is perhaps 160,000 or 180,000, while the United
States have more than twenty times their number,

* The barks of hemlock, pine, fir, and larch, are faid to be
very productive of pot-afh.

of whom two-thirds inhabit scenes much more abundant in wood and timber than Canada and Nova-Scotia. Their custom house books will show what pot-ash those colonies export. Although our writer supposes, that the United States will yield *less than they have heretofore done*, we find, that the return of the treasury exhibited the great quantity of 8,568 tons, though the export, on the medium of 1768, 1769, and 1770, was only 2008 tons, and 5 cwt.

In treating of pot-ash, lord Sheffield takes occasion to digress to the article of coal, and observes, that to encourage the British collieries, and carrying trade, they should prevent the getting of coal on the island of Cape Breton. It was among the disadvantages, which, it was alledged, the United States would sustain by the separation from Great-Britain, that the collieries of Cape Breton were to be particularly barred against them. This, like many other evils, which were apprehended, has vanished on a recurrence to the resources of the country. The collieries on James river will not only abundantly supply the extensive territory watered by the rivers of the Chesapeak and by that bay itself; but they promise to afford a very valuable nursery for seamen in the transportation of their contents to all the sea-ports of the United States. They already furnish coal on terms much lower than the *minimum* of the first cost and charges of importation : and as labour is declining in price and a short water communication, between the mines and the shipping place, is nearly completed,

there is no doubt that foreign coal will be rendered a very lofing commodity, and that it muft finally be excluded from our markets. The interior
country is plentifully fupplied by nature with this
valuable foffil.

HORSES.

Lord Sheffield treats of this article with great
ingenuity. He raifes expectations in the government and people of Great Britain, that the Weft-
Indies may draw fupplies of thefe ufeful animals
from Canada, and confiders Nova-Scotia as having greatly the advantage of Canada and the United States in her capacity for the exportation of
them. It is ftated as certain, that a trade in horfes will be carried on by that province. The diftance of Great-Britain and Ireland do not appear
to reftrain his fanguine hopes, that horfes may be
fhipped to the Weft-Indies from thofe two countries. He proceeds further, and fuggefts the fupply of the probable deficiency of horfes, with mules,
from Barbary, from whence they are to be obtained in abundance, (though at a high price) and from
Porto Rico and the Miffifippi. In fhort, know-
ing the importance of horfes to the Weft-India
planters, he takes great pains to fhew, that they
may relinquifh, without inconvenience, the cheap
and certain fupplies which they formerly enjoyed,
and which the French, Danes, and Dutch now
enjoy by means of deep-waifted American veffels,
manned by perfons accuftomed to the bufinefs.

There is perhaps, no article, in proportion to the value, in which the Britiſh iſlands ſuffer more deeply by the preſent footing of their intercourſe with theſe ſtates, than in that of which we are now treating. This country is particularly fitted for the raiſing of horſes, and affords them in very increaſed numbers. The exportation of them in the year 1770, which was entirely to the Weſt-India iſlands, was, by lord Sheffield's tables, 6,692 : and the exportation of them by the treaſury return, already referred to, was 8,628, beſides 237 mules. The laſt article has been added to the liſt of exports, ſince the year 1770, and promiſes to become very conſiderable, though mules have not a place in lord Sheffield's book among the ſupplies which may be derived from the United States. The Britiſh Weſt-India iſlands are ſtated to have taken off, before the revolution, two fifths of the above number, or 2,676 horſes ; but it appears by the late return that there were ſhipped thither, in thirteen months and a half, no more than 916 horſes and mules; from which it is manifeſt, that the preſent mode of carrying on the trade deprives them of above two-thirds of their former ſupply of theſe animals, which are admitted in the obſervations, to be " *eſſentially neceſſary.*" The price of thoſe they do obtain, muſt of courſe be much enhanced by an unſatisfied demand three-fold greater than the importation, and by the expenſe of conveying them in Britiſh ſhips, which being very generally in the double decked form, are dangerous for the tranſportation of horſes on deck, and carry them at an immenfe freight in the hold. Here is another very injurious inftance of depreffing the Weft-India agriculture. The cafe with the Dutch is very different. Their fugar colonies, though much lefs populous than thofe of Great-Britain, received in the above term, about feven hundred and fixty horfes and mules. The French, as in regard to the other articles of neceffary fupplies, not produced by their own dominions, receive thefe animals, without impediment, in our veffels, and their own, indifcriminately. The precife number, which was fhipped to their iflands, before the revolution, is not afcertained: but, as lord Sheffield alledges, that the whole number exported to the foreign fugar colonies was, in 1770, about 4,015, fome part of which the Dutch and Danes received—and as it appears by the late return, that about 7,000 horfes and mules were fhipped to the French fugar plantations, during its term, it is manifeft, that they have increafed their importations 80, 90, or 100 per cent. It is unneceffary to reiterate here, tha they will receive proportionate advantages in their colonial agriculture, (and to the fhips employed in tranfporting its produce) from fo capital an addition to one of their moft ufeful fupplies.

THAT "FRANCE WILL NOT SUFFER AMERICA TO SUPPLY
HER WITH SHIPS,"

is contradicted by the fact.* That kingdom by rejecting American veffels, would have fo far facrificed her carrying trade to the manufacture of fhips. She wifely purchafes, upon the cheapeft terms, *the cradles* for her marine nurfery. The firft and great object of the maritime powers ought to be, *the increafe of the number of their failors,* which is beft done by multiplying their chances of employment. Among the means of doing this, one of the moft obvious and rational is, *the multiplication of veffels.* The French-built fhips coft from 55 to 60 dollars per ton, when fitted to receive a cargo. and exclufively of fea ftores, infurance, the charges of lading, outward pilotage, and other expenfes incidental to the employment, and not to the building and outfit of a veffel. The American live oak and cedar fhips, to which none are fuperior, coft in the fame fituation, from 33 to 35 dollars, finifhed very completely. If the French require 10,000 tons of new veffels, on any occafion, or in any term of time, they may be procured in the United States, on a computation of the medium price of 34 dollars per ton, for the

---

* Immediately after the firft publication of this paper, the French regulation, confining their flag to native fhips, was received in America. What will be found under this head, which was written before the regulation was known, may ferve as a fincere comment on this new reftriction. A. D. 1791.

fum of 340,000 dollars . but if bought at 55 dollars, the loweft price in France, they would coft the much greater fum of 550,000 dollars. No argument is neceffary to fhow, that fuch a nation, *cœteris paribus,* muft produce feamen more rapidly, than thofe, who refufe thefe cheap veffels.

It would appear much lefs unreafonable, that the government of the United States fhould prohibit the fale of fhips, *(the means of obtaining naval ftrength,)* to foreign nations, than that any of them fhould rejeƈt the great advantage of fo cheap and excellent a fupply. And fhould the French, Britifh, and other foreign nations continue to decline the purchafe of American-built fhips, there can be no doubt, that we fhall take a greater portion of *the carrying trade* for ourfelves and other countries, from that caufe.

THAT THE NAVIGATION ACT GAVE, AND THAT AN ADHERENCE TO IT, WILL SECURE TO GREAT-BRITAIN THE COMMERCE OF THE WORLD.

There is no doubt, that Great-Britain has heretofore obtained, in proportion to the number of its people, a very great fhare of trade both foreign and internal. But the value of her imports in 1774, was not ten per cent. more than that of the imports of France. Holland* had, at the fame

---

* Mr. Eden ftated, fince the American war, that the exports of Holland, in foreign goods only, were 18,000,000l. fterling.

time, a very great trade; as had feveral other
countries in Europe. It would have been beyond
the truth, if lord Sheffield had faid that Britain
had a fifth " of the commerce of the world." It
may appear, at firft view, of little ufe, and even invidious, to notice this remark; *but it is really of
importance to a reafonable and accurate eftimation of
things, to correct fuch extravagancies.* Thefe hyper-
bolical expreffions tend to miflead. They occafion a people erroneoufly to fuppofe, they have
the world at their command, and render the moft
falutary and reafonable arrangements more difficult than they ought to be. They alfo help to
fwell the popular torrent againft a clear-fighted,
honeft, and candid minifter, who may attempt meafures, fit in themfelves, and even neceffary to the
national interefts.

But whatever may have been the degree of truth
in the affertion, that Great-Britain *heretofore* engroffed the commerce of the world, a different
courfe of things has taken place, and is to be expected hereafter, with regard to her and every
other country. It is manifeft, that a prodigious,
and almoft univerfal revolution in the views of
nations, with regard to the carrying trade, has taken place. The extenfion of the fpirit of commerce and the confequent inclination and capacity for naval power, have occafioned this change.
The jealoufy of trade, which gave birth to the
Britifh navigation act, is now felt as well by the
fovereigns, as by the citizens, of every country in

Europe. They have become fenfible, that commerce and navigation are at once great fources of private wealth and of national power. The general prevalence of thefe views is daily producing commercial regulations, (injurious in many particulars to the country making them) intended to fecure to the citizens of each nation thofe benefits, which were formerly enjoyed by the carrying and manufacturing ftates. Thofe, who have heretofore enjoyed the trade of other countries, and in a very extenfive degree, muft neceffarily be the firft to feel the inconveniencies of this change of meafures: and they muft eventually experience them in proportion to their former advantages. The private fhipping of the Hanfe towns and of the United Netherlands, have already felt feverely the confequences of thefe views. Thofe traders, indeed, might once have almoft claimed the commerce of the world. There is confiderable danger, however, that this anxious defire of trade may occafion fome of the maritime nations to give too free and ftrong operation to principles, which are not exceptionable in the prefent ftate of things, if properly directed and reftrained; for it is manifeft, that countries with a great agricultural intereft, will err exceedingly in purfuing, as far as poffible, meafures, which may not be found inconvenient to nations oppofitely circumftanced.

With refpect to Great-Britain, the particular object of her navigation act was to expel the Dutch from her carrying trade, and thus to decreafe the ability of her rivals to maintain and suddenly to increase their navy. Situated as things then were, the British were probably right, as to the object in view: *and from the won derful insensibility of all Europe to the nature and operation of the English marine code*, they gained incidentally, and for a long time, immense advantages in the commerce of other states, for which they originally did not look. *This situation of things however is now thoroughly understood.* The shipping of Britain in consequence, will hereafter find rivals in the private vessels of several foreign countries, and there appears the utmost improbability, that she can continue to retain any extraordinary share of the carrying trade for other nations. The tenure of it is manifestly in the greatest degree precarious; because it absolutely depends on the laws of other countries, and on the improbable continuance of inattention in their commercial citizens.

The value of the carrying trade, it may also be observed, is very materially altered. Instead of being, as formerly, a profitable monopoly (if we may so speak) in the hands of two nations, it is now diffused among ten or twelve. The great advantages, too, which accrued to Britain from cheap provisions—superior and cheap ships—and low wages to seamen, are now lost. Bread and meat, from the increase of manufacturers, are imported into that island—wages have considerably advanced, if we take into the calculation the great fishing bounties—the expenses of ship-building have increafed—the French* are admitted to have obtained the pre-eminence in naval architecture, and it appears from a minute return, exhibited in Anderfon's commerce, that the oak timber of Great-Britain, in forty years proceeding 1771, had decreafed nine-tenths; and that it had advanced in price above 40 per cent. in the courfe of the nineteen antecedent years. It will not be forgotten, that the expenditure of twenty years, including a naval war, in which an unparalleled number of fhips was built, has fince occured further to exhauft their ftock of fhip timber. Nor fhould it be overlooked, that vaft demands were made for this article to replace the private fhipping, which were loft to the Britifh nation by the American revolution. The confumption of fhip timber from 1774 to 1785, appears from the papers of the Britifh fociety for naval architecture, to have been three times as great as in any equal term before.

The fudden command of feamen by means of *impreffment* is too ftrong an operation of the executive power, too great an outrage againft the rights of men, and the facred peace of families, long to be endured in the prefent courfe of European affairs. Thofe prompt exertions of naval ftrength, by which Great-Britain has heretofore gained advantages, will be affected by an alteration in this particular, at leaft fo far as regards unprofitable, unjuft, and ambitious wars, into which all nations are occafionally led.

* See papers of the Britfh fociety for naval architecture.

These remarks, it is presumed, will not be misconstrued, as of an invidious nature. *It is a season requiring a true state of things.* They are intended as dispassionate and reasonable answers to the extravagant assertions and the contemptuous menaces of the writer of the observations, whose doctrines are as pernicious to Great-Britain, as they are injurious to the United States. *" Should a quarrel take place between the American states and Great-Britain, some stout frigates,"* he affirms, *would completely command the commerce of this mighty continent."*

It would not be improper to ask, what argument is this very intelligent writer possessed of, to prove that so great a *permanent* disparity will exist in favour of a nation, whose *exports* are now to their *expenses,* as 18 to 16, over a nation whose exports to their expenses are as 18 to 3 ? Why, can he inform us, should the British exports or imports, neither of which will load 650,000 tons of vessels, afford *a certain and permanent basis* for a powerful navy, if those of the United States, which will lade 650,000 tons of vessels, and are steadily increasing, do not justify, under proper management, expectations equal to a few stout frigates ? Such miscalculations, on the part of any foreign nation, must lead to corresponding improprieties in their deportment towards us, or they must be candidly rejected.

THAT IT MUST ALWAYS BE THE SITUATION OF THE UNITED
STATES TO COURT GREAT-BRITAIN.

To evince the fallacy of this pofition, nothing
more is neceffary than to recollect fome leading
circumftances in the trade of the two countries.
Great Britain exports about £.18,000,000 fterling,
per ann. of which 13,000,000 fterling are her own
manufactures. It will not be pretended, that we,
as the principle cuftomers, are to court the venders
of *thefe goods.** A portion of the remaining
£.5,000,000 is made up of our tobaccoes, rice,
indigoes ginfeng, and other productions, exported
from their dominions in an unmanufactured ftate.
Of thefe, it will not be fuppofed we can be anxious to make *importations.* The greater part of the
remainder is made up of India, Ruffian, German,
and other articles, of foreign growth or manufacture, which Britain cannot furnifh but at fecond
hand ; for which, confequently, we are not under
the neceffity to court her, and which neither we
nor any other nation fhould receive from her European dominions, were we to purfue her navigation principles. The re-fhipped commodities of
Ireland, too, form no inconfiderable item in the
lift of Britifh exports. For thefe we could be under no obligation to Great-Britain, being manufactured goods, on the fhipment of moft of which
to thefe ftates and all the world, the Irifh have

---

* We muft court the arts by which they are manufactured, as
we have wifely done for the laft five or fix years.

long granted a very encouraging bounty. In regard to our exports to Great-Britain, *they consist principally of the precious elements of her manufactures, shipping, and navy*. These are not only (in the language of lord Sheffield, when speaking of the Russian exports) " more precious to her than gold," but are absolute necessaries. Lumber of all kinds, bark, cotton, flax, iron, flaxseed, wax, indigo, pot-ash, tar, pitch, turpentine, skins, and furs, are among the articles here contemplated. To these may be added wheat, flour, and Indian corn, taken in small quantities except when necessity compels large importations; also tobacco and rice, which are consumed in a small proportion in Britain, but contribute to swell her exports, and increase her carrying trade to other countries. 'Tis manifest, that all these exports are much to be desired on her part, and that it would be most profitable to the United States, *to manufacture the raw materials, and to expend the provisions on their own manufacturers;* and to furnish the rice and tobacco, *by the direct voyage,* to those nations which are supplied circuitously through British ports. In another point of view, the intercourse with Great-Britain is not particularly to be courted by the United States. It has been already observed, that we imported of their manufactures, in 1784, £.3,648,007 sterling, and in 1785 £2,308,013, which appear, on a medium of those two years, to have been equal to above one third of *the manufactures* they exported, to *all other foreign nations!* How *immensely beneficial, how indispensibly necessary* to the British manufacturers, are such consumers ? Let it be asked, and candidly answered, if they or we are to court such business ? If any inviting measures are to be adopted by this country, it would be more wise to court the capitalists, manufacturers, and artizans, of the several countries of Europe, which are over-charged with private wealth and population. It may be urged, that we are strongly induced to court Great-Britain for credit. The answer is, that she cannot venture to withhold her fabrics, whatever may be our time of payment ; for in the present state of things, a years absence of British goods from our markets, would give an immense spring to our own manufactures. But there is a strong symptom of the ability of the United States to do without a very extensive credit, from any particular nation, in the abundant supplies of China and East-India goods, which are imported from every part of those countries with which we trade, amounting probably, to more than a fifth of our consumption of foreign commodities. This independency on any particular nation, which is in the highest degree to be desired, will be sensibly promoted by the establishment of our good name in other foreign countries, by strengthening our new and wholesome guards around the rights of property, and by the recent multiplication and extension of banks. Though no such pecuniary institution existed ten years ago, six banks are established now in five different cities ; and their capitals exceed at this time a moiety of our importations. The ac-commodations and facilities which will result from them, muſt exceedingly promote the independency of the American merchant and conſumer, on foreign credits.

THAT " IT WILL NOT BE THE INTEREST OF ANY OF THE GREAT MARITIME POWERS TO PROTECT THE AMERICAN VESSELS FROM THE BARBARY STATES."

The luſt of power has ſeldom given riſe to a leſs reputable ſentiment in the boſom of an individual than that which we are now to notice. Like the inſtruction of the flagitious father to his ſon, to get money, it is adviſed, that *naval ſtrength* ſhould be ſecured, *per fas et nefas*. But it is not aſſerted, that any nation maintains this doctrine. It has been urged in anſwer againſt us, that we import ſlaves, which has in a very great degree ceaſed; for the veſſels from Africa, in the whole returned year, were leſs than four hundred tons. But let the circumſtances of the caſe be examined and candidly conſidered. When high duties on the importation of ſlaves were impoſed before the revolution, by ſome of the colonial aſſemblies, they were rendered of no effect by *the negative of the crown*, upon the ſame principles, that now determine the conduct of many of the European ſhipholders and manufacturers—becauſe the abolition of the ſlave trade would curtail their reſpective advantages. During and ſince the war, moſt of the ſtates have prohibited thoſe importations: ſeveral have aboliſhed ſlavery: and we find as above hinted, that no more than 385 tons of fhipping arrived from Africa in twelve months fubfequent to Auguft 1789, in all the ftates, belonging to us, and all other nations. Whether thefe had on board any flaves, is not known. *Great-Britain* cannot prefs a country, thus conducting itfelf, on the fubject of the flave trade, feeing that her colonies continue to import tens of thoufands per annum.

But it is conceived, that the reverfe of lord Sheffield's pofition is true, and that it is the intereft of moft of the great maritime powers, to purfue meafures, which might tend to free the Americans from the piracies of the Barbary ftates. It may be among the means of transferring to thofe nations, from Great Britain, " *a part of the fovereignty of the ocean"* and " *a part of the commerce of the world, which,* it is alledged, *her naval power has fecured to her."* The balance of power, if it be accurately defined, muft be ftated to comprehend now the balance of *naval* power. To attain and preferve that, the firft ftep is manifeftly to diveft any nation, which may poffefs it, of " the fovereignty of the ocean." That fovereignty can comport with the true interefts and dignity of no other kingdom. It will be more advantageous to the feveral nations, who are not actually the firft in the fcale of naval power, that the United States fhould acquire a portion of the marine force of a nation, too potent by fea, than that fuch a nation, if it really has been the cafe, fhould continue to give law upon the ocean : and it is manifeft, that no one of thofe nations can be satisfied, that any other should prescribe the law there. The destruction of no particular kingdom is alledged to be requisite to the well being of this, or any other country : but it certainly is not necessary, that the other nations of the world should promote, or acquiesce in measures, calculated to support any one kingdom in a naval dictatorship. This degree of marine strength is not requisite for the self-defence of any nation ; and it may evidently be perverted to interrupt the commerce and to disturb the tranquility of Europe. Whether this has been the case, (concerning which no assertion is here made) it remains for the nations concerned severally to determine. If it has been, if it may be, and if it probably will be, then it also remains for them to decide, whether it be their true interest to join in the *honourable* league with the Barbarians against the honest commerce, and the personal liberties of the citizens of the United States.

THAT " THE BRITISH ISLANDS WOULD BE CROUDED WITH DUTCH, FRENCH, AND OTHER FOREIGN VESSELS, IF THEY WERE TO BE LAID OPEN."

A direct contradiction cannot be given to this assertion : but probabilities are strongly against it. The free ports of the French islands are thus laid open ; yet the whole tonnage, which usally passes between them and the United States, in the course of a year, exclusively of their own ships, those of the United States, and those of Great-Britain, do not exceed two per cent. of the whole tonnage employed in the trade; and though the British vessels

have an equal opportunity with the fhips of France
and of thefe ftates, yet they carried but eight fmall
cargoes to all the French iflands, during the returned year. From the nature of the Weft-India trade,
and of the commodities tranfported, it cannot be
fupported, unlefs the veffels be owned by the inhabitants of the iflands, or thofe of this country. Similar facts occur, in examining the trade with the
Dutch ports in the Weft-Indies, and on the main;
and the fame obfervations, it is conceived, would
juftly apply to them. But what could thofe foreign
veffels carry to the Englifh iflands? By the other
Britifh regulations, they could tranfport no *American* articles, and they cannot fhip from their own
dominions, with a chance of profit, a cargo of the co-
modities, which are permitted to be imported from
foreign countries, into the Britifh Weft-Indies.

S E C T I O N V.

THE next errors in the obfervations of lord
Sheffield, on which it is neceffary to animadvert,
are fome which are not inconfiderable, with refpect to the actual and probable

POPULATION OF THE UNITED STATES.

He is of opinion that our population is not likely to increafe as it has done on our coafts; that we
had fallen off in numbers in 1784; and that the
emigration from the United States would be very
confiderable. The ftate of Rhode-Ifland, all of

which lies near the sea, was proved by actual enumeration, in 1783, to contain 51,896 persons. The unhappy condition of that government, and the consequent interruption of its trade, fisheries, and manufactures, from 1786 to the beginning of 1790, occasioned great emigrations from thence into the other states. Yet the census, which was completed before the first day of May, in the present year, amounts to 68,825. Delaware, which, like Rhode-Island, has no back country, and lies upon the coast, was estimated at 35,000 persons, in a return, which lord Sheffield affirmed in 1783, to be too high. Its population is proved, by the actual enumeration just completed, to be 59,094. Connecticut, another state upon the coast, was computed in the same return, which he mentions in 1784, to contain 206,000 persons. It is well known, that its population, in proportion to its territory, was then, and is now, the greatest in the union, and that it has been incessantly sending emigrants to Maine, New-Hampshire, Vermont, New-York, Pennsylvania, Maryland, Virginia, and the western territory: yet the census shows it to contain, at this time, 237,942 inhabitants. New-Jersey, another state without new or unsettled lands, is rated in the return, which lord Sheffield questions, at 150,000, and was proved by an enumeration, which was taken at the moment he hazarded this doubt, to contain 149,435 persons. The census shows its present population to be 184,139. It has no unimproved counties or new lands. New-York was stated at 200,000, and now appears to be

340,120. Pennfylvania, which was faid to be eftimated too high, in 1784, at 320,000, amounts to
434,373. Maffachufetts, including the diftrict of
Maine, is fet down in the difputed eftimation, at
350,000, in 1784 : the cenfus in 1790, proves to
be 475,327. New-Hampfhire, which is found to
contain 141,885, was confidered as having no-
more than 82,200. Maryland, which was eftimat.
ed 220,000, and which has not one county that
does not lie on a navigable river, flowing into the
Atlantic ocean, appears by the cenfus to have
318,729. Virginia, *including* Kentucky, was ftated in the old return to have 400,000, and is
found to contain 747,610, after the feparation of
Kentucky, whofe population is 73,677 more : and
here it is to be remarked, that the ftate of Maffachufetts, though thickly fettled, has manifeftly
gained people in the laft nine years, more rapidly than Kentucky, fuppofing the latter to have
had 10,000 inhabitants or upwards, in 1782 ; and
the part of Virginia, not including Kentucky, has
gained inhabitants much more rapidly than that weftern diftrict. Thefe two facts are mentioned to
prove the error of lord Sheffield's prediction that
our population was not likely to increafe, as it
has done, " on the fea coaft." North-Carolina,
which was ftated at only 200,000, is proved to contain 393,751, exclufively of the weftern country
ceded to congrefs by that ftate in the laft year, the
population of which is found to be about 35,691
more. The population of Vermont is above
85,000. That of South Carolina which was ftat-

ed at 170,000 proves to be 249,073. The population
of the weſtern territory is not yet aſcertained.

The whole return above referred to, is alledged,
by our author, to be too high. Its total is 2,389,300,
and it was made the baſis of congreſſional aſſeſſ-
ments. The beſt accounts, as lord Sheffield affirms,
made the number of whites 1,700,000. There
ſeems, however, from the returns already received,
to be no doubt, that our numbers will prove more
than 3,900,000, by the cenſus taken from Auguſt,
1790, to April, 1791, incluſive. The population
of the United States has therefore advanced 65 *per
centum* on a return in 1782, which lord Sheffield
affirmed, in 1784, to be *exaggerated*.*

The ſimplicity of living amongſt *the great body*
of the American people—the extraordinary facility of obtaining the means of ſubſiſtence—migration to our country—and the non-exiſtence of emigrations from it, though Nova-Scotia is ſo near,
and as lord Sheffield ſays, ſo tempting—theſe circumſtances have occaſioned the United States thus
rapidly to increaſe in population, in the laſt nine
years, though ſeven of them were extremely diſordered and diſcouraging. But now, when agriculture is greatly improved, when laws, religion, morals, liberal and uſeful ſcience, arts, manufactures,
and commerce, are maintained, promoted and extended—lord Sheffield himſelf will believe, that our
population will encreaſe even on the ſea coaſt.

* See the cenſus of 1791 in this volume.

Let foreigners, who fincerely defire information, take up the Philadelphia directory, publifhed by the marfhal of the United States for the diftrict of Pennfylvania, and learn by this fimple but authentic document, the ingredients of which our towns are compofed, even in a ftate whofe territory is not one fourth fettled. It will there be feen, that while our planters' and farmers' fons are fubdividing their lands, or moving forward into lefs populated fcenes, many of the fons of our artificers and manufacturers, and very many perfons of thofe occupations, from foreign countries, are taking their ftations on the vacant lots in our old ftreets, or commencing new ones. *The fober and induftrious journeymen of Europe, who can fcarcely fupport the difficulties and expenfes of living there, often become fuccefsful mafter workmen here.* It may be fafely affirmed, that the Scotch combine the advantages of fobriety, induftry, frugality, and fkill, in as great a degree as any manufacturers in Europe; yet they inceffantly emigrate to us, and are remarkably fuccefsful in their various branches.

EMIGRATION.

Great pains are taken by the writer of the obfervations, to place the emigrants to America in the moft difcouraging circumftances of diftrefs and contempt. " Emigration," fays he, " is the natural refource of the culprit." Thofe, who are acquainted with the hiftory of Europe, fince the beginning of the feventeenth century, and of the colonies fettled

from thence, know, that the emigrants hither have
been, generally fpeaking, *the enterprifing*, and
their followers, or *the oppreffed fubjects of unjuft
civil or religious rulers*—the latter in the greateft
degree.. There is not a ftate in the union which
does not contain one or more fects or churches,
which have fled from religious perfecution. Nothing can be more rational, than that perfons of
fincere piety and tender confciences, fhould feek a
country, in which the affertion of *mere toleration*
is deemed as abfurd, as the denial of *religious liberty* is thought to be criminal. Hence Prefbyterians,
Congregationalifts, Quakers, Baptifts, and others,
have fled hither from England; Seceders and Epif-
copalians from Scotland; Catholics and Prefbyterians from Ireland; Hugunots from France; Pro-
teftants from the dominions of the Catholic princes
of Germany; and Catholics from thofe of the Proteftant princes. Two centuries have not elapfed,
fince all the dominions of the United States were
an howling wildernefs. They now contain near
four millions of people. From whence have they
been derived? In great numbers from various
parts of Europe, by inceffant ftreams of emigration. But it may be afked, are thefe people happy and profperous? Does the foil they cultivate,
yield them any return for their labour? They procure for themfelves comfortable habitations, food,
raiment, and other conveniencies, and have exported in a fingle year, above twenty millions of

dollars in value!* How then can thefe people have been " miferably difappointed in their expectations of profperity here ?"

But lord Sheffield affures all emigrants, that they will be diftreffed, nay, ruined, by taxes; and that our public burdens are heavier than thofe of any country in Europe. It appears, however, that we are now in the middle of the third year of our general government, and notwithftanding all our late arrearages, and the funding of our debts, neither a tax on lands, nor any fpecies of direct tax, is contemplated. No excife upon any article of confumption or ufe is laid or propofed, except a very fmall one on fpirituous liquors, compared with thofe in Europe. Befides this, the impoft, or duty on foreign goods imported is the fole revenue, that is raifed upon the people, and it is, on a medium, lefs in *currency*, than the fame articles pay in *fterling*, in all the principal countries of Europe. Where, then, are thefe infupportable burdens with which this writer attempts to alarm European emigrants?

Under the head of emigration, lord Sheffield has laid himfelf open to a more fevere meafure of juft remark, than it is agreeable to deal out to him. It ought not, however, to be unnoticed,

* The exportations of the year ending on the 30th September, 1792, exceeded 21 millions of dollars. Thofe of the year following were 26,000,000.

that he gravely brings forward a ftory, on the authority of a namelefs letter from Philadelphia, of " two fine Irifh youths being purchafed by a negro fruit feller, in that city, and employed in hawking fruit about the ftreets, and in the meaneft employments." How dangerous muft be the fituation of a government, which has acted upon the information and reafonings brought forward by a mind capable of ufing fuch means to carry his points, admitting the letter were genuine! How unlike a dignified ftatefman does lord Sheffield appear, in exclaiming, after this very little ftory, " *Irifhmen juft emancipated in Europe, go to America to become flaves to a negro!*" and what will be thought when it is known, that in the legiflature of the very ftate (Pennfylvania) in whofe capital he alleges the fact took place, there were, about the time of his publication, no lefs than twenty-eight Irifhmen and fons of Irifhmen, though the whole body confifted of but fixty-nine members? We are willing that the fortunes of the Irifh in this country fhould determine the expediency of their continuing to emigrate hither. As fome pains have been taken by him to excite the apprehenfions of the Germans alfo, it may not be improper to obferve that there have generally been from fifteen to eighteen members of the fame legiflative body, who were natives of Germany or their fons.

It was boldly aſſerted by lord Sheffield, in 1784, that the people of the interior country of America, were " mere nominal ſubjects," and would ſpeedi- ly imitate and multiply the examples of indepen- dence. The regular organization of the govern- ment of the territory north-weſt of the Ohio ſince that time, the arrangements made ſhortly after, for the erection of Kentucky into a ſeparate ſtate, with the conſent of Congreſs and Virginia, the ceſſion of the extenſive country ſouth of the Ohio to Con- greſs in 1790, and its eſtabliſhment as a kind of temporary fief of the general government (with ci- vil officers appointed by the Preſident) to be ad- mitted into the union as an entire new member, when its population ſhould be ſufficiently nume- rous, the adoption of the federal conſtitution by a deliberate act of a ſpecial convention of Vermont, and the formal admiſſions of that ſtate and Ken- tucky into the American union, at their own deſire, and by an act of the legiſlature of the United States, have, as far as poſſible, contradicted the prophecy.

Another opinion, in regard to thoſe diſtant ſcenes, is, that they can derive no benefit from the American ſtates. At this moment, the arm of government is extended, and its funds are appro- priated, to protect them againſt the hoſtilities of the Indians : and the whole regular military force, which it has been thought neceffary to fupport, was raifed, and is now employed in their defence. The Atlantic rivers, from the Miffifippi to the Mohawk, which nature has formed as the channels of their trade, can be cleared of natural and political obftructions only by the meafures of the Atlantic ftates; and no lefs than eight feveral plans to that end are now in preparation or execution in as many different places, under the aufpices of the five ftates, within whofe territories the moft favourable rivers and grounds have been placed by nature.* Congrefs alone can effect the relinquifhment of the pofts, *the keys of the weftern country.* The improvement and opening of the many neceffary roads, leading weftward, muft be done by the acts of the Atlantic ftates, and by their funds. Not a year elapfes without feveral appropriations of money to this object. *By a fincere, juft, and clofe union between the inhabitants of the weftern country and thofe upon the fea coafts, both parties will avoid thofe expenfive, bloody, and frequent ftruggles, which every where difgrace and injure adjacent ftates.*

THAT NO AMERICAN ARTICLES ARE SO NECESSARY TO GREAT-BRTIAIN, AS THE BRITISH MANUFACTURES, &c. ARE TO THE AMERICANS.

Lord Sheffield has already admitted, that raw materials are more precious to Britain than gold: but

---

* A great and expenfive turnpike road has been commenced by Pennfylvania, leading directly weftward towards Pittfburg on the Ohio and Allegany. A. D. 1793.

this was not conceded to America. Thofe things, which are ineftimable, when they are to be drawn from countries, other than the United States, lofe all their value in his eftimation, when to be derived from us. The Britifh manufacturers however well know, that American raw materials (like thofe of Ruffia, the Indies and Ireland) are precious, indeed, to them, becaufe, in addition to their natural value, and their indifpenfible need of them, when once landed in Britain, they cannot be manufactured in America. Timber, plank, boards, mafts, tar, pitch, turpentine, and pig iron for the fupport of their navy and fhipping—indigo, potafh, furs, fkins, flaxfeed, iron, tobacoo, ftaves, fine oil, &c. for the employment of their manufacturers— rice, wheat, and flour for their fubfiftence—and a large catalogue of the moft neceffary fupplies for the Weft-India iflands, which really cannot be obtained elfewhere, without an infupportable addition to their coft, will not be deemed at this time, by a rational and well informed man, of lefs importance to Great-Britain, than the manufactures of that country, which they are affiduoufly endeavouring to difperfe through every quarter of the world, are to us*.

But it is not intended to wafte arguments on this allegation. Every man of information, in the affairs of the two countries, is able to decide on it

* Witnefs the fpecial embaffy to the Chinefe antipodes of Great-Britain.

at firſt view. Little more appears neceſſary than
to remind the parties concerned, that ſuch an aſſertion is among the poſitions, which lord Sheffield
has hazarded, in order that the miſleading tendency of his book may be duly borne in mind by the
ſincere friends of mutually beneficial arrangements.
It may not, however, be amiſs to obſerve, that although the favourable ideas which have been ſuggeſted here by way of anſwer, were juſtified by
faſts and reaſon, when that work was publiſhed,
yet the American ground is not a little meliorated
by the ſubſequent progreſs and preſent ſtate of our
manufaſtures—by the experienced inability of Canada, New-Brunſwick, and Nova-Scotia, to furniſh
the expeſted ſupplies—by the conſequent importations from the United States of timber and lumber
into Great-Britain, and of more than the former
ſupplies into the Weſt-Indies—and by the neceſſary dependence of Europe on the United States for
the precious articles of grain and flour, which has
been recently aſcertained and admitted by unqueſ-
tionable Engliſh authorities.

THE QUALITY OF AMERICAN DISTILLED SPIRITS.

It is not ſurpriſing, that remarks on the bad quality of American ſpirituous liquors ſhould run
through "the obſervations." But the buſineſs of
diſtilling is ſo ſimple, that great improvements
might have been expeſted ſince 1783. Genēva,
in imitation of that of Holland, is now made in
ſome of our ſea ports: the reſtifying of the or-

dinary rums is practised by a few with great succefs.* Peach brandy is made in confiderable quantities, and, when matured, is the moft exquifite fpirit in the world. Should our rice decline in price, it is not doubted, that the manufacture of arrack will be attempted. The ingredients, from which this fpirit is made, have till lately been unafcertained in the United States: but it is now believed, that rice, and coarfe fugar, or melaffes, are really the articles. When the fuccefs of the Americans in the manufacture of malt liquors is remembered, it will not be doubted, that they will have equal fuccefs in that of diftilled fpirits. A principal impediment has hitherto been the free and copious influx of rival foreign liquors, and the general reception of flour, &c. in foreign ports. Every obftruction to our veffels and fales abroad, impofed by the European nations, impels to breweries, diftilleries, and manufactures in general, amongft other modes of creating a demand for our productions, and employment for our capitals.

" IF THE AMERICAN STATES SHOULD ATTEMPT TO PAY THEIR DEBTS, THE LANDS OF THE FARMERS MUST FOR SOMETIME LIE UNDER VERY HEAVY IMPOSITIONS."

This is among the many proofs, which our writer has given, that he did not poffefs the gift of prophecy. The American debt has been confider-

* This branch is very much improved within the laft two years, particularly by the Providence and Rhode-Ifland diftilliries— A. D. 1793.

ably reduced by the fale of ftate and federal lands, and a provifion is made for funding it. A finking fund has alfo been provided. Yet *no* tax upon lands has been introduced among the ways and means. The whole American debt would not require a tax upon each individual, of four pounds fterling, *to extinguifh it forever*. That of Great-Britain would require a tax of more than twenty-four pounds ten fhillings fterling. Our population is rapidly increafing, while theirs is comparatively ftationary. There is a fimilar difproportion in our favour in the ordinary and extraordinary expenfes of government and defence. The French debt is 250 per cent. heavier than ours, in proportion to numbers. *This brief, but very important article will not fail to receive due attention from thofe who fincerely defire to make a juft eftimate of the affairs of the United States;* nor will it efcape the obfervations of thofe foreigners, who may be engaged in refearches into our affairs, or in plans of emigration, fettlement, and landed purchafes in this country. It will alfo be a fource of the moft comfortable reflections to our own citizens. The people of Europe, who have read lord Sheffield's book, will be furprifed to hear that there are no perpetual revenues, no ftamp duties, no window or hearth taxes, no tythes, no excifes upon leather, beer, hops, malt, foap, candles, coal or other fuel, or indeed on any other article in the United States, excepting only about five pence fterling on diftilled fpirits.

" THAT THE AMERICANS COULD NOT HAVE TRADED WITH
THE FRENCH BEFORE THE REVOLUTION TO HALF THE
EXTENT THEY DID, HAD IT NOT BEEN FOR THE SPECIE
THEY TOOK FROM THE BRITISH ISLANDS."

This remark is applied by the writer to our
French Weſt-India trade. To judge of the truth
of it, a compariſon of the preſent with the former
ſtate of that branch of our commerce will be ſufficient. It will not be doubted, that during their
troubles, and (to take a recent term) for a year
preceding the firſt day of May laſt, our imports
and exports from and to the French Weſt-Indies,
were greater than in any year before the war. Yet
our veſſels could not procure ſpecie in the Britiſh
iſlands, being prohibited from entering them.
Pickled and dried fiſh, beef, rice, Indian corn, oats,
beans, peas, onions, Indian meal, boards, plank,
ſcantling, ſhingles, handſpikes, oars, ſquare timber,
ſtaves, heading, hoops, horſes, live ſtock, poultry, boats, and veſſels, &c. to an amount greater than the ſhipments to all the Weſt India iſlands,
other than Britiſh, before the war, have been exported to the French iſlands within the term of one
year. The courſe of things, in ſeveral reſpects, will
probably leſſen our importation of melaſſes and the
taffia, (or rum) which we have been accuſtomed to
draw from thence. Beſides beer and cider, diſtilled
ſpirits are now made from fruit and grain, in ſuch
quantities as to conſtitute more than one-third of
our conſumption and export of ſtrong liquors, other

than wines. Plentiful harvefts of fruit neceffarily
increafe the manufacture from that ingredient;
becaufe it is too perifhable to export. Abundant
harvefts of grain, or low markets abroad, have a
fimilar effect on diftillation from that material.
The meafures of the national affembly of France,
in regard to tobacco, will add to the many objections which before exifted againft the ufual cultivation of it. Barley, rye, and oats, from which
the grain-liquors are principally made, as alfo wheat
and Indian corn, will be produced in much larger
quantities, fhould we decline the cultivation of tobacco in any confiderable degree. If we continue,
after a fhort time, to import choice rums, brandies,
and arrack, to the amount of five per cent. on our
whole confumption, and manufacture the remainder, which will require four millions of bufhels of
barley, rye and oats, and more fo far as we make
beer, we fhall want lefs funds abroad for the purchafe of molaffes, and we fhall confirm the ability
we have fhown, to carry on a trade with the French
iflands, greater than formerly, *without fpecie taken
from the Britifh Weft-Indies.*

" THAT THE UNITED STATES LOST MUCH BY THE SEPARA-
TION FROM GREAT-BRITAIN."

This is an opinion, which it was very natural
for an Englifh writer in 1783 to adopt. It was difficult at that time to compare, with the requifite
certainty and precifion, the benefits in point of
pecuniary advantage, which the United States

might have reasonably expected in a colonial, and in an independent situation. It would be more easily and better done at the present, but cannot be attempted at large in this place. Some ideas on the subject, however, may serve to evince the error of the assertion.

It is true, that by the separation of the two countries, the United States incurred a debt of about £. 15,000,000 sterling, which, however, was entirely spent in the country, as was a great part of the French and *British* expenditures. Great-Britain increased her public debt, in the same time, £. 115,000,000. The whole burden on both sides appears then to be about £. 130,000,000 sterling. There is the strongest probability, from the rapidity of the increase of the British debt, which, in less than a century, grew up from *nothing* to £. 270,000,000, and which is in the present year swelling to a larger size, that, without the American war, the British nation would have been burdened on this day, with at least two hundred millions. Considering the rate in which the objects of taxation or means of revenue have increased in this country, there is reason to believe, that by this time we should have been thought able to endure a proportion of the ways and means requisite to support that debt, equal to our numbers; this would have been above one-fourth of the whole, or *fifty millions sterling*, and is three and one-third times our present debt. It may be said, we paid no such contribution; and the assertion, by refer-

ence to the former public accounts, would appear
on paper to be true: but we were injuriouſly reſtrained, in regard to the ſources of our ſupplies,
and the vents of our produce and manufactures; we
were prohibited from the labour-ſaving modes of
manufacturing; and it is too plain that the prohibitions would have been continued. The impoſt
went into the Britiſh treaſury; our lands were ſubject to quit-rents, which, belonging to the crown,
have either fallen to the preſent government, or
have been entirely aboliſhed. The effects of the
commercial monopoly were prodigious. It may
be ſtrikingly exemplified in the ſingle article of tea.
We have already ſeen that we imported above three
millions of pounds in the year following Auguſt
1789. The medium price of fine and coarſe teas
was above one third of a dollar more favourable to
us in 1790, than in 1774; by which a difference of
a million of dollars, and the whole impoſt on the article, are ſaved to the country.

The facility of naturalization under our preſent
laws, is very much in favour of the introduction of
people, and of arts, manufactures, and capital from
foreign countries. Lands may be held in almoſt
every ſtate, and his occupation or trade may be purſued, immediately on the arrival of an emigrant.
A term much ſhorter than that preſcribed by the
Britiſh ſtatute before the revolution, entitles him to
all the benefits of citizenſhip. It is impoſſible to
eſtimate the value of this circumſtance to a country ſo well calculated to induce emigration, to ſup-

port an increaſed population, and to employ capital
and artificers, as the United States.

Lord Sheffield obſerves, that the Britiſh eſtabliſhment in this country gave it an advantage of
£.370,000 ſterling per annum. He ſhould not
have omitted to mention, that great part of this
ſum was expended on the Floridas, Canada, and
Nova Scotia: and it is to be obſerved, that many
of the articles were imported, and not of our production or manufacture. The mere conſumption
of Britiſh and Iriſh goods by the Britiſh and Iriſh
officers, ſoldiers, and ſailors, ſtationed or employed here, could not benefit the people of America. It is paſt a doubt, that the ſales of the
lands alone, which have fallen to the ſtates and
to the general government, have yielded annually a larger ſum by the purchaſes of citizens
and foreigners. The cuſtoms and quit-rents muſt
alſo have been a full reimburſment. But it is unneceſſary to dwell longer on this article; for what
ever may have been the former opinions of many in
the two countries concerning it, the ſubject is at this
time ſo illumined, and prejudice and miſconcep-
tion are ſo completely done away, that no perſons
of judgment and information now believe, " *the
United States have loſt by the ſeparation from Great-
Britain.*" It is, however, true that the American
ſtates were in a train of proſperity before the revolution, which promiſed greater wealth and happineſs than appeared to await the people of any other
country. Lord Sheffield might reaſonably eſtimate

their prospects very highly. To insure the expected prosperity, however, it was deemed theoretically right, that the provincial " parliaments" (the executive head of the empire by himself or a representative and the legislative houses of each) should enact *all* laws. Though some concessions to what was considered as " *the necessity of the case,*" were frankly made, limiting the practical extension of this sound theory, yet it is plain, that unless it could have been substantially adhered to, in the administration of the American governments, no reliance could have been placed on the continuance of that degree of prosperity, which existed, nor on the attainment of that height, which circumstances otherwise promised. The wonderful advancement of Great-Britain in almost every particular, except her finances, during the present century, and the comparatively small progress of Ireland in the same term, afford a striking example of what might have happened to this country, and furnish the best reasons to believe, that the United States (as to mere emolument) have gained prodigiously by commuting for the great influence and undefined power of two legislative bodies, *actually* rival and then *essentially* foreign, the advantages of governing themselves in all respects, according to the prudent dictates of their own interests. As to the more important article, of *a genuine free constitution,* unexaggerated by political enthusiasm, and unvitiated by any alloying ingredients, America may with modesty affirm, that she is nearer to that *primary object of human desire,* than she would have been in the possession of the moft favourable ground, which her beft friends in Britain ever propofed for her before the feparation

SECTION VI.

I T was intimated, in a preceding part of thefe papers, that the United States have not fuftained any lofs in the important article of fhip-building, which it is propofed now to fhow, in treating of

" SHIPS BUILT FOR ORDINARY COMMERCE AND FOR SALE."

This branch was of confiderable value to the United States before the revolution. Its importance appears greater now, whether it be viewed with regard to the increafed quantity (for there appears good reafon to think it confiderably increafed) or with refpect to the enhanced value of merchant fhips to an independent and maritime country. The quantity built in thefe ftates, on the average of 1769, 1770, and 1771, which are the lateft years in lord Sheffield's tables, was 21,726 tons. An account equally minute, for any recent term, has not been obtained; but it is known, that in fifty-three cuftom-houfe diftricts (and there are fifteen more,)29,606 tons of fhipping were built between the fourth day of March 1790, and the fourth day of March 1791. This is believed to be, in many inftances, the tonnage paid for to the carpenters; and, in thofe cafes, is lefs than the veffels really meafure; as they are a body of workmen, who generally deal liberally. The remaining fifteen

diftricts will not be found to have built in proportion to the fifty three, whofe actual prefent building
is ftated; but the quantity already known, is confiderably beyond the medium of lord Sheffield's
tables, for 1769 to 1771, above mentioned. In
the cafe of New-York, the whole is known, and is
two hundred and thirty-eight tons more than
the former tables. In New-Jerfey, the building
in fome diftricts is unknown, and the difference is
two hundred and eighty-eight tons in favour of
the late return. In Connecticut, the whole of the
building is ftated, and it is five hundred and thirty-four tons in favour of the latter term. In Pennfylvania and Delaware, the whole is alfo known:
and the late return exceeds the former by 3,900
tons. In North-Carolina, a return of three diftricts
(out of five) only is obtained; and it exceeds the
former average by 925 tons. In the ftate of Rhode-
Ifland, the whole is afcertained, and it exceeds the
former average by about 100 tons. The port of
Baltimore alone, in Maryland, exceeds all the fhip-
building of that ftate, in the greateft of the three
years, by near 100 per cent. The veffels built in
Connecticut, in the returned year, are 40 per cent.
more than the medium of lord Sheffield's tables;
and Maffachufetts exceeds the former medium by
3,713 tons*.

It is true, however, that this bufinefs in one of
the principal building ftates, has fallen off; but

* The general increafe fince is very confiderable. A. D. 1793.

there many of the veffels intended for fale, were ufually built; and it is admitted by lord Sheffield;
that thofe were our worft veffels. It is very material to the United States, and entitles us to a larger credit in an accurate eftimation of things, that
much more of our naval military ftores, cordage,
twine, nails and fpikes, fail cloth, plumbers' work,
rofin, fpirits of turpentine, linfeed oil, paints, brafs
and copper work, and other lefs important articles
expended in building and arming fhips, are of the
produce and manufacture of the country, than was
the cafe in 1771. It is alfo an important truth,
that much greater numbers of foreign veffels are
repaired, altered, fupplied with cordage and fail
cloth, painted and otherwife wrought upon by our
various workmen, the money for which, may be
fairly carried to the account of this branch.

At the time when lord Sheffield wrote, it was not
known how much the oak of Great-Britain had decreafed. We have already noticed this point;
and it may be further remarked, that it cannot but
decreafe yet more, as the fupplies of *oak* from the
Baltic, are often intercepted by the competition of
Pruffia, Sweden, Denmark, Ruffia, Portugal, Holland, Spain and France, all but the firft of which
vigoroufly maintain their naval power; and Pruffia has become very confiderable in private fhips.
Lord Sheffield thinks that the cheapnefs of American fhipping arofe from their being ill-found and
deficient in iron. There is little doubt that the
extreme cheapnefs of thofe built for fale, was oc-

cafioned partly by the caufe he mentions: but the
beft double-deck or galley-built fhips, with live-oak
lower timbers, and red-cedar top-timbers, with
white-oak plank on their bottoms, and either that
timber or yellow pine for their top-fides, can be
built and fitted for taking in a cargo, at thirty-four
dollars, or £.7 13s. fterling per ton; and as good a
veffel cannot be procured in Great Britain, France
or Holland, under fifty-five to fixty dollars.*

As the building of coafting and fifhing veffels,
boats in new forms for our improving inland navigation, veffels on various conftructions for public fervice, and for a very diverfified foreign trade, will not
only keep the art of fhip-building at its prefent height,
but will advance it in all refpects, it appears to be
very doubtful, whether we fhould anxioufly defire
to fupply foreigners with fuch cheap means of ri-
valling us in the carrying trade and fifheries. Our

* The papers of the Britifh fociety for naval architecture fhew,
that fhips fit for the Eaft-India fervice are advanced in their coft,
fince 1771, forty fhillings fterling, nearly equal to nine dollars,
per ton.—that timber is confiderably diminifhed in quantity, and
enhanced in value, in the laft twenty years—that the body of working fhipwrights, in 1789, were much inferior to thofe of twenty
years back—and that the late acts of parliament refpecting regif-
ters of fhips and other regulations intended to increafe Britifh fhip-
building, had not operated in their favour. Profitable employment
for *very expenfive and numerous* fhips cannot be created and extended
by a mere legiflative *fiat*. Beyond a certain degree it cannot be
obtained unlefs the reft of the world neglect thofe means which
Great-Britain purfues to increafe and maintain her navigation, foreign trade, and manufactures.

fhip and boat yards are not confined to a fpot, but indeed are more diffufed than formerly. There is no ftate whofe citizens do not purfue the bufinefs, and it is commenced upon the weftern waters. Before the revolution, above half our veffels were paid for by a barter of credit goods for the labour and fkill of the artificer; inftead of which he now generally receives weekly payments in folid coin.

" THAT THE IMPORTS AND EXPORTS OF THE UNITED STATES WILL CONTINUE FOR A LONG TIME THE SAME."

This will be found on examination very erroneous. Pot and pearl afhes are fhipped in an increafed ratio of nineteen to four. The American merchants were once great exporters of iron, hemp, raw hides, and other articles, which they now import in large quantities. The importations of coarfe linens, paper, hats, fhoes, fteel, nails, carriages, malt liquors, and many other articles are confiderably reduced. Should impediments be thrown in the way of our fifheries, fhipping and foreign commerce, there can be no doubt that policy, intereft and feeling will prompt us to purfue with decifion and ardour the objeft of *manufaftures*, which will give employment to our own capital, and that, which we may derive from foreigners. It muft be manifeft, for example, that if we are to receive rum in foreign bottoms, and to be refufed the tranfportation of flour and grain, which are wanted from us in return, we fhall not long continue to ufe foreign fpirits. Our brewers already fupply us with more beer than we confume. No more than 70,000 gallons and 17,500 dozen bottles have been imported in an entire year, ending in Auguft 1790, three times which quantity is made with eafe, by a fingle brewery, on a very modeate fcale. This branch has increafed and flourifhed in the laft two years, and an exportation greater than the importation above ftated, has certainly taken place. The home-made diftilled fpirits are already more than twice as great in quantity, as the fpirits imported. If our tobacco fhips are excluded from France, they will not bring us brandies; and the grain, that will be raifed on our tobacco lands, will yield fpirituous and malt liquors to enable us to relinquifh foreign brandy. Should a confiderable part of our capital be forced out of navigation and foreign trade, the government, without impofing *generally* heavy protecting duties, burdenfome to the nation, may give employment for the money, by holding out effectual encouragement to *one branch of manufactures at a time.* If it be felected with judgment—if the ufe of manual labour be confined within as narrow limits as poffible—if labour-faving machines be ufed—if the raw articles it works on, be made free of impoft duty—if the growth of them be encouraged at home—if a convenient progreffive duty be impofed, there can be little doubt of fuccefs. The example of a well-arranged and fortunate attempt once fet, others will naturally follow; and nations, fome of whofe politicians now grudgingly perceive them to take from us the food they are unable to raife, and who treat as a favour the reception of our precious raw materials, may difcover, when it will be too late, the evils induced by an over-driven fpirit of monopoly *.

" THE CAPACITY OF THE UNITED STATES TO SUPPLY EUROPE WITH GRAIN AND FLOUR."

A recent publication of lord Sheffield's, upon the fubject of the Britifh corn trade, has lately appeared in this country. As in " the obfervations on our commerce," fo in this pamphlet, he endeavours to fhow fallacy in all fuch ideas as favour the importance of the United States to Great-Britain. As this examination has been necelfarily made with

---

* After a very careful eftimate of a number of the principal branches of American manufacture, the writer of this paper does not hefitate to affirm, that the fhoes and boots, fadlery and other articles of leather, gunpowder, fnuff, paper and paper hangings, playing cards, pafteboards, books, linen, cotton, and woolen cloths, hofiery, thread, hats, wool and cotton cards, fet work and watches, manufactures of gold, filver, iron, fteel, brafs, lead, pewter, and copper, cordage, twine, fail-cloth, carriages of all kinds, malt liquors, new fhips and boats, leathern gloves and breeches, parchment, glue, cabinet wares, linfeed oil, foap, candles, potafh, diftilled fpirits, drugs and chemical preparations, and earthen ware, made in the year laft paft, exceed in value the manufactured goods, which Great-Britain fhipped in the fame term, to all foreign nations, but the United States. It will be proper to obferve in this place, that chocolate, cheefe, wafers, ftarch, hair powder, ivory and horn wares, whips, millenary, ftays, windfor chairs, corn fans, wheelbarrows, fpirits of turpentine, paints, brufhes, glafs wares, bricks, ftone and marble wares, *repairs* of veffels, muftard, loaf fugar, falt, the great article of *making up* apparel, coopers' wares, and other things of the nature of manufactures, were not included in the eftimate above mentioned.

little adherence to form or order, and as *the pro-duction and commerce of grain*, conftitute, without any exception, the moft valuable and moft com-manding of our advantages, it will not be impro-per, to take fome notice of this new attempt of his lordfhip's, to diffeminate erroneous information and opinions on American affairs.

According to the lateft of his tables, the Ameri-can *provinces*, in 1770, exported but 46,000 tons of bread, flour, and meal, 578,349 bufhels of In-dian corn, 24,859 bufhels of oats, and 851,240 bufhels of wheat: and he defires it to be believed, that the United States will not be able, in this par-ticular, to exceed their exportations before the re-volution. The return of exports*, fo often men-tioned, contains the following articles.—

724,623 barrels of flour, ⎫
  75,667 do.   of bread, ⎬weighing 77,000 tons.
  99,975 do.   of meal, ⎭
1,124,458 bufhels of wheat,
  21,765 do.   of rye,—-(of which article none
                         was exported in 1770.)
2,102,137 do.   of Indian corn.
  98,842 do.   of oats,
   7,562 do.   of buckwheat, (of which alfo
                      none was exported in 1770.)
  38,752 do.   of peas and beans, (of which alfo
                      none was exported in 1770.)

* *See* the return of exports ending 30th September, 1792. Alfo that ending 30th September, 1793.

It appears, then, that on comparing the acknowledged exports of bread and flour, in 1770, with
thofe of the prefent time, a difference of 50 per
cent. is fhown in favour of our agriculture, and
that we fhip near four times the quantity of Indian
corn, and one-third more of wheat, befides the
new articles of beans, peas, buck-wheat and rye.
The tobacco, exported in the above term, was at
the rate of 36 per cent. per annum more than before the revolution, befides the difference in the
quantity now manufactured. Many circumftances
are combining to turn the attention of the planters
of this article in the grain ftates, towards wheat,
barley, oats, and Indian corn. This is not a new
idea in American farming; for although wheat was
much lower before the revolution than it now is,
the cultivation of tobacco in Virginia and Maryland, was actually declining. The more fouthern
ftates had not then attempted the production of this
article to any confiderable extent. The lands,
which produced the above extra quantity of tobacco, would have yielded 800,000 bufhels of
wheat; the labour would have produced more;
and fuppofing that half the foil and induftry, which
were applied to tobacco in 1789, fhould be appropriated to grain, an addition of 1,400,000 bufhels
might be made to our productions of that article.
To fupply the tobacco, fome of the rich lands of
the more fouthern ftates might be employed in its
cultivation. But lord Sheffield tells the people of
Britain with great gravity, that *only* the weftern
parts of Connecticut, and the ftates of New-York,

New-Jerfey, Delaware, Pennfylvania, Maryland and
Virginia, are capable of yielding wheat. He fhould
have added, that thofe ftates contain twice as much
land as the kingdoms of Great-Britain and Ireland,
thofe iflands being computed at lefs than 100,000
fquare miles by their own geographers. The ftates
of New-Jerfey, Delaware, and Maryland, together
with three-fifths of Pennfylvania, three-fifths of
New-York, and about one half of Virginia, all
which lie fufficiently near to *naturally* navigable
water, to raife grain for exportation, contain above
130,000 fquare miles. Kentucky, North-Carolina,
and the weftern parts of South-Carolina and Georgia, and Vermont, will alfo add confiderably to
our exports of grain, when mills, canals, &c. fhall
encourage the growth and facilitate the tranfportation. But the ftate of population is the point to
which candour and judgment ought to have led a
political economift to advert. He fhould have reflected, that the United States, whofe territory is
about 1,000,000 of fquare miles, are not yet cultivated and inhabited, by more than 4,000,000 people*; that Great-Britain and Ireland, with about a
tenth of the land (or 100,000 fquare miles) have
twice the agricultural population; and that the productive powers of this country, (which appears to
have doubled its people in 25 years, though injured by eight years of a deftructive war,) are *a mean
of human fuftenance,* to which the more prudent

---

* The actual number of the inhabitants of the United States
appears to be from 3,900,000 to 4,000,000. See appendix, paper A. A. D. 1791.

nations of Europe will, and to which all, in the time of need, muft have recourfe. If their governments prevent it, many of their manufacturers and mechanics at leaft muft flee from them. The fupreme law of neceffity will have its due operation, and people, whofe means are rendered, by injudicious regulations, unequal to their wants will certainly refort to thofe fcenes where cheaper food and better wages infure them relief.

It is manifeft that the great increafe of our population has been attended with a very confiderable addition to our exports of eatables. The ftatement made in the beginning of the obfervations, on this article, is a proof of it. Befides this, our fhipments of beef and pork,* are above two and a half times greater than in 1770, of butter four times, of cheefe two and a half times, of potatoes four times, and of rice nearly as great. Add to this, that we have almoft put an end to the importation of malt liquors, (a manufacture from grain,) and that we fhip as much of them as we import— that we have diminifhed our importation of diftilled fpirits, by 1,000,000 of gallons, fince we loft the importation of Britifh rum in our own veffels (though our population is more numerous by 1,500,000 of perfons) which has occafioned the diftillation of grain liquors to the amount probably of 4,000,000 of gallons, requiring near 2,000,000 bufhels of grain, as the raw materials.

* They were five times as great in 1792

Our continuing to export fo large quantities of grain and flour, notwithſtanding this great conſumption of rye, barley, oats, and even wheat in diſtilling and brewing, is a ſtrong proof of our raiſing much more than in former times. But it is not to be forgotten, that conſiderable quantities are conſumed by our *manufacturers*, who are rapidly increaſing. It is extremely difficult to aſcertain the proportion in which theſe valuable citizens contribute to the population of our towns. Their numbers in the city of Philadelphia may aſſiſt to furniſh ſome ground for a reaſonable eſtimate. The ſilverſmiths, brewers, diſtillers, ſhip-carpenters, cabinetmakers, cordwainers, tallow-chandlers, ſoap-boilers, white and blackſmiths, ſteel-makers, turners, braziers, 'coachmakers, copperſmiths, hatters, tailors, weavers, dyers, leather breeches makers, glovers, and ſuch other perſons as may be properly claſſed under the head of *manufacturers* (excluſively of houſe-carpenters, maſons, painters, victuallers, bakers, barbers, and others, who cannot be correctly denominated ſo) appear to be about 2,200 perſons. The city and ſuburbs being found to contain near 43,000 men, women, and children, and it being generally ſuppoſed, that the adult males are about one-fifth of the whole number, it would appear, that of the 8,600 adult males, contained in Philadelphia, above one-fourth are manufacturers, and conſequently, that of the eatables, and home-made drinkables, conſumed in that town, above one-fourth are required for their uſe and that of their wives, children, journeymen, ap

prentices, and fervants: and an addition for the grain
confumed by their horfes and cows may be fairly
made. This ftate of things, it is believed, is exceeded by many of the towns in the eaftern ftates,
and in fome interior fituations,* where it is manifeft that fewer are employed in the learned profeffions, and foreign commerce, and not fo many live
upon their incomes.

It will not be afferted, that the United States
are able to feed all the nations of Europe at the
fame time, nor that they afford any promife
of fo extenfive a capacity in future. Neither are
fuch ideas conveyed by the reprefentation of the
committee of the Britifh privy council, on which
lord Sheffield fo feelingly animadverts. They
reprefent, as the refult of a careful and deliberate
enquiry, their thorough conviction, that the countries of Europe, taken collectively, do not produce, in ordinary years, an aggregate quantity of
grain, larger than what appears requifite for the
confumption of their inhabitants: and they proceed to obferve, that in the event of a failure of
crops, a "*fupply can only be had from America.*" The
reafonable meaning of their reprefentation is, that
as Europe is an extenfive and populous region,
making great, conftant, and inevitable demands for
food, producing in ordinary feafons, that is, ufually, *a mere competent fupply*, but *no excefs*, and as it is

---

* Several inland towns in Pennfylvania, and Winchefter, in
Virginia, have been afcertained to exceed the city of Philadelqhia,
in the proportion of manufacturers.

liable to *partial* and even *general failures* of crops, it muft, in the event of one of thofe *partial* or general misfortunes, look to fome other quarter of the world for relief. With the exception of Barbary, whofe capacity to fupply appears to be much more limited than ours, no other country than America could prefent itfelf to the committee. Great allowances fhould have been made for thofe gentlemen, by lord Sheffield, admitting, for a moment, that they were wrong, as it appears probable they may have been mifled by feveral parts of his treatife on our commerce, which really tend to confirm their doctrine. In that publication, under the head of *wheat and flour,* he obferves, " that Canada, Nova-Scotia, and *the American ftates* are likely to have moft of the corn trade which England had." Our fupplies *to* Nova Scotia have been ftated; and *as they are admitted from us only when neceffity requires them,* the exifting licenfe of the governor of that province to introduce American flour, grain, and live ftock *through the whole of the fummer* (and indeed from May to November) when *the navigation of Canada is open,* will anfwer our enquiries about the capacity of thofe provinces to take away the corn trade from England. Under the fame head, and on the following page, he further fays, " the American ftates were *more than competitors* with us for the wheat trade; they had for fome years engroffed *nearly the whole* of what we had; and it is computed, upon an average of five years, they had received from Spain and Portugal upwards of £.320,000

fterling, per annum, for that grain." It will furely be deemed very reafonable in the committee to
fuppofe that the United Sates, which were faid
to have fupplied the two kingdoms of Spain and
Portugal, for five fucceffive years, with *wheat alone*
to the amount of £.320,000 fterling, could have
furnifhed to Great Britain the lefs fum of £.291,000
fterling, in all kinds of grain and flour, which
they have paid to foreign nations for twenty years
paft. Under the head of " fhips built for fale,"
lord Sheffield again confirms the ideas of the committee, by faying, in very handfome and forcible
language, " America had *robbed* us, at leaft for a
time, of a corn trade, that fome time ago brought
in to us as much as almoft any article of export,'
As his lordfhip confiders an honeft competition of
fellow citizens in the light of *robbery*, the reafona-
blenefs of his other conceptions, will, no doubt, be
duly examined.

Lord Sheffield leads to a material error, affecting the juft eftimation of our corn trade, when he
ftates tobacco to be the principal article of American commerce. It appears, by the return of the
treafury, that *flour* is the moft valuable and (exclufively of the connected articles of bread, wheat
and other grain) it exceeded tobacco by a quarter
of a million of dollars. Wheat (including the
commodities made of it) is one-third more valuable than tobacco; and as this laft production appears to have been advanced in quantity, 36 per

cent. on a comparifon with the exportation of the year 1770, when lord Sheffield ftates it to have been our firft, the increafed importance of wheat is manifefted.*

If we turn our eyes from Great-Britain to other countries, the American grain trade does not appear to be lefs interefting to Europe and her colonies. Spain, Portugal, the wine iflands, the Bahamas, Bermuda, the fugar colonies, the northern Britifh colonies, and the foreign fifheries, regularly demand from us fome of the various articles, which it comprehends. The cultivation of the vine, the advancement of their colonies, the extenfion of commerce, and the increafe of the manufactures of France, which two laft are to be expected in confequence of the revolution in that kingdom, render it highly probable that they will not be able to do without fupplies from other countries. It is the opinion of one of their beft writers,† that they do not ordinarily export more than one-fifteenth of their crop. Should any accident—(the introduction of Britifh and Dutch manufacturers, who are accuftomed to beer, for example)—lead them into breweries, than which nothing is more poffible, that fmall proportion of furplus would be quickly engroffed. There is an highly interefting idea, on this point, which has been recently ftarted, and which may attract the attention of their practical

* See exports of 1792 and 1793.   † Necker.

politicians: the opinion referred to is, that every country which manufactures largely, is in a situation of confiderably lefs danger of want, if its people ordinarily ufe drinks made from *grain ;* becaufe the dreadful confequences of famine may be avoided with certainty and eafe, by converting to the ufe of food, the grain which will be regularly procured from agriculture or importation, to fupply the demands of the brewers and diftillers. The Dutch have been always unable to raife more than a fmall proportion of their bread-ftuff and the modern eftimates of their population countenance the prefumption of a large increafe. They are, moreover, great brewers and diftillers from grain : and their fugar colonies, on the fouthern main, have wonderfully advanced. Thefe fymptoms of new demand, on the part of the European nations, together with the certain requifitions of grain arifing from the univerfal increafe of manufactures and attention to foreign trade, are accompanied by fome important circumftances, which prevent a proportionate production of that indifpenfible neceffary. The growth of private wealth in many parts of Europe, particularly in Britain, the confequent increafe of horfes for equipages and other purpofes of pleafure, the laying out of park grounds, and the diverfion of lands from the lefs profitable production of grain to that of grafs, the declenfion of agriculture in Poland, by reafon of the extreme badnefs of their internal arrangements, the probable increafe of Polifh manufactures, fhould they become free, the continual

efforts of the European manufacturers to draw away
the labourers of the farmers, the greater prevalence
of emigration to their colonies and other countries
among the cultivators, than among the manufacturers, owing to the wretched situation of the agricultural poor in countries, where the high value of
land renders it in effect a monopoly, and the present univerfal attention to political reformation,
which for a time interrupts agriculture, are among
the caufes here contemplated.

But it is not unfair to afk, from what fource are
the maritime countries of Europe to be fupplied,
in the event of a failure of the crops of *one* or *more*
of them, in fo great a degree as from the United
States? The value of grain, flour, meal, and
bread, from the United States greatly exceeds that
of the fame articles from the kingdom of Naples
and its connected ifland of Sicily, which have been
confidered as the granary of the Mediterranean.
Poland, once termed the granary of Europe, is lefs
extenfive including (Lithuania) than the country of
the United States, which furnifhes grain for Europe.
Its exports are not afcertained: but there appear
ftrong prefumptions, that it does not fhip through
Dantzick and Elbing, half as great a value of grain,
and the articles made of grain, as the United States.
Britain, Spain, Portugal, Holland, and lately Flanders, are obliged to import. Ruffia is faid to have
fhipped in 1787, wheat and rye to the amount of near
1,000,000 of bufhels, but imports grain liquors;
and manufactures are growing, and wars are fre-

quent in that kingdom. Sweden imports very large quantities of rye, and ſhips no grain. That article is much the firſt among the imports of Denmark and Norway. Pruſſia produces much corn, and exports ſome: but manufactures are greatly advanced in that kingdom; and the home conſumption of grain will probably equal the production, in a few years. In ſhort, a careful and impartial ſurvey of Europe. will confirm the opinion of the committee of the privy council, that the productions of grain in that quarter of the world, are not generally ſpeaking, more than equal to the conſumption of its inhabitants. A moment's recollection will remind us that even thoſe countries which do not commonly import grain, are, upon the occurrence of ſmall diſappointments, obliged to ſeek it from America, and other foreign ſtates; that ſome parts of Europe conſtantly import from us in large quantities; that all of them ſteadily, or occaſionally, directly, or indirectly, ſupply their colonies from hence; that ſince the manufactures of Great-Britain have been ſo far extended, as to employ ſix elevenths of her people, and ſince the extenſion of her manufacture of grain liquors in particular, her dependence for a portion of her bread upon foreign nations, is proved to be unavoidable, by the moſt ſettled maxims of her own political economiſts; that her real deficiency is *the irremovable want* of the requiſite proportion of agriculturaliſts; and finally, that even in the preſent ſtate of our population, the United States actually contribute much more to the ſupply of the nations of Europe and their colonies, with grain, bread, and flour, than any two, perhaps any three countries in the world; and that their capacity to enlarge that supply, is steadily and rapidly increasing.

This subject has been dwelt upon the longer from its high importance to the United States, and to the general happiness of mankind; and from the new proofs which lord Sheffield has given of a particular indisposition, that Britain should appear to rely on the United States, even in the smallest degree, though we give a greater support to her manufacturers and shipping than any two other foreign nations. It is feared, that nothing beneficial can be expected between the two countries, if the errors and prejudices of so professed a champion against us, have not a very cautious hearing. It will not be deemed unreasonable or improper, to consider in that light a writer, who, in his first book, labours to show, that the production and commerce of grain are bad objects of attention to the American states, because (as he alleges) Europe seldom wants it; and who, in his second book, takes equal pains to prove, that America cannot raise grain for the wants even of Great-Britain itself, when he finds it established on the highest British authority, that their own kingdom and those of other nations in Europe, can only look to America for the deficiency of supply, which the increase of manufactures, of people, of grass and pasturage, of grain liquors, and the uncertainty of seasons, in one or another of them, is constantly producing. He

will prove a bad politician , and a very bad Britifh
patriot, who fhall animate againft the manufactures
of Great-Britain, *the body of the American planters
and farmers*, by promoting a fevere fyftem, which
fhall debar them of a chance of making returns for
an immenfe demand of Britifh fabrics, in the unmanufactured productions of their foil and labour.
But independent of the danger to Britain, from lift-
ening at this time, to fo profeffed an anti-American,
a wife nation will not give too much attention to a
writer, whofe ardent fpirit of monopoly leads him
to attempt to circumvent the fame foreign nation,
in her purfuits of commerce—of manufactures—
and even of her great, beft bufinef , the tillage of
a various and productive foil. If the policy of
England ought to be a dereliction of fome parts of
her fyftem of internal or external commerce in favour of agriculture, let her politicians firmly maintain the doctrine. America will approve their
patriotifm. But in doing this, it furely is not neceffary to depreciate the largeft purchafers of thofe
manufactures, on which the exiftence of more than
half their people depends. It may be well to reflect too that the induftry and foil, which foreign
corn laws may tend to deprive of their accuftomed
object, can be applied to the production of hemp,
flax, wool, cotton, leather, and iron, or their preparation in the form of fabrics to fubftitute for
theirs. It is happy for the United States, that whenever they are injured in the lofs of a vent for any
portion of a particular production, they can create
a market for it by checking the introduction of

some connected foreign commodity, and making a succedaneum for it at home. *See paper S.*

Though it would not be difficult, in purfuing, the examination of lord Sheffield's obfervations, to adduce many more proofs, that his facts are often erroneous, and his obfervations frequently unjuft; and that his predictions have not been verified, but often contradicted by experience, the fubject will not be further purfued. It is confided, that enough has been faid, to induce an attentive revifion of his book. This, it is believed, will be fufficient to lead the Britifh nation to look in future to other fources of information. It may be obferved, in ex-tenuation of his lordfhip's errors, that the circum-ftances of the United States are confiderably alter-ed fince he wrote: but this will not juftfy the con-fidence of his *predictions*, nor apologize for the wild errors of them; and it may not improperly be again remarked to thofe, who are convinced of this great and happy change in our fitua-tion, fince the year 1784, that a conduct on the part of foreigners, which might have been deemed prudent when our political horizon was darkly clouded, would be unwife now, and might be dangerous to fome of their interefts hereafter. Of this lord Sheffield's late book proves him to be not duly fenfible.

The United States have many features of natu-ral ftrength, and many advantages from their local

pofition. The friends of other forms of government will admit, that they have exhibited a highly improved example of a republic, and that they
have pra 6tifed upon the plan, fince it was formed, though not a very long time, with extraordinary fuccefs. They have no occafion to make
war for territory; and they are confiderably removed from the danger of foreign enterprifes aginft
them. Their produ 6tions are remarkably diverfified, and confequently adapted to various purpofes and ufes, and are, with a few exceptions, either
neceffaries of life, or articles of fuch general demand and confumption, as to be nearly as much
fought. Having been recently a part of an intelligent and enterprifing commercial nation, and having a very extenfive fea-coaft, the citizens of America have been infenfibly led to furvey all the regions of foreign commerce, and in paffing through
moft of them, have manifefted, fince the reformation of their political fyftem, every talent requifite for the honourable and lucrative purfuit of
trade. The redundant ftate of private wealth in
feveral foreign nations, promifes every addition
to our a 6tive capital, that occafion can require, if
we preferve *the honeft fpirit* with which the reforms
of the general and ftate governments have been
lately made, and the wifdom with which they have
been adminiftered. The fulnefs of the European
population, and the degree in which every walk,
commercial, manufa 6turing, and agricultural, is
crouded there, afford reafon to expe 6t the fteady

increaſe of our people.* Civil and religious liberty, now ſettled on rational and tried principles,
certify an exemption from all real oppreſſion.

Being diſpoſed to promote the freedom of
commerce, the United States would probably have
made no regulations, but with a view to revenue,
had they not met in almoſt every country, duties
and reſtrictions in their home trade, and charges,
prohibitions and excluſions, in their colonial trade.
But although ſome nations will not permit us to
ſhip them certain of our articles, others withhold
from us certain of theirs, and others impede, abſo-
lutely or in effect, the introduction of our own
goods in our own bottoms, yet we have hitherto
contented ourſelves with a ſmall addition to the
rates of our tariff, and to the tonnage on ſhips,
both together not exceeding £. 87,000, ſterling, *on
all foreign nations taken together.* It will not be
alleged, that this ſum will bear a ſerious compariſon with the injuries our agriculture, manufactures
and commerce ſuſtain from ſeveral of the principal
European powers.

To obtain relief by arrangements as beneficial
to foreign ſtates as to ourſelves, will probably be
the liberal aim of our government. It is confidently expected, that mutual benefits will create and
cement a ſtrong and laſting friendſhip in the çaſe

* Almoſt every comfortable country in Europe, as to the ſtate
of its population, is arrived at an abſolute *plethora.*

of thole nations with which such arrangements
shall be formed; and with regard to others, the
wisdom of the legislature, no doubt, will be sedu-
loufly exercised either temperately to meet them
with the requisite policy and firmnefs, or to trans-
fer from their hands, to those of more equitable
nations, the unrequited benefits they receive from
us—or to derive from our own skill, capital, credit, and industry, the accomodations and supplies
which they have heretofore furnished upon terms
of great advantage to themselves, but which have
been inadequately reciprocated to the United
States.

SECTION VII.

CONTAINING A TABLE OF THE PRINCIPAL RESTRICTIONS,
IMPOSITIONS AND PROHIBITIONS SUSTAINED BY THE
UNITED STATES, IN THEIR TRADE WITH THE BRITISH
DOMINIONS, AND OF THOSE SUSTAINED BY GREAT-BRI-
TAIN IN HER TRADE WITH THE DOMINIONS OF THE
UNITED STATES: ALSO SOME REMARKS ON CERTAIN
PREVALENT TOPICS, RELATIVE TO THE GENERAL BUSI-
NESS BETWEEN THE TWO COUNTRIES.

THE intention of the foregoing examination
being folely the correction of error in the statement
of facts, and in the opinions or conclusions deduced
from them, it has appeared on consideration, not
to be improper to pursue the subject with the same
views, a little further. An idea, that the balance
of favour or indulgence is received by the United
States, frequently appears in the publications, and

is said to prevail in the minds of persons of weight and influence in Great-Britain. It may not therefore be useless to bring up to view the principal facts, relative to the question of reciprocity of commercial regulation. An attempt will be made to throw this statement into the form of a table, as it will be the more clear and impressive.

GREAT-BRITAIN	THE UNITED STATES
Prohibits American vessels from entering into the ports of several parts of her dominions, viz. the West-Indies, Canada, Nova-Scotia, New-Brunswick, Newfoundland, Cape Breton, Hudson's Bay, Honduras Bay, and her East-India spice market.	Admit British vessels into *all* their ports, subject to a tonnage duty of 44 cents, or 24 sterling pence, more than American vessels, and an addition of one tenth to the amount of the impost accruing on their cargoes.
She imposes double light money on American vessels in most of her ports.	They do not impose extra light money on British vessels in any of their ports.
She prohibits the navigating, *ad libitum*, of American vessels, by native or other seamen.	They admit the navigating of British vessels by native or other seamen, *ad libitum*.
She prohibits the employment of American-built ships by her own citizens, in many branches of trade, upon any terms.	They admit the employment of British-built ships by their own citizens, in every branch of trade upon the terms of 44 cents extra per ton, and one tenth extra on the impost arising from their cargoes.
She charges a duty on American sail cloth, made up in the United States for British ships.	They do not charge a duty on British sail-cloth, made up in Great-Britain for American ships.

GREAT-BRITAIN.

She prohibits the importation of goods from several parts of her dominions into others, in American vessels, upon any terms.

She prohibits the importation of goods into Great-Britain, by American vessels from any other country than the U. S.

She prohibits the importation into Great-Britain from the United States, by American vessels, of all goods not produced by the United States.

She prohibits the importation of any goods previously brought into the United States, from the said states into Great-Britain, even in British vessels.

She prohibits the exportation of several articles from Great-Britain to the United States.

She lays duties of various rates upon the exportation of many articles to the United States.

She prohibits the importation of all manufactures from the United States, into her European dominions, and her colonies, unless it be some very simple preparations, and decoctions, requisite to her navy, shipping and manufactures.

She imposes very considerable duties upon some of the *agricul-*

THE UNITED STATES.

They admit the importation of goods from any part of their dominions into another, in British vessels, on the terms of 44 cents per ton extra on the vessel.

They admit the importation of goods into the United States, in British vessels, from *every* country whatever.

They do not prohibit the importation into the United States from Great-Britain, by British vessels, of any goods not produced by Great-Britain.

They do not prohibit the importation of any goods previously brought into Great-Britain, from that kingdom into the United States, in either British or American bottoms.

They do not prohibit the exportation of any article from the United States to Great-Britain.

They do not lay a duty on the exportation of any article whatever to Great-Britain.

They do not prohibit the importation of any manufacture whatever from Great-Britain.

They impose moderate duties (lower than any other foreign

GREAT-BRITAIN.   THE UNITED STATES.

tural productions of the United States, and excludes others by duties equal to their value.

nation by 2 3, and 4 for one) on the *produce and manufactures* of Great-Britain, except in a very few inftances, and exclude fcarcely any articles by duties equal to their value.

She prohibits for confiderable terms of time, fome of the principal *agricultural* productions of the United States, and others at all times.

They prohibit none of the agricultural productions of Great-Britain or her dominions.

It is underftood that by treaty fhe grants fome favours, which are not extended to the United States.

They treat Great-Britain as favourably as any nation whatever, as to fhips, imports, and exports, and in all other refpects.

She prohibits the importation of fome American articles, in American fhips, or any but Britifh fhips, into her European dominions.

They do not prohibit the importation of any Britifh article in Britifh veffels or any but American veffels.

She does not permit an American citizen to import goods into fome of her dominions, and to fell them there even in Britifh veffels. In other parts of her dominions, fhe lays an extra tax on him, or his fales.

They permit a Britifh citizen to import goods into all their ports, in any veffels, and to fell them there without any extra tax on him, or his fales.

She impofes heavy duties on certain articles of the produce of the American fifheries, and infupportable duties on others, in fome parts of her dominions: and in other parts, fhe prohibits their importation.

They impofe only five per cent. on the produce of the Britifh fifheries (which duty is drawn back on exportation) and admit every article derived from them.

She prohibits the confumption of fome American articles, of

They do not prohibit the confumption of any Britifh article

GREAT-BRITAIN.   THE UNITED STATES.

which she permits the importation.	whatever.
She prohibits the importation of American articles from foreign countries into the British dominions, even in her own ships.	They do not prohibit the importation of British articles from foreign countries in any ships.

In detailing the regulations of foreign nations, so various and complex as those of Great-Britain, it is not easy to be correct. The above statement, however, is sincerely believed to contain the substance of the existing British restrictions, prohibitions and impositons, upon commerce, so far as they have any relation to the possible or actual intercourse with the United States. Those which are to be found in the acts of Congress, or which result from them, are few, and are also intended to be correctly given in the table. On a review of the whole of these regulations, it will be perceived, that those of the United States are considerably more favourable to the subjects of the British crown, and their manufactures, produce and navigation, than those of Great-Britain are to the corresponding interests of the citizens of the United States. It has appeared necessary to make a statement in detail and by a comparative contrast, in order that we might render manifest *the absolute and important truth,* that the commercial impediments to Great-Britain in the laws of the United States, are much less considerable than those in the acts of the British parliament are to the United States. Had this ftatement been confined to *the ifland of Great-Britain* alone, on the one part, and our dominions at large, on the other, it would have been found, that our obftructions to Britifh commerce are far lefs than thofe which Britain throws in the way of the commerce of the United States. But it is juft and natural for us, in confidering a *national* fubject, to take into our eftimation the whole of the territories of the Britifh crown, and the whole population, trade, manufactures, and productions thereof, more efpecially as it is plain, that all confiderations, relative to the American fide, are extended to our whole territory and all its appertenances and relative circumftances. Should Great-Britain prove, that exceptions refpecting colonies are as reafonable on her part, as they are fafhionable, ftill it remains to be counterbalanced, that no fuch exceptions are made by us; for we treat the veffels, produce and citizens of *the colonies,* as we treat thofe of Britain. If it is politic and right, that the parliament of Great-Britain fhould exclude us from their colonial trade, then Great-Britain ought not to complain of any *countervailing* regulations, which may exclude her from fome *equivalent* advantage in our trade: and fo in regard to any other country. Should it be proved, that all nations have interdicted their colonial trade to foreigners, it will be no lefs eafy to fhow, that the withholding of any kind of advantage from a foreign nation, by reafon of the particular circumftances of the reftricting party, has always been deemed a juftification for fome correfponding reftriction on the part of the country suffering. But it cannot be proved, that all nations prohibit the participation in their colonial trade to foreigners. The French, the Swedes, the Danes, and the Dutch govern themselves differently from Britain, and from one another. The interdicting rule is not universal. It cannot be rendered permanent, uniform, or precise. It must, therefore, be liable, like other commercial objects, to *legislative discretion and treaty*, and must be involved in the general question of *reciprocity*. Were this not the case, the greatest political absurdities would be induced. Let it be supposed for a moment, that two European nations possess transmarine colonies of equal value, and that one of them grants a perfect freedom of the trade of her colonies to the United States, while the other absolutely refuses that advantage to us. It will not be alleged, that the last of these nations has claims to a participation in the commerce of the United States, equal to those of the former. Further—the distinction taken, with regard to *colonies*, does not apply to all the transmarine dominions of the British crown. Canada, Nova-Scotia, New-Brunswic, Jamaica, and a part of the island of St. Christophers, for example, are *conquered countries*, to whose commerce, considerations other than colonial, apply. And were the idea of colonies strictly adhered to, (viz. the establishment of bodies of natives, who have emigrated from a state, and settled in a new country, politically connected with the old one,) it would be found, that several of the new states of America are more truly colonies of the older ftates, than feveral of the iflands and provinces, which bear the appellation, are colonies of Great-Britain.

As it has been an uniform opinion of lord Shef-field and other perfons in England, that fhip-build-ing would be annihilated in the United States, the prefent ftate of that bufinefs, it is hoped, will deftroy fome material mifcalculations, and will prove, that we do not labour under an inability to carry our own productions without the aid of *any one* foreign nation. If we have not yet encoun-tered the expenfe of a navy, let it be remembered, that Pruffia, which has many more private veffels than Ruffia, has acted the fame part; although the emprefs, of the latter country with fewer merchant-fhips, than any maritime power in Europe, and much fewer than the United States, has neverthe-lefs a very formidable navy.

Nations, which at prefent enjoy any confi-derable portion of the American trade, muft fuf-tain very unfavourable confequences from the con-tinuance of impediments or burdens on our future intercourfe with their dominions. Our exports, being tranfported in our own fhips and thofe of any lefs unkind country, will advance the manu-factures and trade of a nation adjacent and rival to them—or, fent to the colonies of more favourable nations, will greatly increafe the growth of inter-fering colonial productions. It is with the utmoft difficulty that any nation now accomplifhes circuitous supplies of other European countries with our produce ; and it *has become our duty to make foreign nations senfible of the difadvantages of double freights and charges, under which they receive our productions,* the lofs arifing from which, falls in part, upon our farmers, and, in part, upon their citizens, who are the confumers. Aggravating impediments to our trade, are now deeply and conftantly wound-ing the manufaĉturers in Europe, who work up American raw materials, or who fupply us with their fabrics. Duties on our iron, for example, reduced the price, and thus occafioned it to be bought at home to manufaĉture : and fo of other native raw materials. The refufal of cotton, and other raw articles, not of our growth, in any bottoms, from America, makes them cheaper to our manufaĉturers, or to the exporters of them for the ufe of thofe European manufaĉturers, whofe laws will permit them to be received from hence. Impediments in the way of our fhipping, or heavy duties on merchandife from hence, occafion the merchants, as before obferved, in regard to our produce, to fend foreign raw materials to countries, that will admit the veffels and goods upon more eafy terms. Nations, in this enlightened age, will more and more avail themfelves of *the miftakes* that obtain in the commercial regulations of their neighbours and rivals : and the errors of reftrictions and duties, fo far as they fhall be really impolitic, will thus induce a certain and confequent fuffering by thofe who impofe them on us. So, as one country drives our veffels and produce from her ports, others may be thereby induced to open their markets to them. The currents of commerce, like those of the rivers, will certainly be turned from that fide where obstructions are created.

The United States have been led to serious and beneficial reflection on their affairs, by the prevailing disposition to restrict their intercourse with Europe, and the severer regulations of several nations in regard to the commerce of their transmarine dominions. They are prompted to decide, that the immense savings and the extensive advantages they can derive from manufactures, protected by their own laws, render them no less worthy of a share of their capital and industry, than commerce. The importance of this object has been forced upon the minds of many, by European restrictions: and a continuance of those restrictions, will, though gradually, yet infallibly, make converts of the whole nation. So weighty are the considerations relative to manufactures, in the opinions of many, that it begins to be seriously questioned, whether the employment of a share of 20 or 25,000 tons of vessels in the British West-India trade, and of less than half that quantity in the trade to their remaining colonies, ought to induce our consent materially to keep down or diminish any salutary duties on foreign manufactures. The American impost is now very moderate, compared with that of other nations; unquestionably the most so of any which British goods encounter in foreign countries. It does not exceed, on a medium, 8 or 9 per cent.

Were it to be increafed to 14, 20, 25, 28, and even $33\frac{1}{3}$ per cent. as in France, Spain and Portugal—were prohibitions to be added on fome articles, as in thofe countries, and on all articles, as in one or two others, (with a judicious poftponement of the time, for the ftrongeft regulations to take place) what would be the confequences, what the effects upon the tranfplanting of foreign capital and manufactures to the United States? It may be urged, that we fhould be injured by fuch prohibition, or even by the higher rates of duty above mentioned. So far as we did not get manufactures eftablifhed, in the mean time, that might be the cafe; but the fame might be obferved, in regard to the commercial regulations of Great-Britain, fome of which really injure her; and many of which deeply injure Ireland, the Weft-Indies, and the remaining colonies.

If it is in the power of Great-Britain to draw from other countries, the articles fhe obtains from us of better quality, and upon lower terms, which is often afferted to be poffible, it is not to be forgotten, that by ceafing to receive any goods from the United States, the benefit of employing her fhips will be fo far loft. The articles rejected may be fomewhat more difficult for us to fell, and therefore will be neceffarily converted, in a greater degree than at prefent, into manufactures, or they may go to fupply other nations, who now purchafe thofe foreign articles, which it is alledged Britain can procure with more advantage. Among the objections

Great-Britain ought to have to this, the foreign connections we shall be thereby led to form, and the cement it will give to old ones, will not be found the least. But the assertion really is not true. The furs and skins, the oak timber, oak boards, oak planks, staves, potash, pearlash, ginseng the same qualities of rice, some qualities of tobacco, the grain, in case of short European crops, and some of the naval stores cannot be obtained in quantity and quality from other countries.

We are not infrequently reminded, when the loss of the American market and our consumption of British manufactures are spoken of, that, notwithstanding our former non-importation agreements, and the interruptions of the war, the British manufactories were more flourishing, than during the previous peace, when our demand was the greatest. There appear to be some reasons, however, for doubting the truth of this assertion. The tables in Anderson's commerce, already mentioned, state the exports of the year 1774 at £.17,607,447, and those of 1781, at £.11,470,388. This declension was regular, almost every year's exports being less than those of the preceding. These facts are the more remarkable, as the imports of Great-Britain in 1781, were greater than those in 1776, or in any intermediate year, and the prices of raw articles and provisions exported, were higher. It is to be observed, also, that large exports for the British merchants and dealers, who sold extra supplies to their armies and navies in America, the West and

Eaft-Indies, Gibraltar, &c. were made, for the ufe of the great number of officers, foldiers, and fea-men, employed in thofe places. The extra public purchafes of clothing, tents, arms, cordage, fail cloth, porter, and other *manufactured* articles, for their fea and land forces, muft have been immenfe, when we reflect, that about £.14,000,000 per an-num, on an average of the term of the war, was added to their debt, befides the great fums of mo-ney collected and paid within the year; and that the fupplies granted for 1781, exceed thofe of 1774 by £.19,300,000, a larger fum by 100 per cent. than Great-Britain ufually exported in manufac-tures prior to the late treaty of peace. The ex-penditures of fuch a war, muft, indeed, occafion the woolen, linen, leathern and metal branches, and feveral others, to flourifh exceedingly: but the confequences in regard to the increafe of burdens on the people, and to the national prof-perity, muft be viewed in the moft ferious light. In the time of the war, too, foreign manufactures could be lefs eafily introduced into their own markets, which left the demand for confump-tion and importation to be fupplied by their own people. It is to be obferved further, that the eight years which followed 1774, were thofe in which machinery was firft rendered confiderably profita-ble in Great-Britain. Before the American war, the cotton branch was very inconfiderable in that country; but though it has increafed wonderfully fince the peace, it muft have felt a very large ad-vancement during the term in which our regular importations from thence were cut off. Other branches were aided during thofe years, by the introduction of machinery, manual flight and new proceffes, fo as to diminifh the effects of the interruption of the American demand. It is in the higheft degree probable, that the lofs of our confumption would be fenfibly felt at this time. In a feafon of peace, the enormous extra demand for the ufe of their armies and navy does not exift. Ireland now menaces Great-Britain with the diminution of her importations. Such extraordinary *new* inventions of mechanical and chemical aid are not to be expected again—and the United States might derive a very confiderable degree of independency on Britifh manufactures, by the adoption of labour-faving machines, (the peculiar value of which, to them, they are beginning to perceive) in the cotton, flaxen, hempen, metal, and part of the woolen and filken branches, to all of which raw materials they apply. The capacities of the United States for eftablifhing thefe mills, and manufactures in general will be exemplified in the cafe of New-Jerfey, which by a return in 1784, is afcertained to have had then 41 fulling-mills, 8 furnaces, 79 forges, 366 faw-mills, 508 grift-mills, and 192 tan-yards, though her population appears to be about one part in twenty-one of that of the United States. Were the United Netherlands to feize a moment of uneafinefs between us and Great-Britain, and were they to devote their fhipping and immenfe private capital to the fupply and promotion of machine manufactures, they would prove dangerous rivals to England in all foreign markets: and the fame may be faid in regard to the efforts of other countries, if they were ferioufly to undertake manufactures by labour-faving machinery.

It may be fairly afked, what country fupports the navy of Great-Britain, in fo great a degree as the United States, by the employment they give to her fhips? The Ruffian trade furnifhes cargoes for much lefs than 230,000 tons, which is the exact quantity of Britifh veffels that cleared from thefe ftates, in the year following Auguft 1789. The whole Baltic trade of Great-Britain, with all the countries of the various powers that lie within the found, important as it is to her, does not fill more. Their trade with Holland, France, Spain, and Portugal, does not all together employ as many veffels. Their whole fifheries, American colonial trade, and Weft-India trade, do not employ and load more.* And how, it may be further afked, are the United States requited for thus ftrengthening the acknowledged bulwark of Great-Britain, by annually giving a complete lading to the unequalled quantity of 230,000 tons of her private veffels? The whole of the American veffels, which have arrived in our ports, in the fame year, from all

* It appears from a Britifh ftatement of their trade with all the world, and authentic documents publifhed by Congrefs, that their veffels, cleared out from the United States in 1791 and 1792, were about equal in tonnage to all the Britifh veffels cleared out of Great-Britain for Ruffia, Denmark and Norway, Sweden, Pruffia, Poland, Hamburg, Bremen, and Germany in general. A. D. 1793.

the countries and places fubject to the Britifh crown, amount to no more than 43,580 tons. Yet there are not wanting perfons, who will affirm, that the balance of *favour* is given to the United States: and, that Great-Britain is fo far injured by our deportment, as to juftify a retaliation upon us!

There are fome confiderations drawn from the ftate of things in Europe, which ought to render the Britifh commerce with the United States and the confumption of Britifh manufactures by the citizens of this country, matters of greater than former importance. The infufion of republican qualities into the governments of that quarter of the world, will be followed by the extenfion of trade, internal and external. The character of the merchant and manufacturer will be duly efteemed, and large portions of dormant capital, and numerous claffes of inactive men, will be turned by circumftances to employments, which will have loft their ancient imaginary difrepute. The tendency of fuch events, in regard to the fupply of raw materials, and in regard to manufactures which America now draws from Great-Britain, will not be difficult to difcover.

A reliance is fometimes placed upon the difpofition of the fouthern parts of the United States of America, in favour of fuch regulations of commerce, as would be agreeable to Great-Britain— that is, the eafy and unincumbered admiffion of her fhips and manufactures into our ports. What-

ever truth there may be in regard to fome of thofe
ftates, it is known they are far from unanimous,
on that fubject. It may be queftioned, too, whether meafures, which would create difputes, and
interrupt the Britifh trade with America, would
not be difagreeable and inconvenient to the merchants and manufacturers of Great-Britain, as was
manifeftly the cafe on the occafion of the late difference with Ruffia. Ports circumftanced as Li-
verpool and Lancafter, which have large concerns
in fhips and comparatively little other trade but as
carriers and fhipholders, may be difpofed to promote any meafures, that will advance navigation,
at the expenfe of general commerce, manufactures,
and agriculture ; but the great capitalifts and merchants of London, Briftol, and Glafgow, &c. and
the manufacturers of Manchefter, Sheffield, Birmingham, Norwich, Yorkfhire, &c. will view
with due ferioufnefs, the probability of diverting
our trade into other channels, and the deliberate
and decided meafures to promote American manufactures, which the reftraints upon our navigation
and commerce may hereafter produce. The objections of thofe parts of the fouthern ftates, which
may be averfe to further impofitions on foreign
merchandife, will be moderated by their convic-
tions, that American manufacturers may be brought
to confume and work up their productions at home,
and to furnifh them in return by not very flow degrees, with the fupplies they now derive from
abroad.

At the time when this examination was commenced, it was believed, from many symptoms, that the true state of things in this country was little known or understood in Great-Britain. The prejudices naturally arising from so warm a contest as that of 1775, the disorders which grew out of a lax and ill digested government, and the errors incidental to an inexperienced country, suddenly elevated from a colony to an empire—all contributed to deceive and mislead Great-Britain, in her estimation of the United States. The volume of lord Sheffield was supposed to increase the public misconceptions. His work upon the Irish commerce in 1785, represented the American states in the same unfavourable manner in several passages. Symptoms of error in the opinions of other persons of respectable standing in the British community, were, unfortunately, observable. It appeared, therefore, to be a matter of great importance to both nations, that an attempt should be made to point out past and to correct existing mistakes. While it has been desired in doing this, to excite no painful sensations in the minds of those who are connected with the interests of Great-Britain, it has not been deemed necessary or fit to suppress any truths, because they might prove unacceptable to persons, if any such there be, who may want magnanimity enough to receive them with moderation, and to examine them with candour. The facts adduced on this occasion, are certainly not the more true, because they have been asserted in this publication, nor will it be denied, that coming from an American prefs they fhould be examined, on the other fide carefully and thoroughly. Such an examination fhould be defired by the United States, for it was fincerely treated in the beginning as genuine policy in nations, to avoid fhort lived deceptions, and rather to fearch diligently for the ground of common intereft, which can never be afcertained by mifreprefentation, or by erroneous or difingenuous inveftigation. If arrangements beneficial to the two countries can be effected it muft be through means very different from thofe. The minds of well intentioned and able men on both fides fhould be difpationately applied to the neceffary enquiries and difcuffions; the fubject fhould be thoroughly examined and underftood ; and frank admiffions of the advantages derived by either nation from the other, ought to be made. With the lights, which might be thus obtained, it would not be difficult to determine whether the nature of things in the United States and Great-Britain, requires or admits of a treaty of friendfhip or commerce.

S E C T I O N VIII.

A SUPPLEMENTARY NOTE,

CONCERNING THE PROGRESS AND PRESENT STATE OF AMERICAN DOMESTIC, OR HOUSEHOLD MANUFACTURES.

I N the paffage of the obfervations, which forms the head of SECTION III. to which this note be-

longs, the writer predicts, that we shall give a preference to British manufactures; that we shall not
manufacture for ourselves; and that our demand
for British goods will increase, in proportion to
our population. The facts, in opposition to these
ideas, which relate to the supplies drawn from foreign nations, have already been stated; as have
most of those which regard American manufactures,
fabricated by those who pursue them as *a separate
occupation* or *calling*. But lord Sheffield does not
appear to have foreseen the present state of our *family* or *household* manufactures.

The progress and present state of this invaluable
branch of the national industry, exceeds every
idea, it is believed, that has been formed of it,
either in this country or in Europe. In all the
states inhabited almost entirely by white people,
domestic manufactures are known to be very considerable, yielding a considerable surplus for the use
of the other parts of the union. But it is generally supposed, that in the states where the black people are numerous, (and especially near their sea-
coasts, where imported goods can be constantly
and easily obtained) little or no manufactures are
made. The following abstract from a minute
statement of the household manufactures, in one
neighbourhood, of twenty families (rich and poor)
indiscriminately taken, and in a part of Virginia, on a navigable river emptying into the Atlantic ocean, where the whites are, to the blacks, as

one two, will show, that much more is probably made, than is generally believed to be the case.

(1)

Male and female house-keepers,	20
Total number of white and black persons,	301
Fine table linnen, sheeting, shirting, &c. yards,	1,907
Negro clothing, blanketing &c. yards,	1,007
Value of fine cloth &c. per. yard,	cents 60
Value of coarse do. per do.	42
Pairs of fine stockings,	152
Pairs of coarse do.	108
Highest value made in one family,	dolls. 267
Lowest do.	$21\frac{1}{2}$
Total value of the manufactures of the 20 families	1,670
Families which did not manufacture	1
Term	the year 1790.

The following table obtained in the like indiscriminate and impartial way, has also been exhibited from another county of the same state, the situation of which is interior.

(2)

Families, rich and poor,	20
Yards of linen	1,095
Yards of woolen,	344
Yards of cotton	1,681
Pairs of stockings	174
Pairs of shoes made on the estates	237
Total value	dolls. 1,791
Term	the year 1790

A person of reputation, who furnished the latter statement, accompanied it with an assurance, that it might be confidered as a fair average of the *family* manufactures throughout the adjacent counties.

Thefe papers have been obtained under circumftances that juftify a reliance on their truth, and are believed to be very little variant from the medium of the ftate of Viginia. Though they cannot be made the bafis of a fatisfactory eftimate, the following brief one is hazarded merely to fhow the refult. In Virginia (exclufive of Kentucky) 70,825 families appear on the late cenfus. The loweft of the above returns (1,670⅓ dollars) is at the rate of 83⅓ dollars to each family for home-made *hofiery and cloths* of wool, flax, hemp and cotton only. Two-thirds of this rate upon the whole number of families (cutting off a third, to make a moderate calculation, and omitting odd numbers) gives the prodigious fum of 3,900,000 dollars for thofe articles of mere *domeflic* manufacture (exclufively of the work of regular tanners, fhoemakers, blackfmiths, weavers and other tradefmen) in Virginia, and taking the United States at 3,900,000 perfons, would appear to juftify a computation of above 20,000,000 dollars for the whole.

Through fimilar means, but on the examination of other perfons, in the counties of Accomack and Northampton lying on the bay of Chefapeak and the Atlantic ocean, it appears, that 315,000 yards of flaxen cloth are made in a diftrict containing 2,729 families: alfo 45,000 yards of woolen, 30,000

yards of cotton, and 45,000 yards of linen and
woolen cloth, and a quantity of coarfe ftockings
nearly equal to the demand. It is added, that all
the fhoes, and three-fourths of the clothing of that
country, are made by the tradefmen, or within the
families, who refide in it. The raw materials, including the cotton, are the growth of their farms.

Another communication through the fame chan-
nel ftates the manufactures of iron to exceed all
others in Virginia (which muft be erroneous, if
houfehold manufactures, as well as trades be taken
into the calculation) and that the greater part of the
farmers and planters tan the hides of the cattle they
confume.

. Two other communications from the fame ftate
inform, that *the families* in certain vicinities mentioned in them, make on a medium near 200 yards
each of cotton, woolen, and linen goods—and that
five-fixths of the fhoes, cloth, and ftockings, which
are ufed in that country, are made in the houfehold way. Thefe two laft ftatements contemplate
four counties.

Similar information from the interior parts of
South-Carolina (though lefs ftrong and extenfive)
has alfo been obtained, accompanied with a variety
of fpecimens of fubftantial midling and coarfe cotton, woolen, and linen goods, of which it is ftated,
that the inhabitants of that country manufacture,
entirely in the family way, as much as they have

occafion for, " cotton, flax, and hemp, being plentiful, and there being a confiderable ftock of good
fheep ;" " that there is a great deal done in the
houfehold way," and "that the greateft exertions are
made;" " that they have been long in the habit of
doing fomething in family manufactures, but have
improved much in the laft two years; and that the
weaving is done by the females," which leaves the
induftry of the males to be applied to agriculture.

It is well eftablifhed, that fimilar habits prevail
in the interior country of Georgia ; and in the midland and weftern counties of North-Carolina, they
are as attentive to domeftic manufactures as the
people of Virginia.

Such is the ftate of domeftic or houfehold manufactures in the fouthern ftates, where abundance of
very fertile and cheap lands, and a large portion
of black population, are fuppofed, in Europe, and
even in our own country, to have prevented any
confiderable attention to that frugal and induftrious purfuit.

Let us now turn to the northern fcenes, where a
more replete population, and a lefs productive foil
have led to the profecution of many branches of
manufactures as regular trades.

The refult of a careful enquiry, in every county
of the ftate of Connecticut, has been uniform information from twenty-four vicinities, that *domeftic*
manufactures are carried to a very great extent.

The articles, made in the family way, and by perfons engaged ordinarily in the cultivation of the
earth, are woolen and linen cloths including
ing fail-cloth; bed-ticks, fome cotton goods, hofiery, nails, and fpikes, fome filk buttons, hand-
kerchiefs, ribands and ftuffs, fewing filk, threads,
fringe, and pot and pearl afhes. It is obferved,
that there is farcely a family in the ftate of Connecticut, fo rich or fo poor, as not affiduoufly to
attend to domeftic manufactures; that they are extending and improving very faft in quantity, variety,
and quality;—and that confiderable parcels of
houfehold linens, &c. are tranfported out by land
and exported by water to the middle and fouthern
ftates. Here then is *a furplus* of houfehold manufactures fold *out of the ftate.* It as an acknowledged fact, that New-England linens have affected the price and importation of that article from
New-York to Georgia. The foregoing ftatement
is not intended to comprehend the manufactories
of woolen cloths, hats, cotton goods, fail-cloth,
checked and plain linens, fhoes and boots, bell
metal, buttons, wool and cotton cards, flaxfeed
oil, foap, candles, nails, anchors, axes, fpades, fho-
vels, cabinet work, carriages, faddles, books, &c.
&c. conducted as regular and feparate trades by
individuals, companies, and affociations, which are
very confiderable.

An enquiry has alfo been made, by a perfon of
judgment, in the ftate of Maffachufetts, who alleges, that the importations of foreign *manufactures*

into that state, are less by one half, at this time, than they were twenty years ago, though there has been a prodigious increase of population, and though considerable quantities of home made articles, are transported by land and water, to other parts. This is ascribed, in a very great degree, to the domestic manufactures, which are observable in the dresses and furniture of the people, and in the outward cargoes of the coasting and other trading vessels. The informant here contemplated, produced documents to show the magnitude of some of the regular trades, among which were 10,000 dozen pair of cotton and wool cards, much the greater part of which are applied to domestic manufactures throughout the United States, 2,400 pieces of sail-cloth per annum, at a single factory, 100 tons of nails per annum, at the Taunton factory alone, and 150,000 pair of stuff and silk shoes in the single town of Lynn, of which 10,355 pair had been shipped by one family to the Philadelphia market in a single year, although the manufacturers of that city, in the same line, are very expert and numerous.

Another informant has furnished a return, from which it appears, that in the last year thread and silk laces, and edgings, black and white, amounting to 41,979 yards, were manufactured in the family way, and not in regular factories, in the town of Ipswich in Massachusetts, which contains, by the late census, 4,562 men, women, and children. Pattern cards, containing thirty-six specimens of thefe hitherto unnoticed manufactures, have been exhibited. This townfhip comprehending a fmall fea-port, and confequently being open to foreign goods, and the freight of fo compact an article as lace, being very fmall, it will be confidered as a curious fact, that this manufacture fhould have grown up there to fo great a height. It is added in the information, that laces are made in various parts of Maffachufetts, though no where in fo great a degree. It is alfo underftood to be a domeftic manufacture in feveral parts of Connecticut.

The exiftence and continual increafe of domeftic manufactures in Rhode-Ifland and New-Hampfhire, are eftablifhed on fimilar authority :—and the growth of regular trades is very great in the former, in proportion to its population. It is fuppofed to have fucceeded as well as any fcene, in its attempts in the cotton branch, by labour-faving machines. The following parcels of goods were manufactured, in the *family* way, in the firft nine months of 1791, in the town of Providence, though it is a fea-port, and has a number of regular fhops and factories, for making feveral of the fame fpecies of goods.

Linen cloth,	- -	25,265 yards
Cotton do.	- -	5,858 do.
Woolen do.	- -	3,165 do.
Carpeting,	- - -	512 do.
Stockings,	- - -	4,093 pairs.
Gloves and mitts,	- -	859 do.
Fringe,	- - -	260 yards

Three millions of nails (by tale) and 30,000 yards of woolen cloth were made, in 1790, in the town and vicinity of Providence. The industry of farmers and house-wives contributed materially to the manufacture of these articles.

The extent of the woolen branch of domestic manufactures, in New-Hampshire, is evinced by the great number of its fulling mills; for they have no considerable factory employed on that raw material. The same may be observed in regard to the general knowledge of the art of weaving, among the wives and daughters of the farmers in that state. This fact is very frequently observable throughout New-England, and some other parts of the United States. The number of fulling mills in New-Jersey, which has already been stated to be forty-one, is a proof of their domestic manufactures; as they have not any woolen factories. In the vicinity of the town of Reading, in Pennsylvania, are ten fulling mills, which induces the same conclusion there; and they are very numerous throughout the state. The export of flaxseed is equal to that of former times; the manufacture of oil consumes a far greater quantity than heretofore: wherefore a large growth of flax is to be inferred; and as we have very few linen factories, and the exportation of flax has ceased, a great domestic manufacture of linens must exist. The sale of spinning-wheel irons, *in one shop* in the city of Philadelphia, in the course of the last year, has amounted to 1,500 sets, which, though a small fact, is strongly indicative of the extent of domeftic manufactures, as fpinning wheels are rarely, if ever, exported, or ufed in regular factories. The quantity fold is 29 per cent. greater than in any former year. Nail-making is frequently a houfehold bufinefs in New England, a fmall anvil being found no inconvenience in the corner of a farmer's chimney. Bad weather, hours of difengagement from the occupations of the farm, and evenings, are thus rendered feafons of fteady and profitable induftry. Public eftimates of the grain and fruit diftilleries of the United States, have been made at 3,500,000 gallons; much the greater part of which is made by farmers and planters. The importation of cheefe from all countries into the United States, was only forty tons, in the year ending in Auguft 1790: and we exported a much larger quantity in the fame term, from which a great manufacture of that article (in the domeftic way, of courfe) is to be inferred. In fhort, domeftic manufactures are great, various, and almoft *univerfal* in this country.

The implements hitherto ufed in houfehold manufactures, have been of the moft ancient kinds. The art of dying has been advanced in families little further than what was communicated by a receipt as brief as thofe in a book of culinary inftructions; the colouring ingredients have generally been fuch as nature handed to the thrifty houfewife. The operations, from the raw to the manufactured ftate, have often been the fimpleft that can be conceived. Under circumftances like thefe, it

will not be too fanguine to expeĉt that the diffemi-
nation of ufeful inftruĉtion in the praĉtice of dying, in the nature of colours, and concerning
other parts of the bufinefs, the introduĉtion of the
new improvements in the preparing and fpinning
machinery, on a fcale as convenient as the common
weaving apparatus, and the general ufe of the fly-
ing fhuttle, and the double loom, may give a two-
fold value to this moft precious branch of the
national induftry. It will not be deemed one of
the leaft favourable circumftances in the affairs of
a country fo eminently capacitated for agriculture
as the United States, that the profperous courfe of
that great employment of their citizens, is accompanied with an affiduous profecution of this economical domeftic occupation, by perfons of all ages
and fexes, in hours and feafons, which cannot be
employed in agricultural labour or in their ordinary family duties.

S E C T I O N   IX.

AN ADDITIONAL NOTE.

CONCERNING AMERICAN MANUFACTURES IN GENERAL.

THE following reprefentations of the manufactures at prefent exifting in the United States, will
tend to exhibit the ground of reliance which they
afford at this time ; and prefents the moft encouraging affurances of their fteady progrefs to permanent
eftablifhment.

I.

Tanned and tawed leather, dreſſed ſkins, with and without the hair or fur, and manufactures thereof, form one of the beſt eſtabliſhed and moſt import-ant branches. The conſumption and exportation of the following articles made wholly, or in part of leather or ſkins are great, and, in ſeveral inſtan-ces, general, and the importation of them, except-ing the articles of gloves and fur trimmings, is very inconſiderable. Rigging hides, parchment, ſhoes, boots, and ſlippers, common harneſs of all kinds, harneſs and leathern materials for pleaſurable car-riages, ſaddles and bridles, houſings, holſters, ſad-dlebags, portmantuas, boot ſtraps, leathern and hair trunks, fire-buckets, military articles, ſuch as ſlings, belts, cartouch boxes and ſcabbards; leathern breeches and ſome veſts and drawers; mens', youths', and ſome womens' gloves, fur muffs and tippets, li-nings and trimmings of fur for womens' and mens' apparel, ſome chair bottoms, the coatings of wool and cotton cards, and the leathern materials of other manufacturing implements and utenſils; to which may be added glue, being an economical manufac-ture from the otherwiſe uſeleſs parts of raw and dreſſed ſkins and from old leathern articles.

II.

Manufactures from hemp and flax form another very important and well eſtabliſhed branch. Theſe are made as well in regular factories and workshops, as in the household way. Cables, cordage, tarred and untarred; feins and nets of various kinds, twine and pack-thread, fail cloth, tow cloth, white and checked shirtings, sheetings, toweling, table linen, bed ticks, hofiery, fewing thread, and fome thread lace, are the articles manufactured of thefe raw materials. Nearly the whole of the hemp and flax are now of native growth; and as they are productions of every ftate, the fabrics made of them are peculiarly interefting. This circumftance gives breadth and folidity to the foundation of the linen branch, and to all others to which it is common.

III.

Manufactures of iron form a very increafing and ufeful branch. Under this head, the article of nails deferves particular notice, being brought to the footing of a domeftic manufacture in feveral of the ftates. The other fabrics, made of this raw material, are fteel, sheet iron, nail rods, wheel tire, hoops, weights, ftoves, pots and other caftings, fcale beams, plough irons, hoes, and other farming utenfils, the iron and fteel work for pleafurable and working carriages, and for ship-building, anchors, houfehold utenfils of various kinds, fcrew preffes, fome faws and planes, axes and other utenfils for artizans and manufacturers, and *arms* of various kinds. It is reafonable to conclude that the manufacture of military articles has become inconfiderable during the exifting peace. The abundance of mill feats, ore and fuel in the United States, a moft extenfive demand, and the heavy charges of importation, are among the circumftances which have given a refpectable eftablifhment to the iron manufactories.*

IV.

Manufactures of wool and mixtures thereof with cotton and flax, form another branch of peculiar importance, from their being principally the productions of domeftic induftry, at times and feafons which can be fpared from other occupations. Thefe are broad and narrow cloths, chiefly common or coarfe ; coatings, cafimers, ferges, flannels, hofiery, fome blankets, linfey woolfey, and negro cloth in very large quantities, coverlets and counterpanes, mens' and boys' hats, a few carpets, fringe, cord and taffels. This raw material will eventually prove univerfal in the United States, and is already found in every ftate.

The four preceding branches may be thrown into the firft clafs, in regard to prefent importance, and are eftablifhed in *a confiderable degree.* They are increafing rapidly, and particularly the three

* The Indian war and the renewal of our militia fyftem has greatly revived the manufacture of arms. A. D. 1793.

firſt, from the facility of procuring very large quantities of the requiſite raw materials, the introduction of various new implements and machinery, the abundance of fuel, lime, bark, and other articles employed in their manufacture. The latter is ſteadily progreſſive in quantity, and has improved rapidly within the laſt two years.

V.

Manufactures of cotton, and mixtures thereof with flax and hemp, as as alſo with wool, conſtitute a growing and very promiſing branch. In ſeveral of the ſtates, factories of this raw material have been commenced. Very conſiderable quantities of goods are made of it, in the houſehold way, and particularly in the ſouthern ſtates of all of which it is a production. The articles uſually made are corduroys, velverets, jeans, fuſtians and plain and ſtriped cloths, for womens' uſe, hoſiery, thread, fringe, cord and taſſels, counterpanes and coverlets, candlewick, and, when mixed with wool, very large quantities of negro cloth. Connected with this branch is the buſineſs of callico printing, in which ſome promiſing attempts have been made.

VI.

Ships and boats, with their numerous and requiſite appertenances, conſtitute a branch much leſs valuable in money than the preceding; but conſidering how neceſſary they are to agriculture and ma-

nufactures, as well as to commerce and the fisheries, they appear to be of primary importance.
These are constructed upon the moft favourable
terms, and with great perfection.

VII.

Papers of all kinds, form a very beneficial branch,
of confiderable and increafing extent. The fpecies made are paper hangings, playing cards, pafteboards, fullers or prefs papers, fheathing and wrapping paper, writing and printing paper of various
kinds and qualities, except the largeft and moft coftly. Appertenant to this branch is the very increafing and highly ufeful bufinefs of *book printing*. From
the abundance of mill-feats, and the refpectable
eftablifhment of the paper manufactory in fome of
the ftates, it is manifeft, that a much more confiderable faving or gain might be derived to the country, with the requifite attention to the prefervation
of the old and otherwife ufelefs materials.

VIII.

Sugars refined in various degrees, form a branch
fo perfectly eftablifhed as to require little attention, but to the acquifition of the raw material.

IX.

Cabinet wares and turnery, both of the fimpleft
and moft elegant kinds, are made in quantities com-

menfurate with the demand, as well of native as foreign materials. Connected with thefe in fome degree, is the manufacture of many kinds of mufical inftruments, which has gained a footing within a few years, that promifes an eftablifhment adequate to the occafions of the United States. Other manufactures of wood are made in great quantities, fuch as coopers' wares, corn fans, and other implements of hufbandry, almoft every fpecies of mill work, and lately the moft valuable and curious manufacturing machinery in various branches.

X.

Wares of the precious metals, (gold and filver) including fet work, and jewellery, are made in great variety and extent. The lateft addition to this branch is the manufacturing of plated ware, which, however, is not yet confiderable or eftablifhed.

XI.

Manufactures of the mixed metals and of lead and copper, have obtained various degrees of eftablifhment. Thofe of brafs are the moft extenfive; and, combined with iron and wood, there is a confiderable variety. Houfehold utenfils, technical and philofophical inftruments and apparatus, furniture and materials for houfes and carriages, and for the building and furnifhing of fhips, a few barrels and

some furniture of fire arms, are manufactured of
brass. Pewter and hard metal are very much confined to family utensils, distillers worms, printing types,
and buttons. The last article is made with great
neatness and variety in a few shops. Lead is
worked into ball, sheets, and every form requisite
for the building and finishing of houses and vessels,
and for the linings and coverings of wood, which
is exposed to water. Successful attempts to manufacture leaden shot of various sizes, have been
made.

Copper wares of various kinds, are made in the
United States. These are utensils for distillers,
sugar refiners, brewers, and other manufacturers,
and for domestic and ship use, articles to be applied in the building of vessels, and in short, all
those things which are requisite to useful and ordinary purposes.

Tin wares, for military and all other useful purposes, are well manufactured.

XII.

Manufactures from fruits, grain and seeds, are
very considerable. Of the first, distilled spirits
are the whole. Of such liquors from apples, the
quantity is large; of those from peaches, it is
much less, but the quality, when the liquor is
matured, is exquisite: both are increasing. Of
the manufactures from grain and seeds (exclusive

of meal of all kinds and biscuit) there is a greater value. These are distilled spirits, malt liquors, starch, hair powder, wafers and oil. These articles could be made in quantities commensurate with the demand; and the several branches are well understood.

XIII.

The manufacture of gunpowder, has advanced with the greatest rapidity to the point of desire in regard both to quantity and quality. The hazards and expenses of importation, the cheapness of charcoal, of the requisite packages, and of mill seats and mill works, in the United States, are among the principal causes, which have produced so accelerated a progress.

XIV.

Manufactures of glass, of earthen ware, and of stone, mixed with clay, are all in an infant state. From the quantity and variety of the materials which must have been deposited by nature in so extensive a region as the United States, from the abundance of fuel which they contain, from the expense of importation, and loss by fracture, which falls on on glass and earthen wares, from the simplicity of many of these manufactures, and from the great consumption of them, impressions of surprise at this state of them, and a firm persuasion that they will receive the early attention of foreign or American capitalists, are at once produced. Coarse tiles, and bricks of an excellent quality, potters' wares, all in quantities beyond the home confumption, a few ordinary veffels and utenfils of ftone mixed with clay, fome muftard and fnuff bottles, a few flafks or flaggons, a fmall quantity of fheet glafs and of veffels for family ufe, generally of the inferior kinds, are all that are yet made.

XV.

Manufactures from the fat and bones of fea and land animals, form a clafs of confiderable importance. Thefe are the feveral kinds of oil, foap, fpermaceti and tallow candles, articles made of whalebone, fal ammoniac, and volatile falt.

In addition to the above branches or claffes, there are manufactured, (befides the quantities requifite for the home demand) a confiderable value for exportation, of the following mifcellaneous articles—pot afhes and pearl afhes, chewing and fmoking tobacco and fnuff, cheefe, working and pleafureable carriages, Windfor and varnifhed chairs, oil of turpentine and rofin, wool and cotton cards, and other implements and utenfils for manufacturing; and a large value for home confumption of fur hats, brufhes for domeftic and technical purpofes, whips and canes, manufactures of horn, mill ftones and hewn ftone, lampblack, ochres and other painters' colours, fome galenical and chemical preparations, clocks and watches, wearing apparel, and a few manufactures of filk.

[PAPER A.]

Schedule of the whole number of persons within the several districts of the United States, according to an act " providing for the enumeration of the inhabitants of the United States," passed March the 1st, 1790.

DISTRICTS.	Free white males of sixteen years and upwards, including heads of families.	Free white males under sixteen years.	Free white females, including heads of families.	All other free persons.	Slaves.	Total.
* Vermont,	22,435	22,328	40,505	252	16	85,539
New-Hampshire,	36,086	34,851	70,160	630	158	141,185
{ Maine,	24,384	24,748	46,870	538	none.	96,540 }
{ Massachusetts,	95,453	87,289	190,582	5,463	none.	378,787 }
Rhode-Island,	16,019	15,799	32,652	3,407	948	68,825
Connecticut,	60,523	54,403	117,448	2,808	2,764	237,946
New-York,	83,700	78,122	152,320	4,654	21,324	340,120
New-Jersey,	45,251	41,416	83,287	2,762	11,453	184,139
Pennsylvania,	110,788	106,948	206,363	6,537	3,737	434,373
Delaware,	11,783	12,143	22,384	3,899	8,887	59,094
Maryland,	55,915	51,339	101,395	8,043	103,036	319,728
{ Virginia,	110,936	116,135	215,046	12,866	292,627	747,610 }
{ Kentucky,	15,154	17,057	28,922	114	12,430	73,677 }
North-Carolina,	69,988	77,506	140,710	4,975	100,572	393,751
South-Carolina,						249,073
Georgia,	13,103	14,044	25,739	398	29,264	82,548

	Free white males of twenty years and upwards, including heads of families.	Free males under twenty-one years of age.	Free white females, including heads of families.	All other free persons.	Slaves.	Total.
S. W. Territory, N. W. Territory†.	6,271	10,277	15,365	361	3,417	35,691

Truly stated from the original returns deposited in the office of the Secretary of State.

October 24, 1791.   TH: JEFFERSON.

* This return was not signed by the marshal, but was inclosed and referred to in a letter written and signed by him.

‡ The population of the north western government is supposed to be a few thousands, exclusively of the military.   (Note by Editor.)

[PAPER B.]

Abstract of the exports of the United States, from the commencement of the custom-houses in the several states, which was at different times in August, 1789, to the 30th day of September, 1790.

EXPORTED.

	Quantity.		Value.
ASHES, pot,	$7,050\frac{10}{100}$	tons,	dolls. 661,634
Ashes, pearl,	$1,548\frac{55}{100}$	do.	177,459. 50
Apples,	5,898	barrels,	6,318
Boats,	8		372
Bombshells,	10	tons,	100
Bricks,	870,550		2,617. 50
Beer and porter,	472	casks,	4,612
Brandy	97	do.	3,016
Cordials,	236	boxes,	637
Cordage			5,739
Carriages,	220		28,017
Candles, tallow,	149,680	lbs.	14,876
Candles wax	5,274	do.	2,461
Candles, myrtle,	249	do.	52
Cider,	442	barrels,	849
Cotton,	2,027	bales,	58,408
Coffee,	254,752	lbs.	45,753
Chocolate,	29,882	do.	3,537
Cocoa,	10,632	do.	950
Cassia and cinnamon,	9,392	do.	9,715
Deer Skins,			33,009
Duck, American,	77	bolts,	777
Duck, Russia,	220	do.	2,200
Earthen and glass ware,			1,990
Essence spruce,	115	boxes,	600
Flaxseed,	40,019	casks,	236,072
Flax	21,970	lbs.	1,468
Furs,			60,515
Furniture,			8,315

			dolls.
Fishery.			
Fish, dried,	378,721	quintals,	828,531
Fish, pickled,	36,840	barrels,	113,165
Oil, whale,	15,765	do.	124,908
Oil, spermaceti,	5,431	do.	79,542
Candles, do.	70,397	lbs.	27,724
Whalebone,	121,281	do.	20,417
Grain.			
Buckwheat,	7,562	bushels,	2,572
Corn,	2,102,137	do.	1,083,581
Oats,	98,842	do.	20,900
Rye,	21,765	do.	13,181
Wheat,	1,124,458	do.	1,398,998
Ginseng,	813	casks,	47,024
Gunpowder,	5,800	lbs.	861
Gin,	18,025	galls.	16,989
Grindstones,	203		450
Hairpowder,	12,534	lbs.	1,687
Hats,	668		1,392
Hay	2,126	tons,	12,851
Horns,			1,052
Ironmongery,			7,878
Iron, pig,	3,555	tons,	91,379
Iron, bar,	200	do.	16,723
Indigo,	612,119	lbs.	537,379
Live stock.			
Horned cattle,	5,406		99,960
Horses,	8,628		339,516
Mules,	237		8,846
Sheep,	10,058		17,039
Hogs,	5,304		14,481
Poultry,	3,704	doz.	6,263
Lumber.			
Staves & heading,	36,402,301		463,229
Shingles,	67,331,115		120,151
Shook hogsheads,	52,558		32,002
Hoops,	1,908,310		19,598
Boards,	46,747,730		260,213
Handspikes,	2,361	doz.	1,505
Casks,	2,423		3,697
Scantling,	8,719,638	feet,	95,308
Lumber difft. kinds.		feet,	128,503
Timber do.		do.	139,328
Leather,	22,698	lbs.	5,302
Logwood,	264	tons,	3,911
Lignum vitæ,	176	do.	1,760

			dolls.
Lead and shot,	6	do.	810
Mahogany,			18,531
Medicines and drugs,			1,735
Merchandize,			28,156
Molasses,	15,537	gallons,	3,904
Muskets,	100		500
Nankeens,	11	bales,	2,315
Oil, linseed,	119	barrels,	1,962
Provisions.			
Flour,	724,623	barrels,	4,591,293
Bread,	75,667	do.	209,674
Meal,	99,973	do.	302,694
Peas and beans,	38,752	bush.	25,746
Beef,	44,662	barrels,	279,551
Pork,	24,462	do.	208,099
Hams and bacon,	253,555	lbs.	19,728
Butter,	8,379	firkins,	48,587
Cheese,	144,734	lbs.	8,830
Potatoes,	5,318	barrels,	6,009
Tongues,	641	do.	1,598
Onions, vegetables,			22,936
Hogs lard,	6,355	firkins,	31,475
Honey,	165	do.	990
Oysters, pickled,	272	kegs,	272
Pimento,	715	bags,	4,928
Pepper,	6,100	lbs.	1,440
Paper,	169	reams,	381
Paint,	4,650	lbs.	963
Pitch,	8,175	barrels,	17,488
Raw hides,	230		485
Raw silk,	177	lbs.	489
Rosin,	361	barrels,	778
Rice,	100,845	tierces,	1,753,796
Rum, American,	370,331	galls.	135,403
Rum, West-India,	12,623	do.	5,795
Raisins,	213	casks,	1,205
Salt,	31,935	bushels,	8,236
Sago,	2,319	lbs.	455
Soap,	597	boxes,	3,967
Snuff,	15,350	lbs.	5,609
Seeds and roots,			2,135
Shoes and boots,	5,862	pairs,	5,741
Sadlery,			5,541
Starch,			1,125
Sugar, loaf,	16,429	lbs.	3,432

			dolls.
			dolls.
Sugar, brown,	33,358	do.	2,237
Saſſafras,	49,504	do.	555
Steel,	163	bundles,	978
Stones, ſawed,	170		550
Tallow,	200,020	lbs.	20,722
Tobacco,	118,460	hhds.	4,349,567
Tea,	1,672	cheſts,	121,582
Tar,	85,067	barrels,	126,116
Turpentine,	28,326	do.	72,541
Do. ſpirits,	193	do.	1,032
Tow cloth,	67	pieces,	1,274
Vinegar,	24	caſks,	106
Wines,	1,074	pipes,	83,249
Wax,	231,158	lbs.	57,597

	20,194,794
To the North-Weſt coaſt of America,	10,362
Amount of ſeveral returns received }	210,810 84
ſince the 15th February 1791. }	

Total,	* 20,415,966.84

* Quarterly returns, from ſeveral ſmall diſtricts, are deficient

A summary of the value and destination of the exports of the United States, agreeably to the foregoing abstract.

	Dollars.
To the dominions of France, — —	4,698,735.48
To the dominions of Great-Britain, —	9,363,416.47
To the dominions of Spain, —	2,005,907.16
To the dominions of Portugal, —	1,283,462
To the dominions of the United Netherlands,	1,963,880. 9
To the dominions of Denmark, —	224,415.50
To the dominions of Sweden, — —	47,240
To Flanders, — — —	14,298
To Germany, — —	487,787.14
To the Mediterranean, — —	41,298
To the African islands and coast of Africa,	139,984
To the East-Indies, — —	135,181
To the North-West coast of America, —	10,392

Dollars, 20,415,966.84

In addition to the foregoing, a considerable number of packages have been exported from the United States, the value of which be_ ing omitted in the returns from the custom-houses, could not be introduced into this abstract.

TENCH COXE, *Assistant Secretary.*

Treasury department,
Feb. 18*th,* 1791.

CHAPTER IX.

REFLEXIONS ON THE STATE OF THE AMERICAN UNION IN
THE YEAR M,DCC,XCII.

THE apparent profperity of the United States, in the beginning of the year 1792, was attended with ferious doubts in the minds of many refpectable citizens, about particular matters, fome of which are always of importance to the happinefs of a people, and others of which are confidered as peculiarly interefting to this country. A concife examination into *the general ftate of the union* appeared to promife fatisfactory explanations of many of thefe doubts. The reflections, which enter into the compofition of this chapter, were fincerely intended to anfwer that defirable end. They may contain fome errors of fact, and more of opinion and judgment. Yet as there are comprized in them many truths, drawn from fources, which cannot be materially erroneous, and as the opinions have been tefted in fome degree by fubfequent experience and reflection, it is prefumed that a republication of them may tend to inform, at leaft the foreign world. It is certain, that we do not exhibit any obvious fymptoms of a wrong balance of trade, that the expediency of manufactures is rifing in the eftimation of the cultivators, that our exports and fhip-building are increafing, that the property of emigrators contributes to fwell and fully to counter-balance any apparent excefs of our imports, that our aggregate revenue continues to exceed the eftimates, that every good plan requiring capital, which is fet on foot derives it quickly from the confidence of our monied citizens or from foreigners, and in fhort, that the United States are in reality the comfortable original, which is depicted in the following fection.

Reflections on the State of the Union

" Si quid novifti rectius iftis,
" Candidus imperti; fi non his utere mecum."

S E C T I O N I.

DISPASSIONATE enquiries concerning the public interefts, are attended with falutary effects, in every time and in every nation. In a country like that, which we inhabit, fuch examinations are unufally interefting, and may be rendered, it is believed, peculiarly beneficial.

To create the difpofition requifite to the proper acceptation of fuch difquifitions, it is neceffary to call to the public mind the variant characters of the feveral ftates, when they where provinces of a more extended empire—the caufes which produced that difference of character—the means which were devifed to increafe and perpetuate that variation and the ends to which thofe characteriftic differences were intended to be inftrumental. Reflections, duly ferious, upon thefe circumftances will remind the people of the feveral ftates, that they are naturally friends, whofe amity and

union have been too often viewed with jealoufy by rival eyes. They will perceive the wifdom and the high duty of cultivating a fpirit of mutual allowance and conceffion; and a
careful examination of their actual fituation will
convince them, that greater bleffings will refult
from a perfect underftanding, and fedulous cultivation of their interefts at home, than from almoft
any arrangements, which the conceptions of foreign nations will probably lead them to propofe,
or adopt.

The confideration of our prefent fituation and
of fome interefting circumftances which have grown
out of it, are the object of this inveftigation, in
which the benefits to be derived from a liberal intercourfe with foreign nations will not be under-
valued. As no apology is neceffary for fuch an
endeavour, a mifcellaneous enquiry into feveral
matters, which are always deeply interefting to nations, and into others which have refulted from
our public operations, will be profecuted without
further introduction.

CONCERNING THE EXPORTS OF THE UNITED STATES.

It has been apprehended by perfons of obfervation, at home, and the idea has prevailed in the
councils of a foreign nation,* that the exports of

* See the report of a committee of the lords of the Britifh privy
council, publifhed in the gazettes (of March) in Charlefton, South-
Carolina.—American grain has progreffively advanced by equable

the United States for the year preceding October, 1790, were greater in value than could be expected again, by reafon of the prices for grain which were confequent on the fcarcity in France. The exports of the fubfequent year will aid us in tefting this opinion, which attracts the more attention, becaufe it is fometimes fuggefted that agriculture and trade have been injured by the meafures of the general government in regard to the public debt. The firft return of exports, on which this conjecture was founded, includes a term of thirteen months and a half, and amounts to 20,415,966 dollars. From this aggregate value a ninth part is to be deducted, to equalize it with one years exportation, which reduces the fum to 18,147,526 dollars. It is very well known, that the prices of our produce through the year lately returned, and which ended with September 1791, had fallen to their antecedent rates, and it will be perceived on a comparifon, that our exports exceeded in their aggregate

and confiderable fteps, in the laft fifty years. The caufes of this rife are the increafe of fhipping, particularly American; the introduction of foreign fhipping, the increafe of manufacturers in Europe and America, the increafe of mills, particularly in America, the increafe of diftillation and brewing in America, the accumulation of mercantile capital in America, the increafe of commerce among all nations, the fullnefs of population in the European ftates, which formerly exported grain, and the increafe of the circulating medium of the world by mines, banks and bills of exchange. In 1737 wheat was fold for one-third of a dollar in the principal grain ports of the United States: in 1771, 1772, 1773, and 1774, it fold on a medium for near three quarters of a dollar; and in the years 1792, 1793, and 1794, it has fold on a medium for more than a dollar.

value thofe of the former year. The laft return, exclufively of two quarters of Charlefton was

dollars 17,571,551

Thofe two quarters, at the rate of the correfponding term in the preceding year, would be about   700,000

dollars 18,271,551*

There remains not, therefore, the leaft caufe to doubt, that our total exportations were eighteen millions and a quarter, and confequently more than in the antecedent year. It is to be obferved too that the high prices which were current through the time of the firft return, muft have produced an exportation of all the grain that could be carried to market, and none of the old crop could have been left as ufual, to fell with the new. The obvious effect of this muft have been an unufual deduction from the exports in the following year. The valuation of the exports of thefe ftates immediately before the revolution is not precifely afcertained: but the whole exportations from North-America, including the remaining colonies, and Newfoundland, Bermuda, and the Bahamas, were computed to have been in 1771, 15,280,000 dollars. In thefe were comprifed the fhipments between thofe iflands

---

* The exports of the year ending on the 30th September, 1792, are 21,000,000 of dollars. See return thereof in chapter 12. Thofe of the following year exceeded 26,000,000.

and the main, and from province to province
as every veffel, which departed from one American port, to another, was obliged to clear out
her cargo, as if deftined for a foreign country.
It will appear to be fafe to fubtract for the difference produced by thefe two circumftances, one half
of the former exports, when it is remembered that
nearly two-thirds of the quantity of tonnage is probably employed in the intercourfe between the various parts of the prefent union, which is engaged
in that with foreign nations; and that the Britifh
Newfoundland fifhery alone, was eftimated at more
than 2,200,000 dollars in 1775. The increafe of
the tonnage employed in the foreign trade affords
another proof of the increment of our exports.
About 330,000 tons were laden in the prefent
United States in the year 1770, part of which
were deftined for ports now within the union.
About 600,000 tons have been loaded in each of
the two laft years for foreign ports, though our exports being in a much greater degree manufactured,
are now contained in a fmaller proportionate compafs: and boards, fcantling and ftaves, which are
our moft bulky commodities, have not increafed in
half the ratio of the tonnage employed.

An addition may be alfo made to the amount of
the return for the increafed fupplies in provifions,
cordage, and other materials, for the ufe and outfit
of foreign fhips, both of war and trade. Since the
prices of falt provifions have been reduced below
thofe of Ireland, and many articles applicable to

ships' use, have been manufactured here, this item
has become very considerable; and so far as the
articles are sold to foreigners, they are essentially
exports.

Under this head, the increased number of ships
sold to foreign nations, may be fairly mentioned,
and though much has been said of the number formerly disposed of abroad, it is not doubted that a
greater value was sold in that way in the time of the
last return. Of this fact some further illustration
will probably be given in the sequel. It will be sufficient to observe here, that the whole quantity of
tonnage built and native vessels repaired during the
last year, exceeds in value one million of dollars.

The enlarged consumption made within our
country by foreign persons of every description,
who are certainly much more numerous than they
formerly were, is as profitable to the country, as
the same value in exports would have been. This
item will appear to be very considerable, when the
expenditures of foreign ministers, consuls, transient
and resident foreigners, fleets and seamen, are called to mind.

The export trade of the United States and the
great increase of home consumption have placed
the American producers in general on a very advantageous footing. The competition which exists in our markets, between the purchasers for the
account of foreigners of various nations, for our
own merchants, for the great consumption in the

fea-ports and the parts adjacent to the coafts, and
for the ufe of the manufacturers, together with the
occafional fhipments made on their own accounts
by the fouthern planters, by the millers of the middle ftates, and by the owners of the eaftern fifhing
veffels, afford the cultivators and fifhermen fo many alternatives, that they can always obtain the
beft prices, which circumftances will juftify. In
fhort, thefe feveral demands, at once fteady, extenfive and various, efficiently fupport our agriculture:
and though peculiar enterprize and faculties in
commerce and manufactures, the power of capital,
and an intimate knowledge of our trade and interi-
or fyftem, enable a particular nation to participate largely in the exports of the United States,
the remainder of the world receives from us
a very confiderable value, and the variety of demand, which the deftination of our exports proves
to exift, affords us certain relief from the confequences of the commercial errors of any of
thofe countries, whofe citizens are our confumers.
Whenever fuch errors fhall occur—or fo far as
they may have already taken place, to diffufe a
knowledge of our refources among all nations, to
infpire them with confidence in our laws and modes
of dealing, and to convert our commodities by
manufactures, into every fhape, which there occafions and our own may require, will prove a competent and efficacious corrective.

It is fatisfactory to obferve the regular increafe
of manufactured goods in our returns of exported

commodities. The number in each of the two laft years is upwards of one third, in a lift which amounts to near three hundred articles. Hence we may infer, that *the time is really arrived, when foreign trade is increafed and enlivened by home manufactures.* This idea, together with the domeftic commerce produced by them, will be more particularly noticed in another place.

CONCERNING THE MANUFACTURES OF THE UNITED STATES.

In confidering this fubject it will be unneceffary to adduce many arguments to influence the judgment of the eaftern parts of the union. Many of our citizens near the fea-coaft of the middle ftates are equally convinced of the beneficial effects of manufactures. The cultivators in the fouthern and weftern country, and a refpectable proportion of our mercantile citizens are apprehenfive of injury to themfelves and to their country from the purfuit of this object. Thefe are two defcriptions of perfons, whom it is in every view our duty to fatisfy, if the truth and reafon will permit; and it is principally from a due attention to them, that the fubject is propofed to be examined here.

An opinion has prevailed that the fouthern ftates will be facrificed to the eaftern, and in fome degree to the middle ftates, by the plan of manufactures. It is plain, however, that as the foil of the eaftern ftates is not equal to the production of a fufficiency of provifions and raw materials for their own ufe, they muft refort to the middle and

fouthern ftates for feveral raw materials and for
new fupplies of provifions. It is known, too, that
fome valuable articles for manufactures cannot be
produced but in the fouthern ftates, fuch as cotton,
indigo, and rice*, and that tobacco is almoft confined, to them. The fouthern ftates and weftern
country will have confiderable advantages in the
fupport, which the home market of the manufacturers will give at all times, and efpecially in time
of war, (when freights will be high, and fhipping
fcarce) to their agricultural and landed productions. Even now, in profound peace, it is the cafe.
Hemp was delivered in the ports of the middle
ftates, from the lands of the fouthern ftates, at
lefs than five cents per lb. in 1791. Nothing would
have kept it up to that rate, but the rope and twine
manufactories of the middle and eaftern ftates, and
thofe which are growing up among themfelves.
The brewers of Philadelphia draw nearly as much
of their barley from the Chefapeak as they derive
from the lands of Pennfylvania. Thefe and other
facts fhow the beneficial beginning of things. The
manufactures of fhips and cordage throughout the
Union, procure from the fouthern nearly ftates all
their tar, pitch, turpentine, oil of turpentine, and
rofin. The ports of Philadelphia and New-York, take
three-fourths of their fhip timber from them, juftly
preferring veffels of live oak and red cedar to all

* Rice is the raw material for the Eaft-Indian fpirit *arrack*, and
it is neceffary for a particular quality of ftarch ufed by the European manufacturers.

others. The owners of the coal mines of Virginia, enjoy the monoply of all the fupplies for the manufacturers of the more northern ftates, who live in the fea ports: a demand which is increafing rapidly. No lead mine of any confequence is yet worked, except one near the fuperior waters of James river. The fouthern ftates abound with iron, and have much more fuel of all kinds than the northern ftates, and they have ftreams for the moft powerful water works. Few or no very abundant depofits of coal have been yet difcovered further north or eaft than the waters of the Ohio and the Chefapeak, even in internal fituations. The iron manufactures of the United States are already important in value, and immenfely fo in point of utility, or rather of *neceffity*. Buildings, farms, manufactories, fhipping, fifheries, fleets, and armies, all demand them. In fhort the all-important landed intereft would languifh, and its progrefs in profperity would be retarded in the counties of the fouthern ftates, even near the fea, if our prefent manufactures were to be abolifhed, and all future eftablifhments of that kind were to be given up. *But their inland and weftern counties cannot flourifh unlefs manufactures fhall be promoted and introduced among them.* In the counties of Pennfylvania beyond the Allegany mountain, are 63,000 inhabitants, and probably 10,000 of thefe are farmers. The *wool* of that country is yet very inconfiderable—their furs are more abundant. From thefe two raw materials, no lefs than 10,140 wool hats, and 2,200 fur hats are manufactured yearly in thirty three hatters' shops. Sail cloth (which, when manufactured, would be worth 30 cents per lb.) could be made at Pittsburg, Winchester in Virginia, Hillsborough, and Salisbury, in North-Carolina, Camden, in South-Carolina, and Lewisville, in Georgia, out of hemp, the value of which, there, does not exceed 4 or 5 cents. To bring a ton of hemp to the sea-ports from those towns, except Lewisville, costs from 35 to 40 per cent. of its value. To bring a ton weight of sail cloth from the same places to the same ports would not cost above 6 or 8 per cent. and the manufacturers' provisions and fuel are attended with similar savings. Deduct for a moment the demand of foreign commerce from Alexandria and Winchester, and the latter would appear to be most vigorous and flourishing; because it manufactures more, having not so high a market for its provisions and raw materials. These observations apply with equal force to the whole state of Vermont and to all our interior counties. The nation that supplies us with hempen, flaxen, and iron manufactures, takes immense quantities of hemp, flax, and iron from Russia. These Russian raw materials are purchased at the eastern extremity of the Baltic, are transported to another foreign country and manufactured there, are brought hither, and hawled through bad roads, 50, 100, 200, and 300 miles into our most productive counties, which yeild the requisite raw materials. These facts powerfully incite us to foster manufactures of the same kinds, there and elsewhere. Till that shall be the case, we shall continue to drag those raw materials through the same bad roads, and ship them under charges of carting and freight equal to a third, an half, and two thirds of their value, according to the distance. Neglecting and repelling the establishment of manufactures, would occasion immense deductions from the profits of our lands ; and due consideration, it is believed, would convince us, that the best interests, nay the necessities of our landholders require the introduction of some kind of manufactory in almost every vicinity.

The countries south of Pennsylvania are remarkably rich in fossils. Coal, copper, iron, lead, and other minerals are found in either Maryland, Virginia, North or South-Carolina, or Georgia, or all of them. Mineral appearances occur every where. The promotion of manufactures is necessary to draw these forth ; and as they have immense forests of wood, and the most powerful mill-streams, there can be no doubt, that they will be brought into use, as soon as those means shall be adopted.

The family manufactures of the middle and interior counties of Virginia, North-Carolina, and the interior counties of Georgia, South-Carolina, and Maryland, are said to be greater in value, than the articles of foreign manufactures, which they use ; and were they universally awake to the facility, profits, and national importance of this mode of manufacturing, they might extend it much further, without impeding their farming operations, while, at the fame time, they would provide a new ufe for their agricultural productions.

A fingle ftate, Pennfylvania, has upwards of fifty paper mills, which work up materials of no value. The manufactures from thofe mills are computed at two hundred and fifty thoufand dollars—the perfons employed in them do not exceed one hundred and fifty, or two hundred. That ftate contains about one ninth of the people of the United States, and their contributions to the expenfes of the government and the intereft of the public debt, are confequently about 400,000 dollars. Their paper mills, therefore, indemnify them for five-eights of their quota! It appears to be the duty of government to encourage the people in all the ftates to do the fame, efpecially as it can be done by *water-means*, and not by men diverted from their farms. The fouthern ftates do not want a capacity * for this manufacture, which has acquired an eftablifhment in Maryland, and has appeared as far to the fouthward as North-Carolina.

It may be fafely affirmed, that the manufactures of *leather* in the United States exceed in value *all our annual burdens.* We import few or no fhoes.

* They wear cotton and linen more than the northern ftates, whofe climate requires more woolens. Out of the rags of the former paper is made. Out of woolen rags it has not yet been found practicable.

In each of the two laſt years we have procured from abroad no more than 70,000 pair of ſhoes and boots, for 4,000,000 of people. If we uſe only one pair and a half per annum per perſon, at ſeventy-five cents, they will amount to 4,500,000 dollars, which exceeds every demand of the general and ſtate governments.† The hides, ſkins, bark, lime, thread, briſtles, and wax, nay, the very heel-pegs, are all drawn from our lands and farms. Recollecting this, and ſimilar facts, we cannot queſtion the utility of *even handicraft* manufactures to the farmers, planters, and landed intereſt. If the manufacture of ſhoes in this country, were aboliſhed, our annual debt to foreign countries would be increaſed to an amount equal to all our public contributions. Similar obſervations might be made on ſeveral other articles, and to a much greater extent on linen, cotton, and woolen fabrics. Cattle thrive with little attention in the mild winters of the ſouth. That regin being more woody, they have a greater quantity of bark than moſt of the other ſtates.

The manufactures of wool in Great-Britain have been ſtated by their miniſters at £.16,800,000 ſterling—and the ſimple manufactures of liquors in that country are ſaid to conſume twenty-five millions of buſhels of grain. Were there no other proofs, we could not doubt the importance of manufactures to the agriculture of that country. They nouriſh and

† A. D. 1791—2.

fupport it. We make up all our wool—our lands produce cotton with great facility, and we manufacture liquors as eafily as Britain. There is no doubt, that the latter branch already affords to our farmers an *annual market* for 1,500,000 bufhels of grain. This manufacture is well underftood and carried on in all the fouthern ftates.

The objeftion, that manufaftures take the people from agriculture, is not folid as elfewhere obferved; fince women, children, horfes, water, and fire, all work at manufaftures, and perform four-fifths of the labour; and as many manufafturers migrate to the United States, it may be fairly afferted that the *quantity* of agricultural induftry is *increafed* by the impulfe and demand arifing from manufaftures. It may be reafonably afked, whether a farmer does not raife *the more* cotton, flax, hemp, and wool, becaufe his wife and daughters *fpin* and *weave* them, or becaufe a water-work fpins for them ?

The employment of the new medium, the public certificates (which may be taken at £.15,000,000 fterling) in a country that formerly had not £.3,000,000 fterling of medium, renders manufactures neceffary at this time. It may be faid, lands will employ it. But farms fold well at the time when £.3,000,000 fterling was probably the utmoft extent of our medium, and cannot therefore give employment to the additional twelve millions, though they might to a part of it. The firft application of this capital is intended to be made to the manufaturing of cotton, which is peculiar to the fouthern ftates. This is one method by which thofe ftates will be benefited by even that part of the public debt, which they do not own. On this important point more will be faid hereafter. It merits the moft clofe attention and the moft temperate confideration.

More money is employed in manufatures, than in foreign commerce, becaufe the grofs value of exported articles is much lefs than the grofs value of manufatured articles. This will not be doubted, when it is remembered, that fhoes alone amount to fcvcral millions of dollars. Thefe manufatures cannot therefore be deemed lefs important to the fouthern landholders than foreign commerce; and thofe proprietors will not be difpofed to neglet foreign commerce, nor will they confider it as irrelative to their particular or local interefts.

SECTION II.

CONCERNING THE MANUFACTURES OF THE UNITED STATES.

IN purfuing the confideration of American manufatures as beneficial and neceffary to the fouthern ftates, it will be ufeful to take a curfory view of the indications of attachment and difpofition to them, which are difcoverable in that quarter.

Virginia appears to be making a greater *progreſs* in merchant mills than any ſtate in the union, though ſome are yet far before her in thoſe beneficial works. Maryland and Delaware which are in the ſouthern moiety, are ſecond only to Pennſylvania in this branch.* There is little doubt that more *pig and bar iron* is made to the ſouthward of Pennſylvania, than to the northward of it. A lead mine has been opened in Virginia, which is extending its ſupplies through the union, and promiſes fair to be commenſurate with the preſent demand: and there is one which is now worked, in the territory ſouth of the Ohio. But no lead mines are in conſiderable operation in the ſtates north or eaſt of Virginia, though a ſmall beginning upon one in the weſtern parts of Pennſylvania is made. An aſſociation in Virginia, another in the territory ſouth of the Ohio, and a company in the weſtern diſtrict of South-Carolina, have provided themſelves with carding and ſpinning machinery on the Britiſh plans to manufacture their *native* cotton. The planters, in the ſouthern ſtates raiſe quantities of this raw material, unthought of before the war, and until the diſcuſſions of the ſubject of manufactures, which took place ſome time after the treaty of peace. The family manufactures in *cotton* are much greater in the four ſouthernmoſt ſtates, than in the four eaſtern ſtates. There are not wanting conſiderable numbers of *ſheep* in the five ſouth-

* New-York it is conceived, ought to pay more attention to the milling buſineſs.

ern ſtates, yet by the two returns of exports, it appears that no *wool* has been ſent *from thence* to foreign markets. It has been common to receive wool in Pennſylvania from the eaſtern ſtates, though they manufacture ſo much, but it is not known that any is ever received there for ſale from the ſouthern ſtates. Wool has been tranſported to Salem, in North-Carolina, and to Wincheſter, in Virginia, from the city of Philadelphia, for the hat manufactory.

There has been full as great a current of emigration of *flour millers, blackſmiths, tanners, hatters, cabinet-makers, diſtillers, coopers, &c.* to the ſouthern ſtates from thoſe north of them, in proportion to numbers, as of farmers; ſo that the workſhops of the middle and northern ſtates yield a double benefit to their fellow-citizens in the ſouth, in ſupplying them with manufactures, and artizans.

There is greater *variety* in diſtillation in the four ſouthern ſtates than in the four eaſtern—that is, *the manufactory is eſtabliſhed on a broader baſis.* It is alſo more *certain* in the ſouth than in the north. In the latter, molaſſes is the principal ingredient and being from an external ſource, may be loſt to the eaſtern diſtillers. Their manufactory is even now at hazard, unleſs they reſort to the grain of the country to the ſouthward of them. But in the ſouthern ſtates they manufacture ſpirits from molaſſes, peaches, apples, ſeveral kinds of grain, and probably will, as their country is cleared, extend it to *the grape*. This has been tried with fuccefs in the experimental way, at Galliopolis, near the Scioto. The diftillation of arack from rice will probably be commenced if that grain fhould ever fall in price.

The legiflature of North-Carolina made a loan of money fince the late war to affift the introduction of the paper manufactory.

An affociation containing forty of the moft refpectable planters and farmers, in the weftern diftrict of South-Carolina, has been eftablifhed within a few years for the promoting of manufactures, and agriculture. A fubfcription to the amount of about 25,000 dollars, has been made in the territory fouth of the Ohio for the purpofe of carrying on the cotton manufactory.—An indication of zeal not equalled in any middle or northern ftate, confidering that the whole population of the government is 30,000 whites, and 5,000 blacks.

The preparation of tar, pitch, turpentine, fpirits of turpentine, and rofin, in North-Carolina and its vicinity, may be deemed a manufacture as juftly as the making of linfeed oil, pot afh, or ordinary tanning. A very fmall quantity indeed, of thefe articles, will, be made in the ftates north of Virginia becaufe nature forbids; but they will, from obvious reafons, increafe in the fouth.

During the exiftence of the ftate impoft laws, two of the fouthern ftates (Maryland and Virginia) impofed an extra tonnage, not only upon foreign fhips but upon thofe of the other ftates, by which they evinced a ftrong difpofition to encourage the *manufacture of fhips*. The fame two ftates laid duties on the importation of fpirits manufactured in the other parts of the union.

The ftate of Maryland impofed confiderable protecting duties to encourage their own manufactures. The legiflature of Maryland have encouraged the glafs manufactory in that ftate by a confiderable loan. That of Virginia paffed a fpecial act fince the peace, to encourage the manufactory of fnuff and tobacco.

There are more factories of *cordage and cables* in two of the fouthern ftates, (Maryland and Virginia) than in any two of the ftates of New-Jerfey, New-York, Connecticut, and New-Hampfhire. Virginia laid a duty of two-thirds of a dollar on cordage by her ftate impoft law.

The important manufactory of fhips has become greater in each of the three ftates of Maryland, Virginia, and North-Carolina, than it now is in New-Hampfhire. The fouthern ftate of Maryland manufactured in 1790, as many veffels as any two of the northern ftates of New-York, Connecticut, and Rhode-Ifland.

The paper-mill in the United States, which is moft remote from the fea, is to be found in the town of Salem, in North-Carolina, three hundred miles from the ocean. No fuch manufactures as thofe of that village (a Moravian fettlement) in the fouthern ftate of North-Carolina, exift in any part of the union north of Maryland, equally remote from the fea.

There are but two fcenes in the Atlantic counties, in which coal, iron and waterfalls are yet found together in abundance. Thefe fcenes are therefore, peculiarly qualified for the iron branch of manufactures. The city of Richmond on the bank of James' river, in Virginia, which is one of the places contemplated, may be confidered in a permanent view as having an inconteftable natural advantage over any more northern *fea-port*, in this interefting branch. How profitable would it be to Virginia, were all her pig and bar iron paffed under the tilt hammers, or through the rolling and flitting mills, which might be erected at that place.*

Some of the produce of the fisheries, as before obferved, are to be deemed manufactures. The herring and fhad (or river and bay) fifheries, fouth of Pennfylvania are very confiderable. A barrel of herrings is worth, on a medium at the fifhing places, 250 cents. The manufacture of the cafk, the packing, curing, making pickle, and trimming,

* The exiftence of coal on the eaftern boundary of Luzerne county, in Pennfylvania, and in the near parts of Northumberland, and in the wefternmoft parts of Northampton was not afcertained in 1791.

amount to more than one fourth of the fum or twenty five per cent. The cafk and manufacturing of fpirits diftilled from molaffes, does not amount to more than one fixth of the value of the commodity, or 16 2-3 per cent. A barrel of *pickled fifh* of the fouthern ftates may be therefore as juftly deemed a manufacture, as a cafk of country rum. A fimilar comparifon might be made between this article and feveral other fimple manufactures of the middle and eaftern parts of the union. It is not intended to difcufs, at this time, the propriety of granting bounties, but if they were deemed proper grants, there are points of view in which the fouthern ftates would appear to have a much greater intereft in them, than the eaftern ftates.

1ft. As the fouthern ftates cultivate *a greater variety of raw articles*—and are capable of producing *a much larger quantity* of them, all that extenfive clafs of bounties, which are refolvable into an encouragement to the growth of the raw material, will be much more beneficial to them, than to the eaftern ftates, which are more limited both in the kinds and quantities they can bring forward for the bounty.

2dly. The fouthern ftates having extenfive and very rich interior and weftern counties, far from navigable rivers, (which the eaftern have rot) and the productions of thofe fcenes being liable to a long and expenfive land carriage, the bounty would

foon be found *to enable them to bring the fimple ma-*
nufactures and raw materials to the markets on the
fea coafts, which they would not, without the
bounty, attempt to tranfport thither. This will
not be deemed a mere fuggeftion of ingenuity,
when it is remembered that the Britifh and Irifh give
bounties on their fabrics, and even on the bulky
articles of flour, grain, and bifcuit, *to enable the*
exporter to deliver them with advantage in foreign
markets.

It is an obvious truth, that every thing is more
valuable in proportion to the number and extent
of its *ufes,* or the purpofes to which it can be advantageoufly applied. Flax, hemp, wool, filk, cotton, indigo, tobacco, hides, iron, wood, grain, and
cattle, are valuable, where they are wanted merely as exports; but they manifeftly acquire a *new*
or *fecond* value, when wanted to employ, accomo-
date, or nourifh manufacturers. In places from
whence thofe articles cannot be exported, without
a great expenfe of tranfportation, it is very defirable to give them this *fecond ufe ;* but in fituations
too interior to be affected by the demand for
exportation, and where of courfe they are not required for the purpofes of external commerce, this
new ufe *muft* be created for them, or *they will not*
be produced, and agriculture will confequently languifh. *This view of the fubject evinces the indif-*
penfable neceffity of manufactures to the profperity of
the interior and weftern country as before intimated.
Nor will thefe ideas appear, on examination, to be

merely plaufible conjectures. They are no lefs
fupported by the actual ftate of things, than by probability and reafon. The towns of Wafhington,
Pittfburg, Bedford, and Huntingdon, in Pennfylvania, (the neareft of which is 150 miles from a
fea-port, exhibit the ftrongeft proofs, that manufactures are the natural and beft fupport of the interior landed intereft, and are neceffary at once to
the accommodation, the comfort, and the profperity of the cultivators of the middle and weftern
country. The following table contains an account
of the population of thofe villages, which is not exaggerated.

	Washington.	Pittsburg.	Bedford.	Huntingdon.
Clock and watchmakers,	1	1		
Silversmiths,	1			1
Coopers,	1	2	1	
Skin-dressers and breeches makers,	1	1		
Tanners and curriers,	1	2	1	
Tailors,	2		2	3
Cabinet makers,	2	4		2
Blacksmiths,	2	5	3	4
Shoemakers,	2	5	2	4
Hatters,	2	2	1	2
Dyers,	1			
Weavers,	2	2		2
Reedmakers,	1			
Saddlers,	1	3	2	2
Saddletree-makers,	1			
Spinningwheel-makers,	1			
Nailors,	1		1	
Malsters and Brewers,	1	1		
Potters,	1			
Tinners,	1	2		
Distillers,	3		1	
Wheelrights,		3	1	2
Stocking-weavers,		1		1
Gunsmiths,	3			
Ropemakers,		1		
Whitesmiths,		2		
Total of manufacturers,	32	40	15	23
Total families,	*	130	40	85

It appears from this table, that in those county-towns (or seats of justice) in the interior and western parts of Pennsylvania, the necessity for manufactures has occasioned a little congregation of ar-

* The population of Washington is unknown but it is less than that of Pittsburg.

tizans, in the proportion of twenty-seven parts in one hundred, of the whole village in the smallest instance, and in the proportion of thirty seven parts in one hundred, in the largest. The town of Washington, which is the most remote, and is near to the Ohio, has been created since the late war. Its distance is about 300 miles west of Philadelphia. The variety of its manufactures is striking, and it may be safely affirmed, that at the seats of justice, in the counties of Delaware, Bucks, Chester, and Montgomery, which are nearest to Philadelphia, as great a number of manufactures, in propotion to their respective population, does not exist, though the family manufactures are much more considerable in these counties, and though they have very numerous tanneries, iron works, powder-mills, paper-mills, blacksmiths, hatters, shoemakers, weavers, and other valuable workmen, in their villages and scattered throughout their populous townships. This, however, is the case, in some degree, likewise in the townships of the western scene above described.

In the midland counties of Pennsylvania, many precious manufactures have resulted from *a flourishing agriculture*, and, immediately on their birth, have contributed to the prosperity of the cultivators. The borough of Lancaster, which is the largest inland town in the United States, is sixty-six miles from a seaport, and ten from any practised boat navigation. The number of families was in 1786, about 700, of whom 234 were manufacturers. The following is the list of them.

Fourteen hatters, thirty-six shoemakers, four tanners, seventeen saddlers, twenty-five tailors, twenty-five weavers of woolen, linen, and cotton cloth, three stocking weavers, twenty-five white and black smiths, six wheel wrights, eleven coopers, six clock and watchmakers, six tobacco and snuff manufacturers, four dyers, seven gun smiths, five rope makers, four tinners, two brass founders, three skin dressers, one brush maker, seven turners, seven nail makers, five silver smiths, three potters, three brewers, three copper smiths, and two printers in English and German. There were in 1786 also, within thirty-nine miles of the town, seventeen furnaces, forges, rolling mills and slitting mills, and within ten miles of it eighteen grain mills, sixteen saw mills, one fulling mill, four oil mills, five hemp mills, two boreing and grinding mills for gun barrels, and eight tanneries. The increase since 1786, must have been very considerable; for the attention of the United States has been very much turned to manufactures since the year 1787. It may be safely affirmed, that the counties of Lancaster (in which the borough is) York and Berks are among the most vigorous in Pennsylvania, perhaps in the union, and that there are none in the state in which there are more manufactures, is beyond all question. They are all fifty miles or more, from the nearest sea-port.

Information through several channels, affords the greatest reason to believe, that the interior of

Frederick and Elizabeth towns, in Maryland, Stanton, in Virginia, Lexington, in Kentucky, and other towns in the fouthern ftates, would prove on examination, fimilar to thofe of Pennfylvania, and that the improvements in neceffary manufactures are as vifible and as rapid, as thofe in agriculture*.

* The following account of the fize and of the manufactures of Winchefter, in Virginia, is furnifhed by a perfon lately a refident in that place It appears to exceed even the towns of Pennfylvania in the proportion of manufacturers.

There are about two hundred houfes in Winchefter. Provifions and wood are low.

There are four or five tan yards. The demand for leather is fo great, that it is generally fold unfit for ufe.

One rope yard carried on extenfively.

One or two coachmakers. Few carriages are ufed, the roads being yet rough.

The bakers and diftillers brew occafionally.

There are three or four diftilleries in the town. In the neighbourhood there are many.

There are alfo feveral oil mills in the neighbourhood. The price of flaxfeed is 2f. and 2f6 per bufhel, Virginia money.

Grift mills are numerous in the neighbourhood ; and teams are conftantly employed in the tranfportation of flour to Alexandria : diftance eighty miles : carriage $1\frac{1}{4}$ dollar per barrel.

One copperfmith, who carries on his bufinefs very extenfively.

Three tin plate workers.

Eight or ten hatters. Wool hats, of Winchefter make are in much repute, and are vended in large quantities. Price eleven dollars per dozen. Single hat, one dollar.

☞ Note. Wool is one third of a dollar per lb. and *is often ordered up from Philadelphia by the Winchefter hatters.*

Twelve or fifteen faddlers.

☞ Note. This manufacture, as well as the hatting, is in *a flourifhing condition,* and carried on *very extenfively.*

Five or fix blackfmiths—one employed in plating faddle trees.

The reflections arifing from thefe facts are highly fatisfactory, and as they open new and extended views of the refources and capacities of the United States, they muft increafe the prevalent difpofition of the people to improve the interior economy of our country. It is devoutly hoped, that they may alfo contribute to remove the apprehenfions of our fouthern and weftern fellow citizens, in regard to unjuft facrifices of their interefts to thofe of their brethren in other quarters, and that they may lead to fuch further examinations as will finally evince thofe immenfe direct and indirect benefits from American manufactures, which are fincerely believed to pervade *the whole union.*

CONCERNING THE MANUFACTURES OF THE UNITED STATES, AS THEY AFFECT THE MERCANTILE INTEREST.

Many of the fhipholders and merchants trading with foreign countries, fuppofe, but it is believed erroneoufly, that they have no intereft in the promotion of manufactures. It is known that Great-Britain with feventy millions of acres of populated land, fhips fourteen millions (her whole exports being near twenty millions) in her own manufactures. The foreign trade of that kingdom, without manufactures would manifeftly be neither fo

Three or four wheelrights.
Eight or ten tailors.
Eight or nine fhoemakers.
Four or five weavers. Two fpinning wheel makers.
Three or four faddle tree makers.

great nor fo various—for the value of the produce
manufactured is increafed from one hundred to ten
hundred per cent. and more; as is alfo that of the
imported raw materials, which conftitute a great
portion of their trade. The foreign commerce of
the United States, is already enlivened by manufactures. Ships, boats, oars, and handfpikes, bar
iron, fteel, nail rods, carriages of all kinds, hats,
fhoes, cordage, candles, foap, oils of feveral kinds,
ftarch, hair powder, diftilled fpirits, malt liquors,
cabinet wares, plate, puncheon packs, gunpowder,
pot-afhes, bricks, chocolate, muftard, tow linens,
fail-cloth, potter's ware, fadlery and harnefs, wool
and cotton cards, paper and paper hangings, tanned leather, books, fnuff, manufactured tobacco,
and iron manufactures are now frequently exported to foreign countries. Coaftwife there is alfo a
great trade in thefe and many other manufactured
articles, and in raw materials and provifions for the
manufacturers within the United States.

An argument of great importance to the fhipholders, exporters, and underwriters, and indeed
to the cultivators of the earth, in fupport of manufactures is to be drawn from their tendency to promote in an eafy, certain, fafe and cheap way, the
naval capacities and ftrength of the United States.
The tranfportation of provifions, coal, raw materials, and other articles from the fouthern and middle ftates to the northern, and the diffufion of the
manufactures, of the towns on the coaft, throughout
the union, already employs many veffels. The

rice, indigo, cotton, hemp, flax, iron, hides, furs, tar, pitch, turpentine, rofin, wax, tobacco, wood and timber, flour and grain, fhipped from the ftates on, and to the fouthward of the Chefapeak, for the manufacturers in the middle and northern ftates, give employment at this time to a very confiderable portion of our tonnage. This cannot be doubted, when it is remembred, that our coafters are 110,000 tons, though our veffels in *all* the foreign trades probably do not much exceed 150,000 ;* and the former are entirely out of the reach of foreign reftriction, confequently (with the fifhing veffels) are our moft certain dependence. The weight of this circumftance, will be not a little increafed by the recollection, that the coafting trade it uncommonly interefting to a nation without tranfmarine colonies or dominions.

When we confider the fifheries as one of the moft efficacious modes of creating the powers of offence and defence at fea, and that our agriculture and commerce, muft therefore be fupported and defended by our fifhermen, and fifhing veffels, among other means, it will be fatisfactory to the cultivators, and merchants, that they will be promoted by the fuccefs of our manufactures. Skins and furs of fea animals, whalebone, and the head matter of the whale, are ufed by various manufacturers for leather, hats, whips, candles, &c.

* A. D. 1791, and of courfe exclufive of fifhing veffels.

The oils are used by leather dreſſers, ſhipbuilders, &c. and inſtead of candles.

It will be unneceſſary to adduce to our mercantile citizens any arguments to prove, that the United States generally pay a premium on the bills purchaſed for their remittances for European manufactures. The exports, ſales of veſſels, their outward freights and ſales of lands, to foreigners, are the ordinary means applied to the payments for our imports, after deducting that part of them, which belonging to emigrators, is not to be remitted or paid for. It is intereſting to aſcertain the reaſons for our continuing to loſe by the courſe of exchange. The principal cauſe probably is, that we draw ſo very large a proportion of our manufactures from one nation, that there is conſtantly a trebled demand for bills on that country. It is of importance to diſcover how this is to be remedied. *The other European nations have had the eight years of the war almoſt excluſively, and the nine years of the peace, in a fair competition and do not ſupply us with manufactures equivalent to half of the ſtated value of the ſhoes made by ourſelves!* It appears then, that *our own exertions only,* can relieve our merchants from this annual loſs on their remittances for ſeveral million of dollars.

It may not be improper to take a view of the article of diſtilled ſpirits as a commodity, which we are capable of manufacturing to any extent, and which while it will be an aid to agriculture, will alfo be an object of coafting and foreign trade. We have imported, in a fingle year, above eleven millions of gallons of foreign fpirits and molaffes. If one million of gallons of the latter were ufed in fubftance then our imports of fpirits and ingredients made into fpirits, would ftand at ten millions of gallons. The value of thefe, as they coft the country may be fairly taken at one third of a dollar on a medium, and will give 3,333,333 dollars, which is above one-fixth part of the annual value of our exports*. As five millions of bufhels of grain would be confumed in the manufactory of a quantity of fpirits equal to what was imported, in the form of fpirits or ingredients employed to make them, there is no occafion for argument to prove, that *the landed intereft* would be greatly benefited by the manufacture of grain liquors (or fruit liquors) in lieu of the ten millions of gallons drawn from foreign fources. And in regard to *the mercantile intereft*, it may be obferved, that the fupply of a foreign commodity is always precarious, and accordingly the difturbances in the feveral parts of the French empire, and the lofs of their vintage, have deprived us of the ufual importation of their brandies fince the laft autumn, and of the accuftomed fupply of molaffes from the crop of 1792 of their principal colony. Thefe two defalcations will probably amount to fome millions of gallons, and muft produce a void

* A. D. 1791.

in a confiderable branch of our foreign trade, for we fhall not have it in our power to import the brandies and molaffes, nor to export the returns for them, which have employed many thoufand tons of fhipping, and a confiderable part of our mercantile capital and induftry ; nor fhall we be able to export diftilled fpirits, manufactured from molaffes, which has alfo employed our veffels, private funds and induftry. How are the merchant and fhipholder to be relievéd under thefe injuries to their bufinefs ? Manufacturing diftilled fpirits and malt liquors* from native materials will afford confiderable relief. Their capital and veffels may be employed in purchafing and tranf-porting, from the rivers and bays of the United States to the diftilleries and breweries, a part at leaft of the requifite quantities of grain, hops, fuel, and lumber, and of the manufactured liquors, to domeftic or foreign markets. Nor is this a mere probability. It is already an exifting fact. The manufacture of grain liquors in the town of Providence (in Rhode-Ifland) alone, in the firft three months of the prefent year, was equivalent to 12056 cafes of geneva per ann. If the Dutch import grain enough from the north of Europe, to make and diftribute gin throughout the world, from Archangel to Canton, which is really the cafe, it cannot be doubted that the United States, which have the greateft furplus of grain of any country upon earth, which are rapidly increafing it, which are

* See paper T. in the fecond book.

further from their confumers than any nation exporting grain, which have the wood to make the
cafks for it, and the fhipping to tranfport it, and
are themfelves great confumers of malt liquors and
diftilled fpirits, it cannot be doubted that a nation
thus circumftanced, muft be able to manufacture
thofe articles with facility and advantage to any extent of the demand. The benefits to foreign trade
from the manufacture of fhips, cordage, fail-cloth,
and anchors, as neceffary inftruments of commerce, and from thofe articles and pot-afh, foap,
candles, fteel, carriages and other articles, for fale
to foreigners here, or as payments or remittances
to them abroad are already too obvious to need
more than to be enumerated : but too much attention cannot be given to our fituation, qualifications, and profpects in regard to the home manufacture of liquors, confidering the difturbed ftate
of the fugar iflands, the increafed confumption and
prices of all the productions of the cane, the impediments to the ordinary importation of flaves, the
objections to the flave trade which are appearing in
different quarters, the immenfe population of the
manufacturing countries of Europe, and their confequent neceffity to employ in the culture of grain
the lands they recently appropriated to the vine, as
well as the impoffibility of their fparing for the
making of liquors all the barley, rye, and oats,
which were formerly confumed in that manufacture.

There is alfo a confiderable portion of foreign
trade, created by the importation of raw materials

and other neceſſaries for the employment and conſumption of the manufacturers : the articles contemplated are cotton, hemp, bar iron, ſheet iron,
copper and braſs in pigs and ſheets, lapis calaminaris, lead, pewter, wire of every metal, woolen,
cotton, and linen yarns, hempen yarn, hides, ſkins,
and furs, wool, paper for books and hangings, dyers colours, and ſome others, varniſh, printing
types, bullion for gold and ſilverſmiths, gold and
ſilver leaf, glue, mahogany, and other cabinet
woods, molaſſes, and crude ſugars for diſtillers and
refiners, manufacturers tools and implements, ſuch
as vizes, ſcrewplates, anvils, hammers, axes, hatch-
ets, knives, awls, pincers, grindſtones, hatters bow-
ſtrings, &c. glaſs plates for looking glaſs makers
and coach makers, callicoe and linens for printing,
morocco ſkins, and many other commodities, which
are expended in the workſhops or families of our
manufacturers, including foreign articles of apparel, furniture, food and drink.

SECTION III.

A CONTINUATION OF THE REFLEXIONS ON THE MANUFACTURES
OF THE UNITED STATES AS THEY AFFECT THE MERCANTILE
INTEREST.

SOME of the benefits to the coaſting trade
and other parts of the domeſtic commerce reſulting from manufactures, have already been intimated in treating of the manufacture of liquors. Beſides theſe, bark and hides for the tanneries, iron,
lead, ſteel, copper, hemp, flax, wool, cotton, ſilk,

wood, timber, furs, tobacco, flaxfeed, and grain, for the manufacturers of thofe articles, and provifions, fuel, indigo, and other objects of their confumption and ufe, together with the goods made by them, are, and conftantly will be purchafed, tranfported from place to place, and fold; creating a great part of the employment for 110,000 tons of coafting veffels, exercifing a large portion of commercial induftry and fkill, and affording a return of profits, on a very confiderable fum of mercantile capital, employed in the bufinefs. This branch of our trade is of *peculiar* importance; becaufe we have no tranfmarine colonies, and while the redundancy of fhipping owned by moft nations, will leave us but little chance of materially increafing our veffels in the foreign trades, the extenfion we may give by it, in the courfe of ten years, to our home trade and navigation, will probably be very great. We have brought cotton, fugar, and faltpetre to be manufactured, from India, fulphur from the Adriatic, hemp, flax, and iron, from Ruffia, copper from Sweden, furs, indigo, and mahogany, from the gulph of Mexico, and coal for our workmen from England: and we cannot doubt, therefore, that we fhall tranfport thofe commodities and others, from fuch of the ftates as produce them, to thofe which fhall create, or have already eftablifhed, *a manufacturing demand.*

Foreign commerce being limited by the combined value of our imports, and exports,* any mer-

* The negociations and infurances for foreigners are confiderable, but thefe operations require little ufe of capital.

cantile capital, which might accumulate beyond the
sum requisite for those purposes, would want employment of a commercial nature, if the merchant
were not able to have recourse to manufactures.
This is not a mere speculation in possible events;
for considerable trading houses, and others of respectable standing, have actually entered into such
pursuits. Glass-houses, rope-walks, powder-mills,
iron-works, steel-works, slitting and rolling mills,
grist-mills, naileries, sugar refineries, breweries and
distilleries, the manufactory of sail-cloth, and of
woolen, cotton and linen goods, exhibit at this moment numerous proofs of the fact. The commercial states, which do not produce much, will yearly
confirm this truth.

It is too well know to need more than a bare allegation of the truth, that our outward bound vessels are always completely laden, and that they do
not on a medium return half full. It will therefore, increase the profits of the owners of ships, if
the outward cargo can be rendered more valuable
by manufacturing the goods to be exported. This
may be exemplified in regard to wheat and the simple manufacture of superfine flour. A vessel, which
will carry ten thousand bushels of the former, at
the price of a dollar per bushel, will be laden for
10,000 dollars; but the quantity of superfine flour
(3,000 barrels) which the same vessel would receive,
will amount at a proportionate price, to the sum of
15,000 dollars. The same quantity of tonnage,
filled with our bottled porter, distilled spirits, steel,

cordage, ftarch, pearl afhes, carriages, cabinet
wares, plate, candles, foap, linfeed oil, paper, hats,
fhoes, &c. would rife to a much greater value; and
of confequence, the owners of the veffel would be
able to purchafe more goods for the return cargo,
by which the fhip being fuller would make a greater fum in freight back. This circumftance is rendered of the more confequence, by reafon of our
diftance from the greater part of the confumers of
our furplus produce: and it is obvious, that fhips
will be moft profitable in thofe trades, wherein the
meafurement of all our imports, fhall be equal to
the meafurement of all our exports. Veffels, which
depart and return fully laden, cannot fail to enrich
their owners.

No arguments will be neceffary to convince the
judicious and reflecting mind, that the employment of large capitals and of many merchants and
traders is moft certain and eafy, where there are
the greateft number and variety of objects to be
bought and fold. As our commercial towns,
therefore, have offered manufactured commodities to thofe, who come thither to trade, they
have increafed in bufinefs. Pot afh, pearl afh,
country rum, and other domeftic liquors, loaf
fugar, &c. have already contributed to fwell their
exports, by attracting foreign demand, or increafing the number of profitable objects of fhipment.
Thefe will naturally multiply under the hands of
our manufacturers, and inftead of markets, in which
nothing but lumber, tobacco, live-ftock, provifions,

and raw materials were formerly to be obtained, our fea-ports will be converted into magazines, in which not only all thofe articles will ftill be procurable but the various commodities manufactured from them. For thefe goods in whatever fhape, purchafers will never be wanting : *cheap merchandize as certainly attracts buyers, as water finds its level.* Nor is this mere fanguine hope, or ingenious fuggeftion ; for it is an obvious truth, that *the greateft manufacturing nations in the old world, are the greateft traders to foreign parts.* Holland, when moft remarkable for manufactures, traded to the amount of eighty millions of dolars per annum in the commodities of other countries.

A FEW GENERAL REFLECTIONS ON AMERICAN MANUFACTURES.

The political concord and attachments, which grow out of mutual benefits, are the moft rational and permanent. To encourage thefe is *the piety* of American patriotifm. In this view, the cement, which will be given to the national union, by the interchanges of raw materials, provifions, fuel, and manufactures among the feveral ftates, is of ineftimable value. If European nations have fhown difpofitions of amity and mutual forbearance, on thefe confiderations, it cannot be doubted that fifter ftates will evince equal wifdom and virtue. If many parts of our union, from policy or a temporary neceffity for manufactured fupplies, have been willing to exhibit the greateſt liberality toward thoſe foreigners, with whom they have been recently at the wideſt varience, and whom they ſtill conſider as little leſs than hoſtile, it muſt appear very deſireable, that the capacity at once to accommodate thoſe ſtates and engage their regard, ſhould be transferred from diſtant ſtrangers, to our own continent, and our own kindred. If the merchants and manufacturers of the opulent nation with whom the United States ſo long waged war, influenced by the hope of our conſumption, cried aloud for peace, and, on the moment of its return, preſſed with all the courteſies of commerce to our ſhores, the exiſting friendſhip of the ſeveral parts of the union for each other muſt be ſtrengthened by ſimilar influences, as they ſhall be progreſſively created.

The animated proſecution and liberal encouragement of manufactures, is at this moment a great political duty. The national legiſlature has increaſed the impoſt on foreign merchandize, to defray the expences of the Indian war. The continuance of a great part of the duties is to be no longer than that of the hoſtilities, which occaſioned them to be laid. If the interval ſhould be diligently employed in the promotion of manufactures, which theſe duties are calculated to create and to protect, the temporary injuries of the Indian war will be accompanied and followed by great, ſolid, and permanent benefits. The military expence is rendered leſs burdenſome by the employment given to our own workmen. The ſhoes, boots, horſemen's caps,

hats, buckles, buttons, fadlery, fpears, rifles, gun-
powder, and other articles for the ufe of the army,
are made by American manufacturers. It is perceived, that war, which often interrupts foreign
commerce and generally dimnifhes the prices of
agricultural productions for exportation, has in this
inftance no effects of that nature; but by judicious arrangements, may be rendered inftrumental
to the greateft fupport of the landed intereft—*the
manufactures of the United States*. The lamentable
havoc of the field muft inevitably diminifh the
number of our citizens; but there is every reafon
to believe, that thofe, who, in the courfe of the
prefent Indian war, may fall under the banners of
their country, will prove inferior in number to
thofe who will be drawn, by the influence of the
new duties, from foreign countries, to the ftandard
of American manufactures: and although the moft
ufeful arts are no compenfation for the lives of our
compatriots, the acquifition of a greater number of
new citizens will counterbalance *the political evil*
refultiug from fuch a lofs, fo far as it may unhappily occur*.

It is detrimental to the United States, that the
manufactures they confume are drawn from nations,
whofe citizens pay much greater contributions to
their governments than our manufacturers, and
confequently, that we, fo far forth, are fubject to

* It is conceived that the obfervations in the preceding paragraph
apply to the duties laid on account of the Algerine depredations.

their taxes, imposts, and excises. In Great-Britain for example, their national taxes are seven times as large as ours, in proportion to the numbers of people in the two countries ; and their poor rates and church rates are *each* more than double our whole national contributions. The monopolies of those countries fall heavily upon the consumers, among their citizens ; and those, who purchase their fabrics, bear a part of this burden, which lies on their manufacturers. The commercial charges paid by the English East-India company *abroad*, amount to one million of dollars per annum: the freight and the charges in England are about two millions and two-thirds more, exclusively of duties. The company's civil and military charges would, in two years like the present, pay all the expenses of our government, and discharge our national debt*. The restrictions on navigation and trade in the European nations also enhance the price of raw materials and articles of consumption required by their manufacturers, all which fall ultimately upon the people of the United States, so far as their fabrics are consumed here. These considerations should induce our most strenuous exertions, to diminish those indirect burdens, and at the same time they hold out an absolute certainty of a successful issue to our efforts.

In taking a view of the affairs of the United States, and comparing them with the situation of

* A. D. 1791.

moſt of the great commercial nations of Europe, the mind is immediately impreſſed with the peculiarity of their being without tranſmarine colonies. Though ſpeculative politicians have entertained doubts in regard to favourable effeels from ſuch poſſeſſions, taking into view the expences of their improvement, defence and government, no queſtion has been made but that the monopoly of their trade greatly increaſes the commerce of the nations to which they are appertenant. Of ſuch an advantage the United States do not enjoy the benefit ; and conſidering this circumſtance, and the prevailing diſpoſition to reſtriet commerce, our fiſheries, coaſting trade, and *manufaetures* appear to merit extraordinary attention.

The conſideration of manufaetures, upon general principles, has been, for ſeveral years, before the legiſlatures as well of the ſtates, as of the union. The eſtimation of their importance to the landed and national intereſts appears to have been greatly heightened by diſcuſſion and enquiries into faets. *Houſehold* manufaetures, have acquired univerſal and decided approbation. To thoſe which are condueted by labour-ſaving machinery and proceſſes, by horſes and oxen, and which conſequently do not require manual operations, no objeetion has been made. Such of them as can be carried on by the manufaeturers now among us, by thoſe who may migrate hither, by the wives and children of our citizens, and by black women, old men and children, have not been conſidered as diminiſhing the mafs of agricultural induftry, but as manifeftly promoting it by new and extenfive demands.

The prefent difcuffion of the fubject will be terminated by remarking, that although this great fubdivifion of our political economy has been copioufly and freely treated in every mode, it has not only preferved its original importance in the public judgment, but has rifen in the eftimation of the people in every part of the union—*a fate that rarely attends unimportant truths or dangerous errors in an enlightened country.* (See table of duties on foreign manufactures, &c. paper Z.)

CONCERNING THE IMPORTS OF THE UNITED STATES.

This part of the national bufinefs has given rife to doubts, whether the United States are really in a profperous fituation. The apprehenfion is believed, however, to have proceeded from feveral errors. The eftimation of the imports has probably been made from the prices current in America, which are more than the United States pay for them, by the total value of the following particulars. 1ft. Such part of the fhipping charges abroad, as accrue to the benefit of the citizens of the United States, who may be on the fpot to make the fhipment: 2dly, that part of the freight upon them, which is earned by our own veffels: 3dly, that part of the premium of infurance upon them, which is paid to American underwriters or infurers : 4thly, the whole amount of the duties, and cuftom houfe fees, on the goods, which amount to feveral millions of dollars : 5thly,

the amount of the tonnage and fees on foreign veſſels, which are deductions in favour of the country
from the value of the goods imported in them :
6thly, the porterage, ſtoreage, cooperage, weighing,
guaging, meaſuring, commiſſions on ſales here and
other incidental expences on that part of the imports
which belongs to foreigners : 7thly, the profits of
our merchants on that part of the imports which
belongs to them : 8thly, the waſteage of goods
belonging to foreigners between their arrival or time
of valuation and the time of ſale : 9thly, the benefit of credit which is not leſs than two and an half
per cent. on the whole value of our imports : and
10thly, the value of thoſe imported goods which remain in the country, being the property of perſons
intending to become, or who will ultimately become citizens of the United States.   But the apparent or conjectural diſproportion between the exports and imports of the United States, will be conſiderably diminiſhed by the ſales of veſſels to foreigners at home and abroad—the ſales of lands to
them—the expences of foreigners here—the expences of foreign veſſels here, and the coſt of their ſea-
ſtores—the commiſſions on the ſhipments of their
cargoes, and on the diſburſements of their veſſels,
as already obſerved in treating of our exports.
Beſides theſe, the freight of goods ſhipped to foreign
countries in our own veſſels, (not leſs probably
than three millions of dollars) and the profits upon
all the goods exported on the account of our own
citizens, contribute very much to increaſe the fund,
wherewith our imports are purchaſed or paid for.
An eſtimate, which ſhall comprehend all theſe

items at their true value, is neceſſary to form a fatisfactory opinion of the balance on our trade. From
fuch an eſtimation (which has been made) there
would refult no reaſon to doubt our profperity :
nor will this appear queſtionable, when it is remembered, that the outward freights in our veſſels, and
the duties on goods imported, amount together to
6,400,000 dollars, which is more than one third of
our exports. The balance of trade has been aptly
denominated *the metaphyſics of commerce*. To determine it with indifputable certainty requires as accurate and elaborate an inveſtigation as a great me-
taphyſical queſtion : and though this aſſertion proves
nothing, it will infpire us with due caution againſt
haftily adopting unfavourable concluſions.

An opinion fomewhat fingular and of confiderable importance will be hazarded upon this fubject.
*The United States, to make the utmoſt advantage of
things in their prefent improvable fituation, fhould
have little or no balance in their favour on their general commerce.* If their exports, outward freights,
fales of veſſels and lands, &c. amount to twenty-
four millions of dollars per annum, they will find
their true intereſt in importing the whole value in
well felected commodities. It is better for example, that they import molaſſes, hemp, cotton, wool,
bar iron, hides, ſkins, furs, falt-petre, fulphur, copper, tin, braſs, paper, mahogany, &c. to manufacture ; tools for artizans, and materials and utenſils
for conſtructing works, improving waſte lands, and
cultivating farms, and breeding-cattle, horſes, and

sheep; than that they should bring back the equivalent in gold or silver. The sum we annually
import in articles of that nature, more precious to
us than the most precious metals, would constitute
an immense balance in our favour: such, indeed,
as would, in a few years, oppress our country with
too copious a circulating medium, or compel us to
export it.

That the exports and other means of paying for
our imports are much more adequate to the occasion, than they were during several years subsequent
to the peace, is manifest from the state of our private credit in Europe.

A distinction, and it is conceived, a very important one, has been already intimated in favour of
such of our imports as are of a nature adapted to
enhance the value of our lands, or to employ or
assist our citizens: and in regard to those which are
for immediate consumption, the quantity cannot be
in proportion to our former imports, considering
the increase of population. We have actually
almost ceased to import shoes, boots, sadlery,
coarse hats, plate, snuff, manufactured tobacco,
cabinet wares, carriages, wool and cotton cards,
hanging paper, gunpowder, and other articles;
and we have exceedingly diminished our importation of coarse linen and woolen goods, cordage,
copper utensils, tin utensils, malt liquors, loaf sugar, steel, paper, playing cards, glue, wafers, fine
hats, braziery, watches and clocks, cheese, &c:

and we either make thefe articles from native pro-
duftions, by which the whole value is ftruck off
from our imports, or we manufafture them of foreign raw materials, which coft lefs than the goods
ufed to do, efpecially as they often yield a great
freight to our own veffels. Thus the freight of the
molaffes to make rum, imported in one year, at
two dollars per hhd. was not lefs than 140,000 dollars. The fame obfervation occurs as to hemp,
cotton, iron, copper, brafs, tin, faltpetre, fulphur,
mahogany, hides, dye woods, and other raw materials.

From thefe circumftantial evidences, there would
appear to be little danger of miftake, in conclud-
ing, that our imports, on a medium of two or
three years, have not been difproportinate to
our exports, and other fafe and regular means
of balancing the amount of our fupplies. But
though the documents for a comparifon between
the prefent imports, and thofe antecedent to the
revolution, are lefs perfeft than is to be defired,
fome which offer are worthy of attention. Our
imports from Great-Britain in 1770, making fome
addition for thofe from Ireland and adding 20 per
cent. to bring them to their market value, were
worth *here* above £.2,400,000 fterling. In this
item, the information obtained from a report of
the lords of the Britifh privy council, is principally relied on, though a part of it is fupplementary
eftimation. To this fum is to be added, a proportion of the imports into all the American colonies

in 1770, from all the reft of the world, but Great-
Britain, which, after deducting therefrom £.73,000
fterling for the value imported into Bermuda, the
Bahamas, the northern Britifh colonies, and Newfoundland, leaves £1,050,000 fter. for the value here
of this part of our former imports. The total value
of our imports in 1770, would then appear to have
been more than £.3,450,000 or about 15,000,000
dollars, as they would have fold in the American
market, exclufive of the contraband trade, which
was confiderable. This will be feen by a reference
to the firft number of thefe reflexions, to be full
feven millions of dollars more than our exports at
the fame time. If then our imports were to bear
the fame proportion to 18,250,000 dollars (our prefent exports) the former might be above 34,000,000
dollars, without creating more alarm than we had
then reafon to feel. This view of the fubject may
convince us, that our imports were too copious, at
leaft in fome quarters, for feveral years before the
war; and hence we find a heavy load of private
debt was created and remains upon the citizens of
fome of the ftates at this day. Happily for the
United States, the reduction of the prices of fupplies, by the prefent freedom of their commerce,
by the agency of merchants of credit inftead of
planters inexperienced in trade, by the introduction of machinery in Europe, and by their own
manufacturing induftry, has kept down their imports many millions of dollars below that fum, although the impoft and tonnage have directly or indirectly contributed to enhance the nominal amount

without increafing the fum to be paid for them abroad*.

A SKETCH OF THE GENERAL TRADE OF THE UNITED STATES.

In taking a furvey of the American commerce, the attention is pleafingly attracted to the increafe of fhip building, to the new manufactories of articles neceffary to the equipment of veffels, and to the improvement in the art of fhip-building, as well as the fuperior quality of the materials now

U u

* There is a fact, which affects our imports in a manner peculiarly favourable to the United States. Many of the imported articles are not requifite for *daily* or *annual* perfonal confumption, but for permanent landed improvement, and are added in the courfe of our internal operations to the *fixed real propriety* of the country. Landed eftates in the towns and in the country being no where improved to the utmoft point, and being in many places yet in a ftate of nature, a large proportion of the articles of importation not only become at the inftant of ufe, a permanent property, but indeed give life and productivenefs to other property, which the moment before, was an inactive and fruitlefs poffeffion.

For inftance—In 1786 feveral millions of acres, ceded by New-York to Maffachufetts, yielded not one hundred dollars, nor were there one hundred citizens of thefe ftates refident on them. Since that time a very large value in nails, fpikes, hinges, locks, glafs, paints and other imported articles have been converted (with the aid of our own timber, ftone, and lime,) into houfes, barns, mills, workfhops, places of public bufinefs, and of worfhip, &c. and now conftitute *real, fixed, permanent and productive property*, while the teas and fugars, the linens, woolens, and cottons, &c. imported with them have been confumed or worn out. This is yet more ftrongly exemplified in other parts of New-York and Pennfylvania.

ufed in their conftruction. The largeft number of veffels built in any one year before the late war, as far as it can be afcertained, was equal to 24,358 tons; and at leaft 32,000 tons of fuperior quality were built in 1791. The timber and plank are more chofen, and iron is more copioufly ufed at this time, becaufe the veffels are not intended for fale, and the practice of falting them, is becoming very frequent. It is important, too, that the art of fhip-building is diffufed more generally than any other equally important one, which is carried on within the United States.†

† The feveral capacities of the Baltic powers, as to the building of fhips form an interefting object to Europe and America, and are conceived to be as follow. The Swedes have plenty of fir, which quickly decays, and is weak. Yet it is commonly ufed in their trading veffels. Ships of war cannot be relied on, if built of any thing but oak. Of the latter timber the Swedes have fome in Skone and Blekinge, but not enough for their navy. They are faid to have purchafed of the King of Pruffia twice within a dozen years, a great quantity of German oak : at one time 400,000 cubic feet, and at another 200,000 feet at the immenfe price of 5/10 fterling per cubic foot delivered at Carlefcroon. American live-oak is fold in Philadelphia,* after paying a freight from the Carolinas and Georgia as 15d to 18d fterling per foot, and fouthern red cedar at the fame prices : our common white-oak is 9d fterling per foot. The Swedes raife flax but very little hemp, their fupply of which they import from Riga, to make their cordage and fail-cloth. This bulky article in time of war muft coft them high. They have plenty of iron within themfelves.

The Danes import the mafts for their navy, flax and hemp from Ruffia. They make only a part of their fail-cloth, and import

* A. D. 1789.

The export trade in our produce is more beneficial than heretofore to the landed intereſt, becauſe
the cultivators do not, as formerly, anticipate up-

that article both from Ruſſia and Holland. They have little oak
except in Holſtein, which is reſerved for emergencies. The greateſt part of the oak timber for their navy, is purchaſed by contract
from the king of Pruſſia. Their merchant ſhips, it is preſumed,
muſt therefore be of fir, which with their iron they have from Norway.

The Ruſſians have abundance of naval ſtores, flax, hemp, ſail-
cloth, iron, maſts, fir timber and plank for home conſumption and
exportation. *Oak* timber is not plenty in the vicinity of their Baltic
ports. At Archangel they have none. The oak timber for their
navy is ſaid to be brought by their canals and rivers 1200 miles
from their Tartarian kingdom of Cafan. A few ſhips of war have
been built of fir and larch. The Ruſſians have very few merchant
ſhips. Out of every hundred entries in the ſeveral ports of St. Pe-
terſburg, Archangel, Wibourg, Revel, Narva, and Riga not more
than *two* are of their national flag. The Britiſh and Dutch are
their carriers as far as two-thirds or three-fourths of the tonnage
employed.*

The dominions of the king of Pruſſia are the beſt magazine of
oak timber on the Baltic. Having, flax, hemp, timber and iron and
conſiderable manufactures of them, grain, cattle, coal, a ſea-coaſt
more extenſive than the United Netherlands or Ruſſia (excepting the frozen coaſts of Archangel) and being much nearer to the
European fiſheries than the French and Britiſh are to thoſe on
our coaſts, it will not be difficult for the Pruſſian king to advance
his navigation and trade. Indeed his port and territory of Em-
den would enable him to proſecute the fiſheries to advantage, as
alſo the Eaſt-India trade. It is difficult however to judge of things
at ſuch a diſtance. The monopoly of European *oak* is thrown in a
greater degree into the hands of the king of Pruſſia, by the laſt
partition of the devoted territory of Poland.

* A. D. 1789.

on their crops abroad, by ordering out supplies at
the discretion of the European merchant, to be
paid for in shipments of their crops upon their own
account and risque. The planters in Maryland and
Virginia, particularly the tobacco planters, suffer-
ed extremely from an inconsiderate pursuit of that
practice before the revolution. The American
merchant is now more frequently their importer ;
and as he understands the mode of procuring goods
cheap, the real profits of the import and export
trade of the country, are in a greater degree divided between the planter and the trader.

The reduction of the prices of East-India and
China goods, of every species of manufactures in
which labour saving machinery and slight apply,
and of wines, occasion our imports to be obtained
on more favourable terms. This beneficial effect
is increased by the freedom of our import trade,
which lets in the productions and manufactures of
all countries by a direct intercourse with them,
which was formerly either circuitous or forbidden.
From the same cause, superior prices for our produce and manufactured articles have been obtained. If tobacco is becoming an exception, it is to
be remembered, that great prices were obtained
for it till lately, and that the extraordinary quantity raised is sufficient to account for its fall.

The coasting trade has become very great, and
the derangement of the West-India trade must
extend it exceedingly, during the current year,

from the failure of molaffes. The increafe of
manufactures, and foreign reftrictions on other
branches of trade have contributed to elevate
this valuable part of our commerce; and the
former (manufactures) will continue fteadily to
increafe the importance of the coafting bufinefs.
The veffels, which take fupplies of flour, and many
other articles from the middle and northern ftates
to South-Carolina and Georgia, make very frequent voyages, and they return lefs than half laden : but if the planters fhould purfue the culiiva-
tion of hemp, flax, hops, and cotton, they may
come back with full cargoes. A fimilar remark
may be juftly made in regard to the other ftates.

The fifheries would appear not to have recover-
ed their former value; but it is plain, they have
increafed yearly fince 1789: and they are even
now more valuable than they appear to be. The
confumption of oil, whale-bone, fkins of fea animals, fpermaceti, and pickled and dried fifh, is much
greater in the United States at this time, than it
was twenty years ago. The outfits of the fifhing
veffels, too, are more from the induftry and refources of the country, than was formerly the cafe.
Wherefore the general benefits refulting from the
fifheries, are probably not lefs than before the revolution.

Remote as the United States are from all foreign
nations, totally unconnected with their politics,
and having no temptation to wage war for territo-

ry, they cannot but advance in commercial and agricultural prosperity, if they preserve *order* and *justice* at home. Foreign restrictions will be necessarily less rigid, as occasions for supplies and pacific services from the United States shall arise : and these occasions must inevitably exist in every maritime nation, which shall engage in war, even with a country, which is not itself maritime.

The prosecution of manufactures has created some increase of our foreign trade, and will extend it. If we did not pursue that branch of industry, we should not import copper, iron, and hemp, from the Baltic; cotton, saltpetre, raw silk, and white callicoes from India; and cocoa, dyewoods, mahogany, cotton, and hides from the West-Indies, and the southern parts of the American continent. Some of these importations are regularly and extensively made; others are increasing. Without them we should have no intercourse with some of these countries, and much less than we now have with others. In like manner, our intercourse with several countries is increased by manufactured exports. The demand for our potash, distilled spirits, ships and boats, malt liquors, cheese, bar iron, slit iron, steel, gunpowder, carriages, and other articles, occasions a greater and more beneficial trade with many foreign ports. It is impossible to say how rapid and how considerable the progress of this part of our commerce will be. The exported manufactures of Great-Britain, in 1791, were greater than thofe of fifty years ago, by twice the value of our prefent exports.

It is extremely favourable to American commerce, internal and foreign, that a variety of changes have taken place in the affairs of the world, which have opened branches of trade formerly withheld from us by monopoly, or other circumftances. The act of feparation from Great-Britain enabled us to trade to China, and other countries beyond the cape of *Good Hope*, and the enterprife of our citizens foon difcovered the way. The curious perfection of manufacturing machinery in Europe has made it the intereft of the foreign India companies to fell us their piece goods in the markets of the eaft, without taking them at fecond hand.* The misfortunes of St. Domingo have greatly increafed our commerce in indigo, and will have the fame effect upon cotton, and they are impelling us rapidly into an internal trade in native fpirits, which will of courfe lead to external commerce of the fame kind. This will appear to be a matter of great importance, when it is remembered, that fince the late peace, the foreign fpirits imported have in fome years been equal in value to one-fifth of our exports! The failure of fhip-timber, which begins to appear every where in Europe, is enabling the United States to carry on fhip-building upon very ad-

* It is underftood that the Britifh Eaft-India company are likely to be reftrained from importing into Britain feveral kinds of *pia goods.*

vantageous terms. The profitable eftablifhment of feveral banks of perfect credit with the moft wary and judicious citizens and foreigners, is at once a proof, and a great mean of commercial profperity. The growth of cities, towns, and manufactures, has given to the fifheries a more fubftantial bafis in a confiderable home demand, than they formerly had in a foreign one. The banifhment of paper tenders, and ex poft facto laws, and the interdiction of laws impairing the obligations of contracts, have placed our commerce upon a more honourable and folid footing, than it ever was before. The mint, the laws regulating feamen and the fifheries, the appreciation of the public debt, the fpirit of improvement* on roads, rivers, and canals, the difcovery of coal near navigable water, the continual extenfions of the poft-office, the conftant increafe of light houfes on the coafts, the introduction of auxiliary arts, and above all, *the progrefs of agriculture*, have given facilities, ftability, and extenfion to our trade, which, were unknown before the revolution, and which in the diftrefsful derangements of 1786 and 1787, appeared beyond the bounds of reafonable expectation.

* One million and one hundred thoufand dollars were fubfcribed in a fingle feafon to objects of this nature in Pennfylvania alone.

THE IMPORTANCE OF THE AMERICAN FISHERIES CONSIDER-
ED AS A PART OF THE INSTRUMENTS OF NATIONAL DE-
FENCE.

The accurate eftimation of every fubdivifion of
the induftry and wealth of nations fhould occupy
the unremitted attention of the political obferver.
A diligent enquiry after the facts, which appear-
tain to a fubject, never fails to adminifter the moft
ufeful aid to the candid inveftigator: and it fometimes happens, that the fimple adduction of thefe,
affords unqueftionable proofs of great benefits or
injury, in cafes, wherein the general affertions and
reafonings offered, are fuppofed to be mere fug-
geftions of felf-intereft or local prejudice. The
fifheries, it is believed, would prove, on a thorough examination, to be an inftance of this nature. The following ftatement of fome recorded
facts, will be found to warrant ftrong prefumptions,
that their intrinfic value has been hitherto unknown.

It is generally underftood, that the fifheries of
the late American provinces were principally carried on by the people of Maffachufetts and that
fuch is the cafe now, is well afcertained by the returns and reports which have been promulgated by
the federal government. It is alfo generally
known, that the fifheries conftituted by much the
greateft part of the external commerce of that ftate,
and it will be readily admitted, that whatever was
done by its veffels and feamen fhould be principal-

ly afcribed to its fifhing veffels and fifhing men.
By an examination of the records of the three
counties of Suffolk, Effex, and Middlefex, (which
comprife the ports of Bofton, Salem, Beverly,
Newbury-port, Marble-head, Gloucefter, Haver-
hill and Ipfwich) it appears that there were taken,
brought in, and libelled in the maritime court of
thofe three counties, during the laft war, 1095 veffels with their cargoes, and thirteen cargoes, (which
had been taken from veffels probably unloaded at
fea, and abandoned after capture) making in the
whole 1108. It has been ftated by a Britifh pre-
fnier in his place in their parliament, that the number of veffels belonging to Great-Britain in 1774,
was 6219 fail, of which 3908 were Britifh built,
and 2311 American built. What havoc then does
it appear, that thefe fifhermen made among the
Britifh merchantmen? above a fixth of all their
veffels were brought by thefe people, as prizes into the markets of the United States, with cagoes
to an immenfe amount, compofed of every fpeices
of military and domeftic fupply in a feafon of the
utmoft emergency. It appears too, that thefe prizes were no lefs than two fevenths of all the Britifh
built fhips of that nation. But the enquiry goes
further. The opinions of the moft candid and beft
informed eftimators, founded on careful enquiry,
countenance the prefumption, that fifty-five per
cent. of all the veffels captured by the people of
Maffachufetts, during the war, were retaken before
arrival; fo that there is the utmoft probability, that
the whole number of veffels, which were captured

by the shipping of these three counties, was 2450
sail. How great a derangement was this to the British commerce and how heavy must have been the
expence of the salvage paid to the re-captors? How
great the number of marine prisoners? How serious the interruption to the manning of their navy?

The operations, here spoken of, were confined
to what is termed in Massachusetts the middle dis-
trict. The captures in the eastern and southern
districts were much less considerable, but they are
not ascertained at this time. It is computed that
they amounted to at least five hundred and fifty
sail, so that it should appear, that the armed vessels
of our principal fishing state, captured in the
course of the late war, near one half of the
merchant ships, ordinarily belonging to Great-
Britain, and above three-fourths of the number
of her native built vessels. The subject admits
of one more suggestion. It is highly probable,
that many captured vessels, and cargoes of vessels taken and abandoned at sea, were carried into
the ports of powers, who were in alliance with the
United States, which did not appear on the records
of the Massachusetts courts. The vessels of the
other fishing states were remarkably successful in
their operations against the British merchant ships;
and in short, the American fishermen, wherever
bred, operated in their own element, against the
commerce of Great-Britain, with a destructive
activity, vigilance, and efficiency.

There exifts a proof of the extraordinary impreffion made by the veffels of the United States on the Britifh navigation at that time, which cannot be miftaken. This is to be drawn from the rates of infurance on unarmed veffels, which were more exceffive, than in any war of Great-Britain for fifty years paft, although no other maritime nation, with whom they have contended during that time, has been fo deficient in public fhips.

The fifhing trade of the United States, is rendered peculiarly important, as a means of defence or of annoying the commerce of hoftile nations, from the circumftance of our not having yet adopted a naval eftablifhment. The fifhermen, while that continues to be the cafe, muft be tranfmuted by war, as quickly as by a charm, into a corps of privateers-men and their fhips into private veffels of war; becaufe, the navy of any hoftile foreign nation will fufpend the fifheries as long as we remain without a naval force. They are therefore, not only a means of offence and defence, prepared to our hands, like the fifhermen of other nations, but in our peculiar fituation, they will be driven, by imperious neceffity, to live on the fpoils of the commerce of our enemies.

SECTION IV.

CONCERNING THE BANKS ESTABLISHED IN THE UNITED STATES

THESE valuable inſtitutions were unknown to us before the revolution, being added to the political economy in the latter part of the war. The paper emiſſions in the times of the provinces, had yielded ſome of the advantages of bank notes, though with leſs ſafety to thoſe who received them. But the degree in which they were unavoidably recurred to, in the courſe of the war, had completely deſtroyed the utility of paper money in 1781. The ſtate of public credit, and indeed of the public affairs in general, as well as the exigencies of the cultivators, merchants and manufacturers, required an efficient ſubſtitute for an inſtrument of negociation and dealing, of ſo great compaſs. The ſcheme of a bank was preſented in the manner, which is univerſally known, as the moſt probable mean of accommodating the general neceſſities, political, agricultural, and commercial. The promiſes which the plan made were abundantly fulfilled; and at the ſame time a ſtandard of public conduct and action in regard to the rights of property, was unobſervedly erected, at a moment when the recent courſe of events had rendered it very deſireable, as well from political as moral conſiderations. It has been found, accordingly, that the laws which concern property, in the places where banks have been eſtabliſhed, have quickly acquired a ſtability, if they

were good, and have meliorated, if they were before exceptionable, notwithstanding any supposed
or real errors in the plans or administration of the
institutions.

In reflecting upon these establishments, one cannot but call to mind a suggestion, which frequently
occurs, that too large a portion of the capital of
the United States, has been applied to them. Few
pecuniary operations are of as much importance.
In estimating the extent to which we might have
gone with prudence, an examination of the state of
that business in a successful and at the same time
the best known scene of trade in Europe, may be
of some use. In the city of London, the bank of
England (exclusively of that of Scotland) has operated with a capital of more than fifty millions of
dollars about forty-six years. The population of
England, on a medium, during that term, has been
less than double that of the United States at present, yet the capital of its bank has been above
five times the capital of our national bank, and near
five times the amount of all the subscriptions which
are yet* paid into all the banks in the United
States. There, are, moreover a great number of
private banks in the same city, probably not less
than sixty in number, some of which have more
capital stock, than any bank in this country, except that of the United States. The aggregate
amount of their capitals is probably equal to that

of the bank of England. Befides thefe, there are
very many confiderable private banks fcattered
through the kingdom. In addition to thofe,
there are the public and the private banks of
Scotland. If the banks of England and Scotland, public and private, out of London, be equal
to the private banks of London alone, then the
capital of thofe inftitutions in Great-Britain will
be 150,000,000 dollars, or above fourteen times
as many dollars as there are perfons in that kingdom, though the whole of the ftocks of the bank of
the United States, which is paid in, is not equal to
three times the number of their inhabitants. Again:
if the banks of Great-Britain be meafured by the
exports of that ifland, it will be found, that the latter, at their higheft value (90,000,000 of dollars)
are only three-fifths of their aggregate bank capital,
and that our exports, at 18,250,000 dollars, are
above two-thirds more than all our bank capital,
which is actually paid in. Taking the Britifh imports at 80,000,000 of dollars, and thofe of the
United States at 24,000,000, the comparifon will
be ftill more in favour of the difcretion, which has
been obferved in the United States. But a very
important meafure of thefe inftitutions yet remains
to be applied, by which prudent men will be moft
difpofed to teft the fubject—*the ordinary quantity of
fpecie.* The bank capital of Great-Britain being,
as above ftated, about 150,000,000 of dollars, and
the quantum of fpecie being never eftimated at
more than 22,000,000l. fterling, or 97,700,000 dollars, the aggregate bank capitals of the United

States, as now paid in (ten and one half millions
of dollars) would be as prudently, and folidly
founded on a quantity of fpecie a little lefs than
7,000,000 of dollars. Although it would be impoffible to afcertain the precife amount of the fpecie
of the United States, eftimates carefully made, appear to warrant a belief, that it is equal to that
fum. But while examinations like thefe feem to
abate and even entirely to deftroy, the apprehenfion, that we may have purfued the bufinefs of
banking to the injury of agriculture, manufactures,
and commerce, fome circumftances of a prudential
nature are not to be overlooked. When forming
thefe eftablifhments, we may commit errors, perhaps, in carrying into one fcene too great a proportion of the capital appropriated to their creation. Hence the found policy of fubtracting from
the mafs of the bank of the United States, to eftablifh branches at New-York, Bofton, Baltimore,
Charlefton and (as is faid to be intended) in Virginia, miniftering to the convenience, the neceffities,
and the interefts of government, the planter, the
farmer, the merchant, the navigator, the fifherman,
the fhip-builder, the manufacturer, and the mechanic, in fix feveral and variant fcenes, inftead of ac-
cumulating in one great mafs a fuperabundant capital*.

* It ought to diminifh the political jealoufies in regard to the
national bank, that feveral ftate banks were eftablifhed before it,
and feveral fince, which are aggregately of greater force of capital
than the bank of the United States.

It is poffible to err, too, in the difpofition of banking eftablifhments, by fuperadding to thofe which already accommodate any particular fcene, rather than introducing the new inftiutions into pla- ces hitherto without them. The United States contain five or fix great local fubdivifions of trade, refulting principally from the imperious dictates of *the nature of things.* In moft of thofe great fpheres, there is more than one confiderable and flourifh- ing trading town, though there is in each, one which has an acknowledged pre-eminence. When a reafonable portion of bank capital has been intro- duced into one of thefe commercial *metropolies,* the eftablifhment of a new bank would feem to be moft expedient in the trading town of the next degree of confideration. It is true, that fo far as the ope- ration is an employment, or application of the pro- perty of individuals, it muft be left, (within the laws) to their own will; but as the act of incorpo- ration place the fubject within the power of the legiflatures, and within the bounds of their cares and duties, fo it is highly important that thefe in- ftitutions fhould be modified in their original forma tion, upon principles of diftributive juftice in regard to the reafonable accommodation of the marts of commerce, within their fpheres of legiflation, and of all the landed citizens, who refort to them for the fales of their furplus produce, or the purchafe of their fupplies.

A pleafing confequence has refulted from the diftribution of banks through different parts of the

United States. Like all great objects, thefe inftitutions, while operating very beneficially in regard
to the bufinefs of a coutry, are liable to be rendered inftrumental to local party views. Being committed, as in the United States, to many feparate
boards of directors, felected for the fervice on account of their property, integrity, talents, and attention to bufinefs, and whofe primary duties are
the legal, difcreet, and beneficial execution of
their truft, it is not very probable, that they will
deviate, in a dangerous degree, from their proper
walk, into the ground of political combination and
intrigue.

A circumftance obfervable in the bank of the
United States,* will not fail to attract the attention
of cautious men. The portion of public debt, which
enters into the compofition of their ftock, is the
particular contemplated. In this refpect, the bank
of England, and the bank of Ireland (which are
among the beft accredited of thofe inftitutions in
Europe) exceed that of the United States in the
proportion of one third. It is very favourable to
our inftitution, that the national debt, and ordinary
and extraordinary expences of the United States
are much lefs in proportion to wealth and numbers
than thofe of Great-Britain and Ireland, and that
our government is not lefs free from error, nor
more like to be difturbed than theirs. It cannot,
therefore, be more unfafe to confide in our inftitution, which contains three-fourths, than in theirs

* Alfo in the Bank of Pennfylvania. A. D. 1793.

which is wholly compofed of public debt.   It is, moreover, true, and worthy of obfervation, that moft of the other banks in the United States (and particularly the three largeft) have, voluntarily and by their own operations, placed confiderable portions of their ftock upon the credit of the United States, by purchafing largely of the public debt, and by giving at this time extenfive credits founded upon its fecurity.   The market value of the public debt, which if Europe were at peace would be generally greater in fpecie than its nominal amount, renders that part of the bank ftock, which is compofed of it, intrinfically more valuable than that, which is in coin.

CONCERNING THE NATIONAL INDUSTRY.

An enquiry into the knowledge or fkill, affiduity, economy, or frugality, and good management, with which the feveral defcriptions of citizens in the United States purfue their employments, has never yet been made.   The fubject is copious, and would require much previous enquiry and detail.   It is not intended, therefore, in this place to attempt a developement of it; yet it may be ferviceable to beftow upon it a few brief reflections.   The learned profeffions will not be brought into view, as they are not ftrictly of the nature of the object contemplated.   The planters, the farmers, the merchants, the navigators, the fifhermen, the fhipbuilders, the manufacturers and the mechanics, with the perfons immediately employed by them, are all which are conceived to be comprehended in the fubject.   The body of the planters, that is, thofe who cultivate tobacco, rice, indigo, and cotton, are, as a defcription of cultivators, the beft informed perhaps in regard to the objects of their particular purfuit, though it is manifeft, that they have abundant matter for increafed attention in perfecting their cultivation, in afcertaining thofe fpecies of their valuable plants, which are moft excellent, moft certain, and moft productive, in the improvement of their implements of hufbandry, in the acquifition of auxiliary implements and machinery, in perfecting the modes of curing their produce, and preparing it for market, and particularly in the attainment of adequate fubftitutes for the ordinary fpecies of labourers, a fupply of which has become improbable. It appears to be worth their confidering, too, as well with an eye to profit, as humanity, whether an advantageous variation in the employment of fome of the blacks might not be made, by introducing upon every eftate fome of the fimpler manufactures to employ children, old and invalid perfons of both fexes, and particularly the females during thofe frequent terms, when two lives depend upon their health.

The merchants, navigators, fifhermen, and fhipbuilders of the United States may be fafely affirmed to be four defcriptions of our citizens, whofe induftry is as uniformly energetic and well directed, as thofe of any country in the world, though it is certain, that a much ftricter economy prevails among perfons of fome foreign nations engaged in thofe purfuits—an example deferving the moft ferious attention.

The manufacturers, in fome branches, purfue their occupations under the difadvantages of very few errors; yet thofe citizens would be fenfibly bene-fited, were they able to relieve themfelves of cer-tain parts of their labour by the attainment of the auxiliary machinery, which is the purchafe of larger capitals, than are yet engaged in their line. Circumftances, however, of various kinds are dai_ly contributing to remove this inconvenience. The bulk of the manufacturers do not want induftry, nor fkill enough to fucceed in thofe fimple manufac-tures, to which it is moft their intereft to apply themfelves. It may be rather faid, that they ma-nufacture ordinary kinds of fabrics, from the na-ture of the demand, than that they manufacture badly. Their bufinefs is, moreover, progreffively advancing, and has felt, on feveral occafions, fome of them recent, the foftering hand of government.

The mechanic branches have been, till this time, on nearly as good a footing; but thofe employed in the erection of buildings ought now to feek the aid of fuch parts of fcience as have relation to their calling. Rural and city architecture has been too little ftudied. It ought not to be forgotten, that a competent knowledge of it is no lefs conducive to *economy* and *convenience,* than to elegance and fplen-dor.

The most important of all the employments of our citizens, that of *the farmer*, remains to be noticed. It is very much to be feared, that in point of execution, a candid examination would prove that this best of pursuits is most imperfectly conducted. The proofs are, innumerable instances of impoverished lands, precious bodies of meadow lands, in the old settlements of some of the states, which remain in a state of nature, a frequent inattention to the making or preserving of manure, as frequent inattention to the condition of the seed grain, evidenced by the growth of inferior grain in fields of wheat, and by the complexion of the flour in some quarters, the bad condition of *barns*, stables and fences, and in some places the total want of the former, the deficiency of spring-houses or other cool dairies in extensive tracts of country, the want of a trifling stock of bees, the frequent want of orchards, and the neglect of those which have been planted by preceding occupants, the neglect of the sugar tree, the neglect of fallen timber and fuel, accompanied with the extravagant felling of timber trees for fuel, the neglect of household manufactures in many families, the neglect of making pot-ash, the non-use of oxen, and above all, the growth in substance, of large bodies of farmers on lands of an ordinary quaty, while the inhabitants of extensive scenes, hardly extract from much superior lands, sustenance and clothing.

It is a fact very painful to obferve, and unpleafant to reprefent, but it is indubitably true, that *farming* in the grain ftates, their great beft bufinefs, the employment moft precious in free governments, is, too generally fpeaking, the leaft underftood, or the leaft economically and attentively purfued, of any of the occupations which engage the citizens of the United States. It is acknowledged, however with fatisfaction, that great changes have been lately made, and that the energy, fpirit of improvement, and economy, which have been recently difplayed, promife the regular and rapid melioration of the agricultural fyftem. All other things have taken a courfe of great improvement—and it cannot be apprehended that the yeomanry of the United States will permit themfelves to be exceeded by any of their brethren, in the moft valuable characteriftic of good citizens—*ufefulnefs in their proper fphere.*

CONCERNING THE LAWS WHICH INTRENCH UPON THE RIGHTS OF PROPERTY.

It is not remembered, that the acts of the national legiflature have been deemed by any of the poffeffors of any defcription of property, unfavourable to their rights, except the proceedings in regard to the public debt. It is not lefs curious than true, that a part of the community affirm, that the government have injured the country by too much liberality, while another part charge the legiflature with impairing the contract.

In taking a view of this fubject, it fhould be remembered, that the ftate of things, when it was taken up, was in every refpect critical and uncertain. It was difficult to fay what the country could perform, and more fo to tell what they would comply with. It was perceived, on the one hand, that as fuch a ftate of *public credit* as preceded the year 1789, would ruin a government more energetic than that of the United States, fo its immediate melioration was a matter of the moft imperious neceffity. On the other hand, the non-exiftence of one fingle efficient fyftem, *yielding an equitable fpecie intereft,* in any one ftate, and a number of painful facts in the financial operations of fome of the legiflatures, created a conviction, that there was either an inability or difinclination in all to render a fpecie payment in the full extent of the *explicit* contracts. Some of the contracts were found not to be explicit, containing promifes of large fums under the name fpecie, which it could not have been the expectation of the government, at their date, to difcharge, or of the creditor to recieve, in coin; becaufe they promifed to pay as fpecie, what was notorioufly much lefs valuable, than contracts previoufly liquidated at forty nominal dollars for one in real money. The interefting claims of the original creditors alfo, were ftrongly reprefented, while the conduct of every ftate in the union, in its particular finances, had difcountenanced a difcrimination in their favour; and the exifting laws of property were urged againft a reduction of the laft owner's principal: queftions were alfo raifed about the original intrinfic value of the money and property received in many cafes by the United States, leading to the ordaining of a new fcale of depreciation. By infufing into the propofition for a fettlement of the debt, two qualities—*a reduction of the interest* and *a temporary irredeemability of the principal*, which have coft the debtor nothing, and the creditor very little; by vigorous and well devifed efforts to recover credit at home and abroad, an arrangement was formed, and executed, which has given better payment to the creditor than could reafonably have been hoped. It is plain to every obferver, that, but for the indifcretions of fome of the public creditors, who fuperadded to the trials and fluctuations of a convalefcent ftate of credit the late unparalleled difficulties of the holders of the ftock, the three fpecies of the public paper, taken at a medium, would have been worth the nominal value in the market. *Hitherto that has never been the cafe.*

There yet remain, however, in the United States fome laws which affect the rights of property. The operation of inftalment* and valuation laws is not terminated in one or two of the ftates. In one or two others, paper money is a tender for old debts. In one quarter, real eftate is protected as in Great.Britain from execution for debt; and in others, the judgments of the courts are fufpended, if the income of the eftate bears a certain pro-

* A. D. 1792.

portion to the creditors' demand.* In some of the states, preferences are given to the claims of citizens, before those of citizens of the other states, or of foreigners ; and ills exist in the form of insolvent laws. The federal constitution, and those of several of the states, have barred the introduction of these evils in regard to new transactions ; and the states which are not chargeable with them, in regard to past affairs, have reaped, in the last three years an ample reward for their wisdom and virtue. Property may almost be called *the palladium of communities*. Their *moral* safety at least is always at hazard, when that is unwarrantably invaded. In every case wherein difficulties to obtain his own are interposed in the way of the honest and industrious citizen, his loss is not all the public injury. A fellow citizen—perhaps a member of a legislature (and through him a legislature itself) is fatally corrupted.

CONCERNING THE PUBLIC DEBTS.

When it is remembered, that the terms upon which the debts of the states were assumed by congress, are not more favourable than those on which the federal debt was funded, and when it is called to mind, that the unassumed debts of all the states are

---

* The mortgage law of Pennsylvania, and some other states, which exclude " the equity of redemption" create, on the whole, a more favourable ground for the rights of property in those places, than in Great-Britain. Those States are the most flourishing in the union.

lefs valuable in the market than thofe, which were
affumed, it will appear, that the public creditors o f
the union have little reafon to complain. When the
advantages of the *temporary* iredeemability, and of
the opportunity of inveftment in the bank are recol-
lected, that little reafon, if any exifted, appears to be
diffipated. On the other hand, when it is remembered, that long after the promulgation of the funding fyftem and of the bank, the poffeffors of fpecie
might have procured certificates upon very advantageous terms, and that many, who fold after thofe
promulgations wanted confidence enough to hold,
that United States draw a fhare of the profits of the
the bank without furnifhing any of the capital, that
the grant of irredeemability is *temporary*, and fo perfectly *nominal*, that we have now a right to pay off
more than we have money to difcharge; when it is
alfo borne in mind, that the terms given by congrefs to the public creditors, were exceeded (by
law at leaft) in feveral of the ftates, and that two
of them have added to the benefits of their citizens
from the funding fyftem, *without difcriminating in
favour of the original creditor*, or *againft the prefent holder*, the arrangements of the general government appear to be *confiftent with the public interefts*
and *with the wifdom of the ftate legiflatures themfelves*. If the funding fyftem of congrefs has been
thus *equally juft and beneficial with thofe of the
ftates*, it has been accompanied with many advantages which cannot be queftioned. Public credit
is reftored—in confequence of that, the contracts
for all public fupplies are made for cafh on the de-

liveries or performance—the money, thus early
promifed, is paid by anticipation on the proffer of
indubitable fecurity by the various contractors;
and intereft in favour of the United States has
been allowed for the promtitude of her treafury—
500,000 dollars of fpecie claims have been difcharged; and purchafes of the public debt, which bring the
extinguifhed fum to about 2,400,000 dollars,* have
been made, or provided for—a feries of payments
fince the month of September (required by the moft
diftinguifhed ally of the United States, in the late
war) has been made to ferve the occafions of
their unhappy colonifts. Loans upon five per cent.
upon four and a half per cent. and upon four per
cent. intereft, have been effected in two opulent
cities of Europe, folely by means of our reftored
credit, to repay in the hour of need, to that ally,
the monies lent to the United States in a like feafon. All that is due has been paid, part of that
which is not yet due has been anticipated. Monies
anxioufly defired by France, have been difcharged
by mean of loans at a lower intereft. Both nations
are benefited and pleafed; but our country is ho-
noured by the tranfaction. To have neglected our
public credit, would have been to lofe thefe advantages.

It will not be queftioned, that there is in every
walk of life or bufinefs a greater proportion of money
than was obfervable two years ago. Public works

* A. D. 1791.

and buildings of every kind, and of fpecies and values unknown among us till the prefent time, are
undertaking every where. Private buildings, of
equal variety, and comparative value, are fpring-
ing up. The price of lands is greatly advanced.
The raw materials, though raifed in much greater
abundance, fell for larger prices. To what pecuniary caufe fo powerful, fo adequate, can thefe
things be afcribed, as to the fales of part and re-
animation of the whole, of a public debt, ten times
larger than the amount of all the fpecie ordinarily
circulating in the country ? It ought to be admitted however that the found *ftamina* of this country,
and our voluntarily impofing upon ourfelves the
wholefome reftraints of juft government have moft
powerfully co-operated.

The relief of fome of the ftates from all their
burdens, has been another beneficial confequence
of the funding of the debt. It is but a few years
fince one of the moft frugal, vigorous, and productive counties in Pennfylvania rofe againft the col-
lectors of the taxes. The appreciation and fale of
the immenfe mafs of federal fecurities, owned by
that ftate, with the proceeds of her funds have enabled her to difcharge all her obligations, though
fhe has abolifhed her general land tax, and difcon-
tinued her excife, both of which fhe has collected
for forty years.

Some anxiety has been created by the fhare of
our debt, which foreigners have obtained. But
this was a powerful means of bringing the whole

into its prefent beneficial action, by elevating its
actual to its nominal value. It is not at all probable, that it will be drawn from the country. It has
been obferved, in the moft tranquil and profper-
ons condition of Europe, that a great proportion
of the families of thofe foreigners, who have made
large inveftments in the United States, either in
the times of the provinces, or fince the revolution,
have become inhabitants of this country, even
when in its unproductive infant ftate. At this ferious moment, when almoft every tranfatlantic
country feels or apprehends diforders, our chances
are infinitely increafed. The United States, advanced in the means of fubfiftence, of comfort, and
of elegance, now prefent to them an object of
greater defire in a tranquil liberty, which they are
ftruggling to obtain, a teeming agriculture, and a
profperous commerce, both foreign and internal.
Conformable with thefe reflections, we may affirm,
that no great object in our affairs has failed to attract the notice of the foreigners, who have engaged in our funds. The internal navigation of South-
Carolina, North-Carolina, Virginia, Maryland,
Pennfylvania, New-Jerfey, and New-York, are
among the witneffes of this truth. The banks both
national and ftate, the turnpike roads, and toll
bridges, the fales of city eftates, of cultivated farms,
and particularly of unimproved lands, commerce,
fhip-building, manufactures, confirm the fact. Let
us continue to exhibit *a ftrictly honeft fpirit* in our
laws and conftitutions, *an efficient execution* of them
and *an abftinence from unneceffary wars,* and there

cannot exift a doubt, that we fhall draw much more copioufly from the population, the arts, and the funds of Europe, than they will draw from thofe of the United States.

There exifts in the United States one defcription of private difficulties and incumbrances, that muft engage the folicitude of every feeling mind, which, by an examination into the detail and interior of our affairs, has been led to obferve them. The cafes alluded to are thofe of the citizens of two or three of the ftates, who are burdened with heavy foreign debts or claims, which originated before the revolution. Whatever they may be finally adjudged to pay, the fum muft be fo great, and due from fo many perfons, as to give it the refemblance of a public debt: and as in one of thofe ftates it has already occafioned fome facrifices of their principal landed eftates, very far below their value, fo it will probably operate in the others, unlefs fome extenfive means, abundantly adequate the occafion, can be brought to operate, before or at leaft at the time of executing the judgments of the courts, which may be obtained. No refource, competent to the purpofe, appears at all likely to prefent itfelf, unlefs it be the funded debt or ftock of the United States and of the feveral ftates. The method by which this defcription of property can be rendered moft immediately and effectually fubfervient to the interefting purpofe of preventing the deftruction of many families, would feem to be *the fixture of it at a ftable, unfluctuating*

rate, adequate to its proper value, under the exiſting circumſtances of the United States. It is manifeſt, that in ſuch a ſtate of the market, the dealers in the debt and others would ſell out, and
would not buy in again, and that they would ſeek
objeĉts for their money in the trade, the manufactures, the buildings, and the lands of the country,
which might promiſe them more advantage. A
tenth part of the value of the public debts, applied
to the lands of the United States, would raiſe them
every where to their real value, ſo that the debtor,
who might be under a neceſſity to ſell an eſtate,
could diſpoſe of his property, not only without a
ruinous ſacrifice, but probably to uncommon advantage. The proprietors of lands and buildings,
which might be under this probability of ſale,
would ſuſtain no riſque or injury in ſelling their eſtates for the public ſtock.

It may be alledged, that the holders of the debt
will not go into places ſo remote to make inveſt-
ments: but there are faĉts, which appear to warrant a very di fferent opinion. The funds of New-
England have been brought into Pennſylvania, for
inveſtment in lands of ſeveral kinds—the money
of Pennſylvania and Delaware has been inveſted
in mills and lands in Virginia—the greater part of
the iron works of Maryland (the moſt coſtly eſtates
in our country,) were bought and worked by the
capitals of reſidents in Great-Britain before the revolution. The ſame faĉt exiſted in one great inſtance in New-Jerſey. The greateſt cedar ſwamp,

on the waters of the Delaware, that fupplies the
Philadelphia market, is owned in New-England;
and people and veffels from that quarter, are annually fent to perform the bufinefs of it. The
American public creditors, citizens of the United
Netherlands, have recently purchafed eight hun-
dered tracts of land in a part of Pennfylvania, further from Philadelphia than the banks of James
river, York, or Rappahannock. In fhort, if the
hiftory of this country were examined, as it regards' this fubject, it would demonftrate, that the
landed property of it has been conftantly animated
by the application of the monies of diftant capitalifts.*

SECTION V.

CONCERNING THE FOREIGN DEBTS OF THE UNITED STATES.

A T the commencement of the prefent government in 1789, the United States were indebted to
France, Holland. and Spain, and to the foreign officers of the late army, in a fum amounting to near
twelve millions of dollars. Near a million and

---

* A. D. 1794. Great purchafes by late holders of the public debt
and bank ftock in Pennfylvania and New-York, citizens and foreigners, have been made in the diftrict of Maine, in the ftate of Georgia,
in the weftern and northern parts of New-York, in South-Carolina,
in the moft remote parts of Pennfylvania, in the ftate of Kentuckey, in the federal diftrict, in the Norfolk canal, in the Virginia
lead mine.

two-thirds of this fum, was due for arrears of intereft, inattention to which, would have been too
difgraceful to have admitted of a hope of foreign
credit, until meafures were taken for its dicharge.
Above a million and one third of the principal fum
had become due, and the time of other inftalments
was coming round. The refources of the country
had been examined and confidered, but not tried.
The claims of thefe foreign creditors, were originally, the moft delicate in themfelves; and in the
cafe of France, the ftate of her revolntion in the
fummer of 1790, placed her demand in a fituation peculiarly interefting. It was perceived, that
the adoption of the federal conftitution and the
meafures taken to reftore public credit, had made
ftrong and favourable impreffions on the European money lenders: and it was not doubted, that
the arrears of intereft and the principal due,
might be difcharged by loans, upon terms which
would produce very little lofs. The requifite
authorities were given by the legiflature, which
refulted in the borrowing of a fum equal to the
difcharge of all the exigible debt. But as the
occafions of France were likely to be emergent,
and there was reafon to confide, that a firm and
fteady purfuit of the financial fyftem, which had by
that time been adopted, and an adherence to the
upright fpirit of the conftitution, would rapidly
meliorate the credit of the United States, it was
deemed expedient to extend the authorities to borrow, to a fum equal to the whole of the foreign
debt, provided the inftalments, not due, could be

difcharged by means of loans advantageous to the United States. The intereft of above feven millions of the foreign debt, being at the rate of five per cent. per annum, it was not doubted, that the money might be obtained fo as to render the difcharge of the part, not exigible, really advantageous. It has accordingly happened, that a fum adequate to the principal and intereft due, has been borrowed within the terms of the law, fo as to fupport the credit and good faith of the United States, and critically to accommodate France. The further expeƈations of Congrefs have alfo been fulfilled; a confiderable loan at four and one half, and two loans at four per cent. having been effeƈted, fo as to realize an advantage in the difcharge of a large part of the principal, which was at an intereft of five per cent. The United States having thus commuted their foreign debt, further than is due, with honour, and, on a medium of the whole, with advantage, are relieved by thefe operations from any probability of preffure to perform the remainder of their European engagements. The friends of our public credit, of our national fafety and refpeƈtability, and of the freedom of France, among the citizens of the United States, will refleƈt upon this aƈtual courfe of events with cordial fatisfaction.

THE CONCLUSION: BEING MISCELLANEOUS THOUGHTS ON THE GOVERNMENT.

The people of the United States enjoy a peculiar felicity in the poffeffion of principles of government and of civil and religious liberty, more found, more accurately defined, and more extensively reduced to practice, than any preceding republicans. There is not one iota of delegating or delegated power, which is not poffessed, or may not be acquired by every citizen. It is true, that there are in practice, several deviations in the diftribution of power to the various fubdivifions of the country, and to the proprietors of certain defcriptions of property ; but thefe are acknowledged departures from principle, and are known to have arifen out of the antecedent ftate of things. They could not be immediately corrected without violent ftruggles and diforders, and without injury to the property of defcriptions of citizens, too great for the country, at any former period, to compenfate. Mild remedies are, however, daily applied to thefe partial difeafes; and it is manifeft, that the courfe of time is diminifhing, and will finally remove them. The right of legiflative interpofition, on the part of the chief magiftrate, which, in the practice of another country, has been commuted for a dangerous and injurious influence, is here wrought into the effence of the conftitution, and is not only exercifed in the independent and uncontrouled confideration of every refolution and bill, but by the practical application of the qualified negative.

The execution of the office of the chief magiftrate has been attended, through a term of almoft four years, with a circumftance, which to this nation and to the furrounding world requires no commen-

tary—*a native citizen of the United States, transferred from private life to that station, has not, during
so long a term, appointed a single relation to any
office of honour or emolument.*

The senatorial branch of the government has
been created and continued in a mode preferable
to that which is pursued in any other nation.

The representative branch is equally well consti-
tuted.

The military code, for the government of such
troops as are occasionally raised and employed, is
well calculated to produce discipline and efficiency, when time is allowed for the purpose, and consequently to render the United States respectable
in the eyes of foreign nations.

All christian churches are so truly upon an equal
footing, as well in practice as in theory, that there
are and have been in the legislative, executive, and
judicial branches of the general government, persons of the following denominations—Episcopalian,
Presbyterian, Independent or Congregational, Quaker, Lutheran, Reformed, Roman, and probably
others, which do not occur. There have been,
and indeed yet are, a few ecclesiastical distinctions
in the state governments, which reason and time
are rapidly destroying. It is easy to perceive, that
religious liberty, supported by the national constitution, and a great majority of the state constitu-

tions, cannot but attain, in a very fhort time, the fame theoretical and practical perfection in the remainder, which it has acquired in them.

The independency of the judiciary, as well in the tenure of their ftations as in the permanency of their compenfations under the federal conftitution, and in moft of thofe of the ftates, is an advantage over the ancient republics and the generality of modern governments, of ineftimable value in regard to liberty, property and ftability.

The United States, being without tranfmarine or feparated dominions, are exempted from two inconveniencies, which have refulted from them. An immenfe naval force has been found neceffary to defend fuch territories, and to protect the trade with them in time of war, and the difficulty of devifing for them a free legiflation, has hitherto proved infurmountable. The Britifh nation declared, that they had a right to legiflate for their colonies and dominions in America, Afia, and Africa in all cafes whatfoever, and the revolution of the United States turned upon that cardinal point. When we obferve, that the French nation, ardent as they are in the purfuit of liberty, have not yet been able to devife any fyftem of government for their colonies without *a dernier refort* to the legiflature of France, it will be a fource of comfortable reflection to the friends of free and efficient government in thefe ftates, that we are not perplexed

by the neceffity of fo delicate, important, and difficult a political operation.

It has been unfortunate for moft nations, as well
ancient as modern, that they have had no fettled pre-
exifting mode of altering, amending, or renovating
their political fyftem, to which they could refort
without a deviation from the legal courfe of things,
hazarding the public tranquility, and often freedom itfelf.—It is equally happy for the people of
the United States, that in their federal government, and in moft of thofe of the ftates, there exifts a provifion, by which thofe neceffary and defirable ends may be obtained, with whatever
zeal, without recurring to irregularity or violence.*

Fundamental principles being already fettled by
common confent, and being accurately and clearly recorded in the conftitutions, the people cannot
long miftake the nature of a meafure, a law, or a
political maxim, which is really oppofed to thofe
principles ; and when the public judgment is decided
upon any one or more dereliftions of thofe principles of magnitude fufficient to induce an effort for
reform, the will of the people cannot be fuccefsful-
ly refifted or even fufpended. The confequence
of this ftate of things will be, that the mafs of error will not eafily accumulate, fo as to become
infupportable, being kept down by thefe orderly
natural exertions of the community, to relieve
themfelves at an earlier ftage of inconvenience.

* The ineftimable *alterative* powers in the conftitution of the
United States &c. are here contemplated.

Too great a facility to change would, however, be likely to produce fluctuations, injurious to order, peace, property, and industry, and indeed to liberty itself: but as the mode of performing the amendatory or alterative operations is flow, and consequently deliberate, trivial or dangerous changes would be very difficult to accomplish. In this view there appears to be very little probability, that changes from free or representative government, will take place ; or that any modification of hereditary power will be introduced into the governments either of the states or of the union. The people will never deliberately consent to the abrogation of those clauses in the several constitutions, which explicitly provide both in general terms, and in particular detail, for free or republican government. Nor does it seem easy, considering the degree of perfection we have obtained and the certain, constant, and moderate operations of the amendatory clauses, to accumulate sufficient public evil or grievance, to produce one of those convulsions, which the ambitious are wont to seize as the moment to introduce, by force, a despotic government. Even local circumstances conspire to favour the permanency of liberty in these states. Being too remote from any foreign nation, to render a war, requiring a great army, at all necessary, that instrument, so often used by ambitious leaders, is not likely to be placed within the reach of the enemies of freedom, *while the union remains entire.* It is worthy of the most particular observation and remembrance, that a dissolution of our government would immediately open a door to this danger, as the feveral ftates or little confederacies, would each deem it prudent to maintain a larger army, than is now requifite for the whole. The hiftory of Greece will inftruct us that by this more than any other poffible meafure, we fhould be prepared for the military domination of fome modern *Philip*, or fome new *Alexander*. *A ftrong union and a tranquil liberty* would be miferably exchanged for fuch a ftate of things.

It is an evident truth, that the penal laws of thefe ftates have been gradually mitigated fince the epocha of their independence, and it is no lefs true, that the number of crimes does not bear fo great a proportion to the population, as was formerly the cafe, though an univerfal relaxation of the police took place in the late war. It is, an ill fymptom of the actual ftate of things, in a fociety, when *mild laws, ftrictly executed,* are incompetent to the prefervation of order and public happinefs. Our penal codes are, upon the whole, among the leaft fanguinary, and it is believed, they are not cruel, even in thofe unhappy cafes, which impel the community to extremities. The conftitution of the United States has extracted all the gall from the punifhment of offences againft the national fafety, by correcting the power of legiflating concerning them with a mildnefs unknown to the fyftems of moft countries. It is honourable to the humanity and magnanimity of the American people, that this proceeding flowed from them almoft unanimoufly, four years after the revolution war. Future ages will do

juſtice to a nation capable of ſuch an effort, at a
moment ſo particular.

Taking the United States at large, there are few
or no countries in which, at this time, the juſt demands of private creditors can be obtained by a
more certain, a more expeditious, or a leſs expen-
ſive courſe of legal proceſs. There are ſome local
and a very few general defeᴄts yet exiſting; but
they are vaniſhing before the ſpirit of the general
and moſt of the ſtate conſtitutions. There is no
part of the public conduᴄt of this country more
ſtriking, than the firmneſs with which they have applied the cauſtic to ſome inveterate cancers, which
had been derived to their pecuniary ſyſtem, principally from adventitious cauſes. It proves the ex-
iſtence of that virtue and fortitude, which qualify
a nation for republican government. There are
ſome exceptionable circumſtances, yet to be done
away ; but the ſucceſsfull efforts, which have been
made, juſtify a confident expeᴄtation, that they will
yield ere long to the powers and influences which
have eradicated much greater evils of the ſame
kind.

———

THE recent date of theſe refleᴄtions on the ſtate
of the American union, will naturally render them
an intereſting portion of this publication. It may
be matter of entertainment to the curious, and of
inſtruᴄtive information to thoſe, who engage them-

felves in the ftudy of mankind, to know what the
United States have been, have thought, and have
done, in the antecedent ftages of their political exiftence, but to the world in general the real nature
and actual fituation of their affairs at this time, and
the profpects, which appear to arife out of them, are
fubjects of much greater importance.

CHAPTER X.

THE diftance of the United States from the foreign confumers of many of their exported productions, and from all of the manufacturers of their imported fupplies, have been placed among the moft important confiderations in favour of their purfuing, in conjunction with other things, the bufinefs of manufactures. To thefe inducements, of great and manifeft ftrength in times of general peace, the prefent univerfal war among the European powers has added new force. It has become ftill more the intereft of the United States to infufe into their towns and cities further portions of manufacturing capital, induftry and fkill. The following delineation of an eftablifhment, which might be created by foreign or domeftic capital, was intended to exhibit the various and extenfive confequences in favour of the landholders and cultivators, which have invariably refulted from manufacturing towns. Every item in the enumeration, implies a demand for timber, fuel, grain, cattle, beer and other drinks, hemp, flax, wool, iron, flax-feed, or fome other production of our lands and farms. Similar exertions on the fea coaft might be equally or even more fuccefsful, as the manufactures of the productions, as well of the agricul-

tural ſtates as of foreign countries, might be combined with thoſe of the immediate vicinity.

REFLECTIONS ON THE AFFAIRS OF THE UNITED STATES, OCCA-
SIONED BY THE PRESENT WAR IN EUROPE, RECOMMENDED
TO AMERICAN AND FOREIGN CAPITALISTS.

It is highly prudent in every nation, ſeriouſly
to conſider the effects which great events in other
countries may have produced on their affairs, and
to anticipate, in time, the conſequences, in regard
to their intereſts, to which ſuch events may poſſibly
give riſe. The enhancement of the coſt of our
manufactured ſupplies by the demand for the immenſe armaments by land and ſea now making in
Europe, and the impediments to *the cheap tranſportation of our produce* by the recent deduction of
a large proportion of the veſſels, which lately carried them *at peace freights*, with the impoſſibility of
building in time a ſufficient number of ſhips to
perform the ſervice, and to ſupply the purchaſes by
foreign nations, render it a matter of the moſt
comfortable reflection, that we have made ſuch
frequent and full examinations, of our capacities
in the buſineſs of *manufactures;* and that we have
made ſo great progreſs in the eſtabliſhment of many
of the moſt uſeful and neceſſary branches. There
occurs nothing to warrant a belief, that we ſhall
ceaſe to maintain our courſe *in peace.* But it is
manifeſt, that even in that deſirable ſituation, the
inducements to purſue manufactures are not a
little increaſed by the advanced coſt of our ſup-

plies, and *the diminution of our carriers at peace freights* already mentioned. It will be wife then to devife new methods of increafing our manufactures, in order *to cheapen and multiply fupplies, and to extend the home market for our agricultural productions*. It is moreover well worthy of remark, that in confequence of the war in Europe many articles of great importance in the building of houfes, improving new plantations, and fupplying the fettled country, and the induftrious poor, are faid to be prohibited to be exported from Great-Britain, becaufe they can be applied to military purpofes, or may be wanted for themfelves. However reafonable or cuftomary in fimilar circumftances this may be, our citizens muft actually be fubjected thereby to additional expence, and the charges of improving and cultivating real eftates muft be increafed. Manufactures of thefe prohibited kinds of goods are therefore, rendered indifpenfible by the fituation of that country, which is the principal foreign fource of our fupplies.

However improbable or impoffible, war may appear* in the judgment of many or moft of us, it can do no injury to remark, that the coft of our fupplies would be fo much increafed by that worft of all poffible events, and the veffels to carry our produce at peace freights would be fo extremely diminifhed, if our own fhould be involved, that nothing but fome fuch great and vigorous efforts as that fuggefted for confideration, could fave our

* In the fpring of 1793.

cultivators from a very inconvenient expence in procuring supplies, and a reduction of the market prices of many articles of their produce.

. It will be perceived, that the plan is laid upon a scale, which is not likely, at this time, to be carried into execution in any one place. It is necessary, therefore, to remark that it is not intended in any view, but *to exemplify what might be done with a given capital.* The owners, however, of certain great water situations, might safely and advantageously lay out their adjacent grounds in a town plat with such views, and they might sell, or let on ground rents, such ordinary building lots, or such situations for water works, as purchasers or tenants might apply for, leaving the plan to mature by time and the natural attractions and advantages of the several scenes; or improvements might be commenced upon a scale of 5,000, 10,000, 15,000 or 20,000 dollars, as capital might be obtainable, and prudence might appear to justify. In all events, it is conceived, that a profitable attention to our situation may be promoted, and possibly some reflections favourable to the United States, and to the proprietors of particular estates, and many vicinities, may be suggested by the publication of the plan at the present very interesting crisis.

A PLAN FOR ENCOURAGING AGRICULTURE, AND INCREAS-
ING THE VALUE OF FARMS IN THE MIDLAND AND MORE
WESTERN COUNTIES OF PENNSYLVANIA, APPLICABLE TO
SEVERAL OTHER PARTS OF THAT STATE, AND TO MANY
PARTS OF THE UNITED STATES.

In a country, the people, the foil, and the climate of which are well fuited to agriculture, and
which has immenfe natural treafures in the bowels
and on the furface of the earth, *the creation of a
ready, near, and ftable market for its fpontaneous and
agricultural productions, by the introduction and increafe of internal trade and manufactures, is the moft
effectual method to promote hufbandry, and to advance
the interefts of the proprietors and cultivators of the
earth.* This pofition has been affumed, with the
firmeft confidence, by *one,** and maintained and
relied upon afterwards by others, of the moft informed and found minds in Great-Britain, in relation to the internal trade, manufactures, and landed intereft of that kingdom, although it is an ifland
poffeffing uncommon advantages in its artificial
roads, canals, rivers, and bays, which, altogether,
afford the inhabitants a *peculiar* facility in tranf-
porting their furplus produce with very little expenfe to foreign markets.

To a nation inhabiting a great continent, not
yet traverfed by artificial roads and canals, the rivers of which, above their natural navigation, have

* Hume.

been hitherto very little improved, many of whofe people are at this moment clofely fettled upon lands, which actually fink from one fifth to one half the value of their crops, in the mere charges of tranfporting them to the fea-port towns, and others, of whofe inhabitants cannot at prefent fend their produce to a fea-port for its *whole* value, *a thorough fenfe of the truth of the pofition* is a matter of *unequalled* magnitude and importance.

The ftate of things in moft of the counties of Pennfylvania, which are contiguous to, or in the vicinity of the river Sufquehannah and its extenfive branches, is confidered to be really and precifely that, which has been defcribed; and the object of this paper is to fuggeft hints for a plan of relief from the great expence and inconveniencies they at prefent fuftain, by creating a market town for their produce *on the main body of that river*, at fome proper place between the confluence of its eaftern and weftern branches, and the lower end of its prefent navigation.

It is propofed that the fum of five hundred thoufand dollars, to be applied as is herein after mentioned, be raifed in either of the three following methods—that is to fay, *either* by five thoufand fubfcriptions, of one hundred dollars each, to the capital ftock of a company to be temporarily affociated for the purpofe, without any exclufive privileges—*Or*, by the fale of one hundred thoufand lottery tickets, at five dollars each ; or fifty thoufand tickets, at ten dollars each, the whole enhanced amount of which is to be redrawn in prizes agreeably to a fcheme, which will be herein after exhibited—*Or*, by the application of five hundred thoufand dollars, of the monies in the treafury (or otherwife in the command) of the ftate of Pennfylvania.—The inducements to the operation, either to the ftate, to the adventurers in the lottery, or to the fubfcribers of the ftock of the affociated company, will appear in the fequel to be an augmentation of about one hundred per cent. in the value of the property to be embraced —that is, in a profit of about one hundred per cent. on the monies to be raifed or advanced for the purchafe of the lands, and the erection of the buildings.

The application of the above fum of five hundred thoufand dollars, might be as follows :

1ft. In the purchafe of two thoufand acres of land on the *weftern* bank of Sufquehannah, as a town feat to be regularly laid off in *a town or city for inland trade and manufactures*, with ftreets fixty feet wide, in oblongs of five hundred feet, fronting the fouth weftern or *prevalent fummer winds*, by two hundred and twenty feet; each oblong to be interfected by a twenty foot alley, running length-wife, or from north-weft to fouth-eaft, fo as to give *all* the lots *fouth-weft* front expofures, or *fouth-weft* back expofures, and outlets in the rear.

Dollars.

The purchafe of the land, including the farm buildings which may be on it, and water rights, &c. would probably be at fifteen dollars per acre, for two thoufand acres,   30,000

The contents will be a little more than three fquare miles. The fhape might be two miles on the river, by a little more than one mile and one half running from the river.—The number of lots of twenty feet front, and one hundred feet deep, would be about twenty-fix thoufand.

2dly. In the erection of five hundred and ten ftone and brick houfes, of the value of three hundred dollars each (in-clufive of the value of the lots,)   153,000

Two hundred and twenty ftone and brick houfes, of the value of five hundred dollars each,   110,000

Fifty ftone and brick houfes, of the va-lue of eight hundred dollars each,   40,000

Ten ftone and brick houfes, of the va-lue of two thoufand dollars each,   20,000

Four ftone and brick houfes, of the va-lue of fix hundred and fifty dollars each,   2,600

	Dolls.
Two mills for preparing hemp, which would often come down in boats, and on rafts from the rich new lands on the upper waters of Sufquehannah and its branches, one thoufand two hundred and fifty dollars each,	2,500
One mill for preparing flax,	800
One mill of about five hundred fpindles, for fpinning flax, hemp, and combed wool, to be divided into fifty fhares, of one hundred dollars each, to increafe the number of prizes,	5,000
One rope walk,	2,000
Two fmaller ditto one thoufand dollars each,	2,000
Two tan yards, one thoufand five hundred dollars each,	3,000
Two fmaller ditto,	1,500
One paper mill,	1,500
One flaxfeed, hempfeed, and rapefeed oil mill,	1,500
One grift mill,	2,000
Two bake houfes, five hundred dollars each,	1,000

	Dolls.
T~ ~ litting and rolling mills, five thousand dollars each,	10,000
One steel furnace,	3,000
One soap boiler's and tallow chandler's shop,	500
One malt house,	2,000
One brewery,	4,000
Ten grain and fruit distilleries, of various sizes, averaging in value one thousand two hundred and fifty dollars, each,	12,500
One printer's office for the English language,	500
One printer's office for the German language,	300
Six blacksmith's shops, and naileries of various sizes, averaging five hundred dollars each,	3,000
Two cooper's shops, one three hundred, the other two hundred dollars,	500
One cedar cooper's shop,	200
Four hatter's shops, two at five hundred, and two at three hundred dollars,	1,600
One bleach yard and house,	1,000

	Dolls.
Two fulling mills, one a thoufand, the other one thoufand five hundred dollars,	2,500
Two potteries, five hundred dollars each,	1,000
Four wheelwright's and chairmaker's fhops, two at five hundred, and two at four hundred dollars,	1,800
Two copperfmith's fhops, one five hundred, the other four hundred dollars,	900
Two pot-afh works, one three hundred, the other two hundred dollars,	500
One brafs founders's fhop,	600
Two painter's fhops, one five hundred, the other three hundred dollars,	800
Two turner's fhops, one five hundred, the other three hundred dollars,	800
Two water forges, one thoufand five hundred dollars each,	3,000
Four tilt hammer forges, one thoufand dollars each,	4,000
One tobacco and fnuff manufactory,	800
Two boring and grinding mills for guns, fcythes, fickles, &c. at one thoufand dollars each,	2,000

Two ſkin-dreſſer's ſhops, five hundred dollars each,   *Dolls.*   1,000

Four lumber yards on the river, fenced, twenty-five dollars each,   100

Two gun ſmith's ſhops, one five hundred, the other three hundred dollars,   800

Two boat builders yards and ſheds, one four hundred, the other three hundred dollars,   700

Four ſchool houſes, two for each ſex, (part to be German) at three hundred dollars (twelve hundred) and four houſes for the tutors, five hundred (two thouſand) dollars,   3,200

One church for all denominations, to be uſed in rotation by every ſociety, until any one ſhall have a place of worſhip of its own, when that ſociety ſhall loſe its right,   4,000

Two taverns, one four thouſand, the other three thouſand dollars,   7,000

Two ſtables, one in the vicinity of each tavern, for thirty horſes and ten carriages, one thouſand dollars each,   2,000

One hundred buildings, of the value of two hundred and fifty dollars each, half

with, and half without cellars, for tradef- *Dolls.*
men's and manufacturer's shops, stables,
&c. as occasion may require,   25,000

One large scale house to weigh loaded
waggons, to be erected on the market
square,   500

One scale house to weigh hogsheads and
other things, of less than one ton weight,   100

One sail-cloth manufactory,   5,000

One plumber's shop,   300

Two brick kilns, yards and houses, eight
hundred dollars each,   1,600

Two twine and cord factories, five hun-
dred dollars each,   1,000

Four slaughter houses and yards,   1,600

One starch work and dwelling house,   800

One library of three hundred shares, of
ten dollars each, to increase the number of
prizes, to be composed of books relative
to the useful arts and manufactures,   3,000

One parchment manufactory,   500

One glue manufactory,   500

One pump maker's shed and yard,   100

Charges of the superintendence of the   *Dolls.*
execution, at one per cent.   5,000
                                            500,000

The buildings above mentioned will form a town of one thousand houses, useful work shops and factories by water, fire or hand, all of stone or brick, which is larger by near one half than the borough of Lancaster. Being on the river Susquehannah, *a very great and extensive natural canal*, which, with its branches, flows through a country of fifteen millions of acres, and will be connected with the lakes, the position for a town must be considered as warranting a presumption, that the lots would be more valuable.—In order to extend this advantage, the buildings should be erected upon every second, or perhaps every third lot; whereby a number of interval lots would be left, which would be of nearly the same value.—A further advantage would result from such a disposition of the houses, as the vacant lots could be usefully applied to garden purposes, until they should be built upon. As the proposed houses and work shops would be of stone and brick, the possibility of the progress of fire, would be less, if the owners of the interval lots should build *wooden* houses hereafter, than if they were to erect such houses in a compact separate quarter.

The lots, without the scene, which should be first built on, would cost, after throwing out the ſtreets and alleys, about five dollars, and might be moderately eſtimated, were ſuch a town erected, at the medium value of ten dollars.

This town being contemplated as ſuch *an auxiliary* to Philadelphia, as Mancheſter, Leeds, Birmingham, and Sheffield, &c. are to the ſea-ports of Great-Britain, it would be neceſſary to connect it with that city *immediately* and *effectually*, by opening a good road to the Lancaſter turnpike, by whatever might be neceſſary to give it the benefit of the communication with Philadelphia through the Swetara and Tulpohocken canal, through the Brandywine canal, and through the Newport and Wilmington roads, and by all other means which could be deviſed.——It would alſo be proper to connect it with the boroughs of Reading, Lancaſter, York, Carliſle, &c. and with the weſtern, north-weſtern, northern, and other great roads.——Thus circumſtanced, and with the ſupplies of wood-fuel, coal, bark, grain, cattle, hemp, flax, wool, timber, iron, ſtone, lime, forage, &c. which thoſe roads, and the Suſquehannah and its branches, would certainly and permanently afford, this place could not fail to become of very great profit to the ſubſcribers or prize holders, or the ſtate, and to the landed intereſt, both tenants and owners.——The expenſe of tranſportation from the neareſt navigable part of the Suſquehannah by way of Newport, is nine dollars per ton; from Middletown it is twelve dollars per ton, to ſixteen dollars per ton; and as four-fifths of the ſtate are on or weſtward of that river, the immenfe faving, which would be made by a great and ftable market like that contemplated, is equally manifeft and defirable.

It may be afked, whether the owners of the houf-es, fhops, and works would receive applications from tenants? The anfwer is, that they would themfelves be induced to occupy fome of them, that the boroughs in the vicinity have been great-ly extended by the fettlement of tradefmen, manu-facturers and others, who depend upon them and upon the farmer, and that unlefs their inhabitants open canals to the Sufquehannah, or difcover coal in their vicinity, thofe boroughs which are not on that river cannot grow much larger, though the demand for manufacturers is fteadily increafing with our population. It is regretted, that the lat-ter increafe of Lancafter has been inconfiderable. But the water works, and the works by fire, pro-pofed in the plan to be erected, would attract and fupport tradefmen and the workmen requifite to proceed with the goods they would have begun, as is conftantly the cafe in Europe.

It may be fafely affirmed, that no part of the United States, at prefent half as fully populated as the five principal counties on the Sufquehannah, offers fo encouraging or fo certain a profpect for an inland town.—It is, as it were, *the bottom of a great bag or fack, into the upper parts of which natural and agricultural produce is poured from the north-eaft, from the north, and from the weft.*

It will be obferved, that many water works, and
objects requiring the moving power of water, are
particularized in the plan. For which reafon, and
in order to procure all the public and private advantages, which are attainable, it is propofed to
take fome pofition, where the river can be fo drawn
out of its natural bed, as to create thofe mill-feats
and falls. It is confidently affirmed, and is not at
all doubted, that there are not wanting places of
that great and valuable natural capacity.

Doubts may arife about the expediency of erecting fome of the works. It is therefore obferved,
that thofe which are mentioned, are merely offered for confideration; none of them are intended
to be urged: but it is believed, that moft of them
would prove, on examination, eligible.

The greater part of the private emolument would
be realized, it is fuppofed, by the erection of nine
hundred dwelling houfes of various fizes (in any of
which many kinds of manufactories could be purfued) and one hundred fhops for fuch branches, as
by reafon of their producing loud noifes, or unpleafant fmells, or of their requiring greater room,
could not be carried on among women and children, infirm, aged, or fick perfons, or within the
compafs of an appartment in a common dwelling
houfe. In that cafe, however, it would be manifeftly prudent, to bring the unimproved mill-feats
into view, that they might be in the way of early
ufe and employment.

The reafon of extending a view to the immediate erection of thofe water mills and other works
is, that by their very great confumption of the raw
materials and produce, which may be drawn by purchafe from the farmers, they will as early and materially increafe the benefits of the propofed town
to the landholder and cultivator, without taking
any hands from agriculture, or preventing any
from going to it.

It will be proper to afcertain, with precifion and
certainty, what would be a reafonable value of two
thoufand acres of land, *thus purchafed, and thus
built upon,* that the inducements to the operation
may be duly exhibited. The borough of Lancafter will appear to afford a mean of comparifon, not
too favourable, when it is remembered, that a pofition on the *weft* fide of Sufquehannah, would give
the propofed town a moft extenfive and fertile back
country for its fupplies by land, free from the expence and rifque of any ferry ; and that it would
acquire building materials, provifions raw materials, and the infinitely important article, *pit coal,*
the very important articles, *timber* and *bark,* in the
greateft abundance, and on the cheapeft terms, by
means of the navigable waters of the Sufquehannah,
and that its traders and artizans could tranfport
produce and manufactures, and recieve fupplies
from Philadelphia through the canal of Swetara,
without any the leaft expence of carting.

An eftimate of a town, confifting of the kinds and number of buildings particularifed above, may be reafonably made as follows:

Dollars.

The actual firft coft of all the various buildings above mentioned, is ftated to be   500,000

From thefe deduct the value of the four fchools, and the church, feven thoufand two hundred dollars, which would be public, and would be of no value to the owners of the town, as fuch, but as they might reflect value upon the houfes, manufactories and lots: alfo deduct the fum of five thoufand dollars, allowed for the charges of fuperintendance,   12,200

Remain as the actual coft and real value of all the private buildings,   487,800

The value of one hundred lots, to be given for twenty churches, and thirty-two for the market, court houfe, and jail, *nothing*, but as they reflect value on the other property in the town,   000,000

The value of one thoufand and ninety-nine lots, of the fize of twenty by one hundred feet, on which the above pri-

vate buildings and works are to be
erected, when they shall be completed,
at one hundred dollars each, on a medium,

Dolls.

109,900

The value of two thousand one hundred, and ninety-eight interval lots (lying between and among the private and
public buildings, and exclusively of those
without that part of the town plot, proposed to be built upon with the fund of
five hundred thousand dollars) at eighty
dollars on an average,

175,480

The value of one hundred twenty feet
lots, making twenty large lots equal to
one hundred feet square, suitable for
erecting twenty other mills, with the
requisite share of the water right, at five
hundred dollars for each mill seat,

10,000

N. B. These will make, with the improved mill-seats, about forty, and will
not require the height of water or command of a fall to be kept for more than
a quarter of a mile. It is believed *much
more* might be placed against this item.

The value of the exclusive privilege
of keeping ferries, arising out of the
ownership of the grounds, to constitute
prizes,

5,000

The value of twenty-two thoufand   *Dolls.*
lots, accommodated with ftreets and alleys, not within the part built upon as
above, with the woods on them, and on
the ftreets and alleys, for fuel and timber, the ftone, lime, clay, &c. for building, at ten dollars per lot, to conftitute
prizes,   220,000
                                               ─────────
                                               1,008,540
                                               ─────────

The feveral objects in the foregoing eftimate of
one million eight thoufand five hundred and forty
dollars to conftitute prizes, to be drawn by the purchafers of five hundred thoufand dollars worth of
tickets: *a fcheme of a lottery* more protfiable than
moft, which have been exhibited, and which will
moreover yield great advantages to every proprietor
and tenant of lands within the fphere of trade belonging to the town.

Although fuch calculations and eftimates as
thefe ought always to be received with the utmoft
caution, and to be examined with ftrictnefs, yet
there are circumftances, which, it is concieved,
infure fuccefs to a well devifed and well executed
plan in the fcene already mentioned.

A very great and increafing fupply of all thofe
things which can create, maintain, and extend a
town; which can attract, cheaply fupport, and

certainly and thoroughly employ an induſtrious community, *forced by the nature of the river and country into this ſingular ſcene,* juſtify an affirmation, that *no ſuch* ſituations for towns of inland trade and manufactures of *native* productions exiſt in the populated parts of the United States.—To eſtimate the value of the river, and the water works, and their permanent influence upon the proſperity and growth of ſuch a town, let us for a moment ſuppoſe, that twenty ſimilar mills, twenty unimproved mill ſeats, and a copious canal leading to the Suſquehannah, were ſuperadded to the preſent advantages of the borough of Lancaſter.

It cannot but be perceived, that moſt of the American inland towns have been commenced without due attention to the powers of water, the advantages of interior navigation, and a copious and certain ſupply of other fuel, when wood ſhall become ſcarce and dear.—The whole number of the houſes in the towns of ſome of the ſtates is very inconſiderable, which is principally owing to their produce having paſſed on without any natural ſtoppage or heavy expence of tranſportation from their farms to their export market; or to *a ſcarcity of fuel* which has been created, and will be increaſed by their growth.

There will be a peculiar certainty and ſtability in the value of property in ſuch a place as that contemplated, becauſe its trade and manufactures depending upon our own laws, and upon our productions, will not be subjected to the injuries and viciffitudes, which often arife from foreign reftrictions and prohibitions, and from the defalcations of the imports of foreign and precarious tropical productions. On the other hand, every new difcovery of a mineral or foffil, every addition to the articles of cultivation in the great landed fcene, on which it will depend, whether for food or manufactures, will yield frefh nourifhment and employment to its inhabitants.

In addition to the reafons already fuggefted for placing the town upon the *weftern* fide of the Sufquehannah, it ought to be added, with a view to the prefent and all other plans of eftablifhing towns in this climate, that the eaftern and northern fides of all waters in the United States, (the elevation, drynefs of the foil, and other things being equal) are lefs healthy than the fouthern and weftern fides. As it further regards, that great concern, the health and comfort of the citizens, it alfo merits repetition, that by the plan propofed, no inadvertent or uninformed man will be able to build his houfe, or place of bufinefs in fuch a manner as to deprive himfelf of *the bleffing of the fummer winds.*

Altho' great ftrefs has been laid upon a particular fcene in the courfe of this paper, from *a thorough conviction of its fitnefs and value,* it is manifeft, that many of the ideas will apply to fuch of the exifting towns in the ftate of Pennfylvania and elfewhere,

as have a capacity to command, by due exertion,
and at a moderate expence, water falls, coal, or inland navigation——A diligent examination of their
refpective capacities, in thofe particulars, ought,
upon the general principles fuggefted, to be made.
It is alfo clear, that a very large part of thofe advantages may be gained at Harrifburgh, Middletown, the falls of Delaware, at the lower end of
the Schuylkill canal, and moft of the other canals
in the United States, by fuch a power of water as
has been mentioned above. In the ftates of Vermont and Kentuckey, in the weftern parts of Pennfylvania and New-York, in the north weftern and
fouthern governments, and in general *at thofe places
on the eafternmoft, or neareft parts of all the weftern waters, and the fouthern or neareft parts of the
northern waters, where the internal navigation ter-
minates, the whole of the above plan, in a maturer
ftate of their population, will apply, with the moft folid and extenfive benefits to the cultivators and proprietors of the foil.**

WERE two or three manufacturing houfes (or
firms) foreign or American, to make a purchafe of
fome fit fituation to erect a variety of water works,

* The grounds around the lower falls of many of the rivers
emptying into the Atlantic Ocean, are alfo very fuitable for fuch
a plan, becaufe provifions, wood, coal, and raw materials may
be tranfported to them coaftwife and from foreign countries.

and were they to commence two or three feveral manufactories upon a confiderable fcale, and to referve fuitable fituations and a command of water for a number of others which would follow, they could not fail to fucceed in their refpective branches, and they would greatly enhance the value of the purchafed lands. It is unneceffary to repeat, in this place, the numerous circumftances in the fituation and affairs of the United States, which enfure fuccefs to well felected eftablifhments of manufactures, conducted with judgment and prudence.

CHAPTER XI.

ABSTRACT of Goods, Wares, and Merchandize, exported from the United States, from the 1st of October, 1790, to 30th September 1791.

Species of Merchandize.		Quantity.
ASHES, pot,	tons of	3,083$\frac{74}{185}$
pearl,	do.	3,270$\frac{20}{185}$
Apples,	barrels	12,352
Bricks,	number	737,764
Boats,	do.	99
Bellows, smiths,	pair,	4
Beer, Ale and Porter,	gallons	44,526
	dozens	719
Boots,	pair,	482
Boot legs,	do.	17
Brimstone,	pounds	3,280
Blacking or Lampblack,	do.	8,518
Bayberries,	bushels	18
Cider,	barrels	1,694
	dozens	310
Chalk,	pounds	20,000
Cotton,	do.	189,316
Coffee,	do.	962,977
Cocoa,	do.	8,322
Chocolate,	boxes	479
Candles, myrtle,	do.	348
wax,	do.	185
tallow,	do.	2,745
Cordage,	cwt.	3,533
Copper ore,	do.	20
pig,	do.	216
manufactured,	do.	1,480
sheet,	do.	296
Coal,	bushels	3,788
Cranberries,	do.	720
Corks,	grofs	300
Corn fan,	number	1
Canes and Walking-sticks,	do.	598
Cotton and Wool Cards,	dozens	25
Carriages, Coaches, Chairs, &c.	number	85
Waggons and Carts,	do.	25
Duck, American,	pieces	653
Russia,	do.	30

Species of Merchandize.			Quantity.
Grain & Pulse.	Indian Corn,	bushels	1,713,241
	Oats,	do.	116,634
	Buckwheat,	do.	14,499
	Pease & Beans,	do.	165,273
Horns and Tips,		number	119,776
Hides,		do.	704
Hats,		do.	435
Honey,		gallons	1,740
Hops,		pounds	650
Hemp,		do.	1,544
Hay,		tons	2,006
Iron, wrought.	Axes,	number	979
	Hoes,	do.	200
	Drawing Knives,	do.	24
	Scythes,	do.	48
	Locks & Bolts,	do.	2,000
	Shovels	do.	261
	Skimmers & Ladles,	do.	15
	Anchors,	do.	175
	Grapnels,	do.	18
	Musquets,	do.	160
	Cutlasses,	do,	72
	Knives and Forks,	do.	240
	Chests of Carpenters Tools,	do.	4
Iron, castings.	Waggon-boxes,	do.	100
	Pots & Kettles,	do.	808
	Cannon,	do.	37
	Swivels,	do.	8
	Cannon Shot,	do.	1000
	Iron Patterns,	do.	12
Iron, the Ton.	Pig,	tons	4,178¾
	Bar,	do.	349½
	Bundles,	do.	8
	Hoops,	do.	16½
Indigo,		pounds	497,720
Leather, tanned and dressed,		do.	5,424
Lime,		bushels	1,320
Lead. Sheets,		number	45
Pig,		tons	16½
Shot,		pounds	6,473
Live Stock.	Horned Cattle,	number	4,627
	Horses,	do.	6,975
	Mules,	do	444
	Sheep,	do.	10,377

Species of Merchandize.			Quantity.
Drugs & Medicine.	Glauber's Salts,	pounds	1,580
	Sarsaparilla, Pink,	do.	14,900
	Sassafras, Bark,	tons	$3\frac{1}{4}$
	Sassafrass-root,	do.	$34\frac{1}{4}$
Earthen Ware.	Stone,	dozens	55
	Yellow, Queens,	crates	157
Flaxseed,		casks	58,492
Flax,		pounds	18,600
Feathers,		do.	904
Flints,		number	40,000
Frames of	Vessels,	do.	1
	Scows,	do.	6
	Boats,	do.	10
	Houses,	do.	195
	Windows and Doors,	do.	31
Furniture, House.	Tables,	do.	75
	Bedsteads,	do.	18
	Desks,	do.	78
	Bureaus,	do.	21
	Sophas, &c.	do.	59
	Clocks,	do.	8
	Clock-cases,	do.	3
	Chests,	do.	705
	Chairs, Windsor,	do.	5,134
	Chairs, Rush,	do.	738
Fishery.	Fish, dried,	quintals	383,237
	Fish, pickled,	barrels	57,424
	Whale oil,	gallons	447,323
	Spermaceti oil,	do.	134,595
	Spermaceti candles,	boxes	4,560
	Whalebone,	pounds	124,829
Glass Ware,		crates	21
	Window,	boxes	92
Ginseng,		pounds	29,208
Groceries.	Cassia & Cinnamon,	do.	1,778
	Cloves & Mace,	do.	900
	Pepper,	do.	492
	Pimento,	do.	141,701
	Brown Sugar,	do.	73,304
	Loaf Sugar,	do.	1,157
	Other Sugar,	do.	1,200
	Raisins,	do.	400
Grain & Pulse.	Wheat,	bushels	1,018,339
	Rye,	do.	36,737
	Barley,	do.	35

Species of Merchandize.			*Quantity.*
Live Stock.	Deer,	number	4
	Hogs,	do.	16,803
	Poultry,	dozens	10,247
Merchandize, or Foreign Dry Goods,		packages	1,439
Molasses		gallons	12,721
Mill-stones,		number	2
Mustard,		pounds	780
Madder,		do.	1,034
Nails,		do.	130,293
Negro Slaves,		number	24
Nankeens,		pieces	7,072
Nuts,		bushels	1,240
Naval Stores.	Pitch,	barrels	3,978
	Tar,	do.	51,044
	Rosin,	do.	228
	Turpentine,	do.	58,107
	Turpentine, Spirits of,	do.	1,172
Oil, Linseed,		gallons	90
Porcelain, or China Ware,		boxes	2
Powder.	Gun,	pounds	25,854
	Hair,	do.	1,276
Pomatum,		do.	45
Paints,		do.	1,520
Pipes,		boxes	1
Printing Presses,		number	4
Plaister of Paris,		tons	4
Provisions.	Rice,	tierces	96,980
	Flour,	barrels	619,687
	Ship Stuff,	do.	6,484
	Rye Meal,	do.	24,062
	Indian Meal,	do.	70,339
	Buckwheat Meal,	do.	422
	Oatmeal,	do.	6
	Bread,	do.	100,279
	Beef,	do.	62,372
	Pork,	do.	26,635
	Crackers,	kegs	15,346
	Hams and Bacon,	pounds	295,647
	Venison Hams,	do.	600
	Cheese,	do.	129,901
	Lard,	do.	522,715
	Butter,	firkins	16,670
	Sausages,	pounds	250
	Fresh Beef,	do.	92,269
	Ditto Pork,	do.	29,334

Species of Merchandize.				*Quantity.*
Provisions.	Carcases of Mutton,		number,	551
	Neats' Tongues,		barrels,	160
	Oysters, pickled,		kegs,	1,228
	Potatoes,		bushels,	22,263
	Onions,		do.	42,420
Reeds,			number,	15,450
Spirits.	American,		gallons,	513,234
	West-India,		do.	4,742
	French Brandy,		do.	158
	Peach do.		do.	753
	Gin,		do.	10,252
	Ditto,		cases,	3,717
	Ditto,		jugs,	2,039
	Cordials,		cases,	69
Sadlery.	Saddles, men's,		number,	414
	Bridles,		do.	402
	Coach Harness,		setts,	74
	Waggon Geers,		do.	8
Shoes,			pair,	7,046
Soap,			boxes,	691
Sago,			pounds,	2,382
Starch,			do.	160
Snuff,			do.	15,689
Steel,			bundles,	1,375
Raw Silk,			pounds,	153
Silver,			ounces,	103
Salt,			bushels,	4,208
Spruce, Essence of			cases,	94
Seed.	Garden,		pounds,	1,060
	Mustard,		do.	660
	Hay,		do.	60
	Cotton,		bushels,	109
Skins and Furs.				
	Morocco,		number,	132
	Calf, in hair,		do.	402
	Deer,		do.	1,063
	Seal,		do.	2,672
	Bear,		do.	37
	Beaver and Otter,		do.	100
	Deer Skins, dressed,		pounds,	48,031
	Ditto and other do. and Furs,		do.	980
	Ditto and do.		packages,	889
Tobacco, in hogsheads,			number,	101,272
	Manufactured,		pounds,	81,122
Types.			boxes,	3

Species of Merchandize.		Quantity.
Tallow,	pounds,	317,195
Twine,	per 112,	19¾
Tow Cloth,	yards,	6,850
Toys, for children,	dozens,	112½
Tin,	boxes,	9
Manufactured,	dozens,	15½
Teas. Bohea,	chests,	17½
Souchong,	do.	492
Green,	do.	178
Hyson,	do.	2,235¾
Vinegar,	gallons,	2,248
Varnish,	do.	60
Wines. Madeira,	do.	76,466
Other,	do.	32,336
Bottled,	dozens,	6
Wax. Bees,	pounds,	224,538
Myrtle,	do.	2,272
Whips,	numbers,	146
Wood. Staves and Heading,	do.	29,061,590
Shingles,	do.	74,205,976
Shook Casks,	do.	42,032
Casks,	do.	297
Laths,	do.	25,500
Hoops,	do.	1,422,155
Hoop-Poles,	do.	3,450
Masts,	do.	405
Bow-Sprits,	do.	42
Bombs,	do.	74
Spars,	do.	4,983
Hand Spikes,	do.	36,714
Pumps,	do.	80
Boxes and Brakes,	do.	56
Blocks,	do.	7,040
Oars,	do.	28,456
Oar Rafters,	do.	13,080
Treenails,	do.	45,905
Cedar and Oak Knees,	do.	1,067
Breast Hooks,	do.	50
Carlings,	do.	13
Anchor Stocks,	do.	809
Cedar Posts,	do.	10,453
Oak Boards and Plank,	do. feet,	963,822
Pine Boards and Plank,	do.	37,288,928
Other ditto and do.	do.	3,463,673
Scantling,	do.	6,237,496

Species of Merchandize.   *Quantity.*

Wood.

Oak, Pine, &c. Scantling,	feet,	2,180,137
Oak and Pine Timber,	tons,	13,775
Lignumvitæ,	cwt.	1,180
Logwood,	do.	105½
Timber,	number logs,	38,680
Mahogany and Lignumvitæ,	number pieces,	3,251
Oak and Pine Bark,	cords,	499
Oak Bark,	do.	57
Ditto Ground,	hogsheads,	1,040
Maft Hoops,	dozens,	148
Axe Helves,	do.	149
Trufs Hoops,	setts,	15
Yokes and Bows for Oxen,	do.	197
Lock Stocks,	numbers,	4,000
Worm Tubs,	do.	6
Wheel Barrows,	do.	6
Wheels for Carts, &c.	do.	50
Spokes and Fellies,	do.	12,972
Spinning Wheels,	do.	17
Tubs, Pails, Bowls, &c.	do.	204

Value,   *Dollars* 17,571,551 45 *Cts.*

Add for two returns from Charlefton, } 827,651
juft received,

Dollars 18,399,202 45 *Cts.*

See page 412.

A SUMMARY OF THE VALUE AND DESTINATION OF THE FOREGOING EXPORTS.

	Dollars.	Cts.
To the dominions of Ruffia,	3,570	
of Sweden,	21,866	2
of Denmark,	277,273	53
of United Netherlands,	1,634,825	66
of Great-Britain,	7,953,418	21
To the Imperial ports of the Auftrian Netherlands and Germany,	362,010	21
To Hamburg, Bremen and other Hanfe towns,	64,259	25
To the dominions of France,	4,298,762	26
of Spain,	1,301,286	95
of Portugal,	1,039,696	95
To the Italian Ports,	31,726	90
To Morocco,	3,660	50
To the Eaft-Indies, generally,	318,628	46
To Africa, do.	168,477	92
To the Weft-Indies, do.	59,434	36
To the north-weft coaft of America,	3,380	
Uncertain,	29,274	75
Dollars	17,571,551	45
To the above add the amount of two quarterly returns, fince received from Charlefton, South-Carolina,	827,651	
	18,399,202	45

Treafury Department,
October 1ft, 1791.

TENCH COXE,

Affiftant Secretary.

CHAPTER XIII.

A RETURN OF THE IMPORTS INTO THE UNITED STATES, FOR ONE YEAR, ENDING ON THE 30th DAY OF SEPTEMBER, 1790.

Goods, subject to 5 per cent. ad valorem, 13,044,824 90

Ditto,	7½ per cent.		862,977 76
Ditto,	10 per cent.		624,674 59
Ditto,	12½ per cent.		0 0
Ditto,	15 per cent.		3,619 4
Spirits, of Jamaica proof,		gallons,	610,703
Other distilled spirits,		do.	3,067,496
Madeira wine,		do.	256,691
Other wines,		do.	607,561
Beer, ale or porter, in casks,		do.	70,564
Molasses,		do.	5,900,128
Brown sugar,		pounds,	17,380,746
Loaf sugar,		do.	132,837
Other sugars,		do.	177,279
Coffee,		do.	4,013,355
Cocoa,		do.	896,946
Tallow candles,		do.	15,157
Wax and spermaceti candles,		do.	4,224
Cheese,		do.	88,771
Soap,		do.	24,120
Nails and spikes,		do.	1,579,947
Snuff,		do.	2,198
Indigo,		do.	32,283
Cotton, [this article being free, there is no account of it kept by the collectors.]			
Tobacco manufactured,		do.	3,182

In American vessels from India.	Bohea tea,	do.	1,502,995
	Souchong and other black teas,	do.	378,032
	Hyson,	do.	631,310
	Other green teas,	do.	89,515
In American vessels from Europe.	Bohea tea,	do.	298,768
	Souchong, &c.	do.	71,354
	Hyson,	do.	15,736
	Other green teas,	do.	9,212
In Foreign vessels.	Bohea Tea,	do.	9,612
	Souchong, &c.	do.	4,498
	Hyson,	do.	4,644
	Other green teas,	do.	2,528
	Cables,	cwt.	635 1 10
	Tarred cordage,	do.	5257 2 5
	Untarred do. and yarn,	do.	900 3 14
	Twine or packthread,	do.	609 2 8
	Steel unwrought,	do.	5,427 1 2
	Beer, ale, porter or cider, in bottles,	dozens,	17,746
	Wool and cotton cards,	do.	780
	Salt,	bushels,	2,337,920
	Coal,	do.	181,885
	Playing cards,	packs,	19,066
	Pickled fish,	barrels,	3468
	Dried fish,	quintals	3,884 3 12
	Shoes, slippers, &c. of leather,	pairs,	49,003
	Ditto, of silk or stuff,	do.	20,701
	Boots,	do.	746

CHAPTER XIV.

AN ACCOUNT OF THE TONNAGE OF VESSELS, ON WHICH THE DUTY WAS PAID, IN THE UNITED STATES, FROM THE 1st OF OCTOBER 1789, TO THE 30th SEPTEMBER 1790, INCLUSIVELY.

TO WHAT NATION BELONGING.

STATES.	United States.	Mixed, or United States & Foreign.	France.	Great-Britain.	Ireland.	Spain.	United Nether-lands.	Portugal.	Imperial and Germany.	Hamburg and Bremen.	Denmark.	Sweden.	Russia. T.T.	Prussia. T.T.	TOTAL.
	Tons.	Tons.	Tons.	Tons.	Tons.	Tons.	Tons.	Tons.	Tons.	Tons.	Tons.	Tons.			Tons.
New-Hampshire,	13,519	–	34	2,556	–	–	–	–	–	–	–	–	–	–	16,109. 8
Massachusetts,	174,728.10	–	453. 6	19,382. 7	150	–	–	–	–	–	249	–	–	–	194,401. 9
Rhode-Island,	9,526. 5	–	174. 4	95. 9	–	46. 3	–	–	–	–	–	–	–	–	9,841. 9
Connecticut,	30,616.10	–	–	3,458.11	–	–	–	–	–	–	–	–	–	–	34,075. 9
New-York,	48,922. 6	–	1,129	36,843	–	1,807. 3	437. 9	1,762. 6	292.9	–	226. 3	–	–	–	92,737. 9
New-Jersey,	5,624. 7	–	79. 3	267	–	–	–	–	–	–	–	–	–	–	5,970.10
Pennsylvania,	52,987. 4	963.8	3,234. 7	40,202.10	1,800	4,342. 7	736.10	1,086 3	–	–	284. 4	–	–	–	105,638. 5
Delaware,	4,141. 3	–	–	1,782. 9	–	–	3,284	–	–	–	–	–	–	–	5,924
Maryland,	57,608. 2	–	5,176	23,631	–	408	–	–	509	–	–	–	–	–	90,639. 2
Virginia,	43,566. 2	–	2,121. 9	56,333. 8	83. 4	1,104. 4	668. 5	–	–	–	–	182. 9	–	–	104,060. 5
North-Carolina,	19,833. 1	–	65	5,997. 8	213.10	49. 8	–	–	–	–	–	128. 2	–	–	26,287. 5
South-Carolina,	19,777. 2	–	623. 2	20,634. 7	900	952. 7	298. 1	–	–	1.948	1,350	–	–	–	46,483. 7
Georgia,	11,250. 6	–	710. 9	15,767. 4	–	111. 9	–	–	–	–	306. 3	–	–	394	28,540. 7
Grand total,	492,100.10	963.8	13,801. 4	226,953. 4	13,147. 2	8,772. 9	7,228. 3	2,849.9	801.9	1.948	2,415.10	310.11	–	394	761,710. 4

CHAPTER XVI.

CONTAINING A SUMMARY STATEMENT OF THE PRINCIPAL
FACTS, WHICH CHARACTERIZE THE AMERICAN PEOPLE,
AND THEIR COUNTRY OR TERRITORY.

THE people of the United States have exploded thofe principles, by the operation of which religious oppreffions and reftrictions of whatever defcription, have been impofed upon mankind, and, rejecting mere toleration, they have placed upon one common and equal footing every church, fect or fociety of religious men.

They have exploded, in like manner, thofe principles, by the operation of which, civil oppreffions have been inflicted upon mankind; and they have made an unexceeded progrefs in their practice upon the principles of free government.

While the fermentations of a civil and revolutionary conteft were yet operating upon their minds, amidft the warmth of feeling incidental to that ftate of things, they have recently examined with fober attention the imperfections of their national and fubordinate civil eftablifhments : they reflected, with due ferioufnefs, on the numerous inconveniencies, which thofe imperfections had produced, and upon the awful fcenes in which they would probably be called upon *to suffer* or *to act*, if their civil conſtitutions ſhould continue un-amended: and they have ſince exhibited to the world the new and intereſting ſpectacle of a whole people, meeting, as it were, *in their political plain and voluntarily impoſing upon themſelves the whole-ſome and neceſſary reſtraints of juſt government.*

On two occaſions, at the diſtance of four years, perſonal character and the public intereſts have produced *an orderly and unanimous election of the chief magiſtrate of the United States,* without one, even the ſmalleſt, effort or meaſure of pro-curement.

During four years, the ſecond ſtation of execu-tive public employment and all of the third* grade have remained in the ſame hands, nor have any changes taken place in the more ſubordinate, but a few from voluntary reſignations and death.

The public debt is ſmaller in proportion to the preſent wealth and population of the United States than the public debt of any other civilized nation.

The United States (including the operations of the individual ſtates) have ſunk a much greater proportion of their public debt in the laſt ten years, than any other nation in the world.

* A. D. 1793.

The expences of the government are very much lefs, in proportion to wealth and numbers, than thofe of any nation in Europe.

There is no land tax among the national revenues, nor is there any interior tax, or excife upon food, drink, fuel, lights, or any native or foreign manufacture, or native or foreign production, except a duty of about four pence fterling upon domeftic diftilled fpirits*. The greateft part of the public burdens are paid by an import duty on foreign goods, which being drawn back on exportation, it remains only on what is actually confumed. It is in that view the loweft in the world, and operates greatly in favour of American manufactures.

Trade has been encouraged by a drawback of all the import duty on foreign goods, when they are exported, excepting only a very few commodities of a particular nature, which are not defired to be much imported into, or confumed in the United States.

A national mint is eftablifhed under the direction of the ableft practical man in the arts and fciences which this country contains—*David Rittenhoufe.* It is provided by law that the purity and intrinfic value of the filver coin fhall be equal to that of Spain, and of the gold coins to thofe of the ftricteft European nations. The government of

* A. D. 1793.

the United States foregoes all profit from the coinage : a political and wholefome forbearance.

The banks eftablifhed in the feveral cities of Philadelphia, New-York, Bofton, Baltimore, Charlefton, Alexandria, &c. divide a profit of feven and an half to eight and an half per cent. per annum* at prefent, which is paid half yearly.

The intereft of the public debt of the United States is paid quarter yearly with a punctuality abfolute and perfect. There is no tax on property in the funds and banks.

The fhipbuilding of the Uuited States was greater in the year 1792, than in any former year fince the fettlement of the country, and it is much greater in the current year, than it was in the laft. Generally fpeaking, the art of fhipbuilding was never fo well underftood, never fo well executed, nor was there ever a time when fo many of the manufactures requifite for the furniture, tackle, apparel and arming of veffels were made in the United States.

The value of the manufactures of the United States is certainly greater than double the value of their exports in native commodities.

The value of the manufactures of the United States, is much greater than the grofs value of all

* More might be faid with truth.

their imports, including the value of goods exported again.

The manufactures of the United States confist generally of articles of comfort, utility, and necefsity. Articles of luxury, elegance, and fhew are not manufactured in America, excepting a few kinds.

The manufactures of the United States have increafed very rapidly fince the commencement of h e revolutionary war, and particularly in the laft five years.

Houfehold manufactures are carried on within the families of almoft all the farmers and planters, and of a great proportion of the inhabitants of the villages and towns. This practice is increafing under the animating influences of private interest and public fpirit.

The exports of the United States have increafed in the laft two years about fourteen per cent.*

Thofe exports confift in a great degree of the moft necefsary food of man and working animals, and of raw materials, applicable to manufactures of the moft general utility and confumption.

---

* In the laft three years they have increafed from eighteen millions and one quarter : to twenty-fix millions of dollars. September 30th, 1793.

There is not any duty upon the exportation of the produce of the earth, nor can such duty be imposed on any exported commodities : the exportation of produce may be suspended or prohibited.

Produce and all other merchandize may be freely exported in the ships and vessels of all nations (not being alien enemies) without discrimination.

The exports of the United States are five times the amount of the national taxes and duties*.

The amount of the outward freight of the ships and vessels of the United States, at this time, is probably equal to all their national taxes and duties. The inward freight is considerable. The earning of the fishing vessels, in lieu of freight, are also considerable. The coasting freights are greater in value than both the last.

All ships and vessels depart from the United States, fully laden, excepting a part of the East India traders.

A large quantity of tonnage is employed in the coasting trade.

A considerable quantity of tonnage is employed in the cod and whale fisheries.

The imports of the United States are less in value than the exports, deducting the outward freights

---

* They prove to be nearly six times. Sept. 30th, 1793.

of their own ships (which are returned in goods) the nett fales of their ships to foreigners, the property imported by migrators from foreign countries, and the public impoft.

The very great proportion of the imports, which confifts of manufactures, (and from raw materials, which America can produce) affords conftant and inviting opportunities to leffen the balance againft the United States, in their trade with one foreign country, holds out a certain home market to fkilful and induftrious manufacturers in America, and gives promifes to the landholder and farmer, of a very increafing demand for their produce, in which they cannot be deceived.*

The imports of the United States, for confumption, have not been fwelled in proportion to the increafe of their population and wealth. *The reafon is, the conftant introduction of new branches of manufacture, and the great extenfion of the old branches.*

The imports, for confumption, into the United States are compofed of manufactures in a much lefs proportion than heretofore, owing to *the fame two caufes.*

The imports of the United States have almoft ceafed to exhibit certain articles of naval and mili-

* Witnefs the fteady price of our produce, during the embargo. A. D. 1794.

tary fupply, and others of the greateft utility and confumption, owing alfo to *the fame two caufes*.

The imports of the United States, confift in a fmall degree of neceffaries, in a great degree of articles of comfortable accommodation, and in fome degree of luxuries: but the exports confift chiefly of prime neceffaries, with fome articles of mere comfort and utility, and fome of luxury. The following will be found to be the quantities of fome of the principle articles of exportation from the United States, during the year, ending in September, 1792.

3,145,255 bufhels of grain and pulfe (principally wheat, Indian corn, rye, beans and peas.

44,752 horfes, horned cattle, mules, hogs and fheep.

1,469,723 barrels of flour, meal, bifcuit, and rice, reducing cafks of various fizes, to the proportion of flour barrels.

146,909 barrels of tar, pitch, turpentine and rofin.

116,803 barrels of beef, pork, mutton, faufages, oyfters, tripe, &c. reducing cafks of various fizes, to the proportion of beef and pork barrels.

231,776 barrels of dried and pickled fifh, reducing them to barrels of the fame fize.

948,115 gallons of fpirits, diftilled in the United States.

7,823 tons, 12 cwts. and 14 lbs. of pot-afhes and pearl-afhes.

112,428 hogfheads of tobacco.

60,646,861 feet of boards plank, and fcantling.

19,391½ tons of timber.

18,374 pieces of timber.

1,080 cedar and oak fhip knees.

71,693,863 fhingles.

31,760,702 ftaves and hoops.

191 frames of houfes.

73,318 oars, rafters for oars, and handfpikes.

48,860 fhook or knock-down cafks.

52,382 hogfheads of flax feed.*

The imports of the United States are now generally brought directly (and not circuitioufly) from the countries which produced or manufactured them—China, India proper, the ifles of Bourbon and Mauritius, Good Hope, the fouthern fettlements of America and the Weft-Indies, the Wine iflands,

---

* The exports of the year of which the above are a part, amounted to 21,000,000 of Dollars—but the exports of the next following year (ending on the 30th September, 1793) amounted to 5,000,000 more, being 26,000,000 of Dollars. Provifions and raw materials have greatly increafed. Of flour alone there were fhipped 1,013,000 cafks. See paper Y. Book 2d.

the countries on the Mediteranean and Baltic Seas, Great-Britain and Ireland, France, the Netherlands and Germany, Spain and Portugal.

Lefs than half the fhips and veffels belonging to the United States, are fufficient to tranfport all the commodities they confume or import.

Their citizens may be lawfully concerned in any branch of foreign trade, whether carried on from the United States or from any other country.*

Their commerce is diverfified and profperous, and confifts in importing for their own confumption, and for exportation; in the exporting, the coafting and inland trades; the Indian trade; manufactures, fhipping, the fifheries, banking, and infurances on fhips, cargoes, and houfes. There is no branch of commerce foreign or domeftic, in which every diftrict, city, port, and individual, is not equally entitled to be interefted.

The lawful intereft of money is fix per cent. per annum in moft of the ftates: in a few it is feven per cent. in one it is five per cent.

The commanders and other officers of the American fhips are deemed fkilful and judicious; from which caufe, combined with the goodnefs of their

* Except the flave trade, March 1794.

ſhips and of their equipment, inſurances upon their veſſels are generally made in Europe, upon the moſt favourable terms, compared with the correſ-ponding riſques on board of the veſſels of other nations.

The ſeparate American ſtates (with one ſmall exception) have aboliſhed the ſlave trade, and they have in ſome inſtances aboliſhed negro ſlavery ; in others they have adopted efficacious meaſures for its certain but gradual abolition. The importation of ſlaves is diſcontinued, and can never be renew-ed ſo as to interrupt the repoſe of Africa, or en-danger the tranquility of the United States. The ſteady uſe of efficacious *alteratives* is deemed pre-ferable to the immediate application of more ſtrong remedies in a caſe of ſo much momentary and in-trinſic importance.

The clothes, books, houſehold furniture, and the tools or implements of their trade or profeſſion, brought by emigrators to America, are exempted from the import duty, and they may begin their commerce, manufaĉtures, trades or agriculture on the day of their arrival upon the ſame footing as a native citizen.

There is no greater nor other tax upon foreign-ers or their property in the United States, than upon native citizens.

All foreign juriſdiĉion in eccleſiaſtical matters is inconſiſtent with the laws and conſtitutions of the United States; and with the settled judgment of the people.

Almost every known christian church exists in the United States; as also the Hebrew church. There has not been a dispute between any two sects or churches since the revolution. There are no tythes. Marriage and burial fees, small glebes, land-rents, pew-rents, monies at interest and voluntary contributions are the principal means of supporting the clergy. Many of them are also professors and teachers in the universities, colleges, academies and schools, for which interesting stations, pious and learned ministers of religion are deemed particularly suitable. There is no provision in the episcopal, presbyterian or independent church for any clerical person, or character above a rector, or minister of the gospel—and this is generally, if not universally the case. There are some assistant ministers, but no curates, or vicars: also several bishops without salaries.

The poor taxes in the United States are very small, owing to the facility, with which every man and woman, and every child, who is old enough to do the lightest work, can procure a comfortable subsistence. The industrious poor, if frugal and sober, often place themselves, in a few years, above want.

Horses and cattle, and other useful beasts, imported for breeding, are exempted by law from the import duty.

All the lands in the United States are free from tythes.

The medium annual *land rents* of Europe are greater per acre than the medium *purchase* is in the United States; including in the estimate the value of the old improved farms in America, and the great mass of unimproved lands.*

The military regulations and articles of war in the United States, are well calculated to maintain that strict discipline and thorough subordination, which are indispensible to the efficiency of an army. All the officers of the land and sea-forces are, by the constitution appointed by the president, with the advice and consent of the senate.

The production and manufactures of military supplies and articles, enable the United States to derive from their own resources, ships of war, gun-powder, cannon and musket-balls, shells and bombs, cannon and carriages, muskets, rifles and cutlasses, grapnals, anchors, sail cloth, cordage, iron, lead, cartouch-boxes, sword-belts, cartridge-paper, saddles, bridles and holsters, soldiers' and sailors hats, buckles, shoes and boots, leathern breeches, naval stores, sheathing paper, malt and spirituous liquors, manufactured tobacco, soap, candles, lard, butter, beef, pork, bacon, hams,

* A. D. 1793.

peas, biscut, and flour, and other articles for the land or marine service.

The education of youth has engaged a great share of the attention of the legislatures of the states.

Night schools for young men and boys, who are employed at labour or business in the day time, have been long and beneficially supported, and the idea of Sunday schools has been zealously adopted in some places. Free schools for both sexes have been increased. Greater attention, than heretofore, is paid to female education.

The people of the United States are ingenious in the invention, and prompt, and accurate in the execution of mechanism and workmanship for purposes in science, arts, manufactures, navigation, and agriculture. Rittenhouse's planetarium, Franklin's electrical conductor, Godfrey's quadrant improved by Hadley, Rumsey's and Fitch's steam-engines, Leslie's rod pendulum and other horological inventions, the construction of ships, the New-England whale-boat, the construction of flour-mills, the wire-cutter and bender for card makers, Folsom's and Brigg's machinery for cutting nails out of rolled iron, the Philadelphia dray with an inclined plane, Mason's engine for extinguishing fire, the Connecticut steeple clock, which is wound up by the wind, the Franklin fire-place, the Rittenhouse stove, Anderson's threshing machine, Rittenhoufe's inftrument for taking levels, Donnaldfon's hippopotamos and balance lock, and Wynkoop's underlators, are a few of the numerous examples.

It is probable, that all the jewels and diamonds worn by the citizens of the United States, their wives and daughters are lefs in value than thofe which fometimes form a part of the drefs of an individual in feveral countries of Europe. *All capital ftock is kept in action.* There are no *defcriptions* of men in America and very few individuals, at the active times of life, who live without fome purfuit of bufinefs, profeffion, occupation, or trade. *All the citizens are in active habits.*

No country of the fame wealth, intelligence and civilization, has fo few *menial* fervants (ftrictly fpeaking) in the families of perfons of the greateft property.

Family fervants and farming fervants, who emigrate from Europe, and who continue foberly and induftrioufly in family or farm fervice, for one, two or three years, very often find opportunities to better their fituations, by getting into fome little comfortable line of dealing, or trade, or manufacturing, or farming, according to their education, knowledge and qualifications.

America has not many charms for the diffipated and voluptuous part of mankind, but very many indeed for the rational, fober minded and difcreet.

It is a country which affords great opportunities of comfort and prosperity to people of good property, and those of moderate property, and to *the industrious and honest poor ;* a singular and pleasing proof of which last assertion is, that *there are very few, if any, day labourers, in the city and liberties of Philadelphia, of the Quaker church.* That religious society is very numerous, but the sobriety, industry, and frugality which they practice, enables their poor quickly to improve their condition, in a country so favourable to the poorest members of the community.

That part of the tradesmen a nd manufacturers, who live in the country, generally reside on small lots and farms, of one acre to twenty, and not a few upon farms of twenty to one hundred and fifty acres, which they cultivate at leisure times, with their own hands, their wives, children, servants and apprentices, and sometimes by hired labourers, or by letting out fields, for a part of the produce, to some neighbour, who has time or farm hands not fully employed. *This union of manufactures and farming* is found to be very convenient on the grain farms, but it is still more convenient on the grazing and grass farms, where parts of almost every day, and a great part of every year, can be spared from the business of the farm, and employed in some mechanical, handycraft, or manufacturing business. These persons often make domestic and farming carriages, implements and utensils, build houses and barns, tan leather, manufacture hats, fhoes, hofiery, cabinet-work, and other articles of clothing and furniture, to the great convenience and advantage of the neighbourhood. In like manner fome of the farmers, at leifure times and proper feafons, manufacture nails, pot-afh, pearl-afh, ftaves and heading, hoops and handfpikes, axe-handles, maple-fugar, &c. The moft judicious planters in the fouthern ftates are induftrioufly inftructing their negroes, particularly the young, the old, the infirm, and the females in manufactures—a wife and humane meafure.

A large proportion of the moft fuccefsful manufacturers in the United States are perfons, who were journeymen, and in a few inftances were foremen in the work-fhops and manufactories of Europe, who having been fkilfull, fober and frugal, and having thus faved a little money, have fet up for themfelves with great advantage in America. Few have failed to fucceed. There appears to be leaft opening for thofe, who have been ufed to make very fine and coftly articles of luxury and fhew. There is not fo much chance of fuccefs for thofe luxurious branches, *unlefs they are capable of being carried on in a confiderable degree by machinery or water works*; in which cafe they alfo will thrive if the neceffary capital be employed.—There is already fome confumption of thefe fine goods in America, and as free an exportation of them (without duty, or excife) as from any country in the world.

The views of the government of the United States appear by its declarations, and by the ftrong-eſt preſumptive proofs to be *the maintenance of peace, order, liberty and ſafety.* Intrigues at foreign courts and ſecret or open interpoſitions or intermeddling in the affairs of foreign countries, have not been imputed to the government of this nation. They have not manifeſted any inordinate ambition, by ſeeking *conqueſt,* alone or in unity with any other nation, for they have not attempted to eſtabliſh or raiſe a great or unneceſſary navy * or army.

The United States have been prudently and unremitingly attentive to thoſe objeᴄts, which enable a country to purſue, to an happy and profitable iſſue, unambitious, defenſive and neceſſary wars. Amidſt an induſtrious cultivation of the arts of peace, they have maintained and improved *the military organization of the whole maſs of the able bodied citizens.* They have reſtored their public credit, as an indiſpenſible mean of war, and they have ſucceſsfully encouraged all thoſe arts, by which the inſtruments of naval and land armaments may be expeditiouſly procured and created. Their meaſure of retribution to their public creditors, foreign and domeſtic, has been conſidered, by ſome intelligent citizens as even more than juſtice required. From an equal love of juſtice, and from prudential conſiderations, they have, by a formal aᴄt of the peo-

* The intended naval armament was manifeſtly propoſed to reſtrain the pirates of Barbary ; and the meaſures relative to the additional regular troops, the draught of militia, and fortifications are obviouſly grounded on juſtifiable caution and neceſſary defence. April 1794.

ple, fanctioned a treaty recognizing the claims of the fubjects of a foreign country againft whom an infraction and non execution of the fame treaty was alledged. Refraining moft fcrupuloufly from intrigues and influence in the affairs of foreign nations it cannot be doubted, that they will be aware of correfponding intrigues and influence in their domeftic affairs, and that they will check the appearances of fuch attempts with difpleafure and effect.

BOOK II.

BOOK II.

CHAPTER I.

INTRODUCTORY REMARKS.

THE preceding part of this work was prepared for publication in the fummer of the laft year; but the epidemic malady, which occurred in Philadelphia, towards the end of that feafon, prevented the execution of the defign at that time. Some obfervations and documents have fince prefented themfelves, and are intended to be comprifed in the fecond book. Moft of the latter are calculated to render thefe views of our interefts and capacities more particular and more clear. The obfervations principally relate to the prefent ftage of our affairs, and will therefore be the more interefting, if they fhall prove to be founded in truth and reafon.

CHAPTER II.

THERE remain at this time, in moft of the American ftates, extenfive tracts of land, covered with forefts, applicable to every purpofe of human life, for which wood and timber are required. No country, fo well accommodated with navigation and adapted to commerce and manufactures, poffeffes as great a treafure of the fame kind. The manufactures, which can be made immediately of wood, are no lefs numerous than important. Ships, boats, mafts and fpars, oars, hand-fpikes, anchor-ftocks, cafks and other coopers ware of every fize and kind, cabinet wares, and other houfehold furniture, farming and mechanical implements and tools, ftaves, heading, hoops, boards, plank, fcantling, joifts, fquare timber, fhingles, frames of houfes, turners wares, carriages for pleafure and for draught, corn-fans, wheel barrows, meafures, fcale plates, timber for machinery and mills, cannon carriages, gun-ftocks and other military implements for the fea and land fervice are among the objects contemplated.

The manufactures, to which wood is neceffary in the form of fuel, are alfo numerous and important.

Glafs-houfes, potteries, diftilleries, brick-kilns, furnaces, forges, mills for rolling and flitting iron and
other metals, refineries of fugar, black-fmiths and
all other fmiths fhops are among the principal inftances.

The manufactures to produce which, wood is requifite for the making of afhes, are the great articles of foft and hard foap, which are of univerfal
confumption and the very important articles of pot-
afh and pearl-afh.

To all thefe may be added the manufactory of
tanned leather, which demands the bark of various
and innumerable trees.

Of the wooden raw materials and fuel for thefe
invaluable and numerous manufactures, the United
States poffefs, if we may fo fpeak, *an immenfe and
unequalled magazine.* They appear therefore to be
invited to eftablifh *manufactures in wood* by the moft
weighty and obvious confiderations.

But when it is remembered, that this immenfe magazine of wooden materials and fuel will obftruct,
for a time, the cultivation of millions of acres of
the beft lands, we muft feel another and a more
powerful impulfe to the active promotion of manufactures in wood. To enforce thefe general ideas
the following application of them in the manufactory of pot-afhes is here offered:

A METHOD OF CLEARING A FARM LOT OF NEW WOODLAND,
EASILY PRACTICABLE BY PERSONS HAVING NO MORE MO-
NEY OR PROVISIONS THAN ARE SUFFICIENT TO PROVIDE
THE FOOD AND CLOTHING OF THEIR FAMILIES, DURING
THE FIRST YEAR OF THEIR SETTLEMENT.

1ſt. The ſettler in making this clearing muſt take
care to burn the bruſh and wood, in ſuch manner
as to preſerve the aſhes. Out of the wood aſhes,
thus ſaved, he ſhould make as much pot aſh, or
pearl aſh, as he can, and he ſhould diſpoſe of this
for ready money, ſtrong clothing, axes, ſpades,
ploughs, or ſuch other things for his farm, or family, as it would otherwiſe be neceſſary for him to
procure, by ſelling or bartering, grain or cattle,
if he had them to ſpare. It is believed, that the
pot aſh or pearl aſh will procure him as much value as all the expence and labor of the clearing,
during the ſeaſon would be worth in caſh. He
will therefore obtain as much money or goods as
will enable him to hire aſſiſtance, in the next ſeaſon, either to farm, or to clear land, or to make
his improvements, ſo as to ſave his own time, or
labor intirely, for clearing more land, or to help
him in doing it. He muſt again make pot aſh or
pearl aſh, and he muſt again apply the money or
goods, it ſells for, to the clearing of the next ſeaſon.—In this way it is plain, that he will derive
money enough from the clearing and pot aſhes, of
every year, to do much of the ſame in the year following. A man who has 40, 50 or 100 dollars to
ſpare, at the out-ſet, will get his land cleared, in
this manner very faſt indeed. If he has ſugar ma-

ple trees on his land, he may alfo obtain money, by making fugar in February and March, and felling or bartering it for cafh, or goods to be laid out in like manner, in hiring hands the next feafon. If money is fcarce in a new fettlement, and he barters pot afh or maple fugar, for ftrong trowfers, fhirts, hats or jackets, he will find it eafy to procure laborers for fuch neceffaries. It is proper to obferve, that if a man burns his wood and brufh on every part of his newly cleared field, it is doubtful whether he does not injure the foil, by burning the half rotten leaves and light mould, or earth, which have been made from the rotten leaves of many years.—There is an opinion, that the afhes left from burning the trees greatly enrich the land, and that would be certain, if the light mouldy earth and half rotten leaves were not alfo confumed by the fire. The foil of all new countries appears to have for its upper part, a layer or ftratum of half rotten vegetable materials, which are capable of being burned, but which it would be a great benefit to plough into the earth. Potatoes, the beft food for new fettlements, grow abundantly in that rotten vegetable foil. This is very well known.

It appears doubtful, whether the farmers in the long cleared counties of New-England, New-York, and New-Jerfey, do not injure themfelves very much by making pot afh and pearl afh, *confidering how neceffary the wood afhes are to manure* their farms, many of which are impoverifhed, and many naturally light. To carry the fodder and litter from a farm to other places does not appear more improper. But that is allowed to be very bad farming.

2dly. The above method of clearing lands, is obviously important to people of large property, who are defirous of improving their eftates and their country, by clearing their lands expeditiously. They may effect it in two ways; either—1ft. by fetting up pot afh works, at their mills or country ftores, or other central places, and buying wood-afhes of the fettlers of new fertile lands, and making them into pearl afhes, or pot afhes, and then felling them for exportation ; or 2dly. by employing wood-cutters and other laborers, to fell the trees, and oxen or horfes, with chains to bring the wood together for burning, then collecting the heaps of afhes and making pearl afhes, which is a fimple and eafy operation. It is faid to be a fact, and it is highly worthy of notice that the expence of clearing an·acre of land is fully and completely reimburfed, by the nett fales of the pot afhes or pearl afhes, which can be made from the wood afhes, collected after thus burning the trees— Hence it would follow, that if a perfon of fubftance fhould purchafe one thoufand acres of good new wood land, at any fixed or given price, (for example fifteen fhillings, fterling per acre*) and

* This price is mentioned, becaufe it is a low medium of the *land-rents* of Europe, and becaufe great quantities of fine lands, covered with woods, are yet to be purchafed, in America, at and far under that price.

if he fhould be able, by force of money, in one year to clear all the meadow land and half the plough land, by making pot afhes or pearl afhes, in the fecond mode above mentioned, he would immediately raife his property in productivenefs to the level of the good cleared lands of Pennfylvania, New-York, &c. that is to feven, eight, ten, twenty, thirty and forty dollars per acre: for fuch are the prices, according to the quality, advantages of land and water carriages, and proximity to towns and villages. The capital or money employed to make the pot or pearl afhes would be replaced by the fales of them as above mentioned. *This operation, when confidered upon a fcale of 100,000 acres, appears like a new creation of property.*

THE United States have been brought, by flow degrees, to their prefent knowledge of the value of their wood and timber. It is faid to be not more than twenty-five years, fince the fouthern live oak or ever-green oak has been ufed in fhip-building. The importance of pot-afh is by no means duly underftood at this time, in feveral of the beft wooded of thefe ftates. The value of the maple fugar tree is not yet univerfally known. It is faid, that the Hemlock is capable of being made into fhingles fit for home confumption or exportation, in a degree which is not underftood; and the white pine is

more valuable, than is suppofed, for the fame purpofe. The fouthern pitch pine, and even the yellow pine have been suppofed, of late years to be
more fuitable than white oak for beams, carlines,
fills, and other ftraight timbers for fhips and houfes, in places liable to rapid decay. It is little
known, that it is as eafy in America to procure a
beam, for a fhip of war, of white oak or pitch pine,
in one entire piece, as it is difficult, in Great-Britain. The actual and progreffive fcarcity of all
the moft valuable kinds of timber in Europe has
been hitherto noticed in as fmall a degree, as the
diverfified and unequal refources of the United
States in that particular. The demand for wood
and timber throughout the world has been greatly
extended in the prefent century, by the increafe of
the aggregate tonnage of the fleets of public and
private fhips, by manufactures in wood, and by
means of fire, and by the wonderful increafe in the
number and extent of the commercial and manufacturing towns of Europe and America. The tonnage of the Britifh navy for example in 1694, bears
no comparifon to that of 1794, and their private
fhips have undergone a fimilar augmentation. The
whole mafs of the tonnage of the world is now immenfe. A defalcation of timber is percieved in
moft countries, and, in the manner of what has
been faid concerning grain, it may be fafely affirmed, that *the unavoidable deficiencies of European
wood and timber can only be fupplied from America.*
We fhall therefore rapidly arrive at the ufe of our
new lands, through the confumption of our forefts

by the countries and colonies of the old world; and the proceeds of our wood and timber in the mean time will be in lieu of the fales of grain and cattle.

The political importance of thefe great natural productions (wood and timber) is manifeft and ftriking, in this age of manufacturing, and mercantile competition, and of naval rival-fhip and ambition. The value of our forefts to the feekers of the carrying trade and of naval power is greatly increafed by their yielding their poffeffors prodigious quantities of tar, turpentine and pitch. It would be unwife however, in the United States to neglect *the due prefervation of their timber:* and confidering how obvioufly important it is, that we maintain an abundant ftock, it is a comfortable reflection, that the prefent redundance and cheapnefs of American lands enables us to effect *the prefervation and reproduction of our forefts* with lefs inconvenience and expence, than any other civilized nation.

CHAPTER III.

CONTAINING THE TARIFF OF THE UNITED STATES, FOR THE INFORMATION OF MERCHANTS AND MANUFACTURERS.

IT has been frequently obſerved in the courſe of the preceding pages, that the duties laid for the purpoſe of revenue, on foreign manufactures imported into the United States, are a great encouragement to ſimilar articles, which are or ſhall be manufactured in this country. It is indiſpenſibly neceſſary to a view of our affairs, that the advantages ariſing from the American impoſt to the manufacturer of any domeſtic fabric ſhould be diſtinctly exhibited. This will be moſt eaſily effected by the following complete table of the duties payable by law on all goods, wares and merchandize, imported into the United States of America, after the laſt day of June 1794, and of the articles which are free from impoſt. It may be proper to obſerve, that theſe duties are in the caſe of importations in veſſels of the United States, and that the rates are ten per cent. higher in foreign ſhips.

(For the Tariff ſee the next page.)

[Paper Z.]

A

ARMS, fire and fide, not otherwife enumerated,	15	per cent. ad val.
Apparatus, philofophical, efpecially imported for any feminary of learning,	free	
Ale, beer and porter, in cafks,	8	cents per gallon.
——————————— in bottles,	8	ditto.
Artificial flowers, feathers and other ornaments for womens head dreffes,	15	per cent. ad val.
Annifeed,	15	ditto.
Articles of all kinds of the growth, product or manufactures of the United States, fpirits excepted,	free	
Anchors,	10	

B

Brafs cannon, teutenague, and wire, fee cannon,	free	
—— Iron or fteel locks, hinges, hoes, anvils and vizes,	10	
—— All other manufactures of brafs,	15	
Balls and balfams (fee powders, paftes, &c.)	15	
Beer, ale and porter in cafks,	8	cents per gallon.
———————————— in bottles	8	
Bricks and tiles,	15	per cent. ad val.
Bonnets and caps (fee hats)	15	
Boots,	75	per pair.
Books, blank,	10	per cent. ad val.
Books of perfons who come to refide in the United States,	free	
Buttons of every kind,	15	
Buckles, fhoe and knee,	15	
Brufhes,	10	
Bullion,	free	

C

Cannon of brafs, from May 22, 1794, to May 22, 1795,	free	
————————— after the 22d May, 1795,	15	
Carriages (fee coaches)	20	
Cards, playing,	25	cents per pack.
—— wool and cotton,	50	cents per dozen.
Cables and tarred cordage,	180	cents per cwt.
Cabinet wares,	15	per cent. ad val.
Caps and bonnets (fee hats)	15	

Carpets and carpeting,	15	per cent. ad val.
Cartridge paper,	15	
Candles of tallow,	2	cents per lb.
———— of wax or ſpermaceti,	6	
Capers,	15	per cent. ad val.
Canes, walking ſticks and whips,	10	
Cambricks,	10	
Cheeſe,	7	cents per lb.
China ware,	15	per cent. ad val.
Cinnamon, cloves, currants and comfits,	15	
Chintzes and coloured calicoes or muſlins, and all printed, ſtained or coloured goods or manufactures of cotton or of linen, or of both, or of which cotton or linen is the material of chief value,	12½	
Cocoa,	4	cents per pound.
Chocolate,	3	
Clogs and goloſhoes (ſee ſhoes)	15	cents per pair.
Cordage, tarred,	180	cents per cwt.
———— and yarn untarred,	225	
Coſmetics,	15	per cent. ad val.
Coal,	5	cents per buſhel.
Colours, (ſee painters)	15	per cent. ad val.
Copper manufactures,	15	
———— in plates, pigs and bars,	free	
Compoſitions for the teeth or gums (ſee dentrifice)	15	
Coffee,	5	cents per pound.
Cotton,	3	
Cotton or linen manufactures, or of both, or of which cotton or linen is the material of chief value, being printed, ſtained or coloured,	12½	per cent. ad val.
———— not printed, ſtained or coloured,	10	
Clocks and watches, or parts of either,	15	
Coaches, chariots, phaetons, chairs, chaiſes, ſolos or other carriages, or parts of carriages,	20	
Clothing ready made,	10	
Clothes, books, houſhold furniture, and the tools or implements of the trade or profeſſion of perſons who come to reſide in the United States,	free	
Cutlaſſes, from May 22, 1794, to May 22, 1795,	free	
———— after the 22d May, 1795,	15	

D

Dates and figs,	15	per cent. ad val.
Dentrifice powders, tinctures, preparations and compositions for the teeth or gums,	15	
Dolls dreffed and undreffed,	15	
Drugs medicinal, except thofe commonly ufed for dying,	15	
Drugs and wood for dying,	free	

E

Earthen and ftone wares,	15	
Effences, (fee powders, paftes, &c.)	15	

F

Fans,	15	
Fayal wine,	20	cents per gallon.
Feathers and other ornaments for womens head dreffes,	15	per cent. ad val.
Fringes commonly ufed by upholfterers, coachmakers and fadlers,	15	
Figs,	15	
Flowers, artificial,	15	
Floor cloths and mats,	15	
Fruits of all kinds,	15	
Furs of every kind undreffed,	free	

G

Glafs, black quart bottles,	10	
——— window glafs,	15	
———all other glafs, and manufactures thereof,	20	
Glauber falts,	200	cents per cwt.
Gauzes,	10	per cent. ad val.
Geneva (fee fpirits)		
Ginger,	15	per cent. ad val.
Golofhoes (fee fhoes)	15	cents per pair.
Gloves of leather,	15	per cent. ad val.
——— all other gloves and mittens,	15	
Gold, filver, and plated ware,	15	
Gold and filver lace	15	
Goods, wares and merchandize imported directly from China or India in fhips or veffels not of the United except teas, China ware, and all other articles liable to higher rates of duties,		
Goods, wares and merchandize intended to be re-exported to a foreign port or place, in the fame fhip or veffel in		

which they fhall be imported—and all
articles of the growth, product or manufacture of the United States, fpirits
excepted,   free

Goods, wares and merchandize not herein otherwife paticularly enumerated
and defcribed,   10   per cent. ad val.

Glue,   15

Gun powder, from May 22, 1794, to
May 22, 1795.   free

——— after the 22d May, 1795,   10

H

Hangers,   15

Hair powder,   15

Hats—of beaver, felt, wool, or a mixture
of any of them,   15

—— all other hats, caps and bonnets,   15

Hemp,   100 cents per cwt.

Hides, raw,   free

Houfhold furniture of perfons who come
to refide in the United States,   free

I

Implements of the trade or profeffion of
perfons who come to refide in the
United States,   free

Indigo,   25   cents per pound.

Iron wire,   free

—— caft, flit and rolled,   15

—— fteel or brafs locks, hinges, hoes,
anvils, and vizes,   10

—— all other manufactures of Iron, fteel
or brafs, or of which either of thefe
metals is the article of chief value, not
being otherwife particularly enume-
rated,   15   per cent. ad val.

J.

Jewellery and pafte work,   15

L.

Lace of gold and filver,   15

Laces and lawns,   10

Laces, lines, fringes taffels and trimmings,
commonly ufed by upholfterers, coachmakers and fadlers,   15

Lampblack,   10

Lapis calaminaris,   free

Leather, tanned and tawed, and all manufactures of leather or of which leather

is the article of chief value, not otherwife particularly enumerated, 15 per cent. ad val.

Lead and mufket ball, from May 22,
1794, to May 22, 1795, free

———————— after May 22, 1795, 1 cent per pound.

———— All other manufactures of lead, or
in which lead is the chief article, 1

Lemons and limes, 15 per cent. ad val.

Linen or cotton manufactures, or of both
or of which cotton or linen is the material of chief value, printed, ftained or
coloured, $12\frac{1}{2}$

———— not printed, ftained or coloured, 10

Lifbon and Oporto wines, 25 cents per gallon.

Looking glaffes, 20 per cent. ad val.

M.

Manufactures of tin, pewter and copper, 15

———————— of iron, fteel or brafs, not
otherwife particularly enumerated, 15

———————— of leather, not otherwife
particularly enumerated, 15

———————— of lead not otherwife particularly enumerated, 1 cent per pound.

———————— of cotton or linen, or of
both, printed, ftained or coloured, $12\frac{1}{2}$ per cent. ad. val.

———————— of ditto, not printed, ftained or coloured, 10

———————— of glafs (fee glafs)

———————— of tobacco (fee fnuff and
tobacco)

———————— of wood (fee cabinet wares
and wood)

———————— of the United States, fpirits
excepted, free

Mats and floor cloths, 15

Malt, 10 cents per bufhel.

Marble, flate and other ftone bricks, tiles,
tables, mortars and other utenfils of
marble or flate, and generally all ftone
and earthen ware, 15 per cent. ad val.

Madeira wines (fee wines)

Mace, 15

Medicinal drugs, except thofe commonly ufed in dying, 15

Merchandize, goods and wares, imported directly from China or India, in fhips
or veffels not of the United States ex-

cept teas, china ware, and all other articles liable to higher rates of duties,

Merchandize, goods and wares, intended to be re-exported to a foreign port or place in the same ship or vessel in which they shall be imported—and all articles of the growth, product or manufacture of the United States—spirits excepted, free

Merchandize, goods and wares not herein otherwise particularly enumerated and described, 10 per cent. ad. val.

Mittens (see gloves) 15

Millenary, ready made, 15

Molasses, 3 cents per gallon.

Muskets and firelocks, with bayonets suited to the same, and musket ball, from May 22, 1794, to May 22, 1795, free

———— after the 22d May, 1795, 15 per cent. ad val.

Muskets and fire locks, without bayonets, 15

Mustard in flour, 15

Muslins and muslinets, printed, stained or coloured, 12½

———— not printed, stained or coloured, 10

N.

Nails, 2 cents per pound.

Nankeens, 12½ per cent. ad val.

Nutmegs, 15

O.

Oranges, 15

Ornaments for womens head dresses, 15

Ointments, oils and odors (see powders, pastes, &c.) 15

Olives, 15

Oil, 15

Oporto and Lisbon wine, 25 cents per gallon.

P.

Paper hangings, 15 per cent. ad val.

———— writing and wrapping, 10

———— sheathing and cartridge, 15

Painters colours, whether dry or ground in oil, except those commonly used in dying, 15

Packthread and twine, 400 cents per cwt.

Paste boards, parchment and vellum, 10 per cent. ad val.

Paste work and jewellery, 15

Phaetons, see coaches, 20

Plaister of Paris, free

Pewter manufactures,	15	per cent. ad. val.
———old,	free	
Pepper,	6	cents per pound.
Perfumes,	15	per cent. ad val.
Pistols, from May 22, 1794, to May 22, 1795,	free	
——— after the 22d May, 1795,	15	
Pictures and prints,	10	
Pimento,	4	cents per pound.
Pickles of all sorts,	15	per cent. ad val.
Printed, stained or coloured goods, or manufactures of cotton, or of linen, or of both,	12½	
Philosophical apparatus, specially imported for any seminary of learning,	free	
Porter, beer and ale, in casks,	8	cents per gallon.
——————————— in bottles,	8	
Powder for the hair,	15	per cent. ad val.
——— gun powder, from May 22, 1794, to May 22, 1795,	free	
——— after the 22d May, 1795,	10	
Powders, pastes, balls, balsams, ointments, oils, waters, washes, tinctures, essences or other preparations or compositions commonly called sweet scents, odors, perfumes, or cosmetics—and all powders or preparations for the teeth or gums,	15	
Plumbs and prunes,	15	

R.

Raisins,	15	
Raw hides and skins,	free	
Rum, see spirits,		

S.

Salt, see note*	12	cents per bushel.
Salts, glauber,	200	cents per cwt.
Stained, printed or coloured goods or manufactures of cotton, or of linen, or of both,	12½	per cent. ad val.
Salt petre,	free	
Saint Lucar wines,	30	cents per gallon.
Starch,	15	per cent. ad val.
Sail cloth,	10	
Slate, stone and stone ware,	15	
Saddles,	10	
Sattins and other wrought silks,	10	
Steel,	100	cents per cwt.

—— iron, or brafs locks, hinges, hoes, anvils and vizes,	10	per cent. ad val.
—— all other manufactures of steel,	15	
Sheathing and cartridge paper,	15	
Sherry wine,	33	cents per gallon.
Sea ftores of fhips or veffels,	free	
Spermaceti candles,	6	cents per pound.
Sweet fcents, (fee powders, paftes, &c.)	15	per cent. ad val.
Spirits diftilled in foreign countries, viz.		
From grain, Firft proof,	28	cents per gallon.
Second do.	29	
Third do.	31	
Fourth do.	34	
Fifth do.	40	
Sixth do.	50	
From other materials.		
Firft proof,	25	
Second do.	25	
Third do.	28	
Fourth do.	32	
Fifth do.	38	
Sixth do.	46	

Spirits diftilled in the United States, imported after the fifth day of June, 1794, in the fame fhip or veffel in which they had been previoufly exported from the the United States, viz.

From molaffes.

Firft proof,	13	cents per gallon.
Second do.	14	
Third do.	15	
Fourth do.	17	
Fifth do.	21	
Sixth do.	28	

From materials of the growth or produce of the United States.

Firft proof,	7	
Second do.	8	
Third do.	9	
Fourth do.	11	
Fifth do.	13	
Sixth do.	18	
Spikes,	1	cent per pound.
Silver and plated ware,	15	per cent. ad. val.
——lace,	15	
Skins, raw	free	

Shoes and slippers of silk,	25	cents per pair.
———other shoes and slippers for men and women, clogs and goloshoes,	15	
———other shoes and slippers for children,	10	
Swords and cutlasses, from May 22, 1794, to May 22, 1795,	free	
——— after May 22, 1795,	15	per cent. ad. val.
Stockings,	15	
Stone and earthen ware,	15	
Soap,	2	cents per pound.
Solos and other carriages,	20	per cent. ad. val.
Sulphur,	free	

Sugars. From July 1st, to Sept. 30, 1794, inclusively.

Brown,	$1\frac{1}{2}$	cent per pound,
Clayed,	$3\frac{1}{2}$	
Lump,	$3\frac{1}{2}$	
Loaf,	5	
Other refined,	$2\frac{1}{2}$	

From and after Sept. 30, 1794.

Brown,	$1\frac{1}{2}$
Clayed,	$3\frac{1}{2}$
Lump,	$6\frac{1}{2}$
Loaf,	9
Other refined,	$6\frac{1}{2}$

Sugar candy,	10	per cent. ad. val.
Snuff. From July 1st, to Sept. 30. 1794, inclusively,	10	
———From and after the 30th of Sept. 1794,	22	

T.

Tassels and trimmings commonly used by upholsterers, coachmakers, and sadlers,	11	
Tables of marble, slate, other or stone,	15	per cent. ad. val.
Tallow candles,	2	cents per pound.

Teas. From China and India,

Bohea,	10
Souchong and other black teas,	18
Hyson,	32
Other green teas,	20

From Europe.

Bohea,	12
Souchong and other black teas,	21
Hyson,	40

Other green tea,	24	per cent. ad val.
From any other place.		
Bohea,	15	
Souchong and other black teas,	27	
Hyson,	50	
Other green teas,	30	
Teneriffe wine,	20	cents per gallon.
Twine and pack thread,	400	cents per cwt.
Tin manufactures,	15	per cent. ad. val.
——in pigs and plates,	free	
Tinctures, (fee powders, pastes, &c.)	15	
Tiles and bricks,	15	
Toys, not otherwise enumerated,	10	
Tobacco, manufactured,		
————From July 1st, to Sept. 30th, 1794, inclusively,	6	cents per pound.
————From and after the 30th of Sept. 1794,	10	
Tools of the trade or profession of persons, who come to reside in the United States,	free	

V.

Velvets and velverets,	10	per cent. ad. val.

W.

Wares of tin, pewter and copper,	15	
——— earthen or stone,	15	
——— china,	15	
——— gold, silver, and plated,	15	
——— goods and merchandize imported directly from China or India in ships or vessels not of the United States, except teas, china ware, and all other articles liable to higher rates of duties,		
——— goods and merchandize of the growth, produce or manufacture of the United States, (spirits excepted,)	free	
Wafers,	15	
Waters and washes, (see powders, pastes, &c.)	15	
Walking sticks, whips and canes,	'10	
Wax candles,	6	
Watches and clocks, or parts of either,	15	cents per pound.
Wines, London particular Madeira,	56	per cent. ad. val.
——— London market, do.	49	cents per gallon.
——— Other, do.	40	
——— Sherry,	33	
——— St. Lucar,	30	

——— Lisbon and Oporto,	25	cents per gallon.
——— Teneriffe and Fayal,	20	
——— All other wines (not to exceed thirty cents per gallon in American veffels. or thirty-two cents per gallon in foreign veffels)	40	per cent. ad val.
Window glafs,	15	
Wire of brafs and iron,	free	
Wool and cotton cards,	50	cents per dozen.
Wool unmanufactured,	free	
Wood (unmanufactured)	free	
Wood manufactured (exclufive of cabinet wares)	12½	

Y.

Yarn untarred,	225	cents per cwt.
All other goods, not before particularly enumerated and defcribed,	10	per cent. ad val.

To the encouragement to the manufactures of the United States refulting from the foregoing table, very confiderable additions are to be made for freight, infurance, commiffions, porterages, cofts of packages, premiums on bills, or other loffes on remittances to Europe. The aggregate of thefe is unufually high at this juncture, for a feafon of peace.

There is no duty on exports, nor is there any prohibition of exportation, excepting the temporary inftances of certain military articles.

NOTE. *The duties on Salt are at the rate of 12 cents per bufhel of 56 lb. or lefs.*

CHAPTER IV.

A STATEMENT OF THE TONNAGE OF VESSELS, WHICH HAVE PAID DUTY IN THE PORTS OF THE UNITED STATES OF AMERICA, BETWEEN THE 1ſt DAY OF OCTOBER, 1791, AND THE 30th DAY OF SEPTEMBER, 1792, INCLUDING THE COASTING AND FISHING VESSELS.

To what nation belonging.	*Tons.*
THE United States,	549,279
The United States and foreign nations, jointly,	407
France,	24,443
Great-Britain,	209,646
Spain,	3,148
United Netherlands,	3,123
Portugal,	2,843
Hamburg and Bremen,	5,677
Denmark,	752
Sweden,	943
Total,	800,261

TREASURY DEPARTMENT, REVENUE-OFFICE,
JANUARY 21ſt, 1794.

TENCH COXE, Commiſſioner of the Revenue.

CHAPTER V.

AN ABSTRACT OF GOODS, WARES, AND MERCHANDIZE, EX-
PORTED FROM THE UNITED STATES, FROM THE 1ſt OCTO-
BER, 1792, TO 30th SEPTEMBER, 1793.

Species of Merchandize.		*Quantity.*	
Aſhes, pot	tons of	4,359	9
pearl	do.	1,807	6
Apples,	barrels	8,994	
Bark of oak,	hogſheads	3,108	
———	cords	444	
——— eſſence of,	gallons	208	
Bricks,	number	683,070	
Boats,	do.	73	
Boots,	pairs	1,167	
Shoes,	do.	15,102	
Beer, porter and cider,	gallons	137,631	
bottled,	dozens	776	
Blacking or lampblack,	pounds	70	
———	hogſheads	100	
Bellows'Smith,	pairs	1	
Cotton,	bags	2,438	
Chalk,	tons	16	
Candles, Wax	boxes	48	
Myrtle,	do.	18	
Spermaceti,	do.	5,874	
Tallow,	do.	9,857	
Cordage,	tons	469	19
Coal,	buſhels	14,719	
Cranberries,	do.	166	
Cards, Wool and Cotton	dozens	34	
Coffee,	hogſheads	3,895	
	tierces	1,914	
	barrels	10,175	
	bags	1,789	
	pounds	10,764,549	
Cocoa,	hogſheads	12	
	tierces	55	
	barrels	180	
	bags	336	
	pounds	133,675	

Species of Merchandize.		Quantity.
Carriages. Coaches, chaises & chairs,	number	54
Waggons, carts & drays,	do.	48
Wheel-barrows, &c.	do.	44
Copper,	packages	146
Duck,	pieces	2,630
Drugs and medicine,	pounds of	52,720
——————— ————,	packages	281
Saffafras,	tons	67 10
Earthen-ware,	crates	175
Flaxseed,	casks	51,708
Flax,	pounds	1,474
Furniture, House	packages,	44
Tables, bureaus, &c.	number	175
Windfor chairs,	do.	3,884
Chefts,	do.	201
Fifhery. Fifh dried,	quintals	372,825
——, pickled,	barrels	45,440
Oil of whale,	gallons	512,780
Oil, fpermaceti	do.	140,056
Whale-bone,	pounds	202,620
Grain and Pulfe. Wheat,	bufhels	1,450,575
Rye,	do.	1,305
Barley,	do.	30
Indian Corn,	do.	1,233,761
Buckwheat,	do.	330
Oats,	do.	78,524
Peas and Beans,	do.	40,620
Groceries. Loaf Sugar,	hogfheads	9
——————,	tierces	6
——————,	barrels	59
——————,	pounds	27,554
Brown Sugar,	do.	4,539,809
Chocolate,	do.	7,432
Raifins,	do.	84,800
Almonds,	do.	13,900
Pimento,	do.	114,255
Cloves,	do.	500
Pepper,	do.	14,361
Ginger,	bags	478
Caffia and Cinnamon,	packages	351
Glafs,	boxes	47
——,	packages	13
Ginfeng,	pounds	71,550
——–,	packages	188
Grindftones,	number	38
Hides,	do.	9,78

Species of Merchandize.			Quantity.	
Horns and Tips,		number	91,142	
Hats,		do.	2,777	
Honey,		gallons	732	
Hops,		packages	73	
Hay,		tons	1,871	
Iron.	Nails,	casks	144	
	Axes, Spades, and Hoes,	number	951	
	Anchors,	do.	11	
	Grapnels,	do.	215	
	Pots, kettles, & other castings,	do.	6,117	
	———,	casks	3	
	Cannon,	number	43	
	Shot,	tons		13
	Pig,	do.	2,089	
	Bar,	do.	763	2
	Hoops,	do.	27	11
Indigo,		casks	462	
———,		pounds	690,989	
Ivory,		packages	10	
Lead.	Pig,	number	241	
	Shot,	pounds	952	
	Sheet,	tons	1	
Leather,		pounds	17,301	
———,		packages	52	
Lime,		bushels	748	
Live Stock.	Horned Cattle,	number	3,728	
	Horses,	do.	4,613	
	Mules,	do.	1,105	
	Sheep,	do.	12,064	
	Hogs,	do.	9,934	
	Poultry,	dozens	6,428	
Merchandize, or Dry Goods,		packages of	4,136	
	Nankeens,	pieces	10,972	
	Tow Cloth,	yards	14,947	
Molasses,		gallons	28,733	
Mill-stones,		number	2	
Naval Stores.	Pitch,	barrels	8,338	
	Tar,	do.	67,961	
	Rosin,	do.	1,715	
	Turpentine,	do.	36,957	
	Spirits of Turpentine,	casks	93	
Negro Slaves,		number	21	
Nuts,		bushels	502	
Oil.	Linseed,	gallons	1,183	
	Sweet,	boxes & baskets	1,168	
Powder.	Gun,	qr. casks	1,286	

Species of Merchandize.		*Quantity.*
Powder. Hair,	pounds	12,810
Paper,	reams	75
Pipes,	groce	48
Paints,	kegs	102
Pearl,	boxes	67
Provisions. Rice,	tierces	134,611
Flour,	barrels	1,074,639
Bread,	do.	76,653
Crackers,	kegs	43,306
Rye Meal,	barrels	12,695
Indian Meal,	do.	37,943
Ship Stuff,	do.	3,871
Buckwheat,	do.	146
Beef,	do.	75,106
Pork,	do.	38,563
Neat's Tongues,	kegs	867
Tongues and Sounds,	do.	209
Hams and Bacon,	pounds	521,483
Butter,	firkins	9,190
Cheese,	pounds	146,269
Lard,	do.	597,297
Sausages,	do.	2,863
Pickled Oysters	kegs & pots	1,561
Potatoes,	bushels	20,367
Onions,	bushels & bunches	269,380
Reeds,	number	123,276
Spirits, American	gallons	665,522
Foreign,	do.	224,614
Gin,	cases	10,761
Sadlery. Saddles,	number	1,114
Bridles	do.	997
Harness	setts	20
Soap,	boxes	6,620
Starch,	pounds	5,440
Snuff,	do.	35,559
Salt,	bushels	1,107
Spruce, essence of	boxes	81
Silk, raw	pounds	104
Silver Sweepings,	casks	7
Skins and Furrs,	pounds	426,318
——, packages,	number	1,123
——,	do.	27,446
Tobacco,	hogsheads	59,947
——, Manufactured	pounds	137,784
Tallow,	do.	309,366
Twine,	do.	3,760

Species of Merchandize.		Quantity.
Tin,	boxes	121
Teas. Bohea,	pounds	21,521
Souchong,	do.	3,020
Hyfon,	do.	17,672
Other Green,	do.	7,725
Vinegar,	gallons	3,473
Varnifh,	cafks	24
Wines. Madeira,	gallons	49,180
Other Wines,	do.	180,929
Bottled,	dozens	1,330
Wax. Bees,	pounds	272,800
Myrtle,	do.	1,273
Wood. Lumber,	feet	65,846,024
Timber,	tons	21,838
———,	pieces	12,272
Dye wood,	tons	319 10
Staves and heading,	number	29,734,854
Shingles,	do.	80,813,357
Hoops and poles,	do.	2,304,853
Shooks,	do.	37,863
Empty cafks,	do.	6,944
Mafts and fpars,	do.	5,052
Oars,	do.	20,251
Handfpikes,	do.	19,169
Pumps,	do.	43
Blocks,	do.	4,814
Treenails,	do.	91,632
Spokes and Fellies,	do.	22,076
Lock ftocks,	do.	600
Cords of wood,	do.	1,119
Frames of houfes,	do.	311
——— of veffels,	do.	2
Cart wheels,	do.	78
Yokes and bows,	pairs	696
Maft hoops,	dozens	27
Tubs, pails, &c.	do.	95

Value of Goods, Wares, and Merchandize, Exported from the United States.

	Dollars.
New-Hampſhire, - - - - -	198,197
Maſſachuſetts, - - - - - -	3,676,412
Rhode-Iſland - - - - -	616,416
Connecticut - - - - - -	770,239
New-York - - - - -	2,934,370
New-Jerſey - - - - - -	54,176
Pennſylvania - - - - - -	6,958,736
Delaware - - - - - -	71,242
Maryland - - - - - -	3,687,119
Virginia - - - - - -	2,984,317
North-Carolina - - - -	363,307
South-Carolina - - - - -	3,195,874
Georgia - - - - -	501,383
Total,	26,011,788

[NOTE.] Sundry returns from ſmall ports, not yet received.

A Summary of the Value and Deſtination of the Exports of the United States, agreeably to the foregoing Abſtract.

	Dollars.
To the dominions of Ruſſia - - -	5,769
the dominions of Sweden - - -	301,427
the dominions of Denmark - - -	870,508
the dominions of the United Netherlands -	3,169,536
the dominions of Great-Britain - -	8,431,239
the Imperial ports of the Auſtrian Netherlands and Germany - - -	1,013,347
Hamburg, Bremen, and other Hanſe Towns	792,537
the dominions of France - -	7,050,498
the dominions of Spain - - -	2,237,950
the dominions of Portugal - -	997,590
the Italian Ports, - - -	220,688
Morocco - - - -	2,094
the Eaſt-Indies, generally - - -	253,131
Africa, generally - - -	251,343
the Weſt-Indies, generally - - -	399,559
the North-Weſt Coaſt of America - -	1,586
Uncertain - - - -	3,986
Total,	26,011,788

Treaſury Department, Revenue-Office, March 20th, 1794.
TENCH COXE, *Commiſſioner of the Revenue.*

CHAPTER VI.

MISCELLANEOUS FACTS AND OBSERVATIONS CONCERNING THE STATE OF PENNSYLVANIA, SUPPLEMENTARY TO THE FOURTH CHAPTER OF THE FIRST BOOK.

IT has been already affirmed, that the bufinefs of fhip building is in a courfe of extraordinary profperity in the United States. From the books of the Infpector General of American commerce, under the Britifh government, it appears, that there were built in Pennfylvania in the year 1769, no more than 1649 tons of new veffels; in the year 1770, 2354 tons; and in the year 1771, only 1307 tons. The return of new veffels, built in the ftate of Pennfylvania, during the year 1793, though a grievous epidemic malady was introduced, in that term, into its only fea-port, exhibits the number of 8145 tons. Thefe veffels were generally built of the fouthern live oak and cedar, and were confequently, of the firft clafs in value and excellency. This great increafe of fo capital a vehicle of commerce, is an evidence as well of the growth of trade, as of fhip building. It is, however, proper to obferve, that the meafurement of 1771, was much lefs accurate, than that of 1793. The medium of the actual tonnage of the three former years, mentioned above, was perhaps 2,300 tons.

But there is a stronger proof of the growth of trade in the port of Philadelphia, and in the state of Pennsylvania. This results from the astonishing increase of exports. The aggregate value of all the commodities shipped from Philadelphia, to foreign countries, during one year, ending on the 30th September, 1792, was   3,820,646 *Dols.*

The aggregate value of the like exports, from Philadelphia, during one year, ending on the 30th September, 1793, was   6,958,736 *Dols.*

The aggregate value of the like exports, from Philadelphia, during one *half* of a year, ending on the 31st of March, 1794, was   3,533,397 *Dols.*

It is to be remembered also, that the epidemic malady, already mentioned, and the embargo in the last spring, interrupted the commerce of Philadelphia, during a term of nearly five months, in the close of 1793 and the beginning of 1794.

The exports of the state of Pennsylvania, during the year, ending on the 30th September 1793, were more than one fourth (*i. e.* nearly seven twenty sixth parts) of the exports of the whole of the United States. The tranfportation of merchandize and domeftic manufactures, coaft-wife, and by land were alfo very great.

The catalogue of books at this time for fale, and which have been publifhed by lefs than a dozen of the bookfellers of Philadelphia, contains three hundred and twenty fetts of different books, of one volume in duodecimo to eighteen volumes in quarto; alfo many charts, maps, and pamphlets, fmall hiftories and chapman's books. This precious branch, which diffufes indifpenfible knowledge in every line, yields large profits to the manufacturers, the artizans, and the United States, upon a fmall capital, in fheep-fkins, lead, lamp-black and ufelefs rags.

There are eftablifhed in the city of Philadelphia, three incorporated banks, which may be fafely affirmed to be in full and perfect credit, and to yield a better dividend, or half yearly profit, to their ftockholders, than any fimilar inftitutions in Europe: they are,

1. The Bank of North-America, eftablifhed in the year 1781.

2. The Bank of the United States, eftablifhed in 1791.

3. The Bank of Pennfylvania, eftablifhed in 1792.

The United States of America are interested to an amount much lefs than a major part of the ftock in the fecond; and the ftate of Pennfylvania in a fimilar degree in the third. They are all banks of difcount and depofit, and iffue notes payable in fpecie, on demand to the bearer. Their organization is upon a plan and on principles nearly uniform, and very much like to thofe of the Bank of England. Foreigners are confiderably interefted in all of them. The Bank of the United States has many proprietors in other parts of this country. It has branches, or fubordinate offices, in Bofton, New-York, Baltimore and Charlefton.

The following table is extracted from authentic documents. The third column fhews, in detail, the number of *taxable* inhabitants of each of the exifting counties of Pennfylvania, and of the city of Philadelphia. The two preceding columns exhibit the number of the like inhabitants in two feveral years prior to the revolution.

A COMPARATIVE VIEW OF THE NUMBER OF THE *TAXABLE* INHABI-
TANTS OE PENNSYLVANIA, IN THREE SEVERAL YEARS BEFORE
AND SINCE THE AMERICAN REVOLUTION.

	A. D. 1760.	A. D. 1770.	A. D. 1793.
The city of Philadelphia,			7088
The county of Philadelphia,	8321	10455	6885
The county of Montgomery,			4360
The county of Delaware,	4761	5483	2216
The county of Chefter,			5270
The county of Lancafter,	5631	6608	6409
The county of Dauphin,			3481
The county of Bucks,	3148	3177	4644
The county of Northampton,	1987	2793	4697
The county of Luzerne,			1409
The county of Allegheny,			2510
The county of Huntingdon,			1717
The county of Wafhington,			5045
The county of Fayette,	1501	3521	2844
The county of Mifflin,			2468
The county of Cumberland,			3869
The county of Bedford,			2881
The county of Weftmoreland,			3451
The county of York,	3302	4426	6974
The county of Franklin,			3570
The county of Berks,	3016	3302	5511
The county of Northumberland,			3878
	31667	39765	91177
	A. D. 1760.	A. D. 1770.	A. D. 1793.

On this interefting document, a fingle remark is
fufficient irrefragably to evince, that the profperity
of Pennfylvania is much greater at this time, than
it was in the year 1770. The ratio of the increafe
of taxable perfons in 1793 would have been equal
to the proportion between the years 1760 and 1770,
if the taxables in 1793, had been 68,000 ; but they
over run that number by more than 23,000. It
may be truly obferved, that the redundant population of New-England, the old counties of New-
York, New-Jerfey, the Delaware ftate, and Maryland, muft have migrated into Pennfylvania in
great numbers during the late war.

The following valuable table, relative to Pennfylvania, has been received from the editor of " le
" Niveau de l'Europe & de l'Amerique,"* and is
inferted in this volume with his permiffion.

* " A comparative view of Europe and America," by M.
Egron, of Philadelphia. It may ferve any confiderable public or
private interefts in this country, if documents elucidating fuch
interefts, fhould be tranfmitted to M. Egron, by the perfons
concerned.

It is a curious fact, that the price of produce at Pittfburg, three hundred miles from Philadelphia, is higher by fifty per cent. at this time, than it was fifty years ago in the city of Philadelphia. In the year 1739, wheat was fold in that port for two fhillings and nine pence per bufhel, flour for feven fhillings and three pence per cwt. and Indian corn for one fhilling and fix pence per bufhel. Thefe truths are interefting to the interior land holder and to the political econimift. The invention and information of the American cultivators and ftatefmen at the prefent time with the capital and numbers of the former, are powerful auxiliaries, which did not exift in the year 1739. The diftillation of fpirits of the higheft proof, the production of filk, the fupplies of the army, the cultivation of tobacco, hemp, and flax, the manufactory of falt, cheefe, butter, pot-afh, flaxfeed oil, leather, fteel, rolled, and flit iron, and the fineft flour, with furnaces, forges, canals, and turnpikes, greatly reduce the charges of tranfportation, and increafe the value of natural and agricultural productions in the midland and weftern counties. Thefe advantages may perhaps be eafily extended, if the city of Philadelphia and the interior towns and villages will purfue fuch of the ideas, fuggefted in the tenth chapter of the firft book, as may be convenient to their fituation, and to the pecuniary circumftances of their inhabitants.

The interior of Pennfylvania is peculiarly adapted and impelled to the manufactory of glafs, earth-

en ware, ftone ware, and iron ware. The forefts
on the Delaware, Lehigh, Lehiwaxen, Schuylkill,
Sufquehanna, and its two branches, and on Juniata, and Penn's creek, are now fo near to a great
population, that immenfe quantities of thofe feveral manufactures might be delivered by 'water carriage. On the completion of the canals they might
be tranfported, in like manner, to Philadelphia and
from thence to foreign countries.

The healthinefs of the climate of Philadelphia is
evinced by the fact that although it was eftablifhed
very long after the two next largeft towns in the
United States, New-York and Bofton, yet it is little
fhort of the fize of both. The city and county of
New-York, and the towns of Bofton and Charlef-
town, contained in 1791 no more than 52,752 perfons: the city and county of Philadelphia contained in the fame year 54,391 perfons. The counties
of New-York and Philadelphia are both very fmall
and much lefs than any other in their refpective
ftates. The latter is moft populous. It muft be
admitted, that this increafe is to be afcribed in
fome degree to the general profperity of Pennfylvania, New-Jerfey and the peninfula between the
Delaware and Chefapeak bays.

A more direct proof of the healthinefs of Philadelphia is to be deduced from the books of the
Difpenfary, a public charity from which medicine,
advice and affiftance are extended to the poor,
under every diforder and difeafe, without expenfe.

In the year 1790 the patients, which were under the care of the inftitution, amounted to 1892 poor citizens and foreigners. Of thefe only fixty-three died. The want of proper food, raiment, bedding, nurfes, cleanlinefs, and fafe and comfortable apartments, muft have contributed to the mortality of a part of thefe, as the patients were generally working people and all *paupers*, and the funds of the Difpenfary are applied in a very fmall degree to thofe articles. Medicine, advice and affiftance are the chief objects of their plan.

A malignant fever fimilar to that of 1793 obtained an entrance into a few families in the clofe of the fummer of 1794, but as the difeafe did not fpread or extend in Philadelphia, though it did fpread in the fmall airy town of New-Haven in Connecticut, and in the fuburbs of Baltimore upon Fell's point, it is manifeft that the climate of Philadelphia is not more difpofed to that kind of malady than other large towns. Indeed the three inftances of 1794 would prove it to be lefs difpofed to promote fuch difeafes, than fmaller towns.

It may be confidered as a fact ftrongly in favour of the induftry, fobriety and tranquility of the city of Philadelphia, that its breweries exceed, in the quantity of their manufactured liquor, thofe of all the fea-ports in the United States. The corporation of the city wifely favour houfes for the retail fale of beer and other malt liquors. Good regulations on the fubject of intoxicating liquors are infinitely important to health, morals, induſtry, property and good government: or in other words to the lives, proſperity, honor and happineſs of the people.

The number of ſlaves of all ages and ſexes in the city of Philadelphia has been gradually worn down to 273; and there are not more than 3000 in the ſtate of Pennſylvania. The laws and conſtitution prevent their increaſe, and are ſilently and ſteadily working the abolition of ſlavery. The migration hither of a free yeomanry has been increaſed by the very limited number of ſlaves.

The variety and extent of the foreign commercial correſpondence of the city of Philadelphia is very great. This is evinced by a well known faĉt, that in all the great branches of foreign trade the Philadelphians have taken a very conſiderable ſhare. They commenced the American trade with India and China; they have purſued the commerce of Ruſſia, though hemp and iron are two of the ſtaple articles of Pennſylvania; they have entered more largely into the Dutch trade than New-York, though it is well known that Philadelphia did little and New-York much in that branch of commerce before the revolution; Philadelphia carries on much more trade, both external and internal in commodities not of her produĉtion, than any other port; which will appear to be clear, when it is remembered how much of its ſupplies and of thoſe of the adjacent country are drawn from native manufactures, that its imports are very great and its exports are near feven twenty fixth parts of the whole fhipments of the United States, and that it has a very large fhare of the coafting trade.

It is very extraordinary, that Philadelphia has never yet engaged in the cod and whale fifheries, though Britain and France have carried on the former on the American coafts, and they and the Dutch have purfued the whale fifhery in very diftant feas. Thefe, it appears, may fhortly become very good objects for the accumulated capital of Philadelphia.

There are in that city two incorporated companies for the infuranee of houfes and other buildings againft fire, and two for the infurance of fhips and merchandize againft the dangers of the feas, enemies, &c.—Of thefe corporations (one againft fire) exifted before and three have been eftablifhed fince the revolution : further proofs of the acceffion of capital and expanfion of the powers, capacities, and operations of that profperous city.

Philadelphia is remarkably well accommodated by natural depofits of excellent materials for build- and improvements in its vicinity, and indeed within its boundaries : brick-clay, gravel, fand, limeftone, and quarries of common ftone and marble, with great forefts of white and yellow pine, oak, cedar and other wood and timber on the waters of the rivers Delaware and Schuylkill, which bound its eaftern and weftern extremities.

The penal code of Pennfylvania, though never fevere or cruel, has been greatly mitigated within a few years. In moft inftances ignominious, painful and fanguinary punifhments have been commuted for a ferious and edifying folitude, a fober and ftrictly temperate regimen, and a conftant, regular, ufeful and very induftrious employment. Experience appears to be in favour of the experiment.

It does not appear, that any of the American ftates make fo large quantities of pig iron and bar iron as Pennfylvania, nor is there any ftate which appears to have in its bowels fo much pit coal in fituations favourable to manufactures of American productions and internal trade.

It is eftimated, that taking into the calculation the extent and number of the exifting forges and furnances of Pennfylvania, the new iron works of the laft feven years are equal to one half of all thofe, which had been erected in the ftate during and before the year 1787.

———————

OTHER and fimilar remarks might be added to this chapter, concerning the ftate of Pennfylvania, but enough has been faid in this and the former chapter* to give a general idea of that important member of the American union. This addition has been neceſſarily very miſcellaneous and without any regular plan.

* See Chapter 4. Book I.

CHAPTER VII.

CONTAINING A VIEW OF THE SUBJECT OF FOREIGN DISTILLED
SPIRITS, EXTRACED FROM A PUBLICATION IN THE YEAR 1789.

[PAPER T.]

THE quantity of foreign liquors, imported into the United States, is very great. The feveral fpecies, commonly introduced, wines excepted, are unhappily the moft injurious to health both of body and mind. Ardent intoxicating fpirits, grofs and unripened, form the prefent importations; viz. the rum of Great-Britain, Denmark, and Holland—the brandies of France and Spain—and the geneva of Holland. We may compute them at two millions of dollars, to which they certainly amount, befides rum made in the United States of foreign molaffes: a diftreffing fum, indeed, if it were paid even for neceffaries, which Providence had been pleafed to withhold from us. a grievous fum, as it is paid (in provifions and other articles of prime neceffity or univerfal value,) for a poifonous luxury: an alarming fum, comparing it with any reafonable eftimate of our national revenues. When we reflect on this prodigious expenfe, no argument is neceffary to convince us how defirable it is to vary, fo far as we can, the kinds of liquors confumed, and to obtain fubftitutes on lefs

difadvantageous terms. Some ideas to thefe ends
are here propofed for confideration.

If we fuppofe the rum, brandy, and geneva, imported, as above, into the United States, to be
worth, on a medium, three fhillings and four pence
Pennfylvania money, or forty ninetieths of a dollar per gallon—then the quantity, fo eftimated at
two millions of dollars, will be four millions five
hundred thoufand gallons.* By a mixture of three
parts of water with one of rum, gin or brandy, we
fhall have eighteen millions of gallons of drink, as
ftrong as porter or the ftouteft beer. This quantity is equal to five hundred and fixty-two thoufand
five hundred barrels of thofe malt liquors, worth,
at thirty-three fhillings and four-pence (or four
dollars and forty ninetieths) the fum of nine hundred and thirty-feven thoufand five hundred pounds,
or two millions five hundred thoufand dollars,
which immenfe value would arife from the barley
and hops of our farms, and the ftaves and hoops
cut out of our woods. The quantity of barley, neceffary to make thefe five hundred and fixty-two
thoufand five hundred barrels of ftout beer or porter, at four bufhels to a barrel, is two millions two
hundred and fifty thoufand bufhels, exclufive of
the hops, ftaves, hoops, and firewood, neceffary in

---

* It appears by the public returns of 1792, that 4,869,992
gallons of diftilled fpirits were imported into the United States
during that year.

the manufactory. How comfortable to the country would such a manufacture be, in which few labourers are wanted, and wherein fire and horses perform so great a part of the work!—Imposts upon foreign liquors appear, in this view of the subject, to be a wholesome and efficient encouragement to agriculture, impelling us to what we ought to do, and very easily can perform. The superior virtues, both moral and political, of a country, which consumes malt liquors, instead of distilled spirits, need only to be mentioned.

In addition to these substitutes for foreign liquors, drawn from native productions, we may add cider and metheglin; of which large quantities can be made, and which will come into more general use, as agriculture advances, and economy prevails. We might mention also the spirits of fruit and grain; but it must be acknowledged that the domestic manufacture of ardent spirits from fruits and grain, threatens this country, no less than foreign liquors, with much public and private evil. Beer and cider would yield the farmer as great benefits, and are subject to fewer disadvantages. The friends of internal peace and order, and of practical religion—the advocates and promoters of American manufactures—the great body of farmers and planters—in short, all classes of our citizens have manifestly an interest in promoting the manufacture and consumption of those valuable articles, beer, porter, cider, and metheglin.

This review of our refources for the expenfive article of liquors, is taken with a defign to place the fubject properly before us. Its magnitude will infpire us with a difpofition to proportionate exertions. Sufficient means prefent themfelves, by which we may be relieved of this immenfe tribute to foreign nations, fome of whom require us not only to give them in exchange articles of the firft intrinfic value, but even to pay them for bringing it to our own ports.

CHAPTER VIII.

THE foreign and domeſtic debts of the United
States of America, as they appeared upon
their public books on the firſt day of the current
year, 1794, amounted to a little more than ſeventy-
four millions of dollars. From this ſum ſeven or
eight millions are to be deduɛted, being different
kinds of ſtock purchaſed in by means of the ſink-
ing fund or due upon the books or upon certificates
from the United States to ſeveral of the members of
the union: that is to themſelves. Of the entire balance, about fourteen millions will not bear intereſt
until the year 1800. Much of the debt bears an
intereſt at one half of the eſtabliſhed rate of this
country. Some of it bears an intereſt of two-thirds,
ſome of three-fourths, and ſome of four-fifths of
the medium of the legal intereſt of the ſtates. It
therefore reſults that forty-eight millions of dollars
in ſpecie, about £.11,000,000 ſterling, would pur-
chaſe or diſcharge all the debts of the United
States, which they owe to individuals, or to bodies
politic other than themſelves.

The revenues of the United States were eſtimated in 1791 at 3,329,750 dollars; and in 1792 at

3,700,000 dollars. They have always exceeded
the eftimates.

The revenues of 1793, and 1794, are very much
advanced and are in full proportion to the commerce, agriculture, and profperity of the country.
The furplus revenue of 1793 was eftimated at
2,300,000 dollars. It was appropriated by law to
the means of public ftrength and defence.

CHAPTER IX.

MISCELLANEOUS REFLECTIONS UPON CERTAIN IMPORTANT FACTS AND CONSIDERATIONS, WHICH OCCUR, AT THE PRESENT TIME, IN THE AFFAIRS OF THE UNITED STATES; INTENDED AS A CONCLUSION TO THIS COLLECTION.

THE critical ſtate of things during the laſt twelve months between the United States and the kingdom of Great-Britain renders it highly intereſting to reflect, for a moment, on the preſent condition of our mutual commerce.

It is eſtabliſhed by a recent inveſtigation in Great-Britain, that in the year 1791 the United States of America took from that kingdom (excluſive of Ireland and the Britiſh Eaſt-Indies, from which they import many manufactures) the immenſe value, in Britiſh manufactures, of

Sterling, £.3,929,771 12 8

In the ſame year France, now at war with England, took, as the equivalent for the advantages of Mr. Eden's treaty, only   576,632 6 10

And Ruſſia took 281,243l. 1s. Denmark and Norway 219,803l. 11s. Sweden 36,259l. 4s. 6d. Poland 39,833l. 16s. 9d. Pruſſia 43,402l. 16s. 2d. Germany 778-213l. 3s. 2d. Holland 692,725l.

8s. 3d. Auftrian Flanders 387,399l
7d.* Portugal & Madeira 657,388l
7s. 3d. Spain and the Canaries
582,914l. 4s. 3d. Gibraltar and
the Streights (partly Britifh demand) 224,673l. 16s. 9d. Italy
932,148l. 9s. 1d. Turkey 99,206l.
1s. 8d. the foreign Weft-Indies
462l. 12s. 3d. and Florida 15,300l.
15s. 1d. in all   £·4,990,974   7   11

From the latter fum of £·4,990,974 7 11, it is
neceffary to deduct confiderably for the confumption of Gibraltar, where, it is prefumed, the confumption of Britifh goods extends to every manufactured convenience and neceffary—not only fine
cloths and linens, but malt liquors, cheefe, foap
and candles, loaf fugar, fhoes, hats, caft iron
utenfils, &c. &c.

It is well known, that feveral of the foreign nations which take off the above Britifh manufactures, fend in return to Britain great quantities of
their own fabrics ; for example, Ruffia fends hemp-
en and flaxen manufactures, and milled iron articles, probably to a greater amount than her above
demand of £·281,000 fterling ; and though Germany and Holland can fhip very little value in raw
materials, provifions, or lumber, yet their exports

---

* The French have checked, for a feafon, the Flemifh, German, and Dutch demand of Britifh goods.

to Great-Britain in 1791 were £.1,569,000 sterling. This large amount must have included a greater value of Dutch and German manufactures, than the difference between our import from Britain, and that of all those foreigners. The same remark applies to the British trade with France, Ruffia, Flanders, &c. and indeed the United States of America promote the demand of all those countries for British manufactures, by permitting Britain to send us foreign goods to the value of nearly a million and a half of dollars per annum. Hence it appears almost certain, that the United States of America take from Great-Britain *a greater balance of manufactured goods*, than is taken from Great-Britain by all those foreign nations. The important question occurs: how ought a wise and just nation to conduct themselves towards such great customers and consumers? If an error should be made in the decision, it will be prejudicial to the United States, and pernicious in the extreme to the commerce of Great-Britain.

The weight of the inducements to an equitable and generous deportment on the part of Great-Britain is not a little increased by similar facts in relation to the employment of her ships. It appears from a British statement of her trade with all the world and from the promulgated documents of Congress, that the vessels of that country, loaded in the United States in 1791 and 1792, were about equal in tonnage to all the British vessels cleared out of Great-Britain for Ruſſia, Denmark and Norway, Sweden, Pruſſia, Poland, Hamburg, Bremen, and Germany in general.

A ſolution of the extraordinary increaſe of imports from Great-Britain, into the United States, will be uſeful to ourſelves.

The aſtoniſhing proſperity of this country, in conſequence of the reſtoration of union and order in 1789, is a very principal cauſe. Since that time our exports (including a freight upon them) have increaſed by more than two millions ſterling. Our conſumption is therefore more free (perhaps too much ſo) as to the quantity, and particularly as to *the quality* of the commodities ; and the new buildings and repairs of old ones, requiring glaſs, hardware, &c. have exceeded thoſe of all former times. The population of thoſe ſtates is known to advance, under common circumſtances, at the rate of five per cent. per annum. The proſperity of our country, and the diſorders of France, of her neighbours in Europe, and of her colonies, have occaſioned a great and moſt rapid increaſe of people, part of which may be temporary. Theſe conſume fine goods.* The exportations of Britiſh goods from this country to foreign markets ſhould be taken in-

---

* The ſum paid by one foreign nation, to tranſient refugees from the diſordered parts of its territories, ſojourning in the United States in the ſummer of 1794, is ſaid to have been no leſs than 60,000 dollars per month, equal to 720,000 dollars per annum.

to the eſtimate, particularly the French colonies.
The ſails and furniture of the extraordinary quantity of new veſſels, built in our ports, is alſo to be
noted : nor is the quantity of furniture and goods
brought in by European emigrators to be forgotten. The ſtock on hand in the wholeſale and retail ſtores throughout the country (the ſurplus of
importations) is very great, though the coarſe and
ſubſtantial articles for building, apparel and furniture, are generally ſold between the arrivals of the
ſpring and fall veſſels: and laſtly the tools, implements and materials for works and manufaƈtories, to
be built and eſtabliſhed among us, are not inconſiderable, but are a new demand on our part, which
has been created ſince 1775, and which has been
greatly extended in the laſt ten years.

It is particularly worthy of calm remark on both
ſides of the Atlantic, that the exports of manufactures from Great-Britain to Canada in the year before mentioned (1791) was no more than 243,000l.
ſterling, being leſs than one ſixteenth part of our
demand. In that ſmall ſum was included, of courſe,
the ſupply of Britiſh manufaƈtures for the Canadian
Indian trade. Let conſiderate men determine then,
whether that branch of commerce (the fur-trade)
is of ſufficient importance to juſtify the hazard of
a difference with the United States. The whole
importation (furs included) from Canada and Hudſon's bay, into Great-Britain, amounted in 1791,
to no more than 135,000l. ſterling. Had a war appeared to ariſe about ſuch a trifle, it might have

been fufpected on reflexion, that political confiderations were the true and fecret caufe. To acquire
a portion of our territory would probably have been
deemed the real object of our neighbour. To fruf-
trate or prevent a difmemberment of our country
would have been the honeft and avowed object of the
people of the United States. But it feemed good
to Providence to fave the two nations from the
deftroying fcourge of war.

It has been confidently expected by many in this
country, that the re-animation, acceffion and accumulation of its capital would gradually relieve us
from the alledged neceffity of trading with thofe
who could beft afford us the accommodation of
credit. The expectation was reafonable, and it
therefore will not be difappointed. The merchants
of the United States are now prepared to purchafe
very large portions of their fupplies with ready money in the beft and original markets. When the
diforders and immenfe military demand on the continent of Europe fhall ceafe, it is not at all doubted,
that this ability will plainly appear, wherever the
nature of the market fhall afford an adequate temptation. It is not alledged here, that this ability will
materially vary the foreign fources of our fupplies,
whatever may be the cafe: but it obviates much of
the arguments drawn from the confideration of credit.

It is believed, that mifcalculations of the refources and faculties of the United States have affected

the mutual interefts of this country and of feveral nations, with which we have intercourfe. Many of thefe errors have been touched in the preceding pages. One more is intended to be noticed here. It is an opinion, which has been maintained, that *the United States would be deftitute of revenue were any circumftances to interrupt their Britifh trade.* The importations into the United States were very confiderable in the moft difficult years of the late war. The prize goods (and thefe pay duty) were of great value. It is certain, that the revenue from foreign and domeftic fpirits amounts, at this time, to one million, fix hundred and fifty thoufand dollars, of which a very large part is drawn from fources other than Britifh. The revenue from wines, China goods, and molaffes, are entirely from other fources, as thofe from coffee, fugar and cocoa are in a large degree. Ruffia and the Hanfe towns now, and Rotterdam, Amfterdam, Oftend, France and Italy, in tranquil times, would furnifh great fupplies for money and produce, and fome of them for credit. Thefe would yield us revenue of courfe.—If unhappily a war were to take place, neutral bottoms, with cargoes belonging to themfelves, would afford large fupplies, which the political claims of Great-Britain prevented in the revolutionary war. Every European country would maintain its right to trade with America,*

* The armed neutrality, and the prefent armament of Denmark and Sweden, afford ferious leffons on this fubject—as alfo the conduct of Portugal and Holland towards the United States.

acknowledged independent by that country, which then upheld a claim to check all intercourse between her and the foreign world. That trade would also yield us revenue.—So far as the manufactures of the United States might diminish the importations from foreign countries, it is obvious that our citizens could *well* afford to pay a proportionate tax. If we should save the whole value of a bale of linens for example, by making it at home, we could have no difficulty in raising or paying one tenth of its value in the form a land-tax, or some other equitable and reasonable contribution. The modes of revenue of all nations are unfolded to us, and we have no reason to doubt that our law-makers are less able to devise original plans of taxation, than those of other countries. An useful lesson upon this subject may be obtained by considering how much more easy and effectual have been the financial measures of the United States, since 1786, 1787 and 1788, than was expected by unwise and unkind observers in those three years. The short question is this.—Has America the substance, wherewithal to defray the expences of her political existence? Let those, who are capable, compare her present operations in every line with those of 1775: and let them also compare the public contributions of this happy people with those of the nations of the old world—taking duly into view the productions and exportations of each. Let them also remember that the depredations on the British commerce, in the late war, were *great indeed*, and that the exertions of that day could be far exceeded at this time.

It is highly favourable to the character, the energy, and safety of the United States, that the importation of flaves has ceafed, that the increafe of white population and gradual emancipation have reduced the proportion of thofe unhappy, and once dangerous people to a very fafe point indeed in the nine middle and northern ftates, and that a very extraordinary increafe of white population has taken place in the fouthern ftates. The fubdivifion of lands and of all other property, by the recent laws of defcent, facilitates and occafions the fales of farms to the people of the more northern ftates, and to European emigrants; and promotes the rapid courfe by which the whites are overnumbering the blacks. Kentucky, the Southern Territory of Congrefs, the weftern parts of Maryland, Virginia, and the Carolinas, are not in the moft remote danger of inconvenience from the negroes. The low and level counties of Maryland, Virginia, North-Carolina, and South-Carolina, where the blacks are moft numerous, are fo near to the fea, that the tranfportation of a force by water, were it unexpectediy to become neceffary, and the collection of the neighbouring and interior militia, would enfure the immediate fuppreffion of any diforderly movement. The midland and interior counties being inhabited almoft entirely by whites, no refuge could be had there. The number of flaves in the United States is fomewhat more than thofe of French St. Domingo, but the white people of this country are one hundred times as many as the white people of that colony were at the commencement of the exifting diforders in that ifland : and are far more energetic, and better armed.

It will be pleafing to the friends of religious liberty to perceive, that no evils whatever have refulted in America from the non-exiftence of an eftablifhed church, nor from an entire feparation of ecclefiaftical influence from the civil power.

It has been fometimes feared, that the luxuries and diffipations of Europe would be quickly introduced, with their capital, into the United States. Moft of thofe, who have come among us have been led hither by ferious views of advantage or driven by misfortune. Hence it is true, that we really have no ftriking examples of diffipation or expenfe among the families, who have chofen America for their home. They have been duly fobered by their plans of emolument, or by reflection on the loffes and difficulties, which have conftrained them to leave their native country. It is really true that they have rather accommodated themfelves to the American modes of life, than purfued or introduced thofe of Europe. A fact equally beneficial to them and to us. It is, however, highly prudent to remember, that the United States having become by their independence in fome fenfe, " *the colony of all Europe*" further wholefome provifions in our laws, calculated effectually to prevent inconveniencies, which might arife from the fudden introduction to power of perfons of every variety of cha-

racter, difpofition and property, are truly worthy
of legiflative confideration. But while we obey
this obvious and folemn dictate of prudence, let us
not ceafe to be perfectly equitable, kind, and
generous to thofe foreigners who may defire to
fet down among us: and particularly let them
fully enjoy the rights of religion, protection,
occupation, profeffion and property. When the
courfe in which thefe ftates have wifely march-
ed to the goal of freedom, civil and religious,
is duly remembered, it will be fafe to affirm,
that no general defcription of foreigners are likely
to be indifpenfible auxiliaries to the American
people in thofe important objects, immediately on
their arrival. When the wifdom, which any perfon
may have brought with him fhall be fufficiently directed by his experience and knowledge of thofe
things, which belong to our peace and which concern our general interefts, and when he fhall have
manifefted a fufficient common intereft in this community, thofe temporary precautions, which prudence may at firft require, will become unneceffary. This principle of caution is not a new one. It
will be fatisfactory to prudent men at home and
abroad, that the conftitution of the United States
and thofe of the feveral ftates have been framed
with confiderable attention to its obvious expediency.

It is not unfavourable to the form of government
adopted by this country, that no monarchy in the
civilized world, exercifed over an equally nume-

rous people, has been fo well able to maintain internal tranquility and foreign peace in this day of general convulfion and diforder. The recent inftance of oppofition to a law of the union has evinced the difpofition of the people of America to maintain their government, the efficiency of the conftituted authorities, and the alacrity of the body of militia of four feveral ftates. This prompt exertion will be deemed, on ferious reflection, no inconfiderable proof of an unalterable determination to maintain order and the civil power, when it is remembered that the rejection of a fimilar law was attempted in England, within the prefent century, and actually effected by tumultuous influences on their legiflature itfelf, equal therefore to the late diforders in the fouth weftern counties of Pennfylvania. In the United States it may be at leaft affirmed, that the fecondary confideration of *a particular mode of revenue* has been put out of queftion in order to maintain the primary object of *an efficient republican government.*

It appears from a very incomplete but authentic note of the veffels built in the United States during the eighteen months following the 31ft day of December 1792, that they amounted to nearly 80,000 tons. The ports of Nantucket, Bofton, Alexandria, the two Wilmingtons, Edenton, and (for one year of the time) Baltimore, and feveral others of inferior confequence were, not included in the return. The quantity built at Philadelphia was 10,204 tons, although the epidemic malady of 1793, fufpended the bufinefs for one entire quarter. The diftrict of Maine appears to have built 15476 tons, though fome of the returns from thence are deficient. During the firft year of the exifting general government (from March, 1789, to March, 1790) the whole fhip-building of the United States was 17 to 18,000 tons, and in the fecond year, ending in March, 1791, it was about 32,000 tons. Such has been *the progrefs* and fuch is *the prefent ftate* of the firft of our mechanic arts.

It is of fome importance to the harmony between the United States and foreign countries, that circumftances of unfavourable difcrimination againft us are gradually wearing out of the fyftems of thofe countries. An inftance of this, but little noticed in America or Great-Britain, has occurred in the regulations of the latter country with refpect to foreign manufactures. Before April, 1792, no manufactured articles of the United States could be imported into that kingdom. This exceptionable difcrimination operated againft us only. On the firft of that month the annual order of the king of Great-Britain in council legalized the introduction of American manufactures upon the footing of the moft favoured foreign nations. The two countries have thus placed each other on an equal ground in that particular, excepting that Britain has done that by a temporary executive order which the government of the United States have done, upon the principles of impartiality, by reiterated legiflative acts. The exiftence of the late rigid prohibition of our manufactures in Great-Britain, though formerly of little importance, would have been of confiderable inconvenience to us in the event of a war between that country and the maritime powers in the north of Europe. Tanned leather, rolled and flit iron, fteel, cannon ball, cordage and flaxen and hempen yarns for example (fome or all of them) are imported into Great-Britan to a large amount from thofe nothern nations. Thefe articles on the occurrence of fuch war, we could fupply to confiderable advantage. Grain fpirits, ftarch, malt, foap, candles, and tawed fkins, and other articles muft become redundant and cheap in the United States and a foreign market for them may be found defireable. The powers now at war have doubtlefs confumed no fmall value of thefe articles from America during the laft three years. Holland, the Auftrian Netherlands, the Hanfe towns, the European ports of France, and the colonies of feveral nations have received by ordinary importation from the United States confiderable manufactures of grain, of the fat of animals, of wood, of iron, of leather and fkins, of flax and hemp, and of fur.

Terrifying reports of danger from the American Indians have been widely circulated in fome foreign countries. It is a fact, however, that there is not the moft remote poffibility of injury from thofe favages to more than a twentieth or thirtieth part of the inhabitants of this country. Nineteen in twenty or twenty-nine in thirty of our people are as free from that danger, as the people of Germany, or Great-Britain. All the counties on and near the atlantic ocean, all the midland counties and all the firſt ranges of the weſtern counties are perfectly ſafe and even undiſturbed. In the unconnected range of frontier counties, the inhabitants are often partially alarmed in the time of an actual Indian war, and it is true that they ſometimes ſuffer. But this has little effect upon them as is proved by facts, which ſpeak more ſtrongly than any thing, that can be ſaid upon the ſubject. The old frontier county of Cumberland in Pennſylvania, for example, contained, in the year 1760, no more than 1501 taxable inhabitanst, and in the year 1770 no more than 3521 taxable inhabitants. It had a narrow front on the weſtern bank of the river Suſquehanna, and extended from thence over the Allegheney mountain beyond the head of the Ohio to the weſtern limits of the ſtate. By a public return of 1793,* it appears that the counties, erected ſince out of the original county of Cumberland are inhabited by the increaſed number of 24,785 taxable inhabitants. Four of them, which are beyond the Allegheney mountain, and neareſt to the Indians, contain nearly one third more than thoſe four which lie between that mountain and the river Suſquehanna. Much the moſt populous of the whole eight, is the county of Waſhington, which lies the neareſt to the Indians, and has in it near 24,000 inhabitants of all ages and ſexes.

* See Chapter VI. Book II. for a comparative view of the taxable inhabitants of Pennſylvania at three periods.

The great prices of American exports, both the
fpontaneous productions of the earth and the fruits
of cultivation, which have been obtained in our
home market, during the laft fix years, together
with the prodigious increafe of fome of them, have
given an immenfe fpring to the landed property
and the agricultural interefts of the United States.
For example our whole export of flour in 1786,
fuppofing it to be 300,000 barrels, at five dollars,
has been advanced to nearly 1,100,000 barrels in
1793 at feven dollars. It is to be remembered alfo that as very great improvements in agricultural
fkill and economy are obvioufly practicable in this
country, much confequent increafe may be reafonably expected. The commerce, which has refulted from this great natural caufe, *the profperity of
agriculture,* is of the moft fatisfactory and unfluctuating kind. Thofe, who have nearly 800,000 barrels of flour to fell and fhip in 1793 more than
they had in 1786, will have fo much the more to
do in their banks, their infurance offices, their
counting houfes, their tradefmens fhops and on
their wharves; fo much more for their millers to
grind, and for their coafters to tranfport, fo much
more to employ their outward fhips, and fo much
more to fill their inward veffels, and in fhort, fo
much more of all the pleafing and profitable details
of an honeft, intelligent and flourifhing commerce,
folidly founded upon, and infeparably blended with
the profperity of the farmer, the planter, the gra-
zier, the iron mafter, and the land holder of every
defcription.